S·A

Special A

RYU & JUN & MEGUMI
SEVEN YEARS old

Volume 15

Story & Art by

Maki Minami

STORY

★At the tender age of 6, carpenter's daughter Hikari Hanazono suffered her first loss to the wealthy Kei Takishima in a wrestling match. Now the hardworking Hikari has followed Kei to the most elite school for the rich just to beat him! I call this story "Overthrow Takishima! Rise Above Perpetual Second Place!!" It's the story of Hikari's sweat, tears and passion, with a little bit of love thrown in! ★ Going into her second year, Hikari is tied at 2nd place with a transfer student named Iori Tokiwa. Hikari and Iori hit it off once they discover a common goal—first place! Hikari eventually realizes that Kei is jealous of their new bond, so she tries to back off and get some space from Iori.

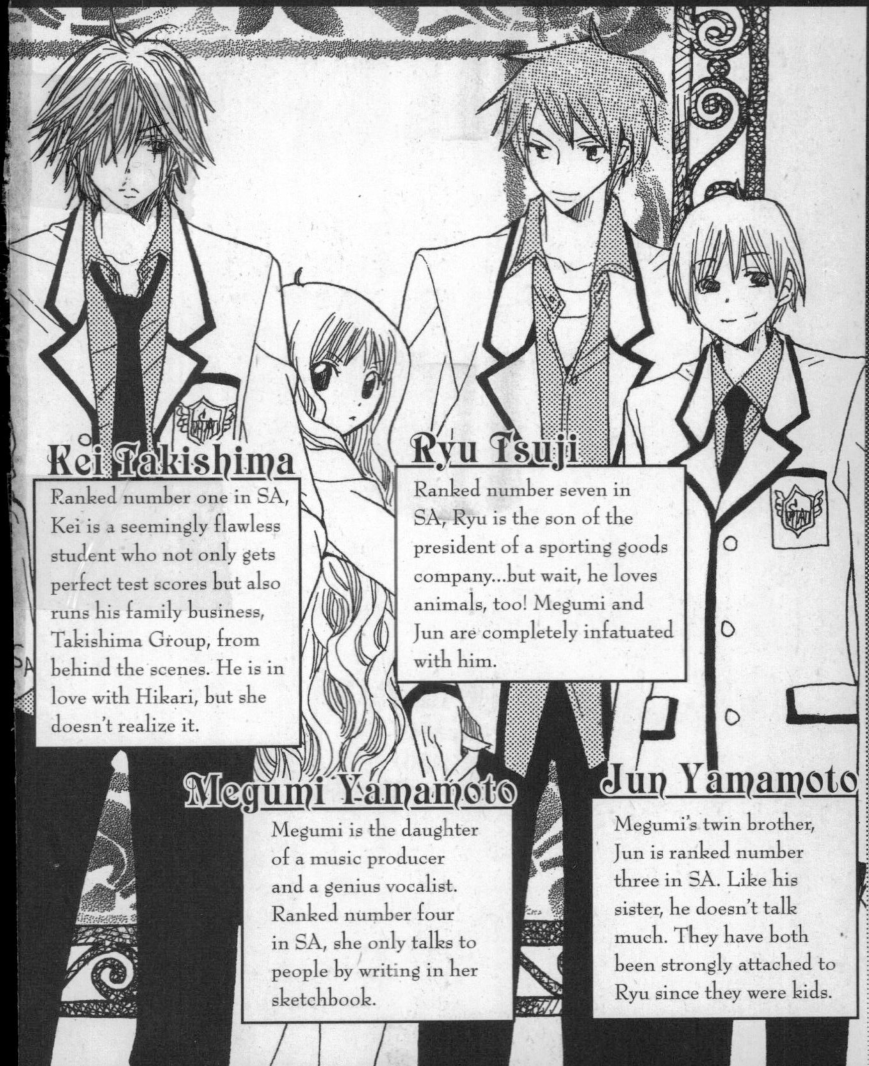
Kei Takishima
Ranked number one in SA, Kei is a seemingly flawless student who not only gets perfect test scores but also runs his family business, Takishima Group, from behind the scenes. He is in love with Hikari, but she doesn't realize it.
Ryu Tsuji
Ranked number seven in SA, Ryu is the son of the president of a sporting goods company...but wait, he loves animals, too! Megumi and Jun are completely infatuated with him.
Megumi Yamamoto
Megumi is the daughter of a music producer and a genius vocalist. Ranked number four in SA, she only talks to people by writing in her sketchbook.
Jun Yamamoto
Megumi's twin brother, Jun is ranked number three in SA. Like his sister, he doesn't talk much. They have both been strongly attached to Ryu since they were kids.

S·A CHARACTERS

What is "Special A"?

Hikari goes to an elite school called Hakusenkan High School. This school divides each grade level into groups A through F, according to the students' test scores. Group A includes only the top seven students in each class. Then the top seven students from all grades' A groups are put into a group called Special A, which is considered much higher than all others. Known as SA, they are "the elite among the elite."

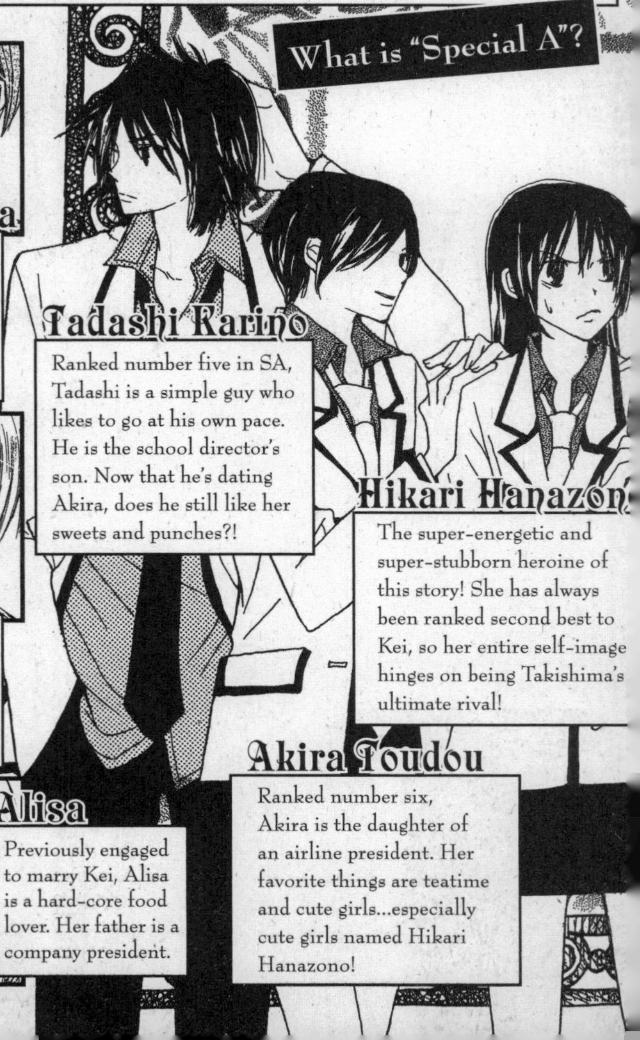

Hikari Hanazono

The super-energetic and super-stubborn heroine of this story! She has always been ranked second best to Kei, so her entire self-image hinges on being Takishima's ultimate rival!

Tadashi Karino

Ranked number five in SA, Tadashi is a simple guy who likes to go at his own pace. He is the school director's son. Now that he's dating Akira, does he still like her sweets and punches?!

Akira Toudou

Ranked number six, Akira is the daughter of an airline president. Her favorite things are teatime and cute girls...especially cute girls named Hikari Hanazono!

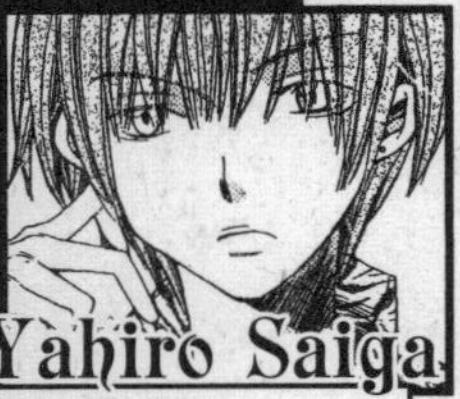

Yahiro Saiga

A childhood friend of Kei and Akira. His family is richer than the Takishima Group.

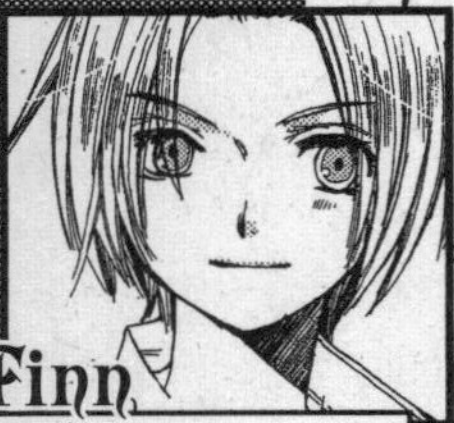

Finn

The prince of a foreign country. He traveled to Japan to make Hikari his bride. (He's really a girl.)

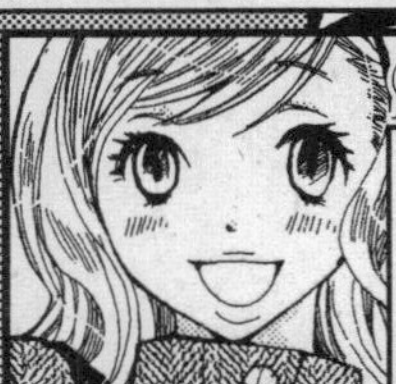

Alisa

Previously engaged to marry Kei, Alisa is a hard-core food lover. Her father is a company president.

Contents

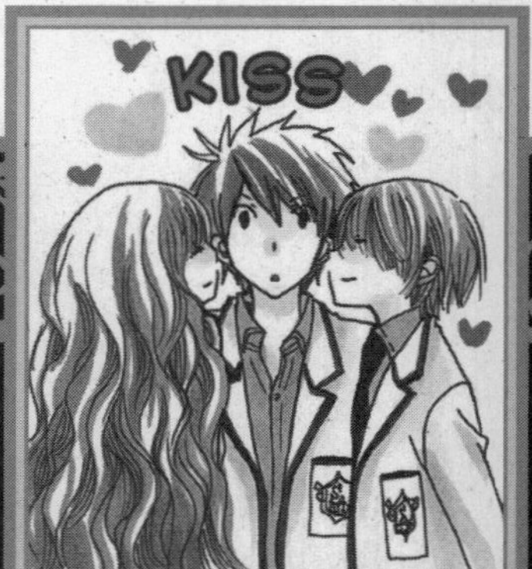

KISS

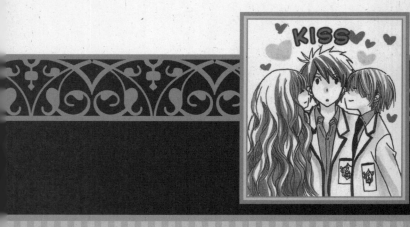

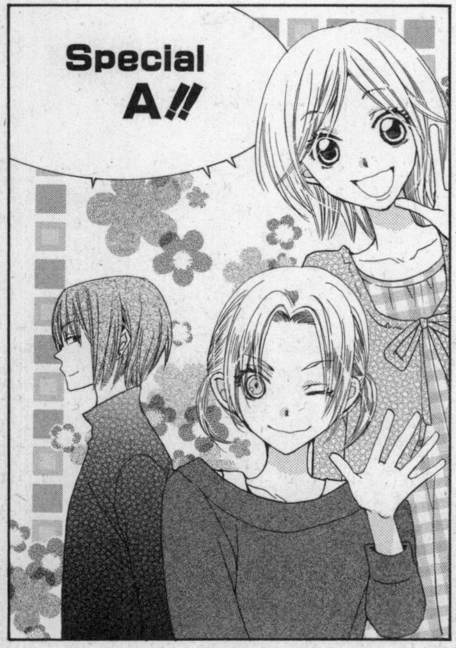
Special A!!

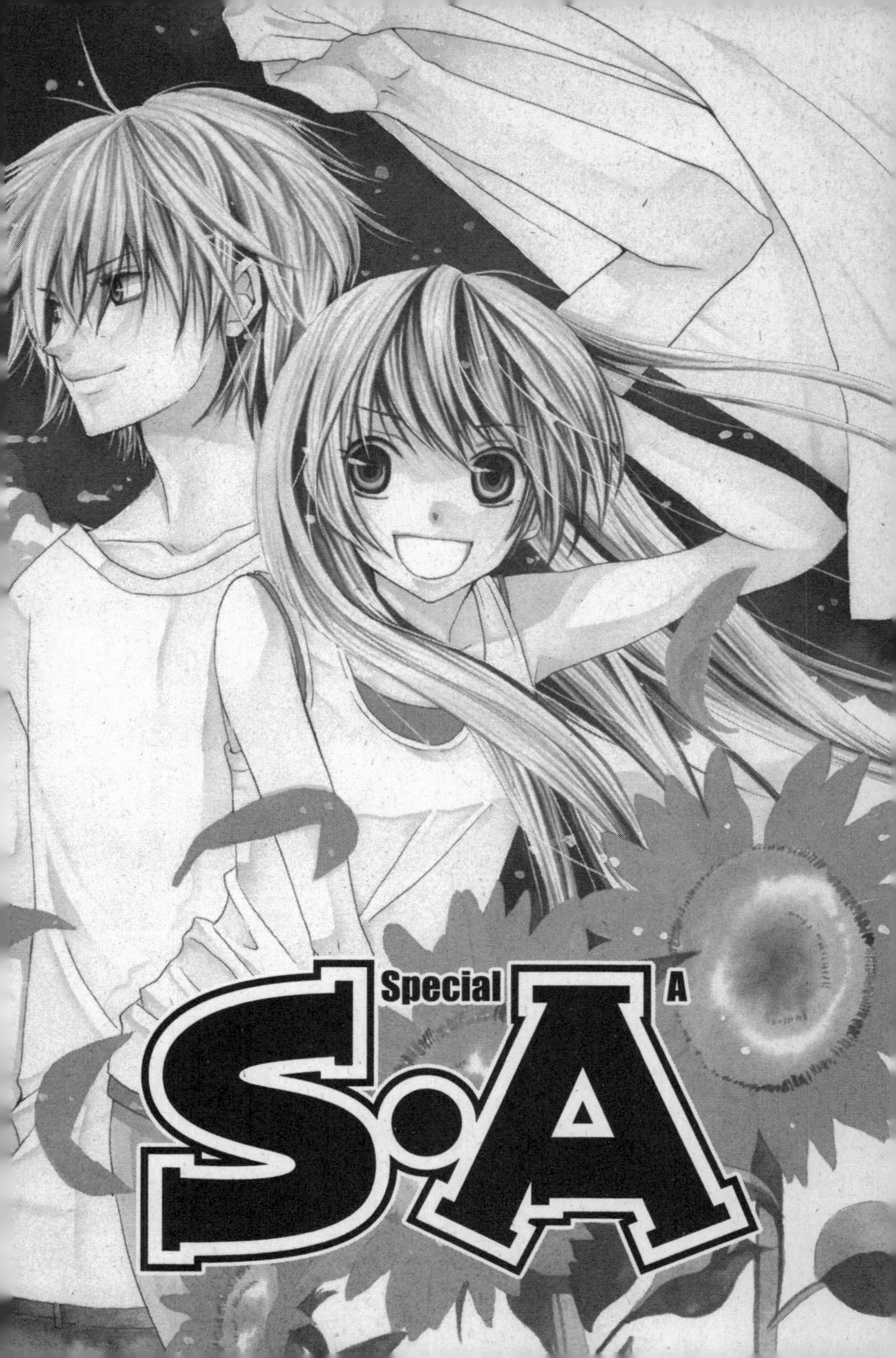
Special A
S.A

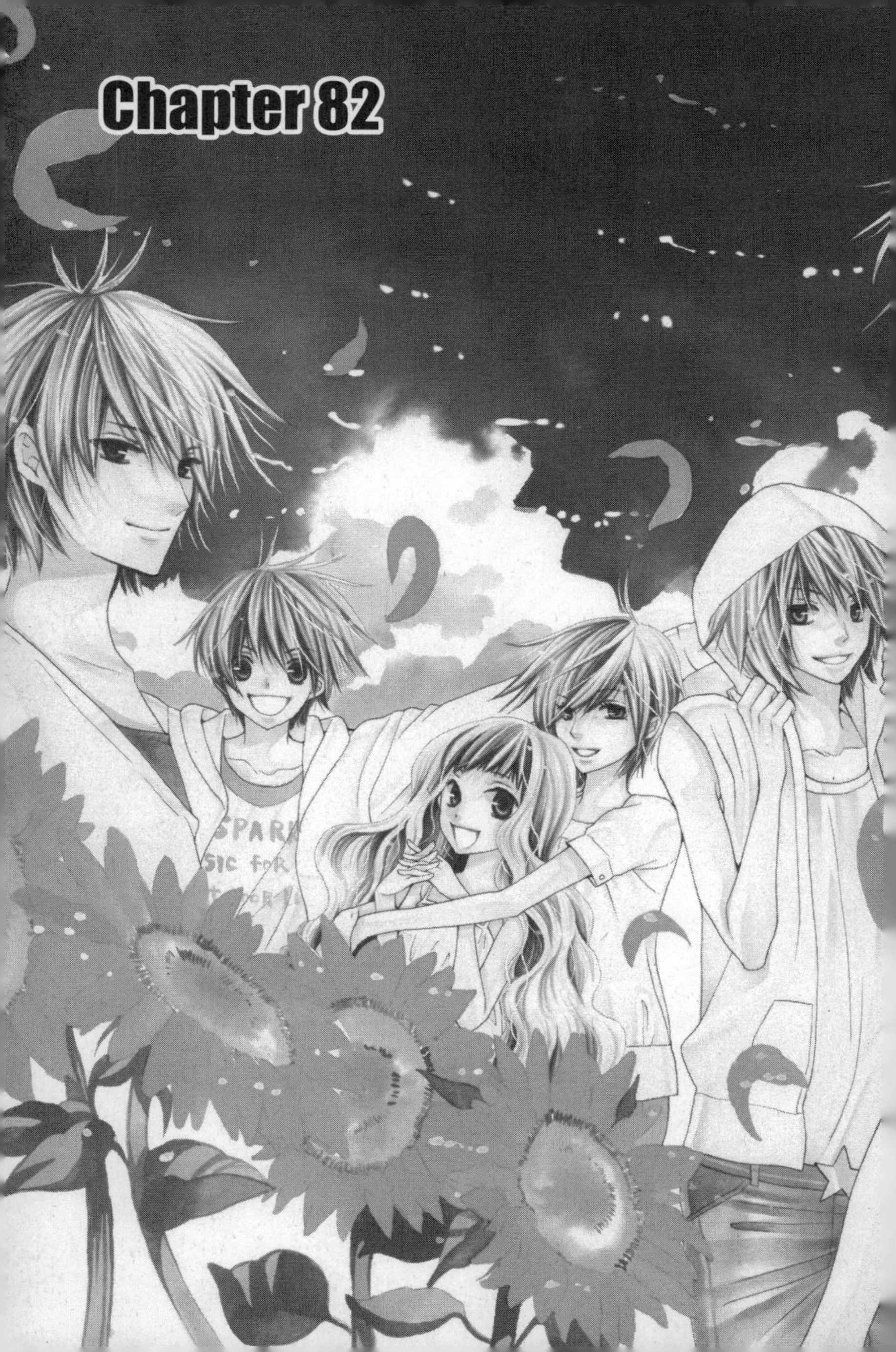
Chapter 82

Special・a……

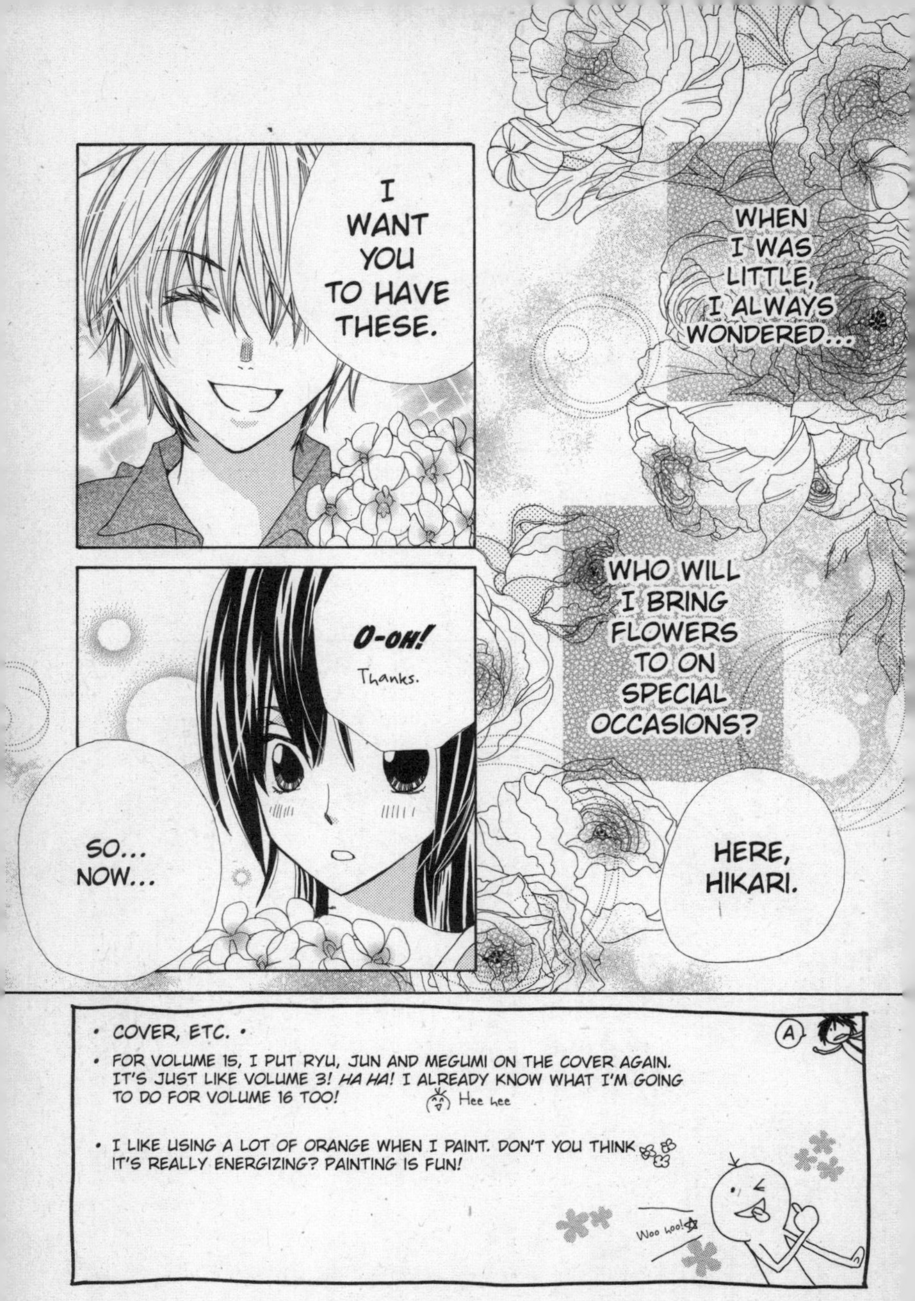
WHEN I WAS LITTLE, I ALWAYS WONDERED...
WHO WILL I BRING FLOWERS TO ON SPECIAL OCCASIONS?
HERE, HIKARI.
I WANT YOU TO HAVE THESE.
O-OH!
Thanks.
SO... NOW...

• COVER, ETC. •

• FOR VOLUME 15, I PUT RYU, JUN AND MEGUMI ON THE COVER AGAIN. IT'S JUST LIKE VOLUME 3! *HA HA!* I ALREADY KNOW WHAT I'M GOING TO DO FOR VOLUME 16 TOO! Hee hee

• I LIKE USING A LOT OF ORANGE WHEN I PAINT. DON'T YOU THINK IT'S REALLY ENERGIZING? PAINTING IS FUN!

Woo woo!

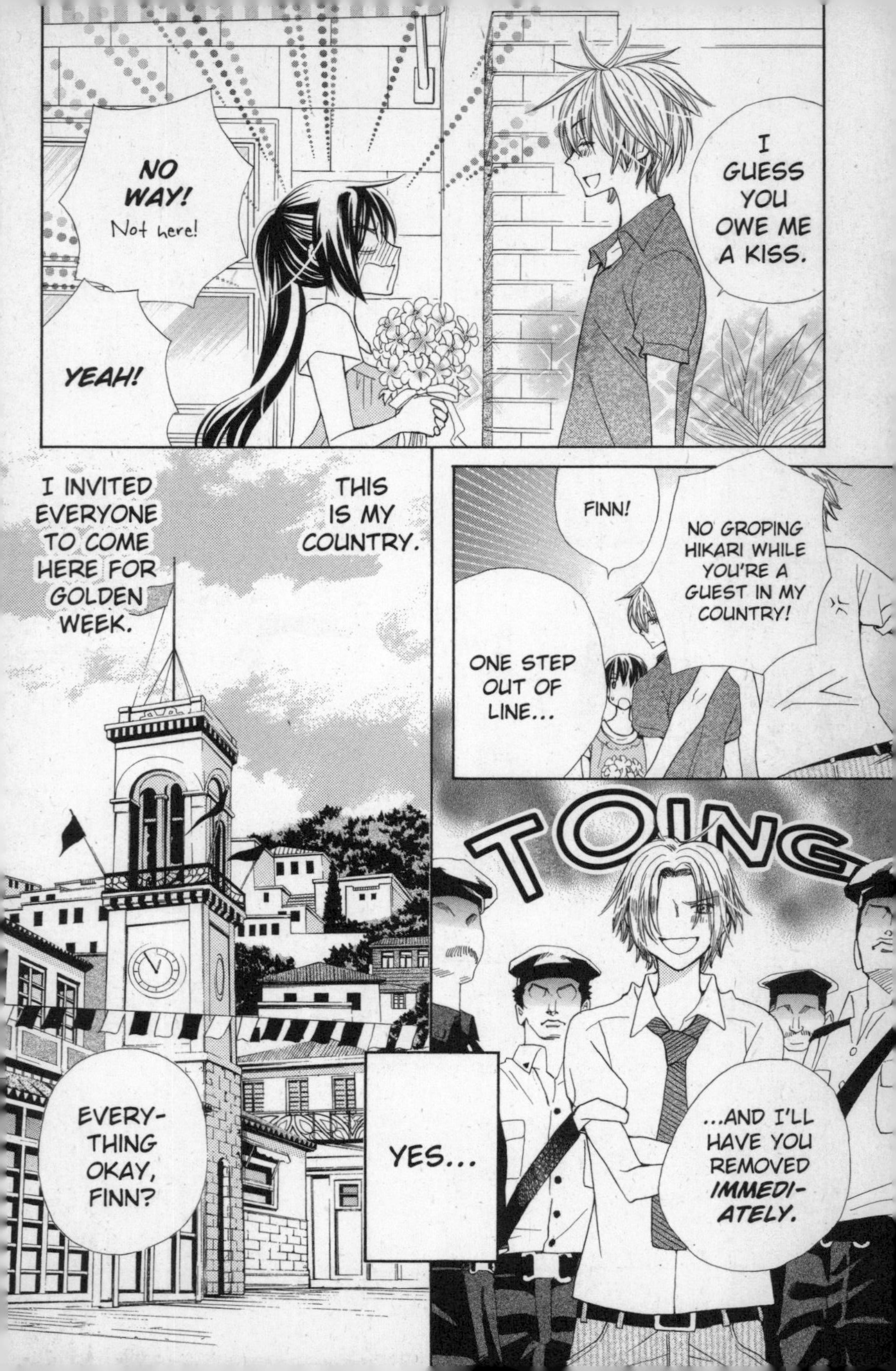
I GUESS YOU OWE ME A KISS.
NO WAY!
Not here!
YEAH!
FINN!
NO GROPING HIKARI WHILE YOU'RE A GUEST IN MY COUNTRY!
ONE STEP OUT OF LINE...
TOING
...AND I'LL HAVE YOU REMOVED IMMEDI-ATELY.
YES...
THIS IS MY COUNTRY.
I INVITED EVERYONE TO COME HERE FOR GOLDEN WEEK.
EVERY-THING OKAY, FINN?

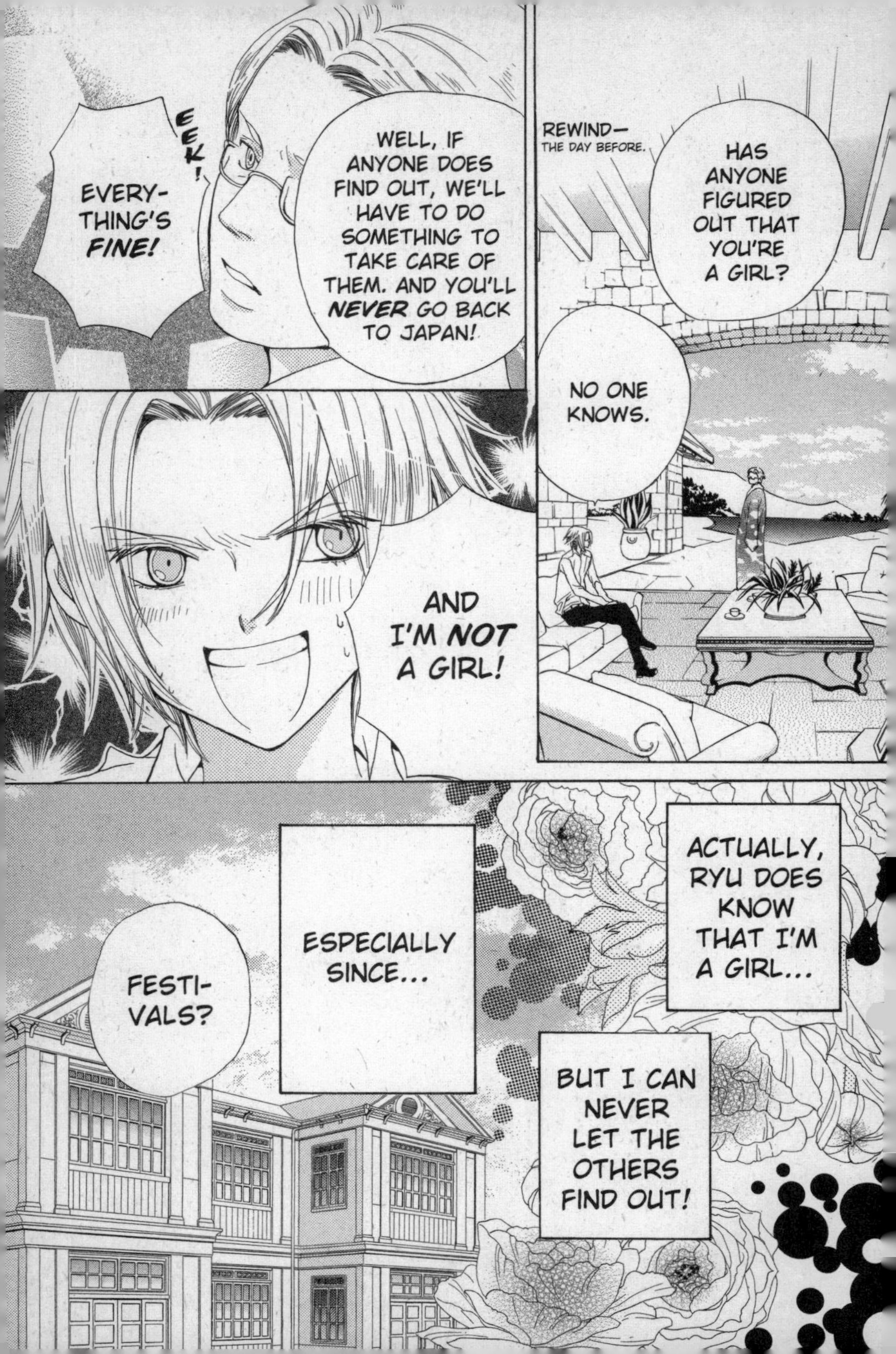
REWIND—
THE DAY BEFORE.
HAS ANYONE FIGURED OUT THAT YOU'RE A GIRL?
NO ONE KNOWS.
WELL, IF ANYONE DOES FIND OUT, WE'LL HAVE TO DO SOMETHING TO TAKE CARE OF THEM. AND YOU'LL NEVER GO BACK TO JAPAN!
EEK!
EVERYTHING'S FINE!
AND I'M NOT A GIRL!
ACTUALLY, RYU DOES KNOW THAT I'M A GIRL...
BUT I CAN NEVER LET THE OTHERS FIND OUT!
ESPECIALLY SINCE...
FESTIVALS?

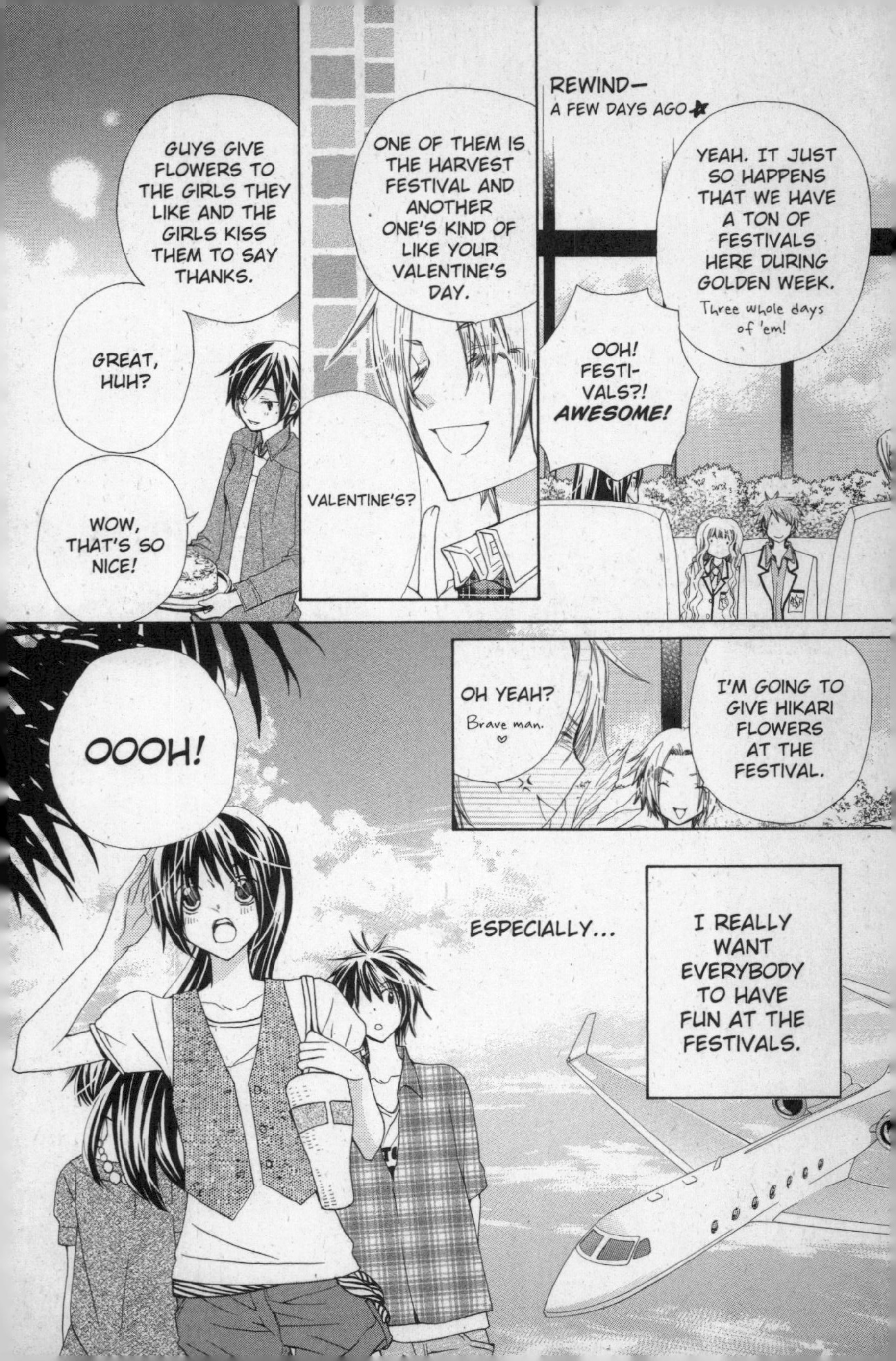
REWIND—
A FEW DAYS AGO
YEAH. IT JUST SO HAPPENS THAT WE HAVE A TON OF FESTIVALS HERE DURING GOLDEN WEEK.
Three whole days of 'em!
OOH! FESTI-VALS?! **AWESOME!**
ONE OF THEM IS THE HARVEST FESTIVAL AND ANOTHER ONE'S KIND OF LIKE YOUR VALENTINE'S DAY.
VALENTINE'S?
GUYS GIVE FLOWERS TO THE GIRLS THEY LIKE AND THE GIRLS KISS THEM TO SAY THANKS.
GREAT, HUH?
WOW, THAT'S SO NICE!
I'M GOING TO GIVE HIKARI FLOWERS AT THE FESTIVAL.
OH YEAH?
Brave man.
OOOH!
ESPECIALLY...
I REALLY WANT EVERYBODY TO HAVE FUN AT THE FESTIVALS.

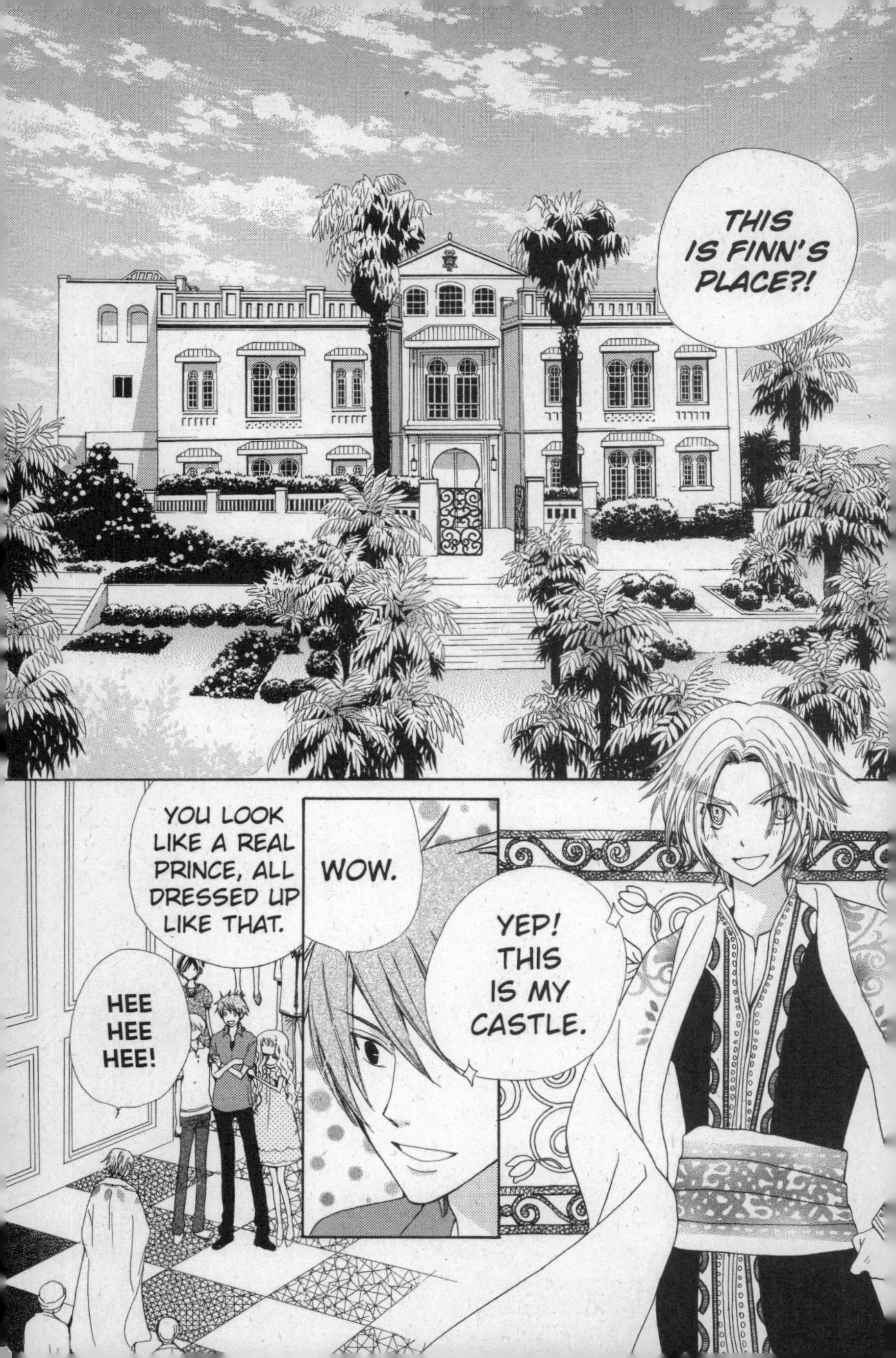
THIS IS FINN'S PLACE?!
YEP! THIS IS MY CASTLE.
WOW.
YOU LOOK LIKE A REAL PRINCE, ALL DRESSED UP LIKE THAT.
HEE HEE HEE!

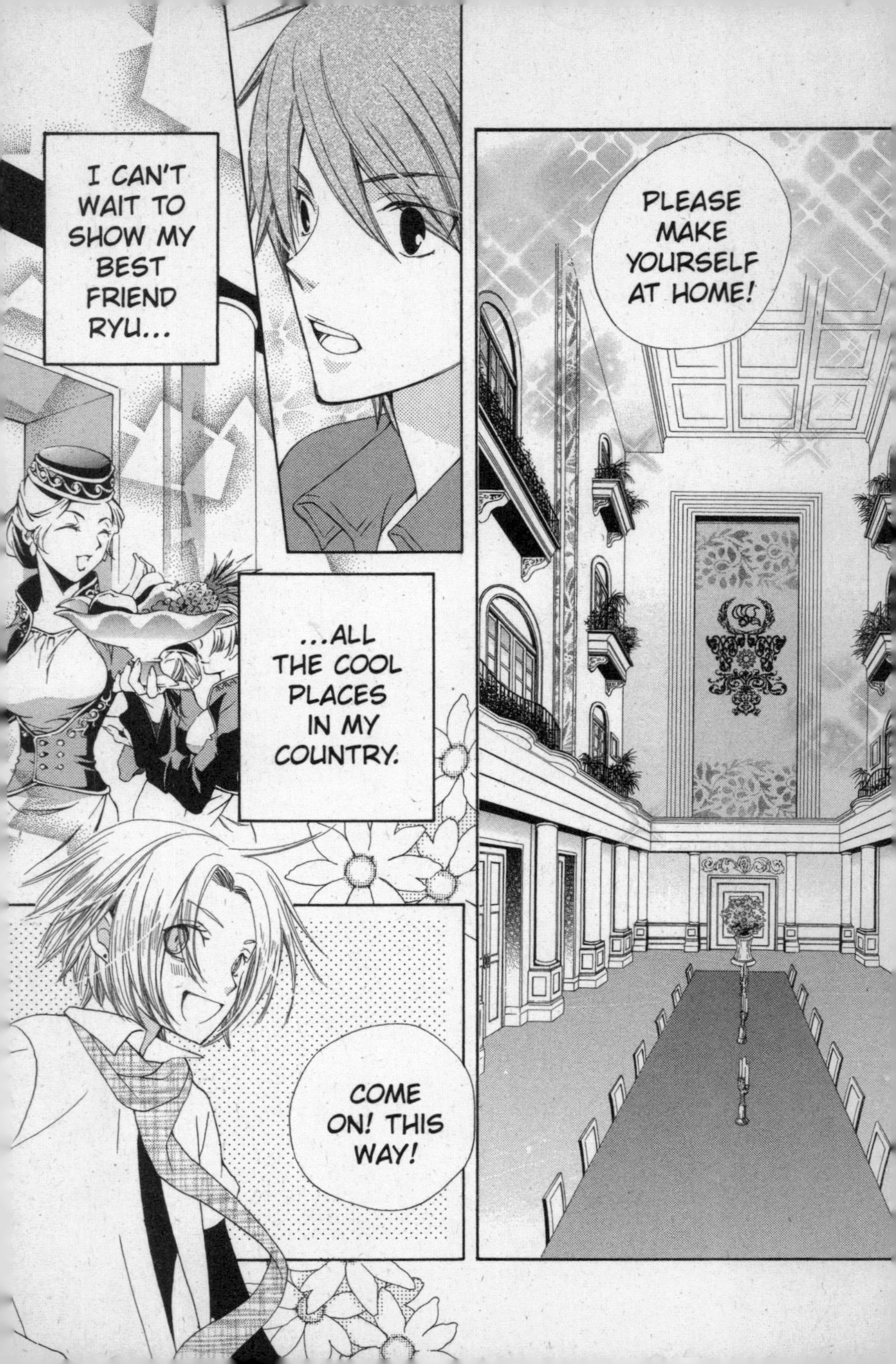
PLEASE MAKE YOURSELF AT HOME!
I CAN'T WAIT TO SHOW MY BEST FRIEND RYU...
...ALL THE COOL PLACES IN MY COUNTRY.
COME ON! THIS WAY!

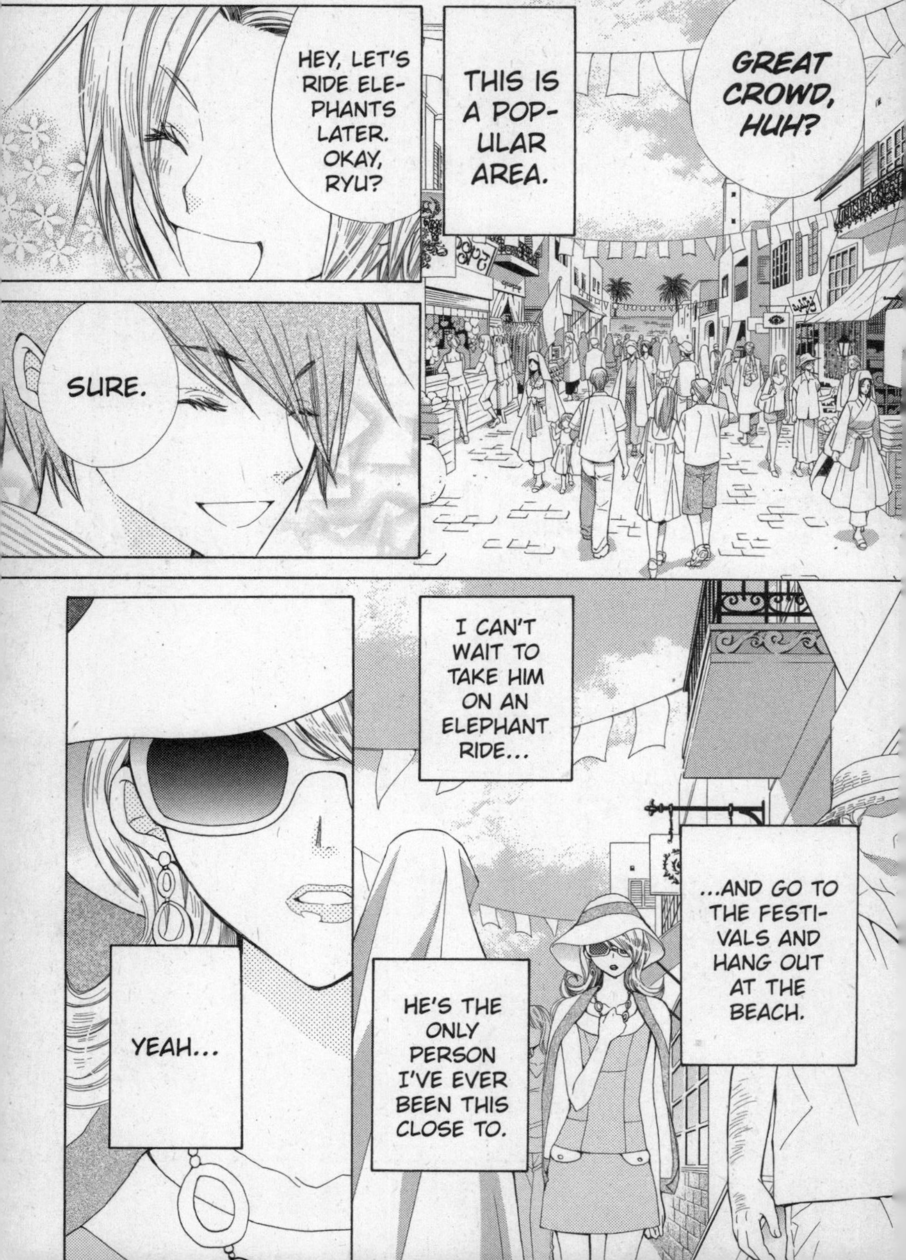
GREAT CROWD, HUH?
THIS IS A POPULAR AREA.
HEY, LET'S RIDE ELEPHANTS LATER. OKAY, RYU?
SURE.
...AND GO TO THE FESTIVALS AND HANG OUT AT THE BEACH.
I CAN'T WAIT TO TAKE HIM ON AN ELEPHANT RIDE...
HE'S THE ONLY PERSON I'VE EVER BEEN THIS CLOSE TO.
YEAH...

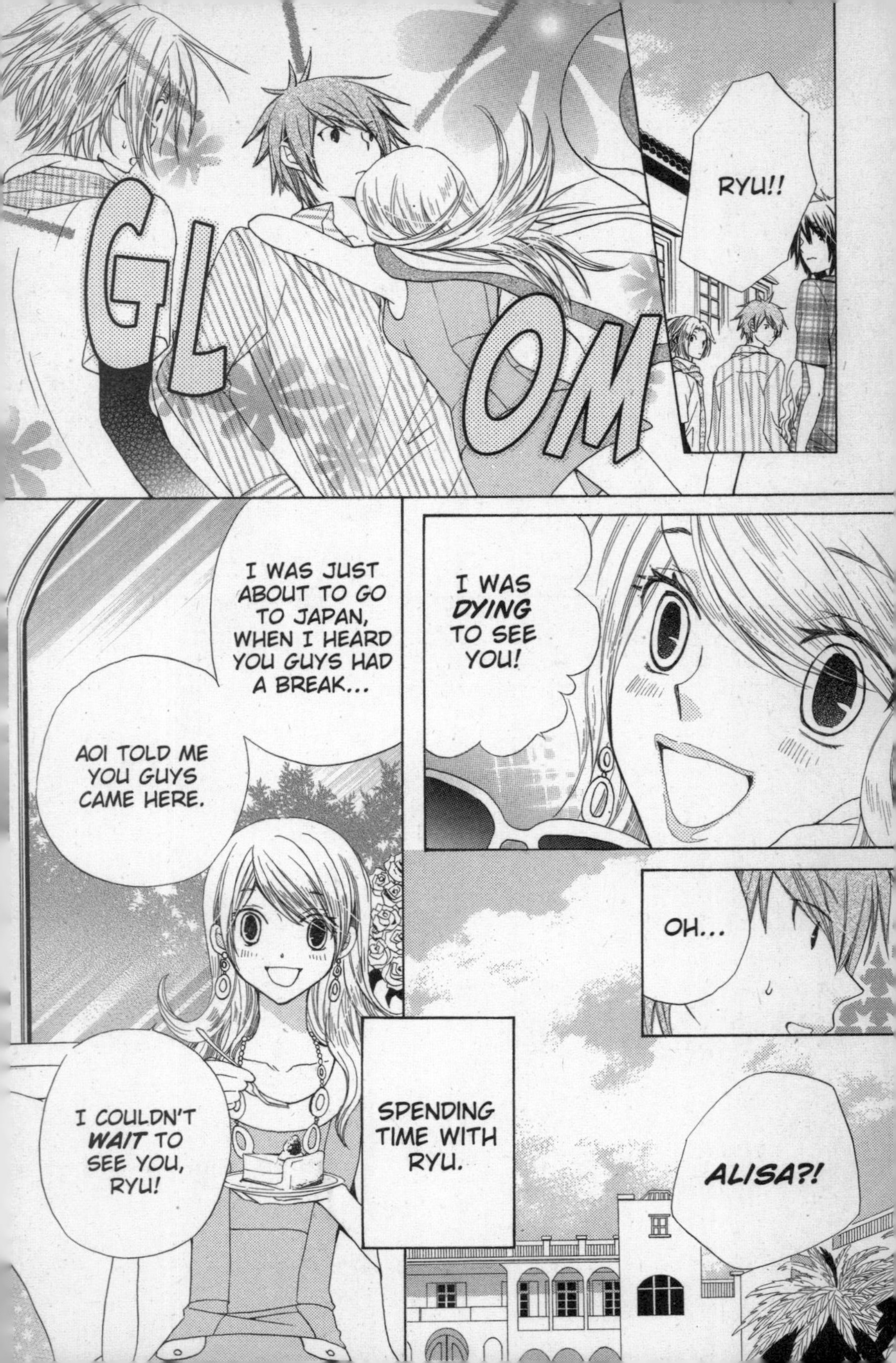
RYU!!
GLOM
I WAS DYING TO SEE YOU!
OH...
ALISA?!
SPENDING TIME WITH RYU.
I WAS JUST ABOUT TO GO TO JAPAN, WHEN I HEARD YOU GUYS HAD A BREAK...
AOI TOLD ME YOU GUYS CAME HERE.
I COULDN'T WAIT TO SEE YOU, RYU!

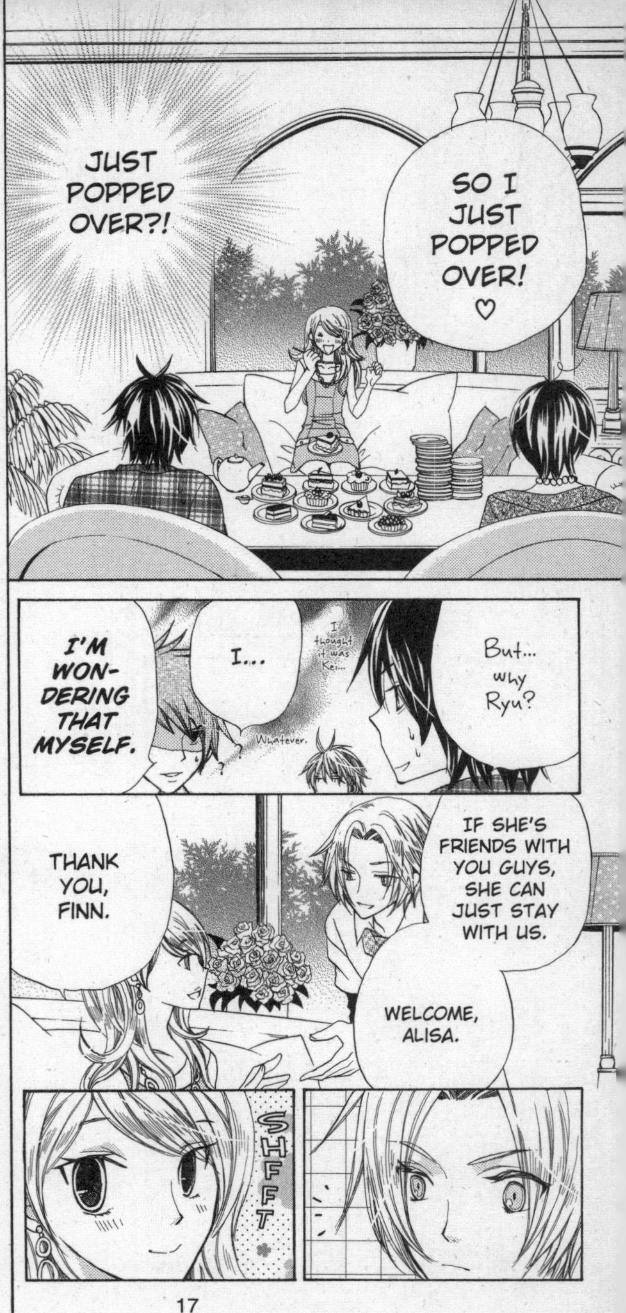
SO I JUST POPPED OVER! ♡
JUST POPPED OVER?!
But... why Ryu?
I thought it was Kei...
I...
Whatever.
I'M WON-DERING THAT MYSELF.
IF SHE'S FRIENDS WITH YOU GUYS, SHE CAN JUST STAY WITH US.
WELCOME, ALISA.
THANK YOU, FINN.
SHFFT

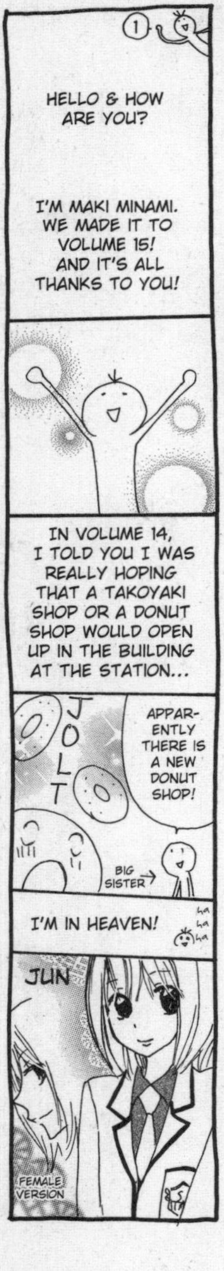
1
HELLO & HOW ARE YOU?
I'M MAKI MINAMI. WE MADE IT TO VOLUME 15! AND IT'S ALL THANKS TO YOU!
IN VOLUME 14, I TOLD YOU I WAS REALLY HOPING THAT A TAKOYAKI SHOP OR A DONUT SHOP WOULD OPEN UP IN THE BUILDING AT THE STATION...
APPAR-ENTLY THERE IS A NEW DONUT SHOP!
JOLT
BIG SISTER
I'M IN HEAVEN!
ha ha ha
JUN
FEMALE VERSION

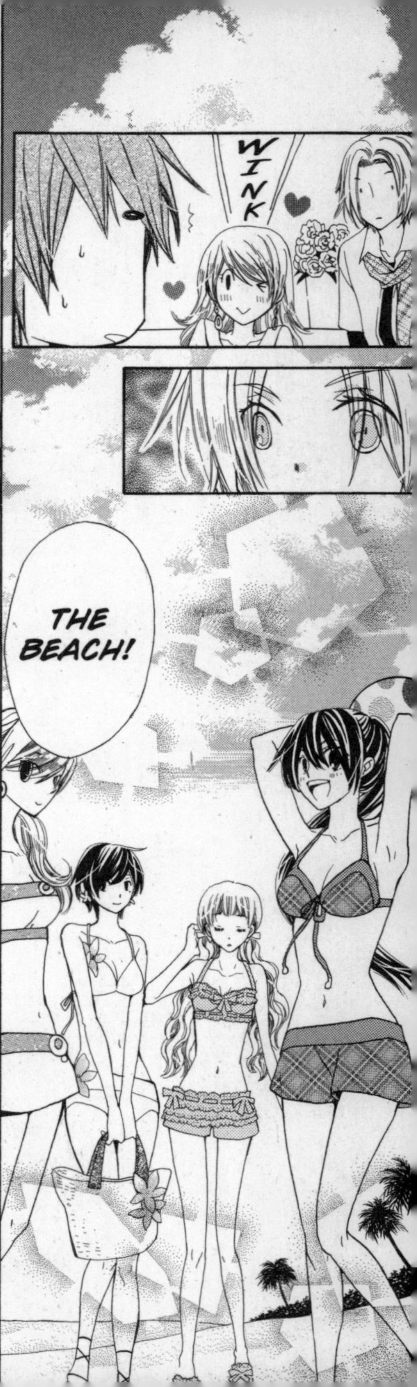
WINK
THE BEACH!
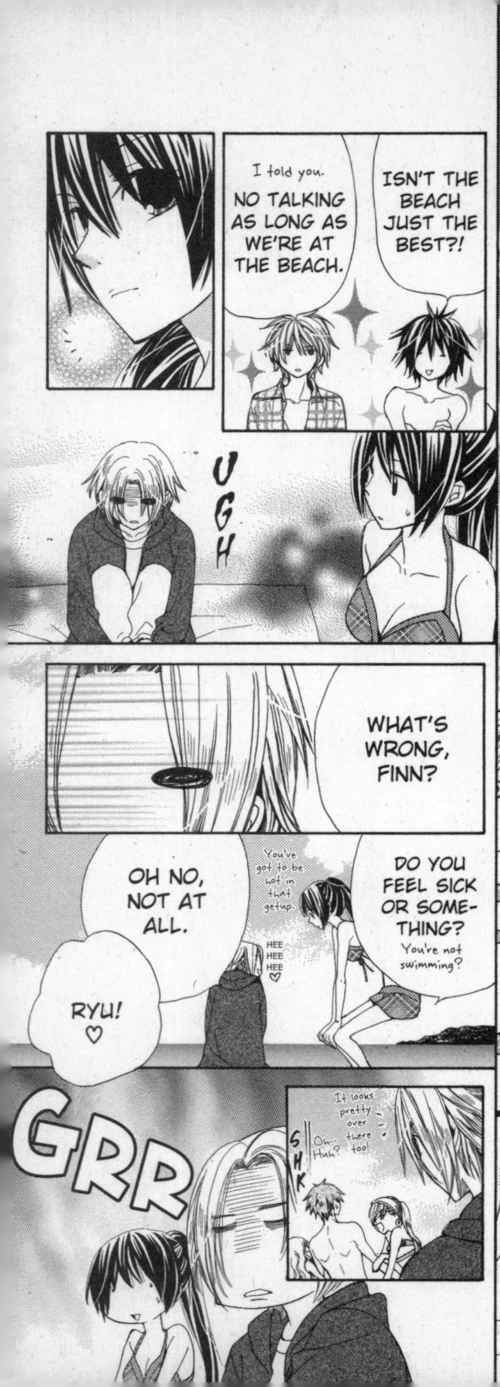
ISN'T THE BEACH JUST THE BEST?!
I told you.
NO TALKING AS LONG AS WE'RE AT THE BEACH.
UGH
WHAT'S WRONG, FINN?
DO YOU FEEL SICK OR SOME-THING?
You're not swimming?
You've got to be hot in that getup.
HEE HEE HEE ♡
OH NO, NOT AT ALL.
RYU! ♡
It looks pretty over there too!
Oh... Huh?
SHK
GRR

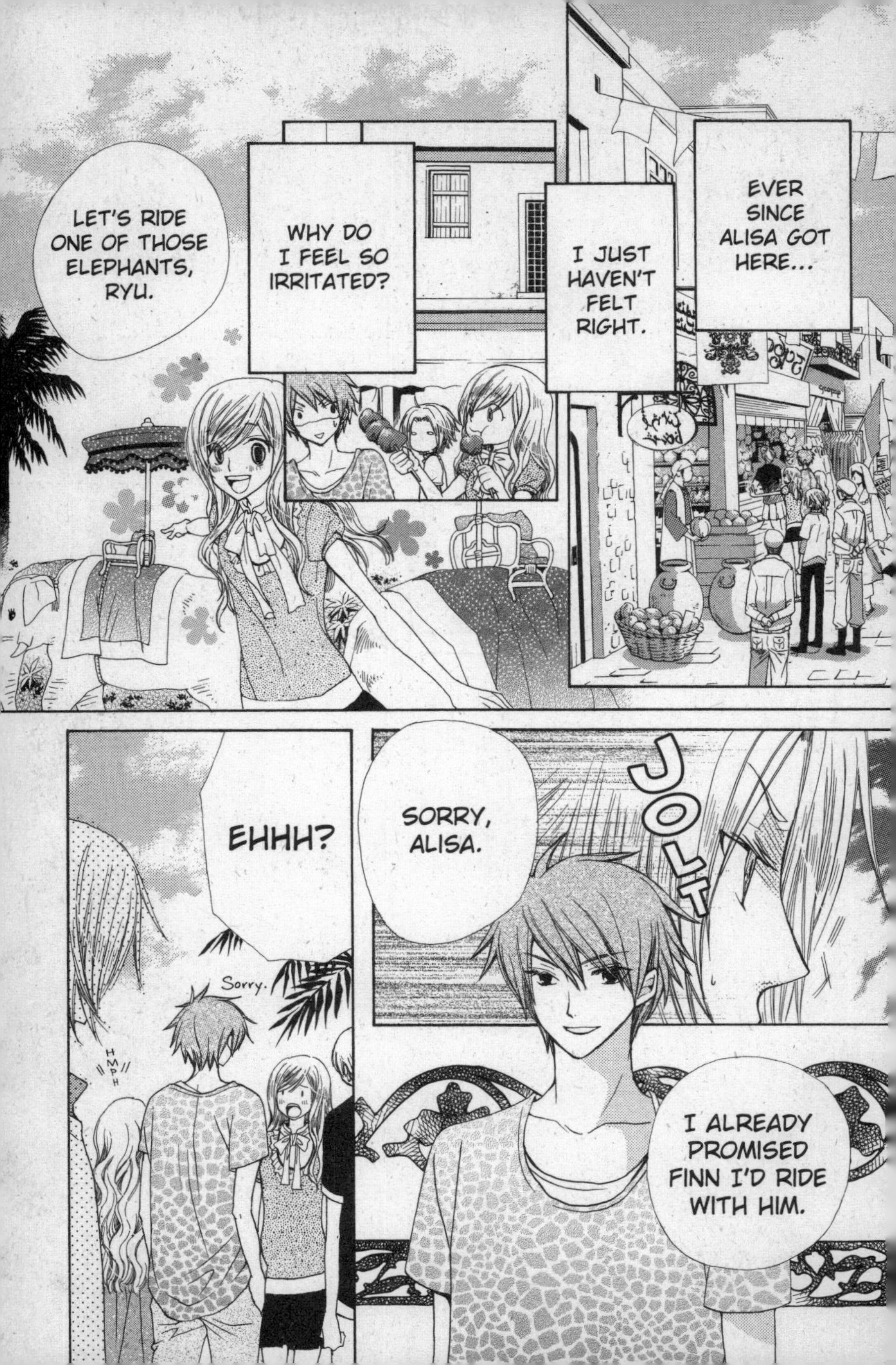
EVER SINCE ALISA GOT HERE...
I JUST HAVEN'T FELT RIGHT.
WHY DO I FEEL SO IRRITATED?
LET'S RIDE ONE OF THOSE ELEPHANTS, RYU.
JOLT
SORRY, ALISA.
I ALREADY PROMISED FINN I'D RIDE WITH HIM.
EHHH?
Sorry.
HMPH

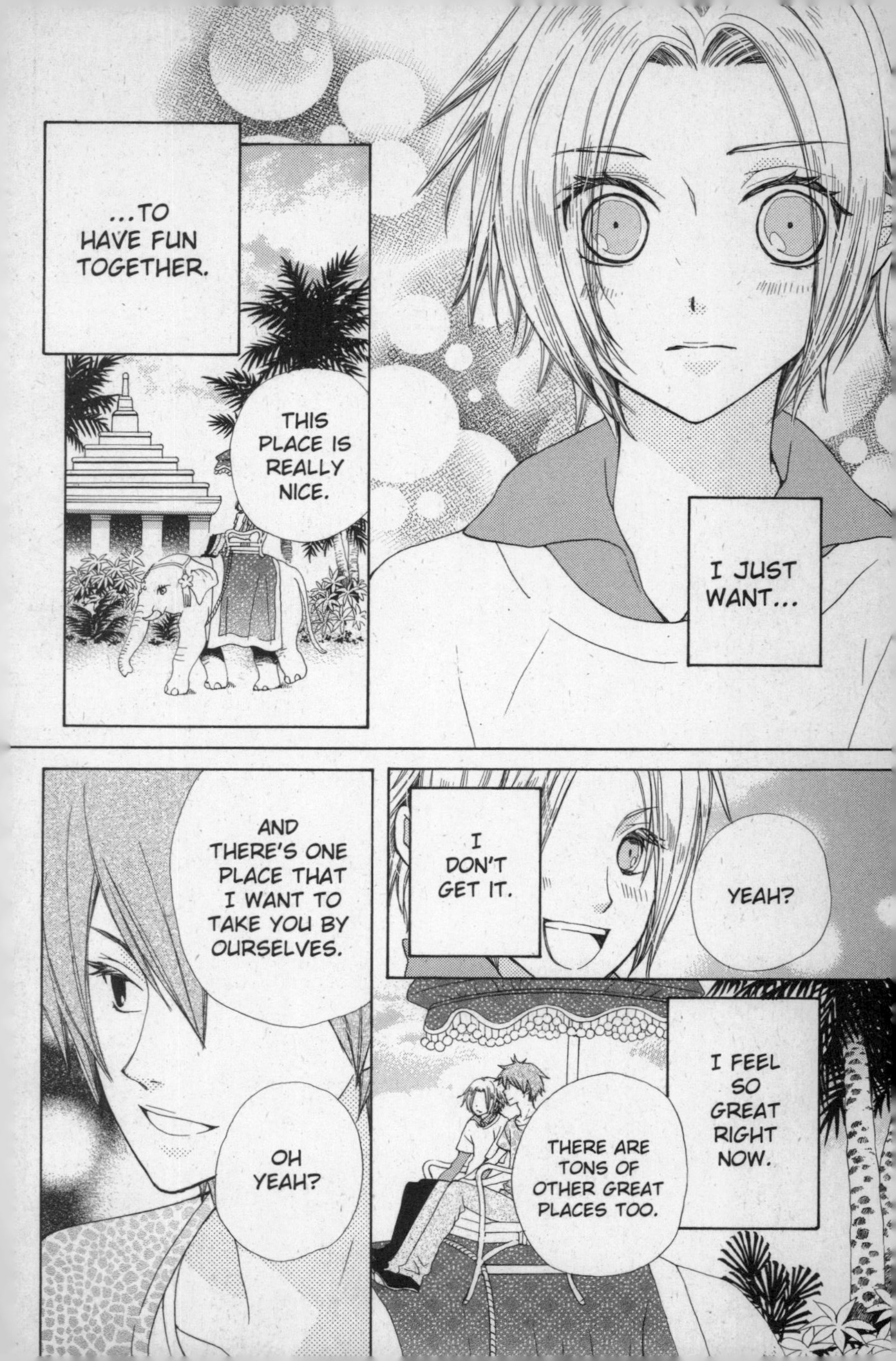
I JUST WANT...
...TO HAVE FUN TOGETHER.
THIS PLACE IS REALLY NICE.
YEAH?
I DON'T GET IT.
I FEEL SO GREAT RIGHT NOW.
THERE ARE TONS OF OTHER GREAT PLACES TOO.
AND THERE'S ONE PLACE THAT I WANT TO TAKE YOU BY OURSELVES.
OH YEAH?

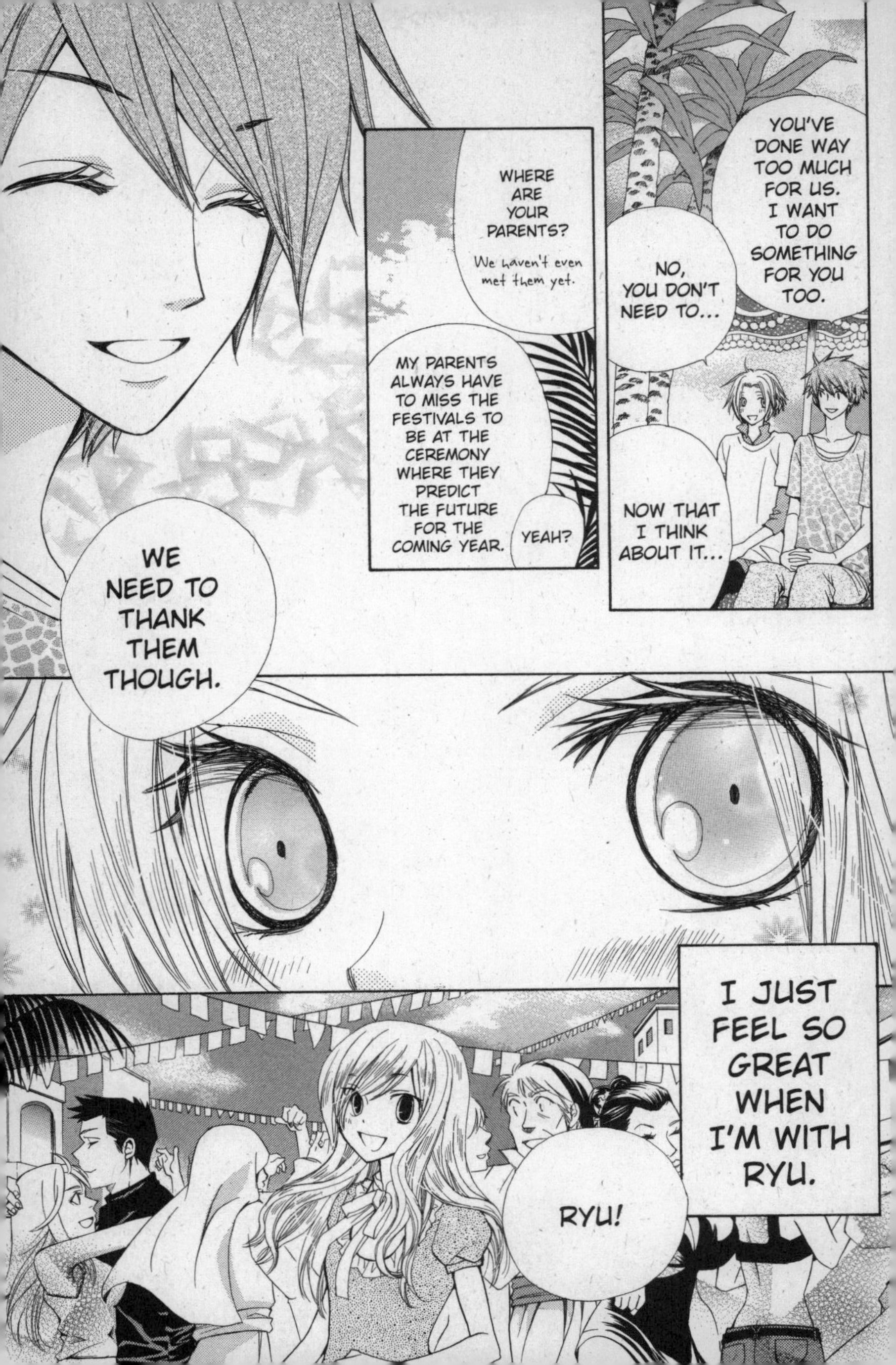
YOU'VE DONE WAY TOO MUCH FOR US. I WANT TO DO SOMETHING FOR YOU TOO.
NO, YOU DON'T NEED TO...
NOW THAT I THINK ABOUT IT...
WHERE ARE YOUR PARENTS?
We haven't even met them yet.
MY PARENTS ALWAYS HAVE TO MISS THE FESTIVALS TO BE AT THE CEREMONY WHERE THEY PREDICT THE FUTURE FOR THE COMING YEAR.
YEAH?
WE NEED TO THANK THEM THOUGH.
I JUST FEEL SO GREAT WHEN I'M WITH RYU.
RYU!

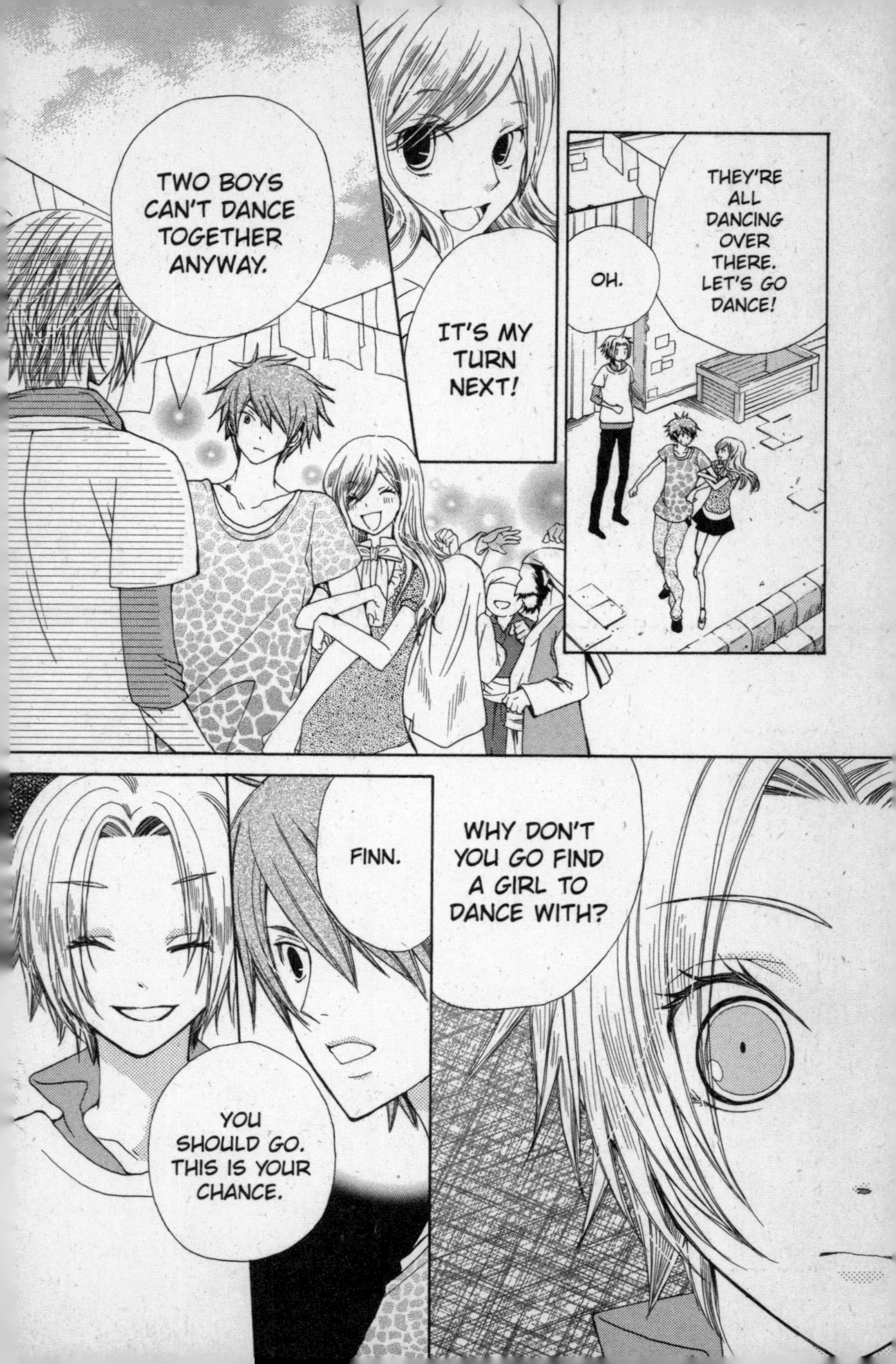
THEY'RE ALL DANCING OVER THERE. LET'S GO DANCE!
OH.
IT'S MY TURN NEXT!
TWO BOYS CAN'T DANCE TOGETHER ANYWAY.
WHY DON'T YOU GO FIND A GIRL TO DANCE WITH?
FINN.
YOU SHOULD GO. THIS IS YOUR CHANCE.

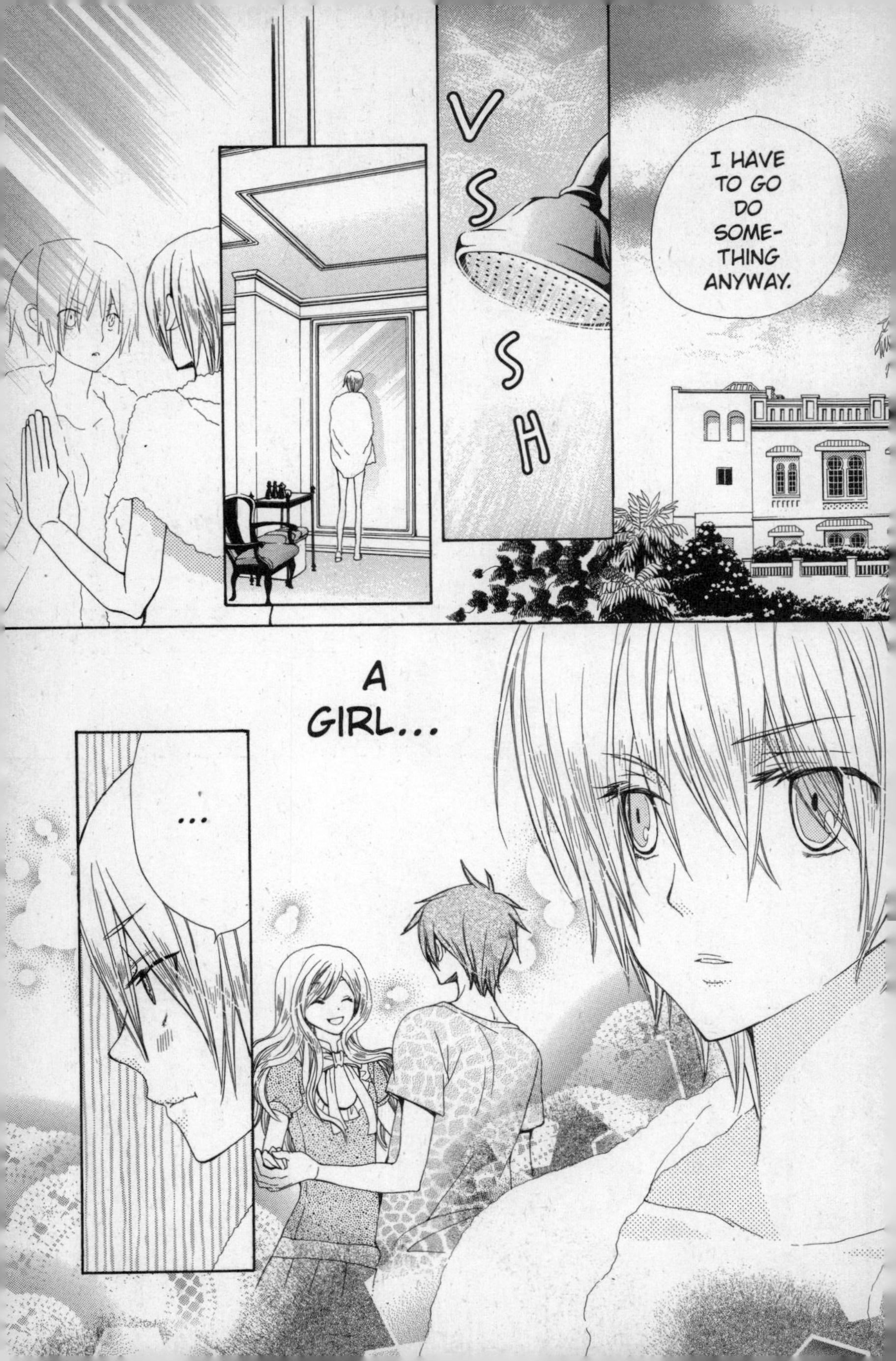
I HAVE TO GO DO SOME-THING ANYWAY.
VSSH
A GIRL...
...

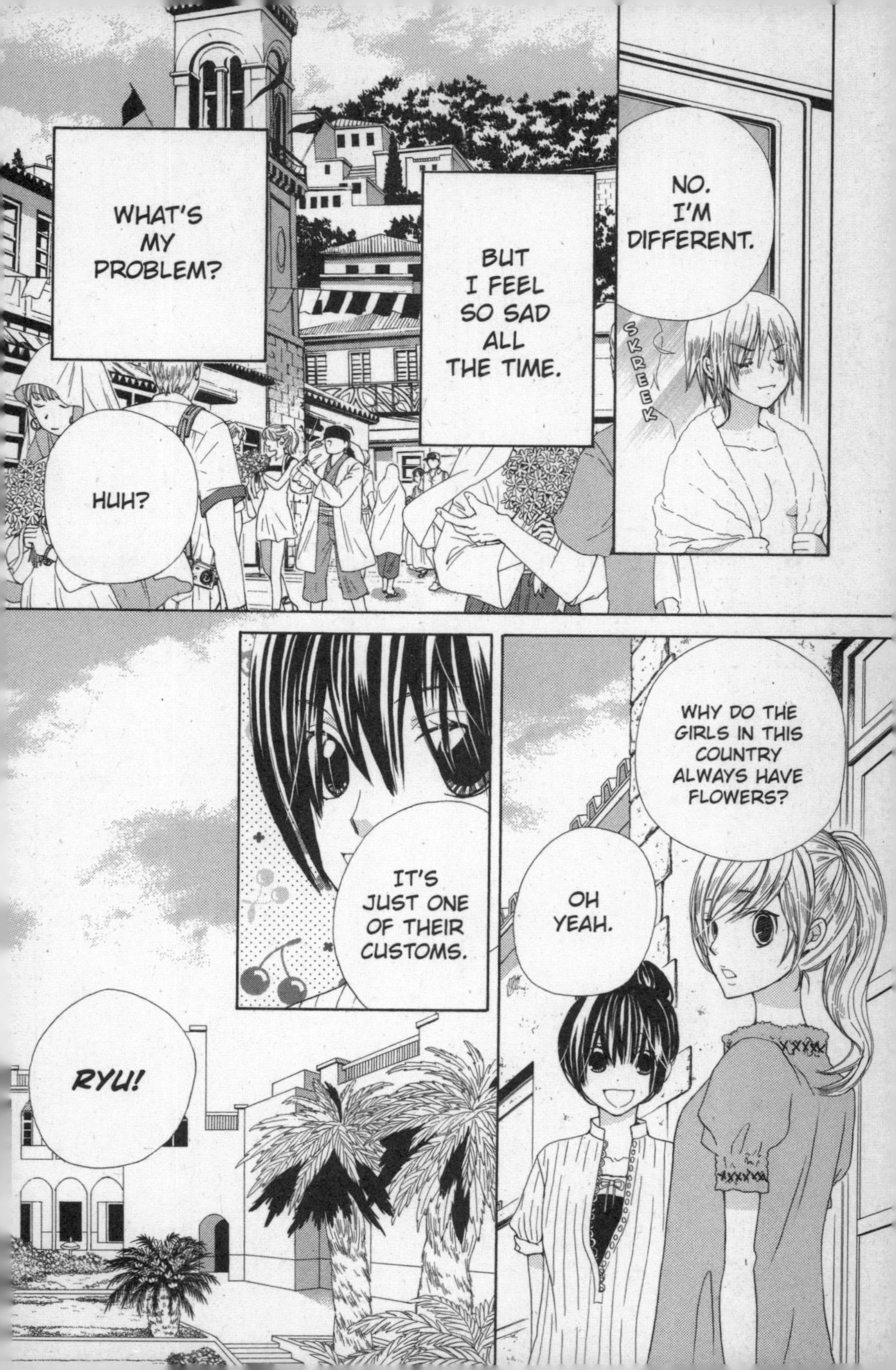
NO. I'M DIFFERENT.
SKREEEK
BUT I FEEL SO SAD ALL THE TIME.
WHAT'S MY PROBLEM?
HUH?
WHY DO THE GIRLS IN THIS COUNTRY ALWAYS HAVE FLOWERS?
OH YEAH.
IT'S JUST ONE OF THEIR CUSTOMS.
RYU!

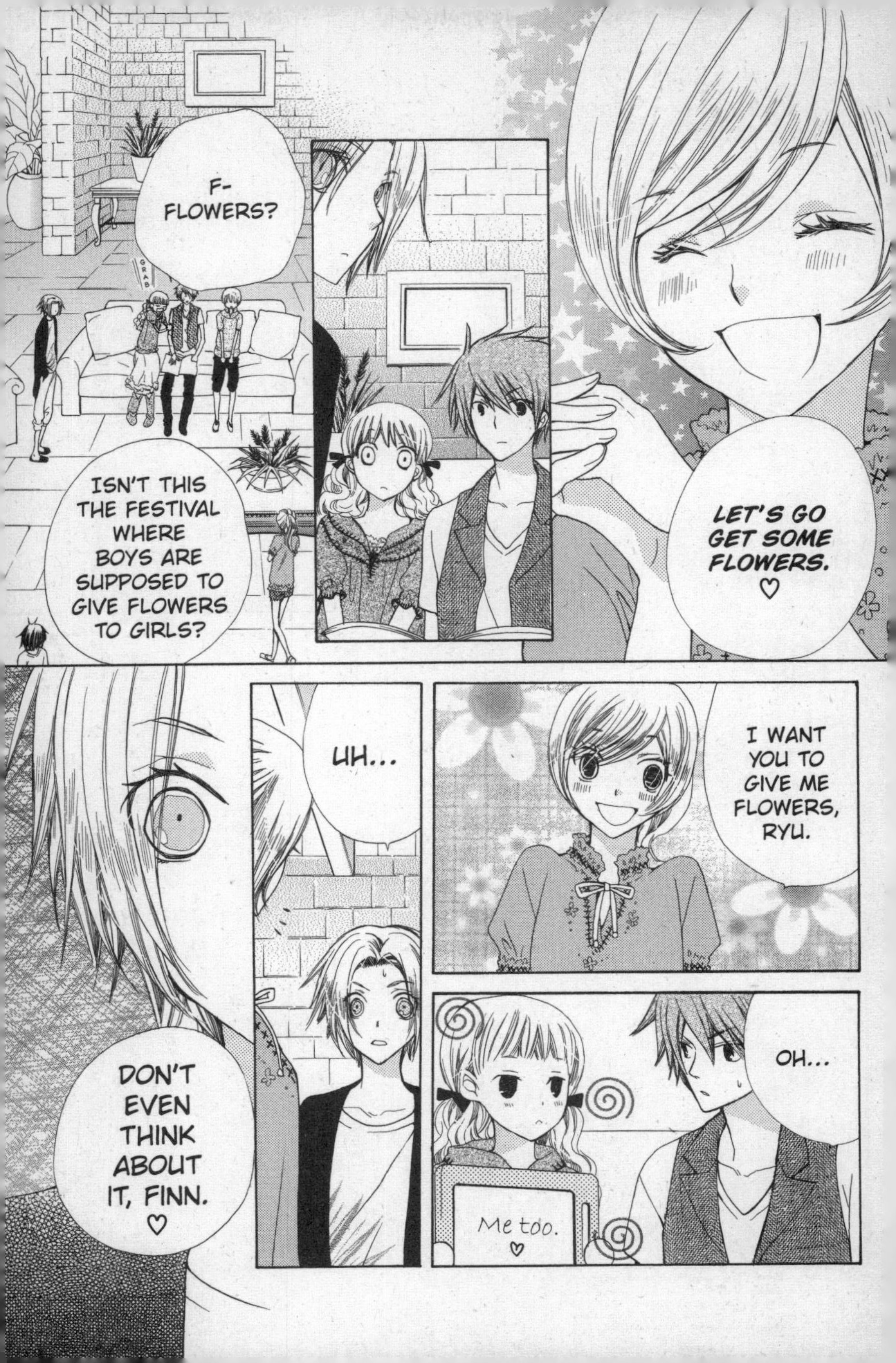
LET'S GO GET SOME FLOWERS. ♡
F- FLOWERS?
GRAB
ISN'T THIS THE FESTIVAL WHERE BOYS ARE SUPPOSED TO GIVE FLOWERS TO GIRLS?
I WANT YOU TO GIVE ME FLOWERS, RYU.
OH...
Me too. ♡
UH...
DON'T EVEN THINK ABOUT IT, FINN. ♡

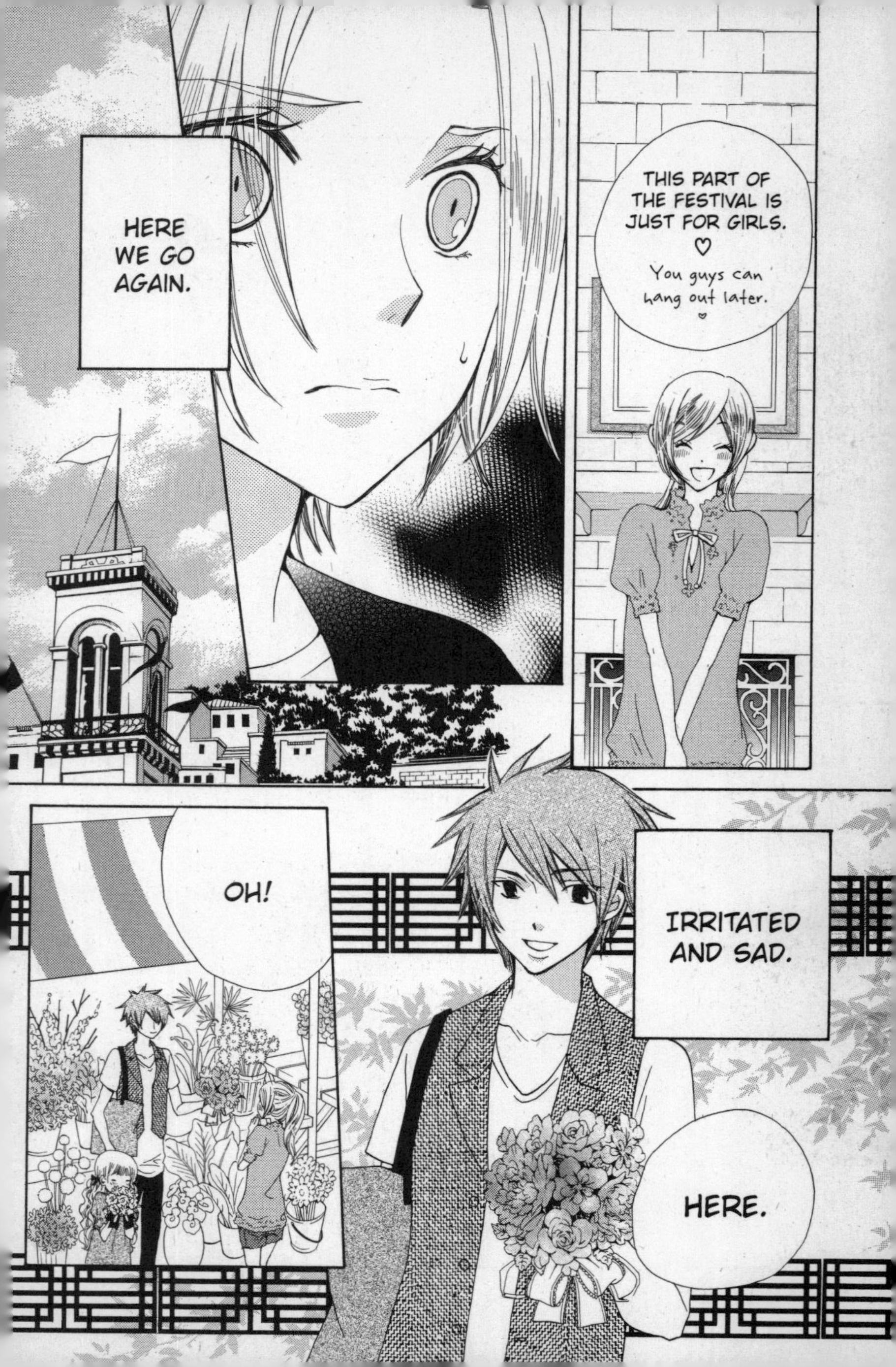
THIS PART OF THE FESTIVAL IS JUST FOR GIRLS. ♡
You guys can hang out later. ♡
HERE WE GO AGAIN.
IRRITATED AND SAD.
HERE.
OH!

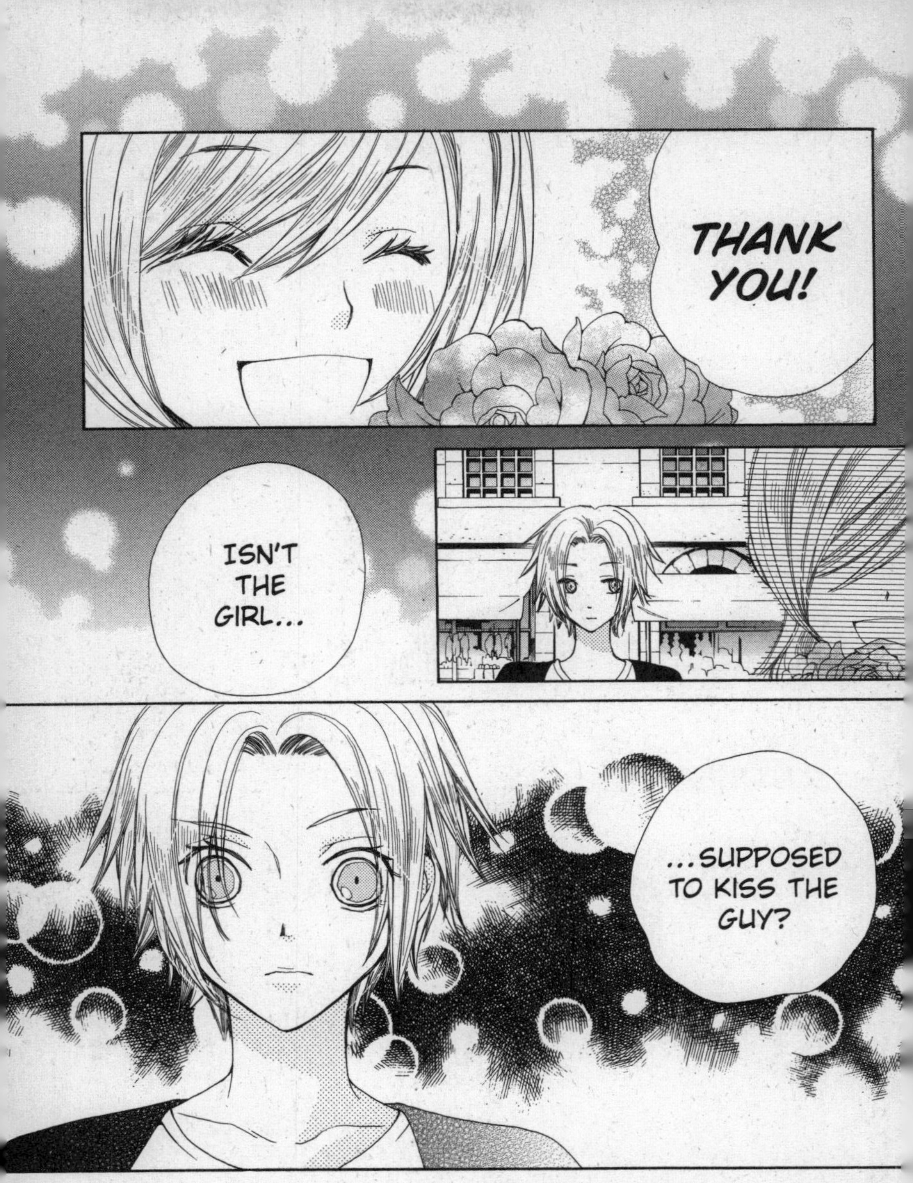
THANK YOU!
ISN'T THE GIRL...
...SUPPOSED TO KISS THE GUY?
IT'S WEIRD.

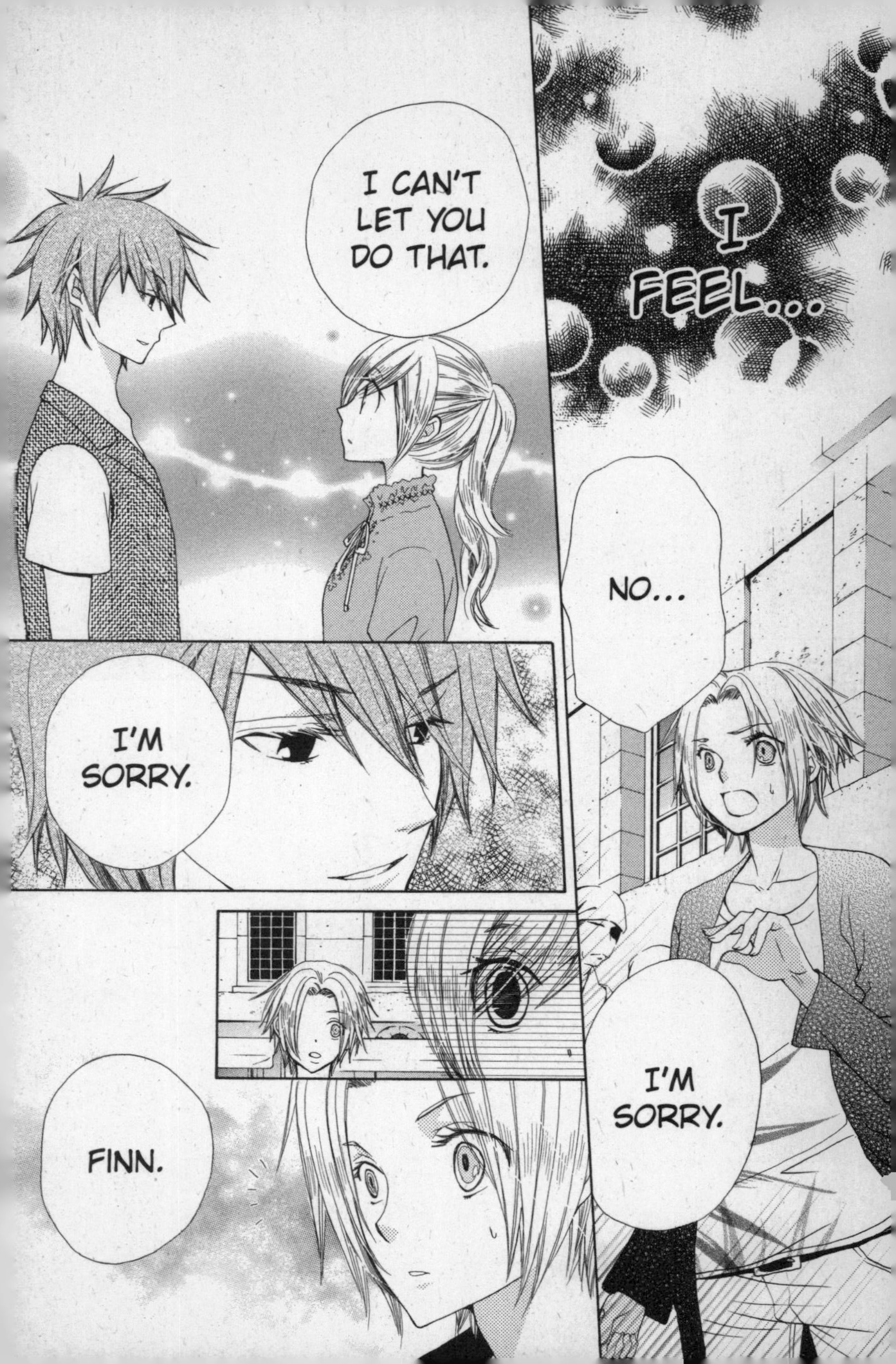
I FEEL...
NO...
I'M SORRY.
I CAN'T LET YOU DO THAT.
I'M SORRY.
FINN.

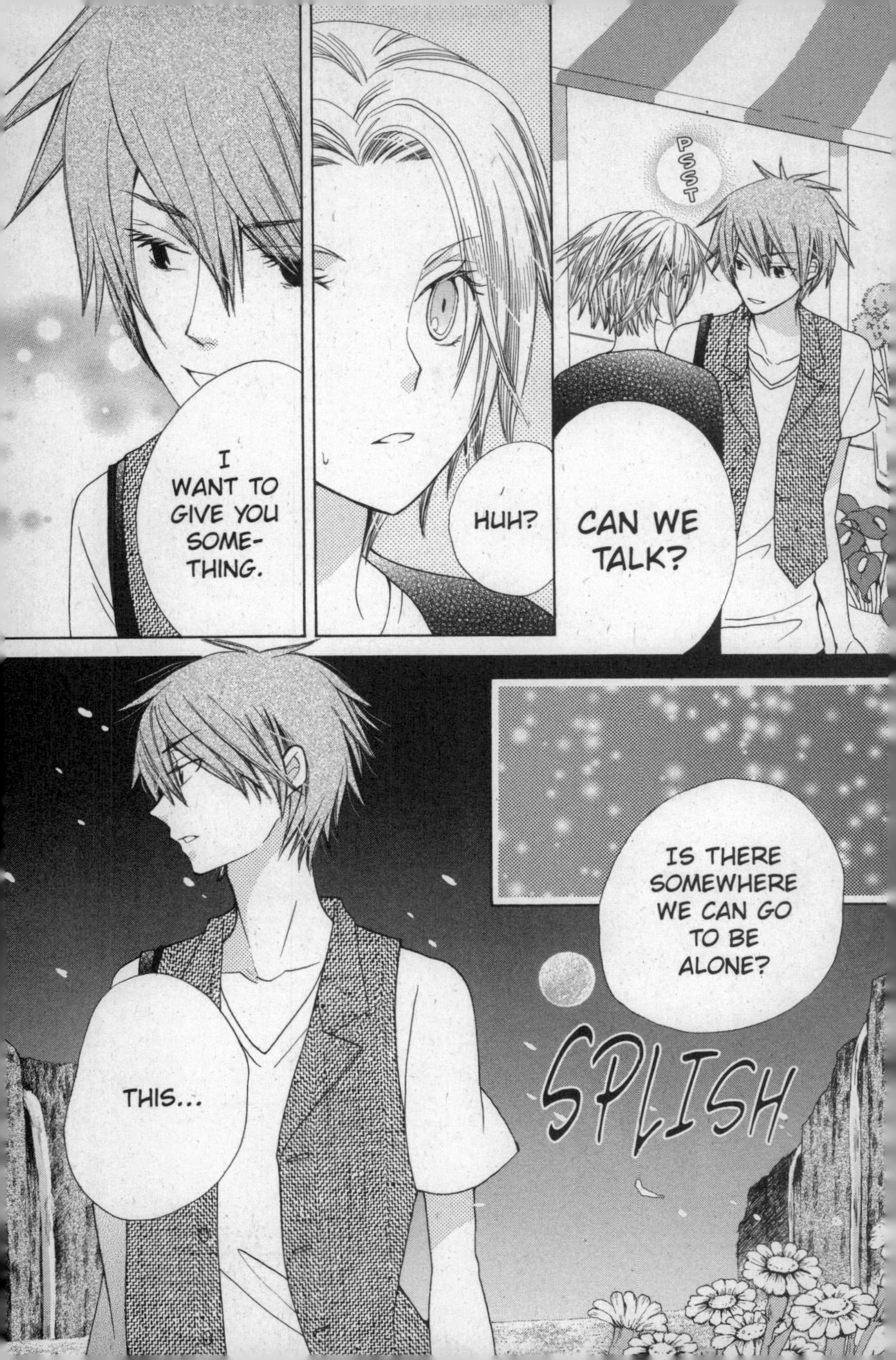
PSST
CAN WE TALK?
HUH?
I WANT TO GIVE YOU SOME-THING.
IS THERE SOMEWHERE WE CAN GO TO BE ALONE?
SPLISH
THIS...

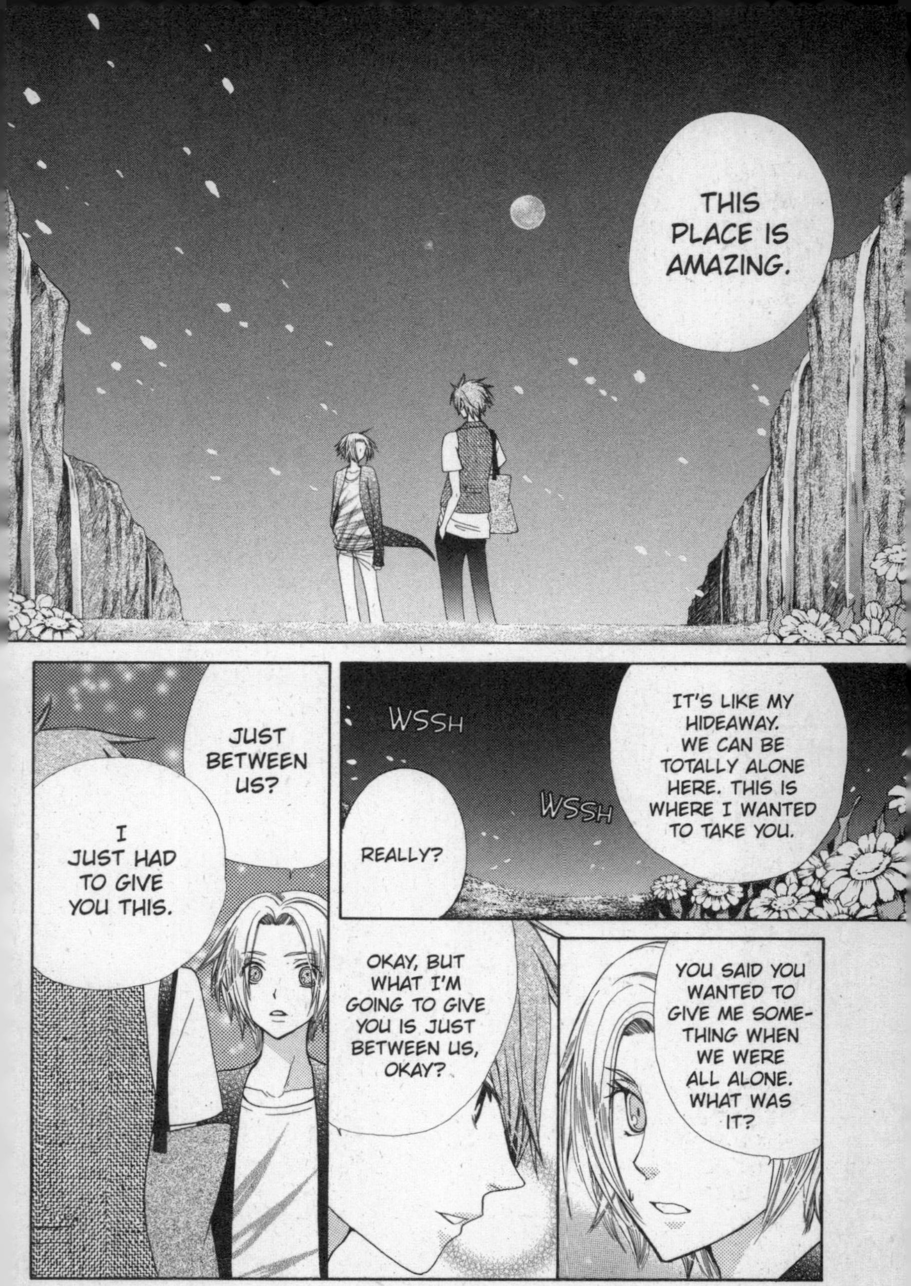
THIS PLACE IS AMAZING.
IT'S LIKE MY HIDEAWAY. WE CAN BE TOTALLY ALONE HERE. THIS IS WHERE I WANTED TO TAKE YOU.
WSSH
WSSH
REALLY?
YOU SAID YOU WANTED TO GIVE ME SOME-THING WHEN WE WERE ALL ALONE. WHAT WAS IT?
OKAY, BUT WHAT I'M GOING TO GIVE YOU IS JUST BETWEEN US, OKAY?
JUST BETWEEN US?
I JUST HAD TO GIVE YOU THIS.

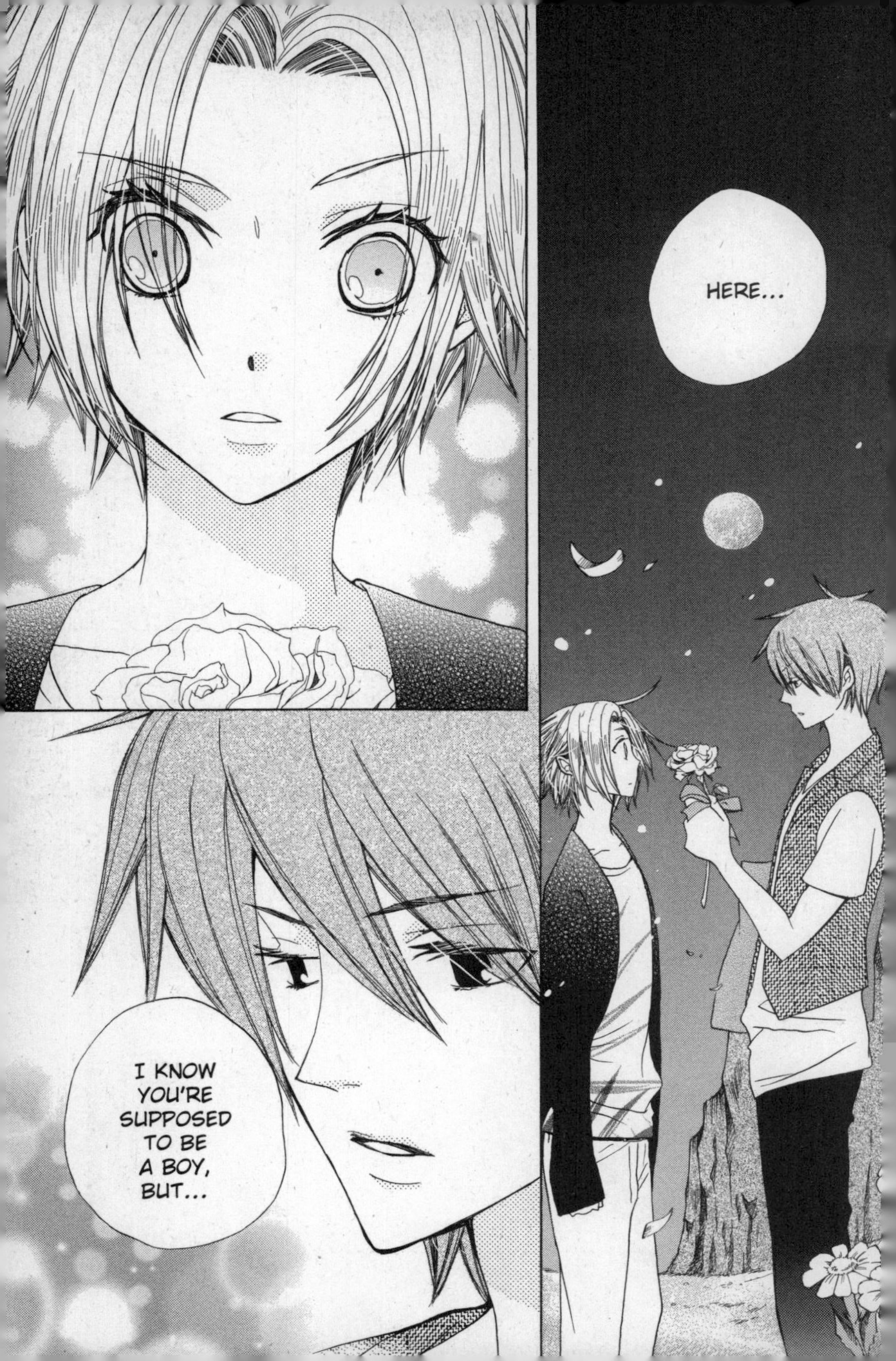
HERE...
I KNOW YOU'RE SUPPOSED TO BE A BOY, BUT...

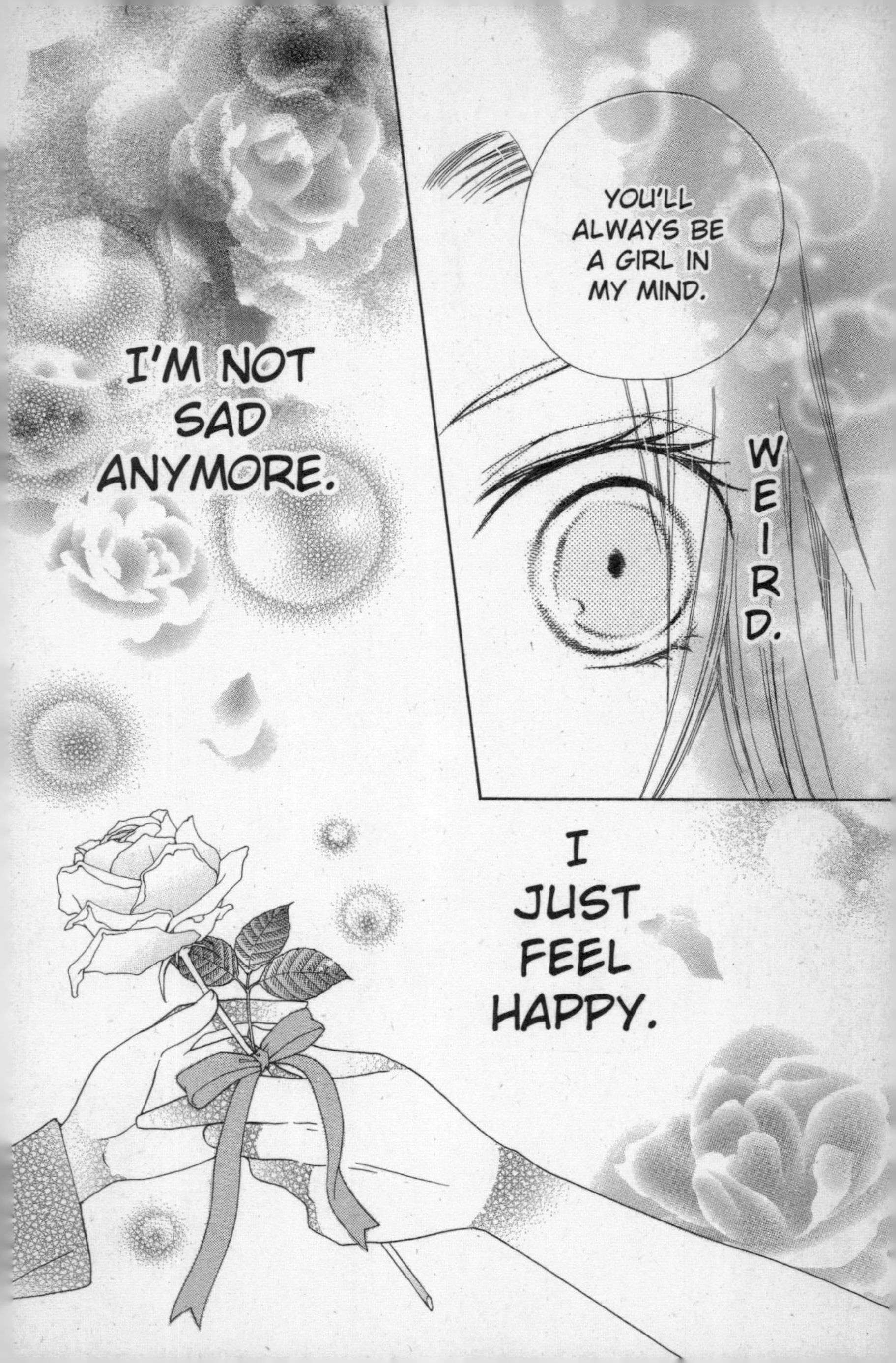
YOU'LL ALWAYS BE A GIRL IN MY MIND.
WEIRD.
I'M NOT SAD ANYMORE.
I JUST FEEL HAPPY.

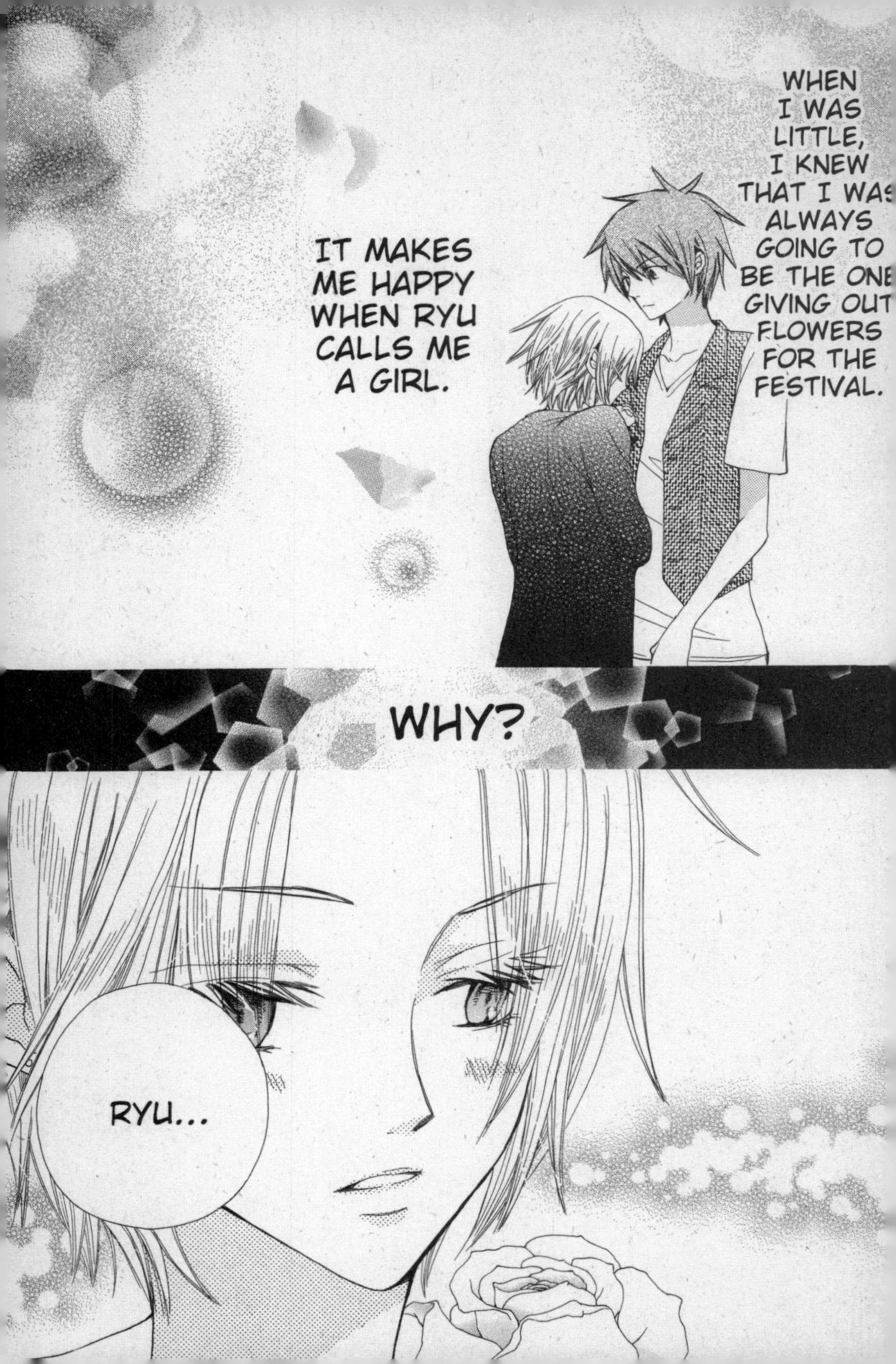
WHEN I WAS LITTLE, I KNEW THAT I WAS ALWAYS GOING TO BE THE ONE GIVING OUT FLOWERS FOR THE FESTIVAL.
IT MAKES ME HAPPY WHEN RYU CALLS ME A GIRL.
WHY?
RYU...

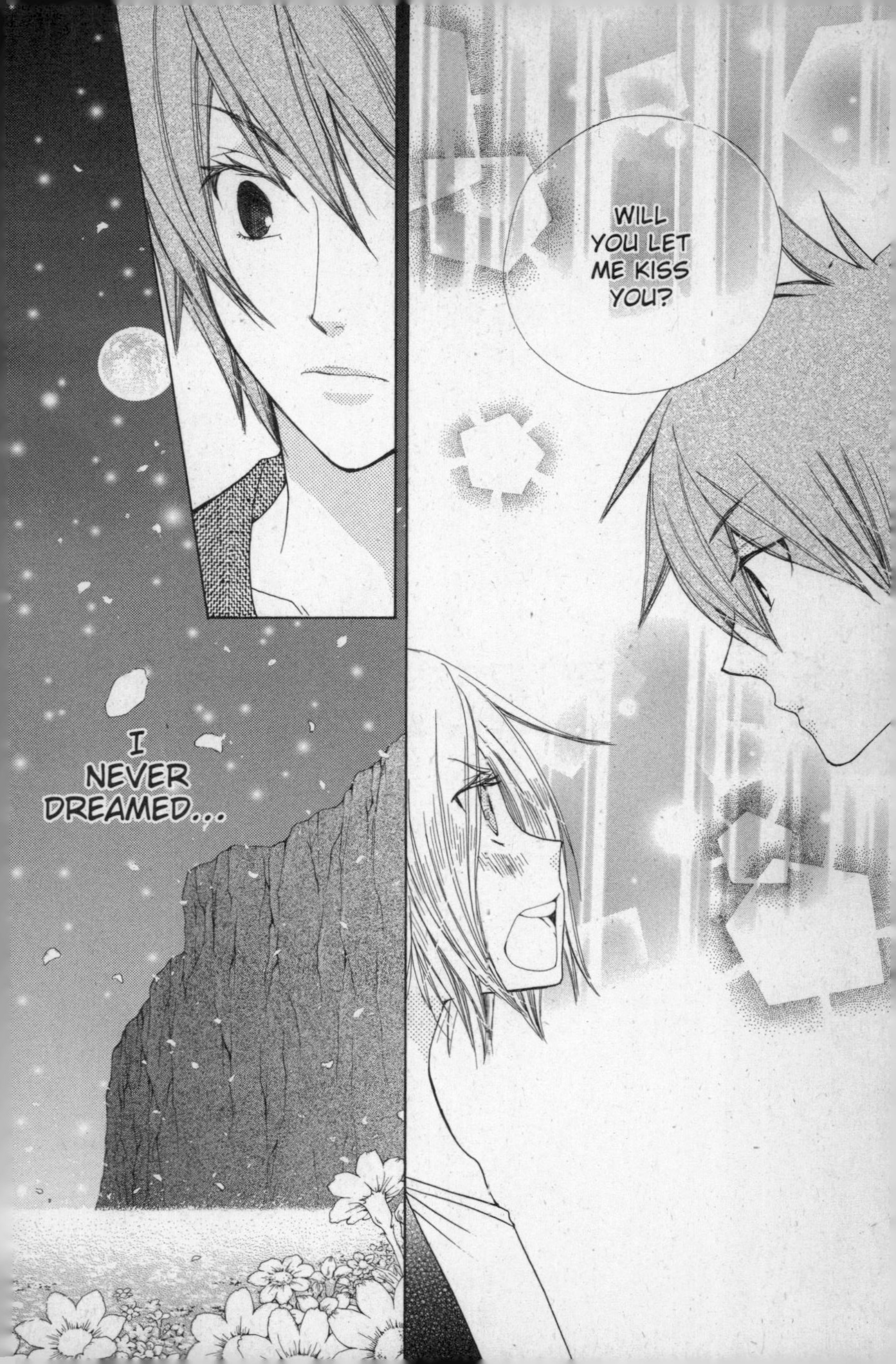
WILL YOU LET ME KISS YOU?
I NEVER DREAMED...

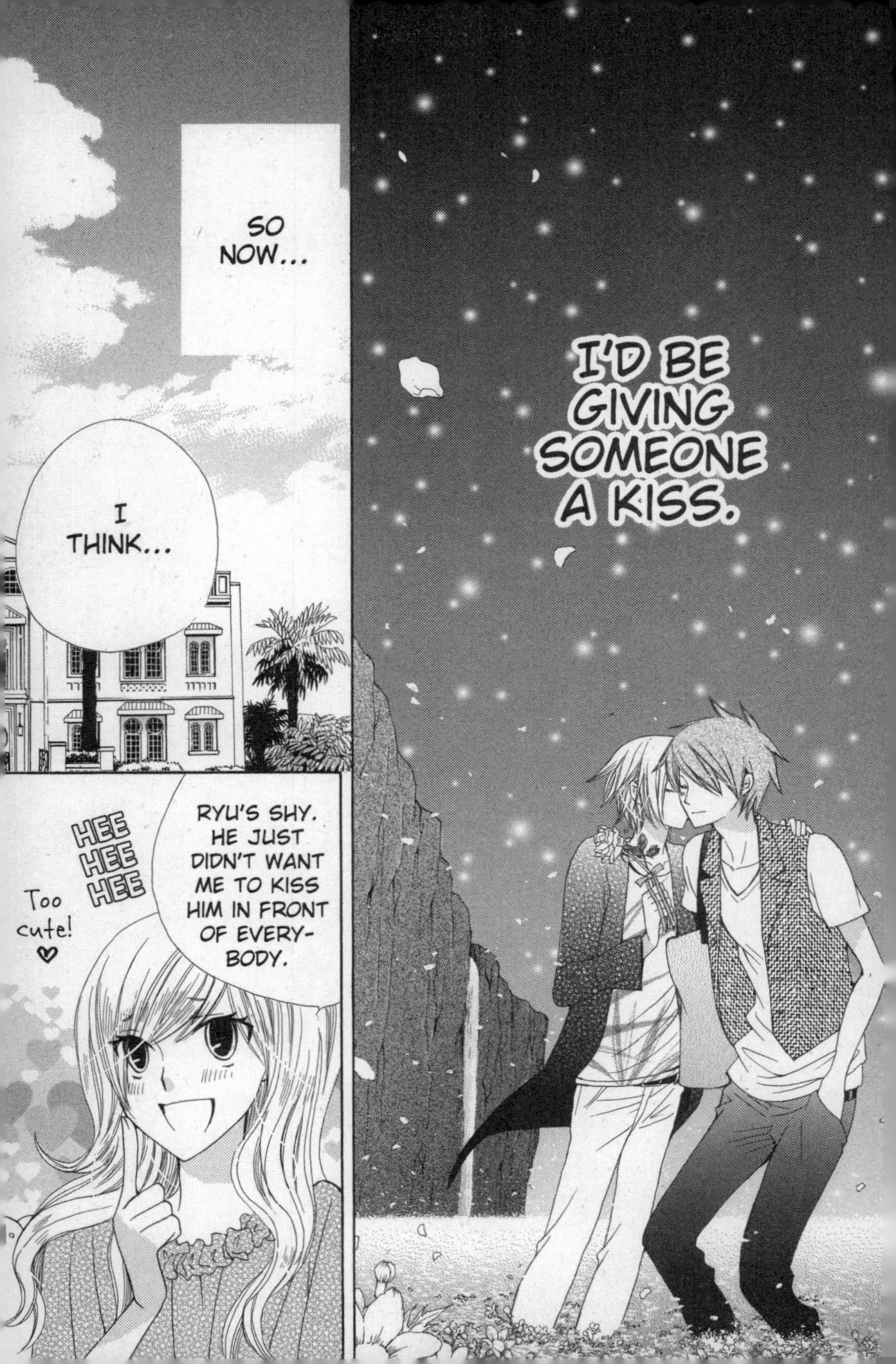

SO NOW...
I THINK...
I'D BE GIVING SOMEONE A KISS.
RYU'S SHY. HE JUST DIDN'T WANT ME TO KISS HIM IN FRONT OF EVERY-BODY.
HEE HEE HEE
Too cute! ♥

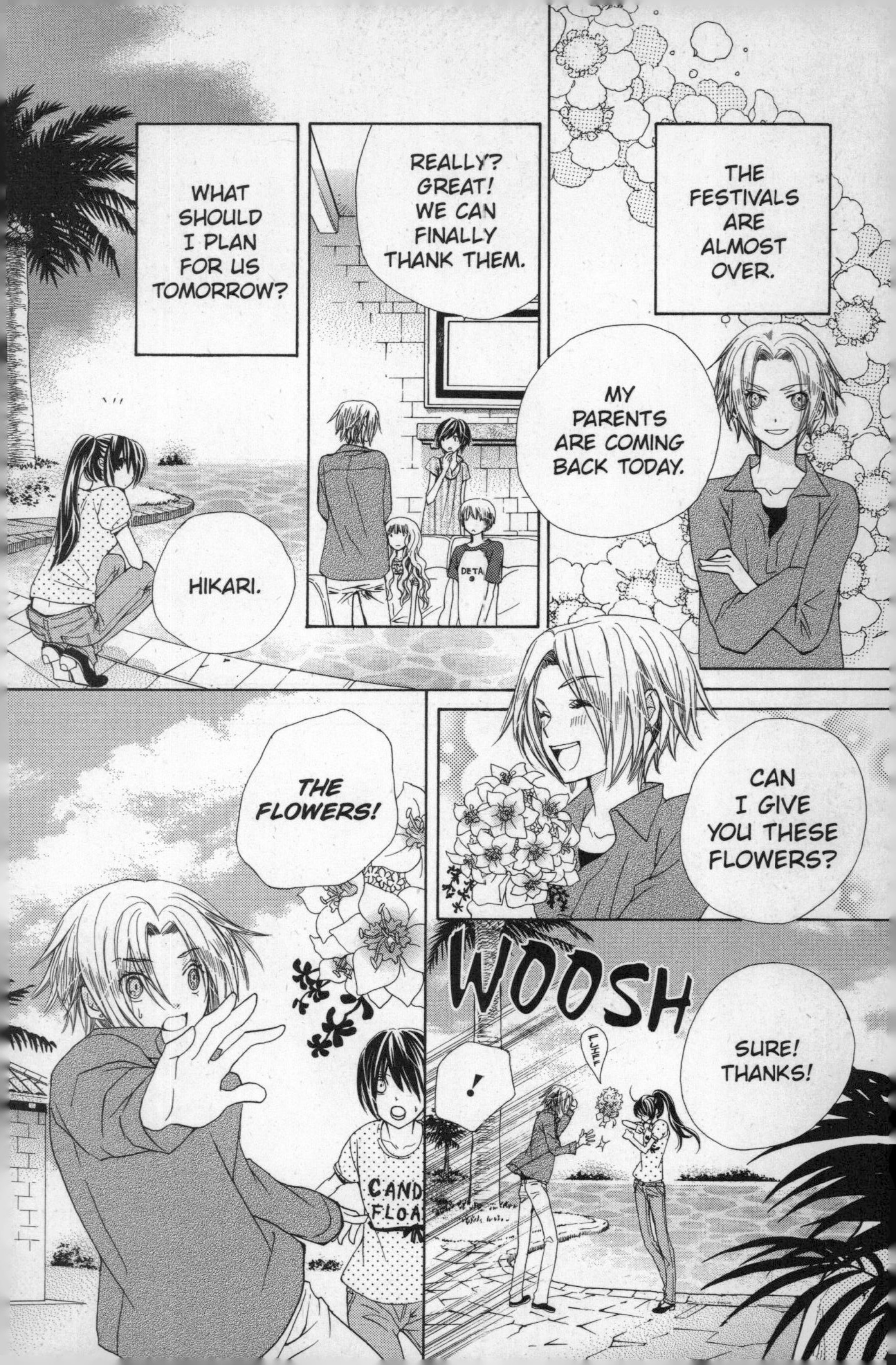
THE FESTIVALS ARE ALMOST OVER.
MY PARENTS ARE COMING BACK TODAY.
REALLY? GREAT! WE CAN FINALLY THANK THEM.
WHAT SHOULD I PLAN FOR US TOMORROW?
HIKARI.
CAN I GIVE YOU THESE FLOWERS?
WOOSH
SURE! THANKS!
!
THE FLOWERS!

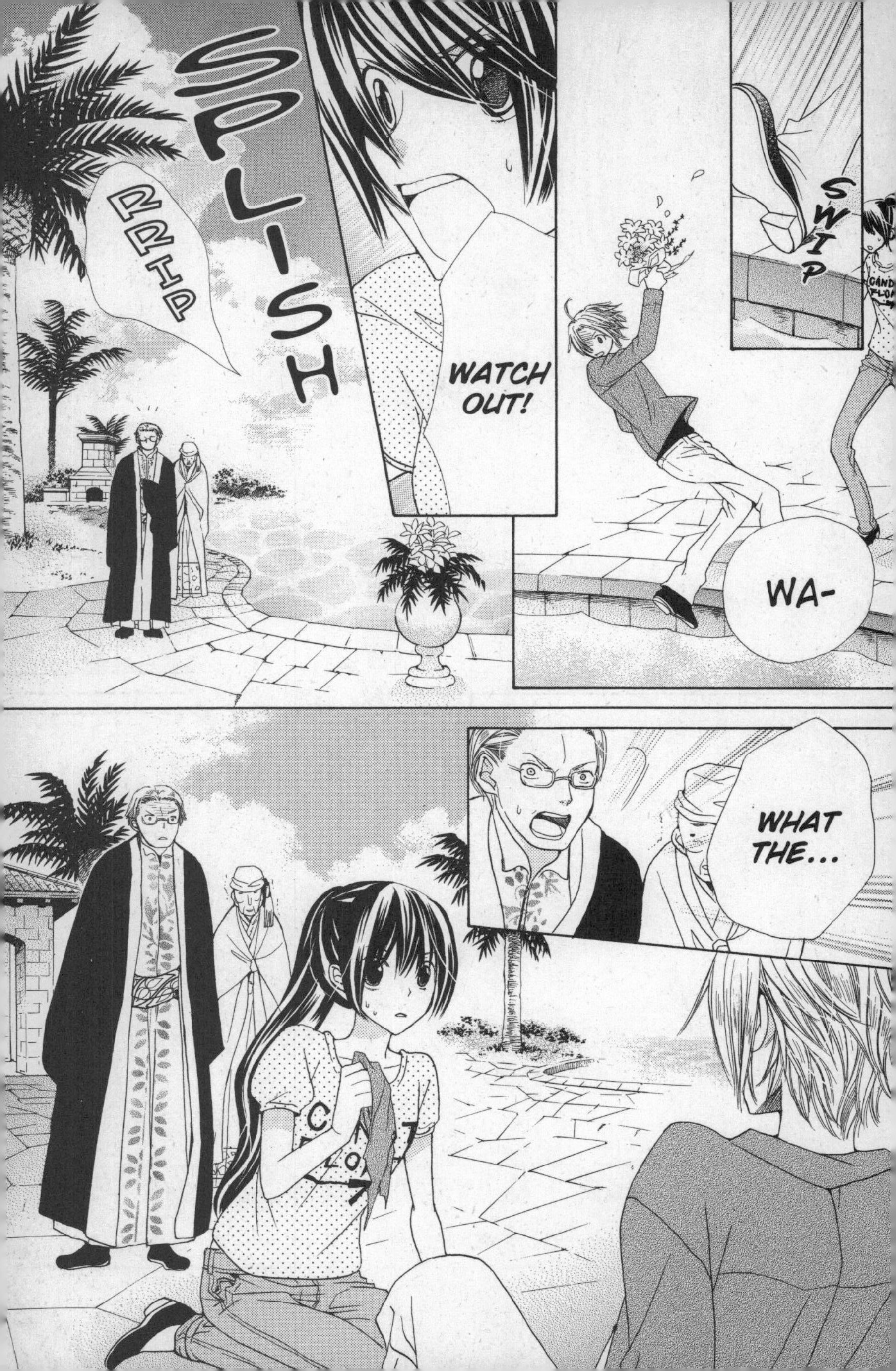
SWIP
WA-
WATCH OUT!
SPLISH
RRIP
WHAT THE...

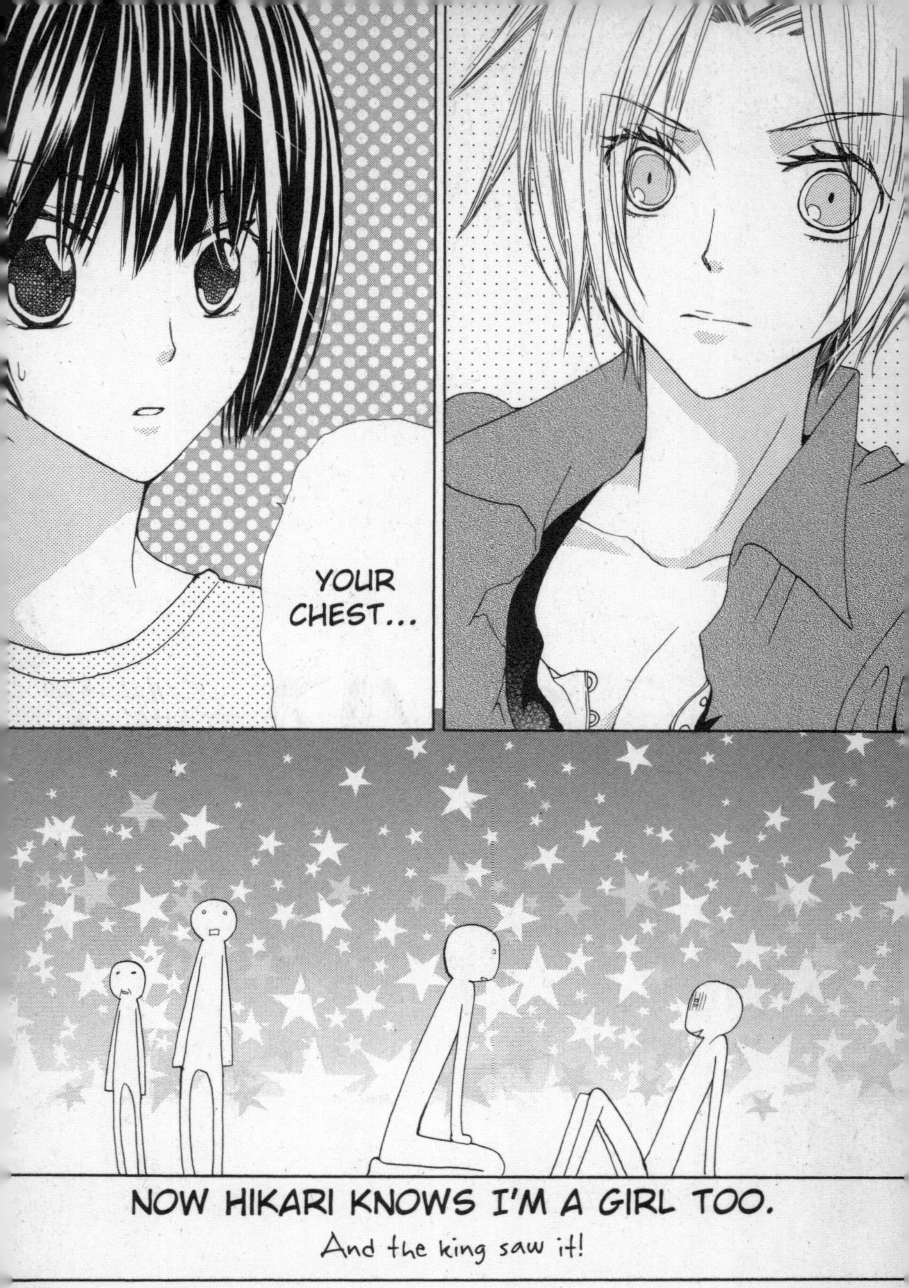
YOUR CHEST...

NOW HIKARI KNOWS I'M A GIRL TOO.

And the king saw it!

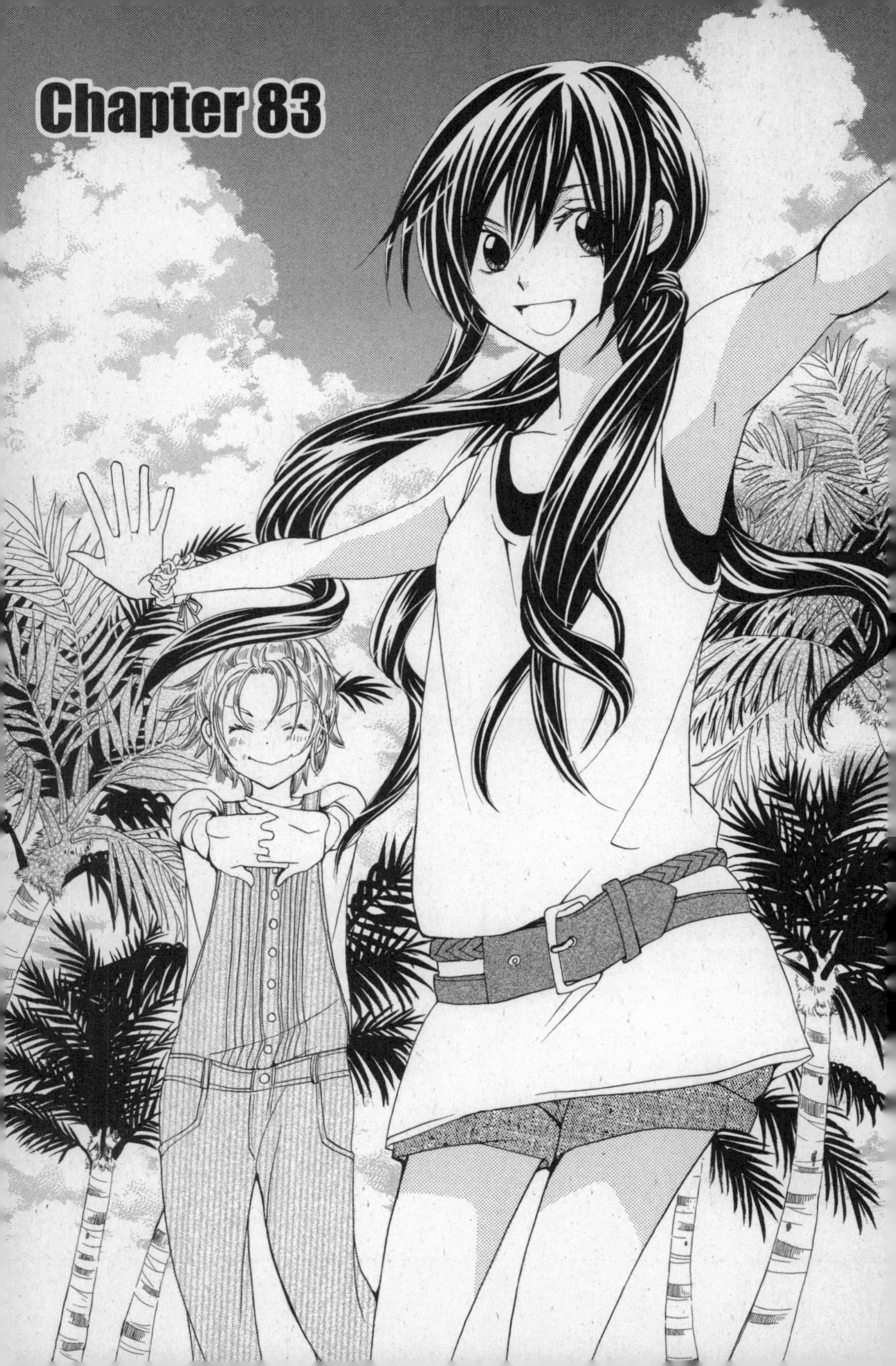
Chapter 83

MY SECRET'S OUT.

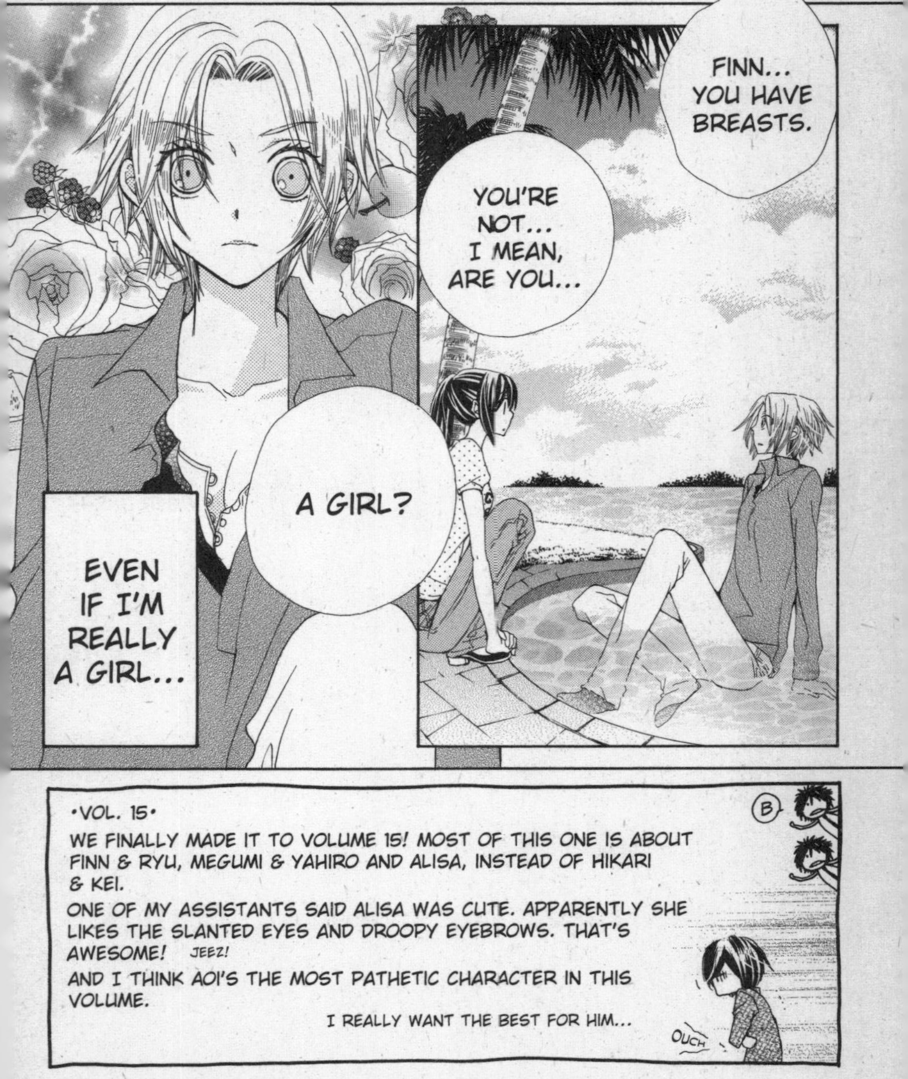
FINN... YOU HAVE BREASTS.
YOU'RE NOT... I MEAN, ARE YOU...
A GIRL?
EVEN IF I'M REALLY A GIRL...

•VOL. 15•

WE FINALLY MADE IT TO VOLUME 15! MOST OF THIS ONE IS ABOUT FINN & RYU, MEGUMI & YAHIRO AND ALISA, INSTEAD OF HIKARI & KEI.

ONE OF MY ASSISTANTS SAID ALISA WAS CUTE. APPARENTLY SHE LIKES THE SLANTED EYES AND DROOPY EYEBROWS. THAT'S AWESOME! JEEZ!

AND I THINK AOI'S THE MOST PATHETIC CHARACTER IN THIS VOLUME.

I REALLY WANT THE BEST FOR HIM...

OUCH

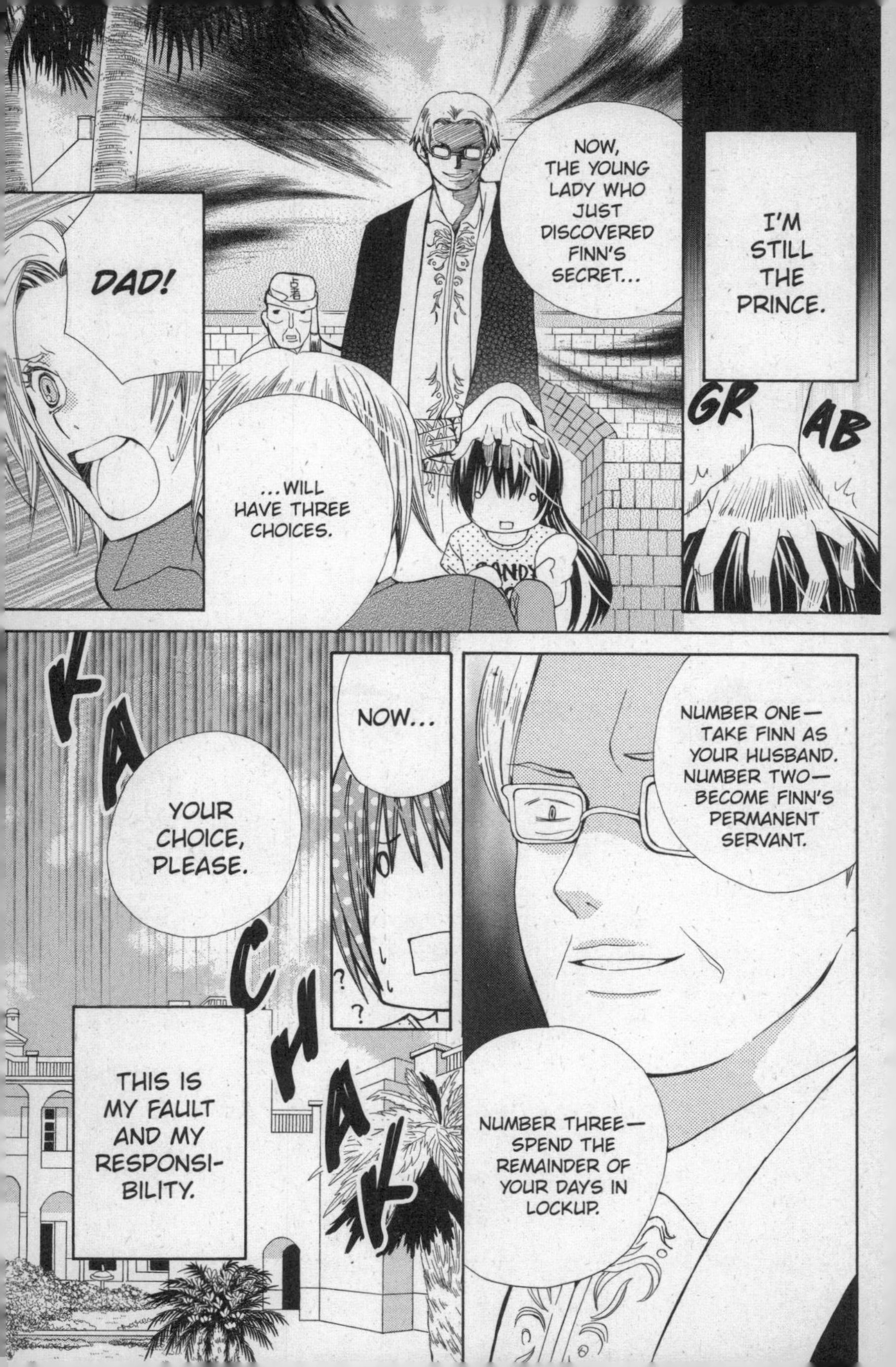
I'M STILL THE PRINCE.
GRAB
NOW, THE YOUNG LADY WHO JUST DISCOVERED FINN'S SECRET...
...WILL HAVE THREE CHOICES.
DAD!
NUMBER ONE— TAKE FINN AS YOUR HUSBAND. NUMBER TWO— BECOME FINN'S PERMANENT SERVANT.
NUMBER THREE— SPEND THE REMAINDER OF YOUR DAYS IN LOCKUP.
NOW...
?
?
YOUR CHOICE, PLEASE.
KACHAK
THIS IS MY FAULT AND MY RESPONSI-BILITY.

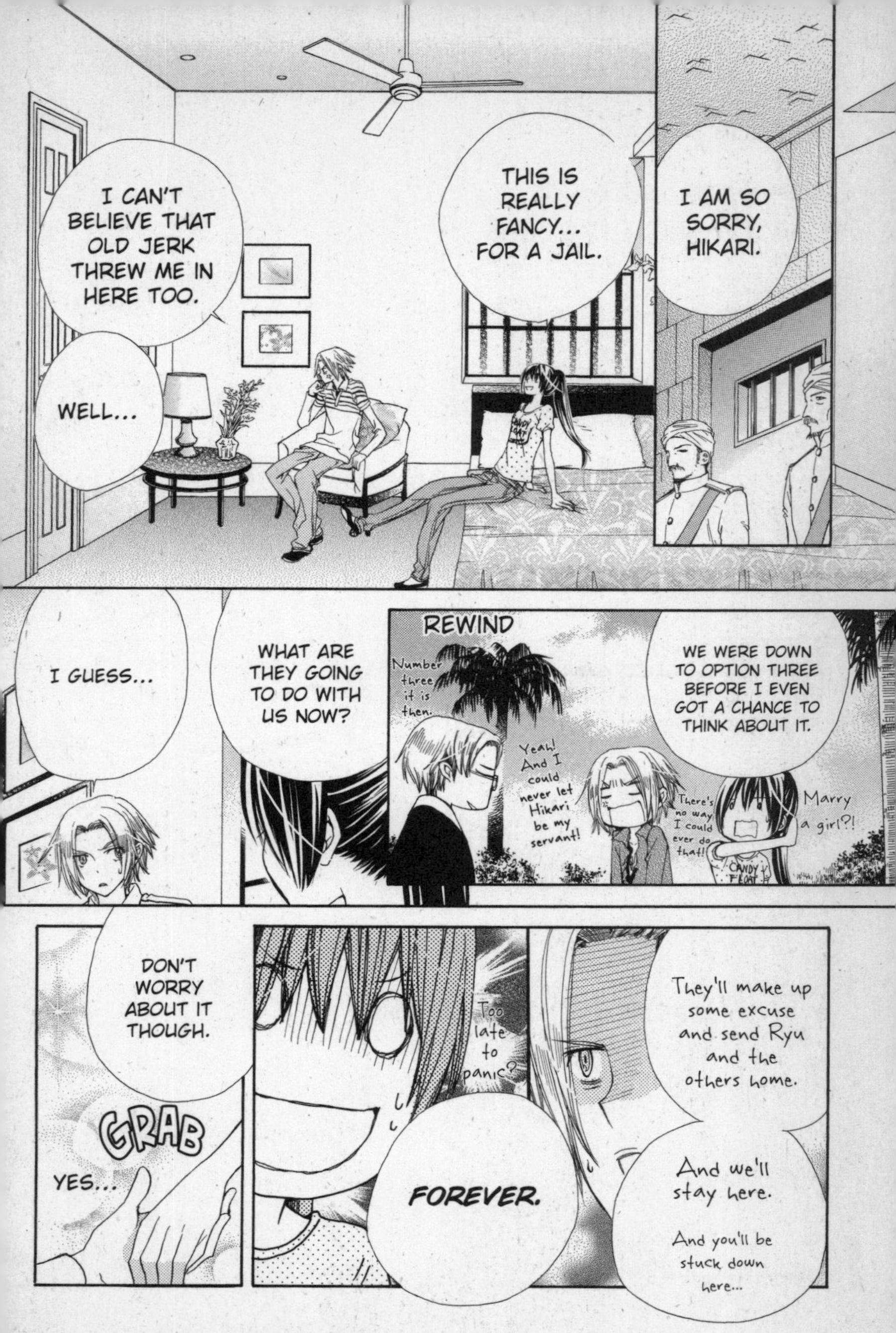
I AM SO SORRY, HIKARI.
THIS IS REALLY FANCY... FOR A JAIL.
I CAN'T BELIEVE THAT OLD JERK THREW ME IN HERE TOO.
WELL...
REWIND
WE WERE DOWN TO OPTION THREE BEFORE I EVEN GOT A CHANCE TO THINK ABOUT IT.
Marry a girl?!
There's no way I could ever do that!
Yeah! And I could never let Hikari be my servant!
Number three it is then.
WHAT ARE THEY GOING TO DO WITH US NOW?
I GUESS...
They'll make up some excuse and send Ryu and the others home.
And we'll stay here.
And you'll be stuck down here...
FOREVER.
Too late to panic?
DON'T WORRY ABOUT IT THOUGH.
GRAB
YES...

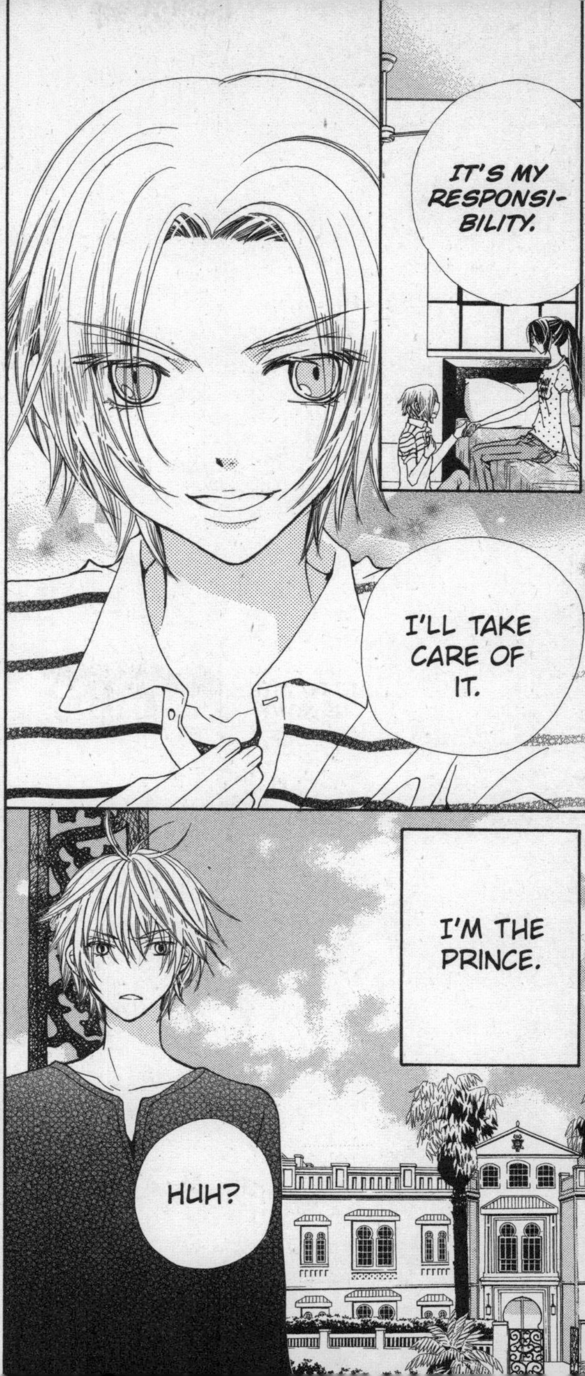
IT'S MY RESPONSI-BILITY.
I'LL TAKE CARE OF IT.
I'M THE PRINCE.
HUH?

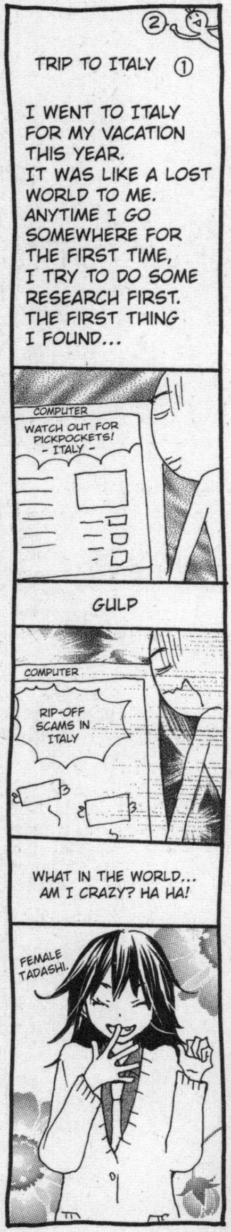
TRIP TO ITALY ①
I WENT TO ITALY FOR MY VACATION THIS YEAR. IT WAS LIKE A LOST WORLD TO ME. ANYTIME I GO SOMEWHERE FOR THE FIRST TIME, I TRY TO DO SOME RESEARCH FIRST. THE FIRST THING I FOUND...
COMPUTER
WATCH OUT FOR PICKPOCKETS! - ITALY -
GULP
COMPUTER
RIP-OFF SCAMS IN ITALY
WHAT IN THE WORLD... AM I CRAZY? HA HA!
FEMALE TADASHI.

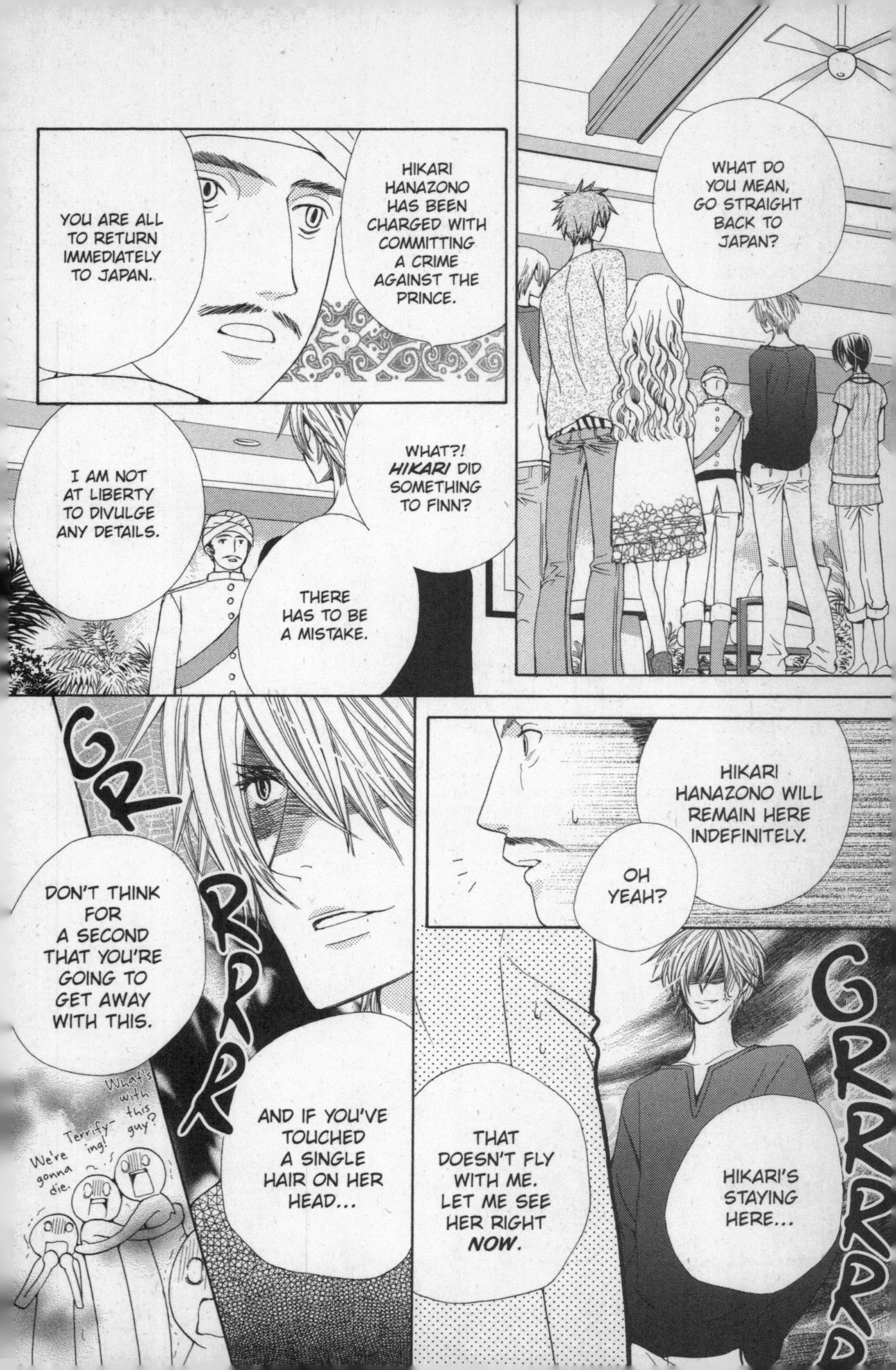
WHAT DO YOU MEAN, GO STRAIGHT BACK TO JAPAN?
HIKARI HANAZONO HAS BEEN CHARGED WITH COMMITTING A CRIME AGAINST THE PRINCE.
YOU ARE ALL TO RETURN IMMEDIATELY TO JAPAN.
WHAT?! *HIKARI* DID SOMETHING TO FINN?
THERE HAS TO BE A MISTAKE.
I AM NOT AT LIBERTY TO DIVULGE ANY DETAILS.
HIKARI HANAZONO WILL REMAIN HERE INDEFINITELY.
OH YEAH?
GRRRRRR
HIKARI'S STAYING HERE...
THAT DOESN'T FLY WITH ME. LET ME SEE HER RIGHT *NOW*.
GRRRRR
DON'T THINK FOR A SECOND THAT YOU'RE GOING TO GET AWAY WITH THIS.
AND IF YOU'VE TOUCHED A SINGLE HAIR ON HER HEAD...
What's with this guy?
Terrify-ing!
We're gonna die.

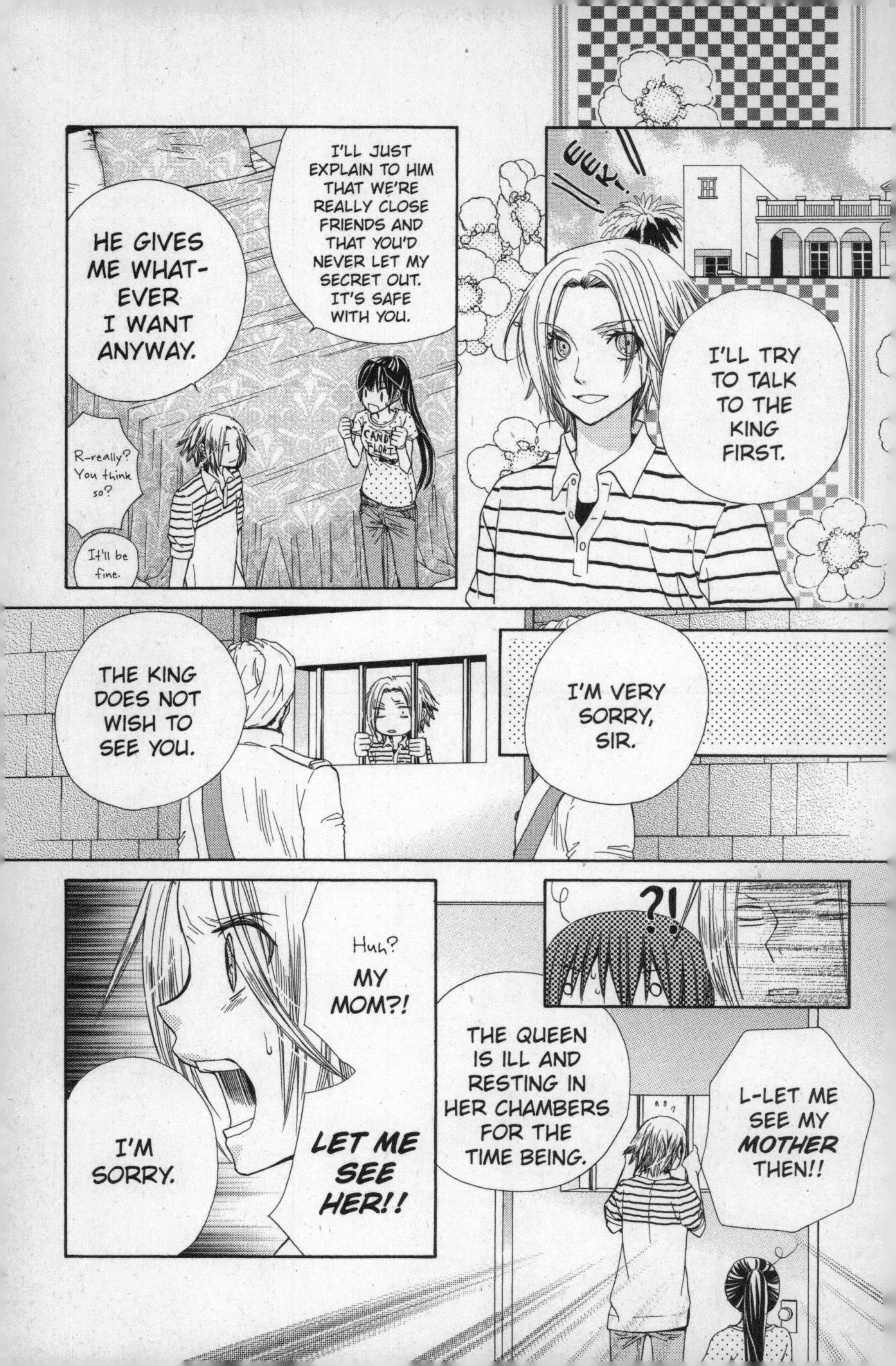

WUXY-!
I'LL TRY TO TALK TO THE KING FIRST.
I'LL JUST EXPLAIN TO HIM THAT WE'RE REALLY CLOSE FRIENDS AND THAT YOU'D NEVER LET MY SECRET OUT. IT'S SAFE WITH YOU.
HE GIVES ME WHATEVER I WANT ANYWAY.
R-really? You think so?
It'll be fine.
I'M VERY SORRY, SIR.
THE KING DOES NOT WISH TO SEE YOU.
?!
THE QUEEN IS ILL AND RESTING IN HER CHAMBERS FOR THE TIME BEING.
L-LET ME SEE MY MOTHER THEN!!
Huh? MY MOM?!
LET ME SEE HER!!
I'M SORRY.

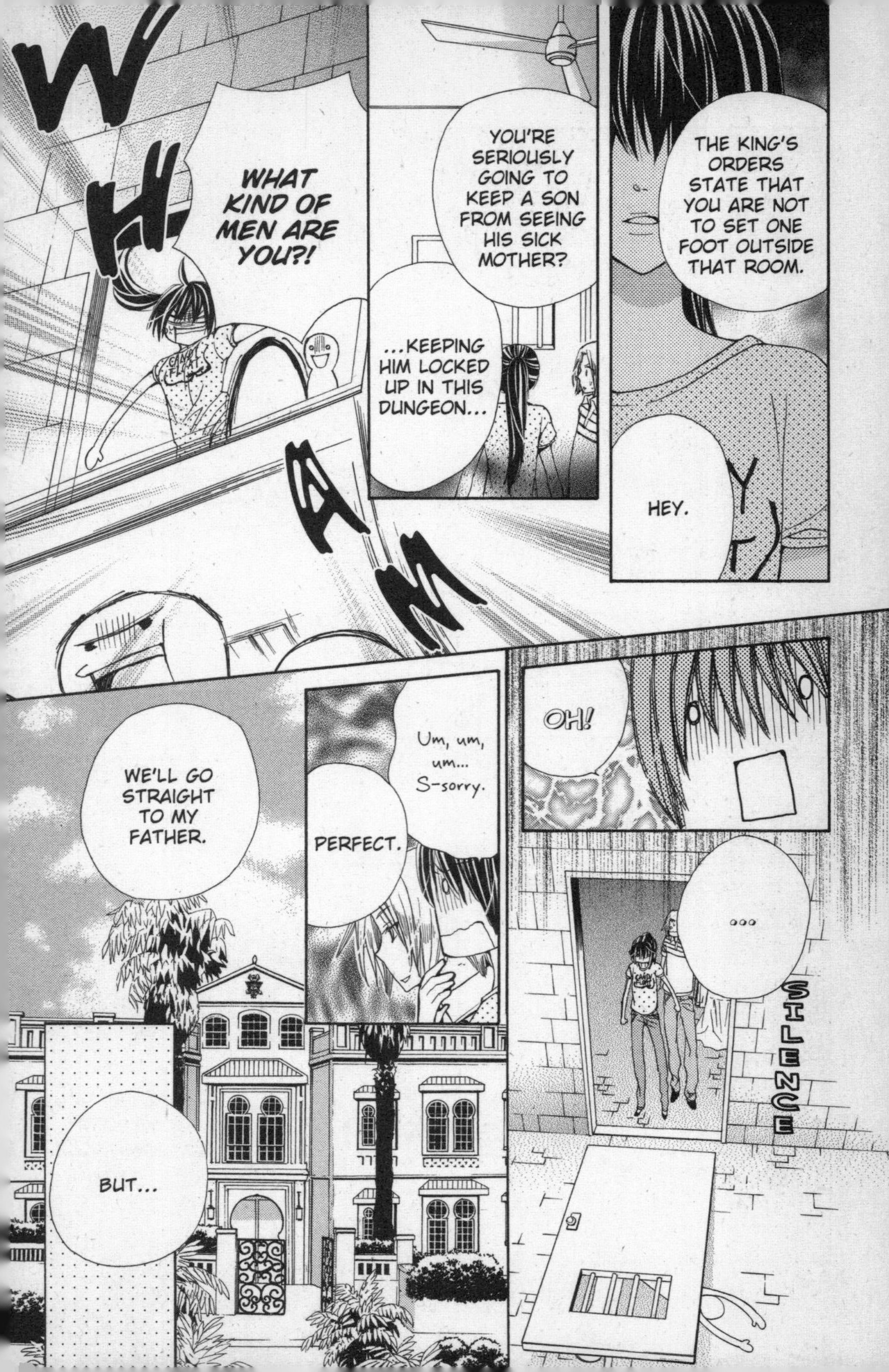
THE KING'S ORDERS STATE THAT YOU ARE NOT TO SET ONE FOOT OUTSIDE THAT ROOM.
HEY.
YOU'RE SERIOUSLY GOING TO KEEP A SON FROM SEEING HIS SICK MOTHER?
...KEEPING HIM LOCKED UP IN THIS DUNGEON...
WHAM
WHAT KIND OF MEN ARE YOU?!
OH!
...
SILENCE
Um, um, um... S-sorry.
PERFECT.
WE'LL GO STRAIGHT TO MY FATHER.
BUT...

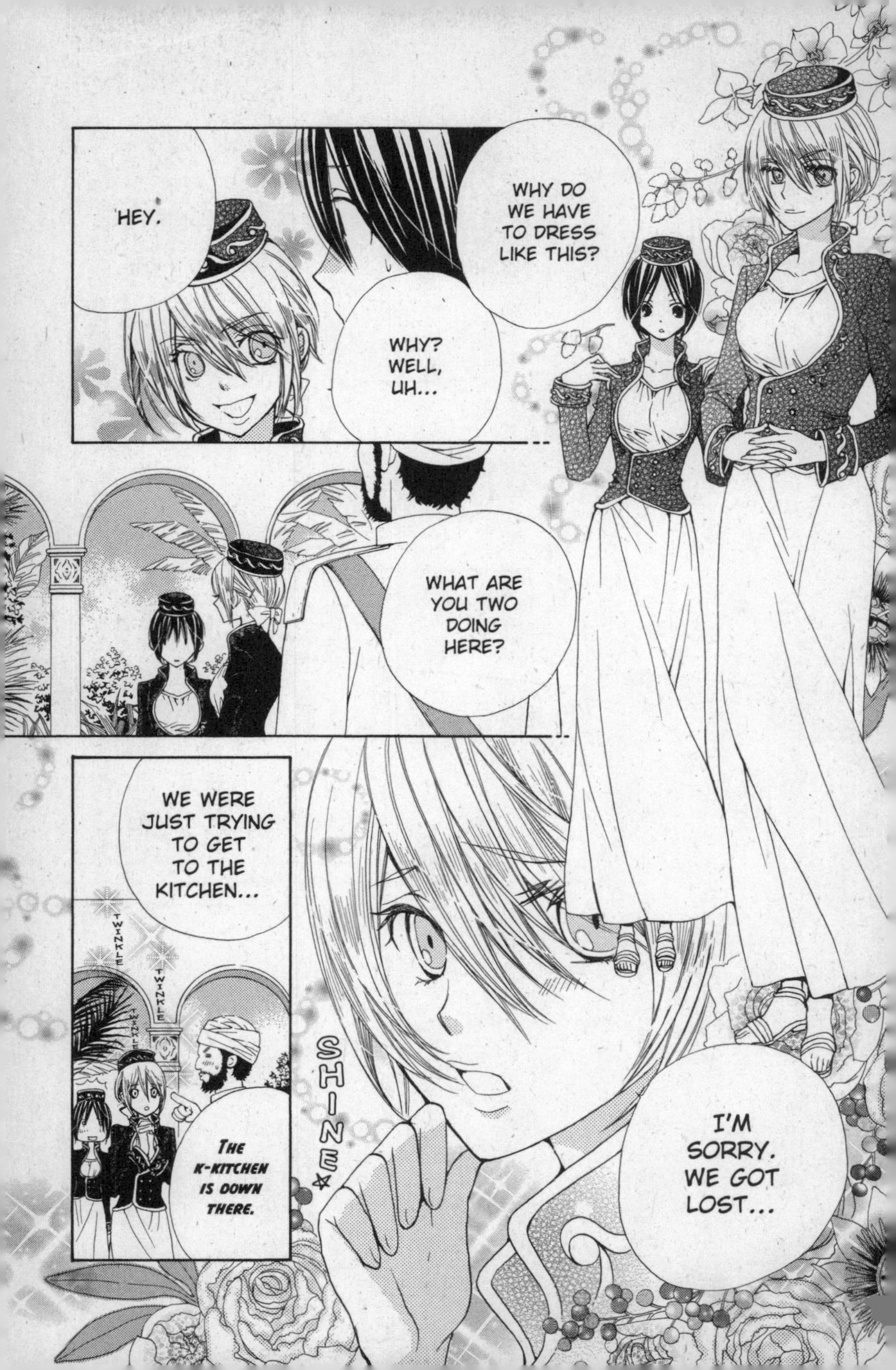
WHY DO WE HAVE TO DRESS LIKE THIS?
WHY? WELL, UH...
HEY.
WHAT ARE YOU TWO DOING HERE?
I'M SORRY. WE GOT LOST...
SHINE☆
WE WERE JUST TRYING TO GET TO THE KITCHEN...
TWINKLE
TWINKLE
TWINKLE
THE K-KITCHEN IS DOWN THERE.

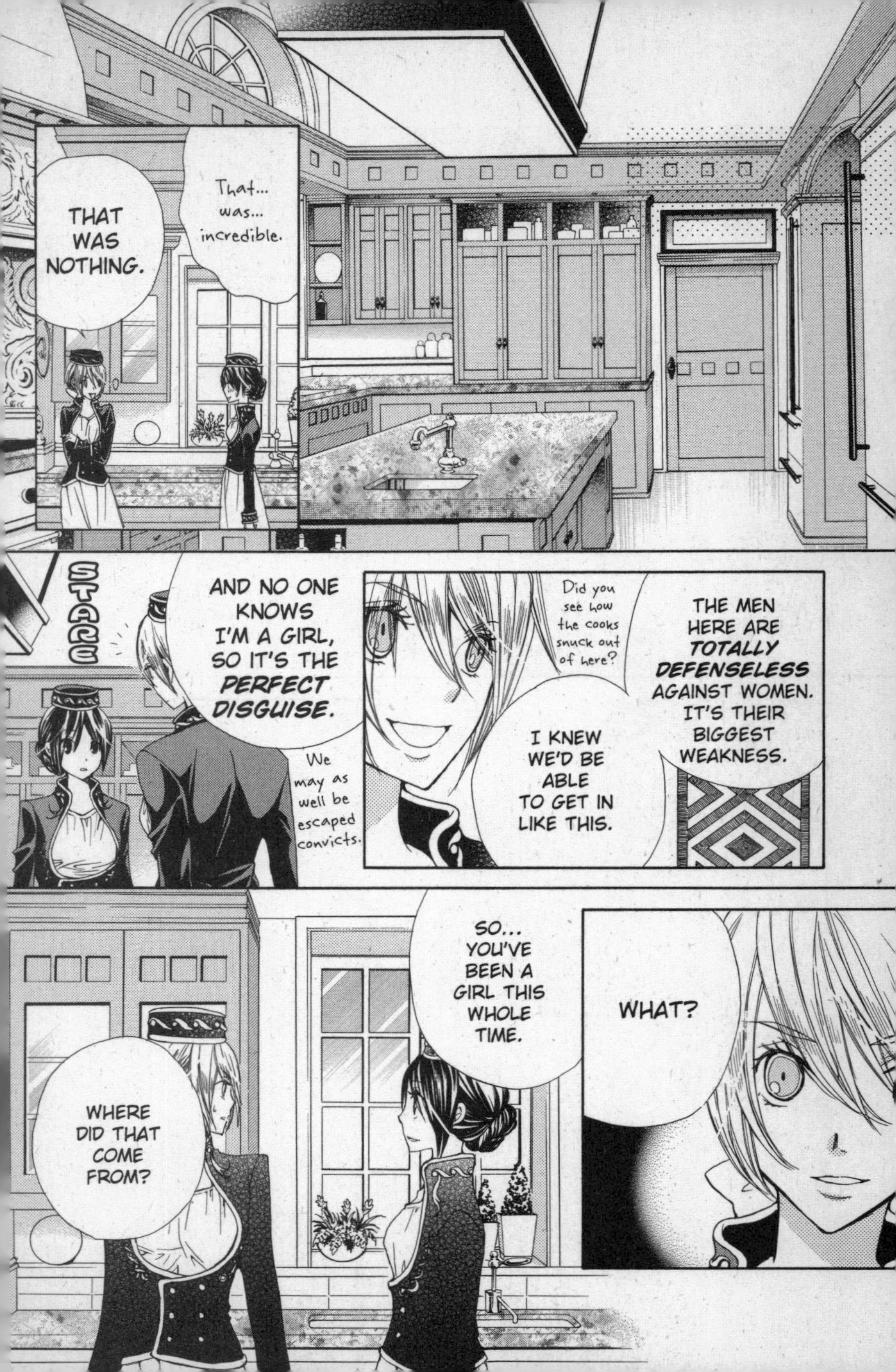
That... was... incredible.
THAT WAS NOTHING.
THE MEN HERE ARE TOTALLY DEFENSELESS AGAINST WOMEN. IT'S THEIR BIGGEST WEAKNESS.
Did you see how the cooks snuck out of here?
I KNEW WE'D BE ABLE TO GET IN LIKE THIS.
AND NO ONE KNOWS I'M A GIRL, SO IT'S THE PERFECT DISGUISE.
STARE
We may as well be escaped convicts.
WHAT?
SO... YOU'VE BEEN A GIRL THIS WHOLE TIME.
WHERE DID THAT COME FROM?

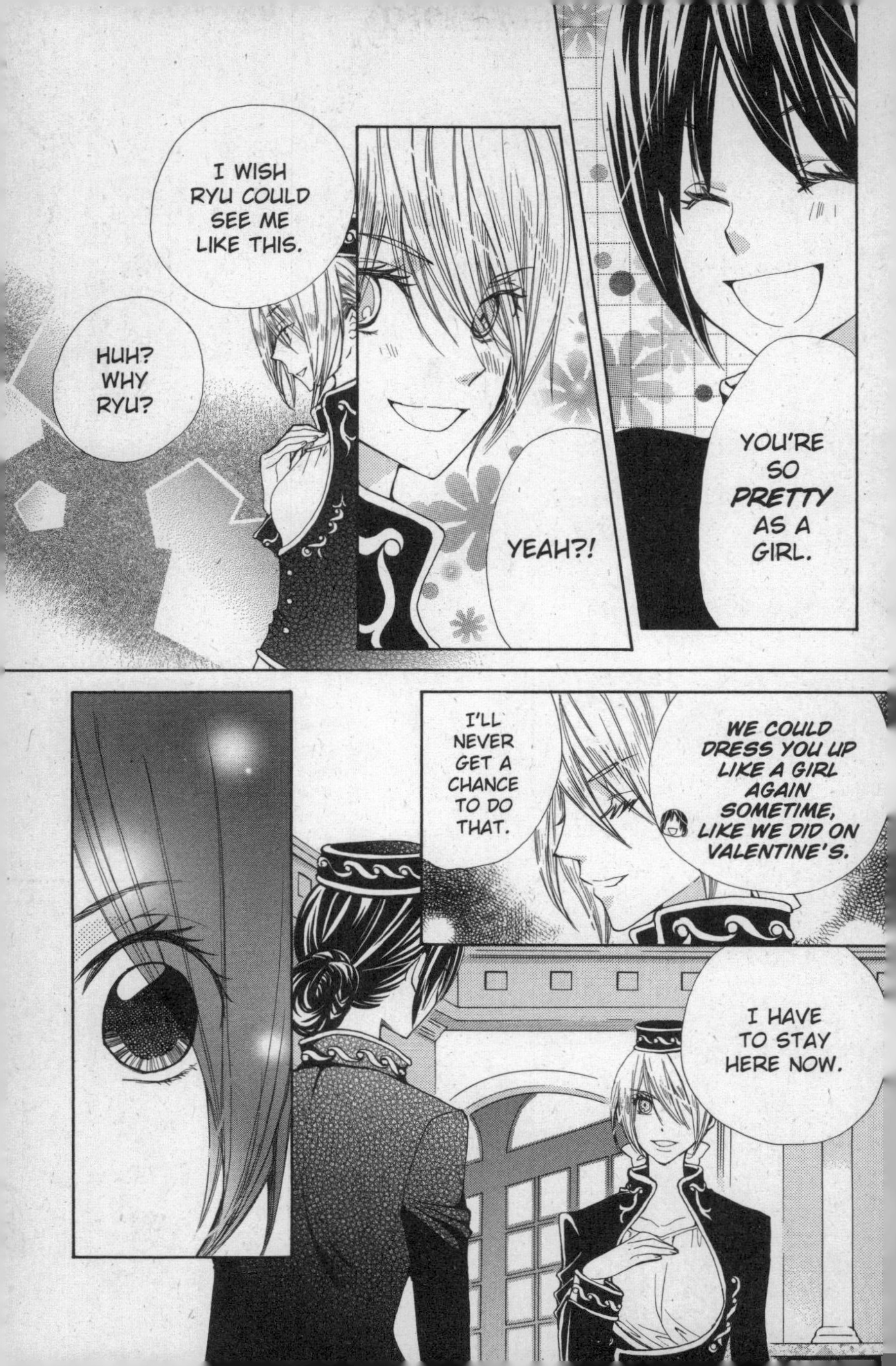
YOU'RE SO PRETTY AS A GIRL.
YEAH?!
I WISH RYU COULD SEE ME LIKE THIS.
HUH? WHY RYU?
WE COULD DRESS YOU UP LIKE A GIRL AGAIN SOMETIME, LIKE WE DID ON VALENTINE'S.
I'LL NEVER GET A CHANCE TO DO THAT.
I HAVE TO STAY HERE NOW.

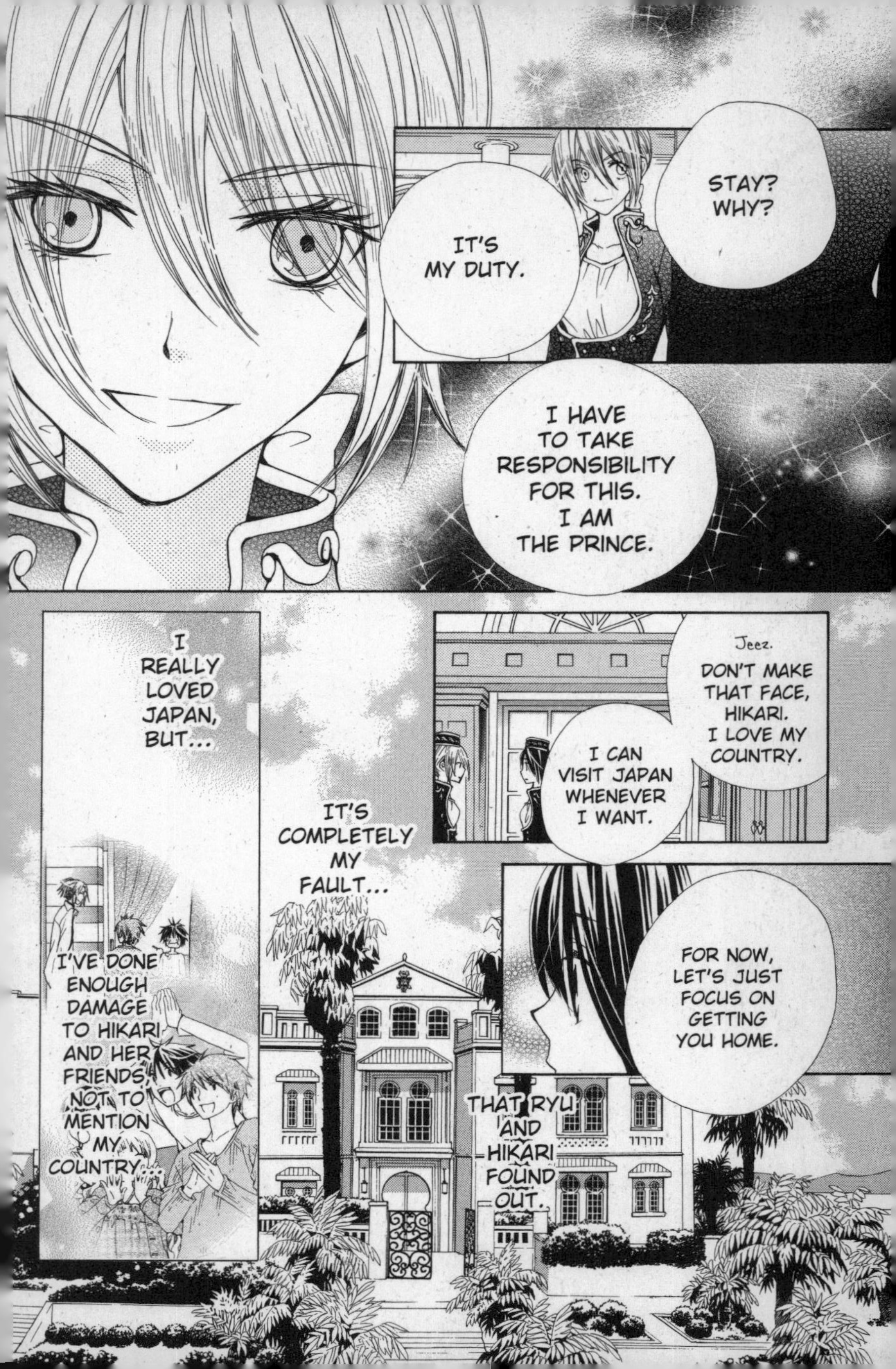
STAY? WHY?
IT'S MY DUTY.
I HAVE TO TAKE RESPONSIBILITY FOR THIS. I AM THE PRINCE.
Jeez.
DON'T MAKE THAT FACE, HIKARI. I LOVE MY COUNTRY.
I CAN VISIT JAPAN WHENEVER I WANT.
FOR NOW, LET'S JUST FOCUS ON GETTING YOU HOME.
IT'S COMPLETELY MY FAULT...
THAT RYU AND HIKARI FOUND OUT.
I REALLY LOVED JAPAN, BUT...
I'VE DONE ENOUGH DAMAGE TO HIKARI AND HER FRIENDS, NOT TO MENTION MY COUNTRY...

THERE'S NO WAY I COULD GO BACK TO JAPAN.

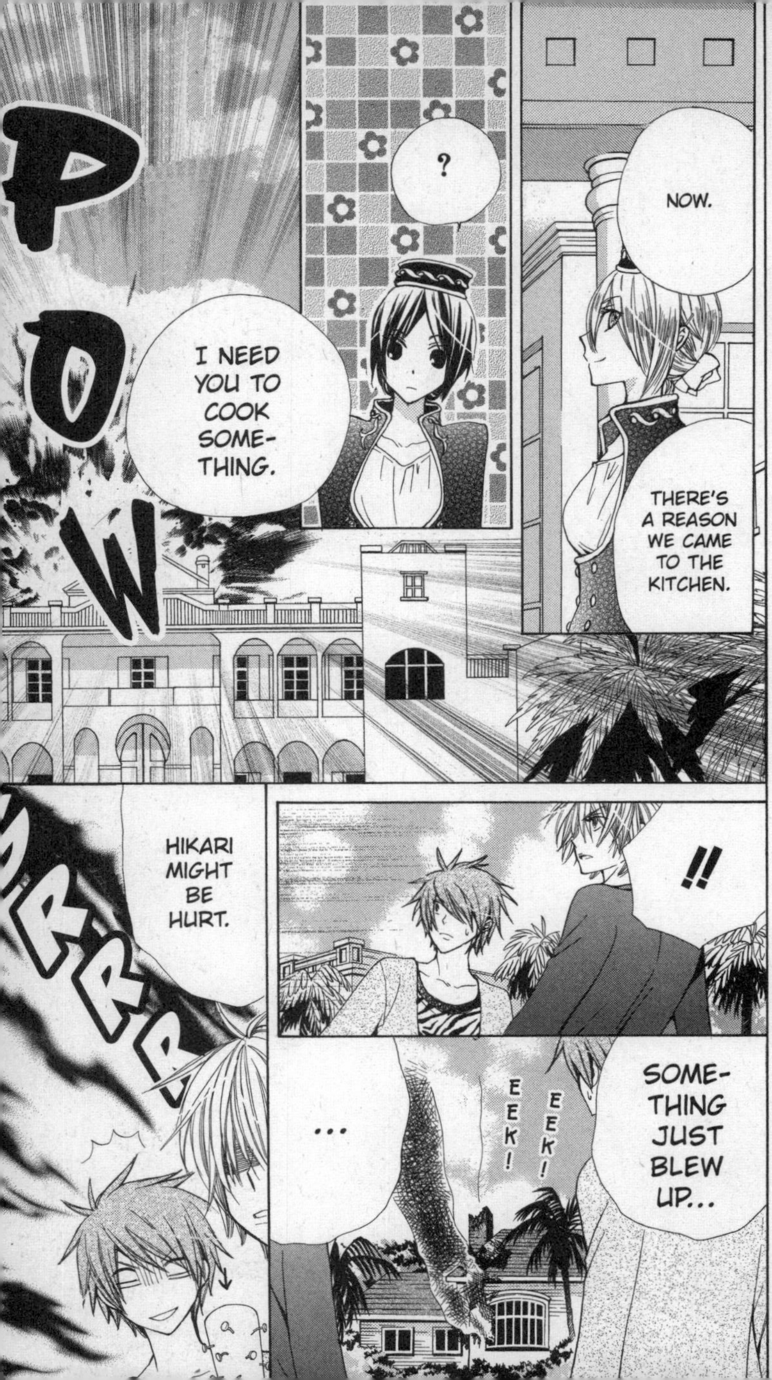

NOW.
THERE'S A REASON WE CAME TO THE KITCHEN.
?
I NEED YOU TO COOK SOME-THING.
POW
!!
HIKARI MIGHT BE HURT.
RRR
SOME-THING JUST BLEW UP...
EEK! EEK!
...

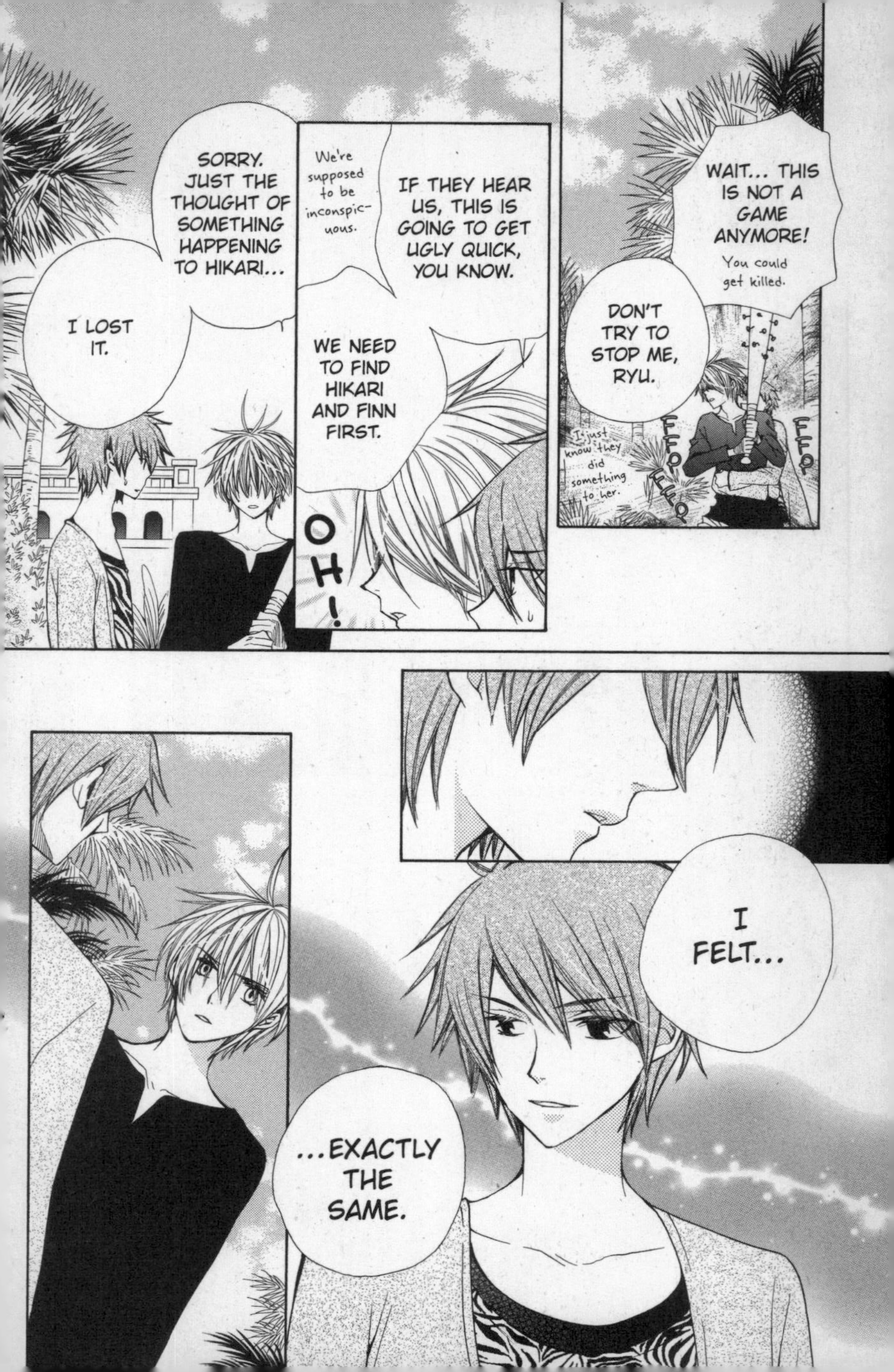
WAIT... THIS IS NOT A GAME ANYMORE!
You could get killed.
DON'T TRY TO STOP ME, RYU.
I just know they did something to her.
We're supposed to be inconspicuous.
IF THEY HEAR US, THIS IS GOING TO GET UGLY QUICK, YOU KNOW.
WE NEED TO FIND HIKARI AND FINN FIRST.
OH!
SORRY. JUST THE THOUGHT OF SOMETHING HAPPENING TO HIKARI...
I LOST IT.
I FELT...
...EXACTLY THE SAME.

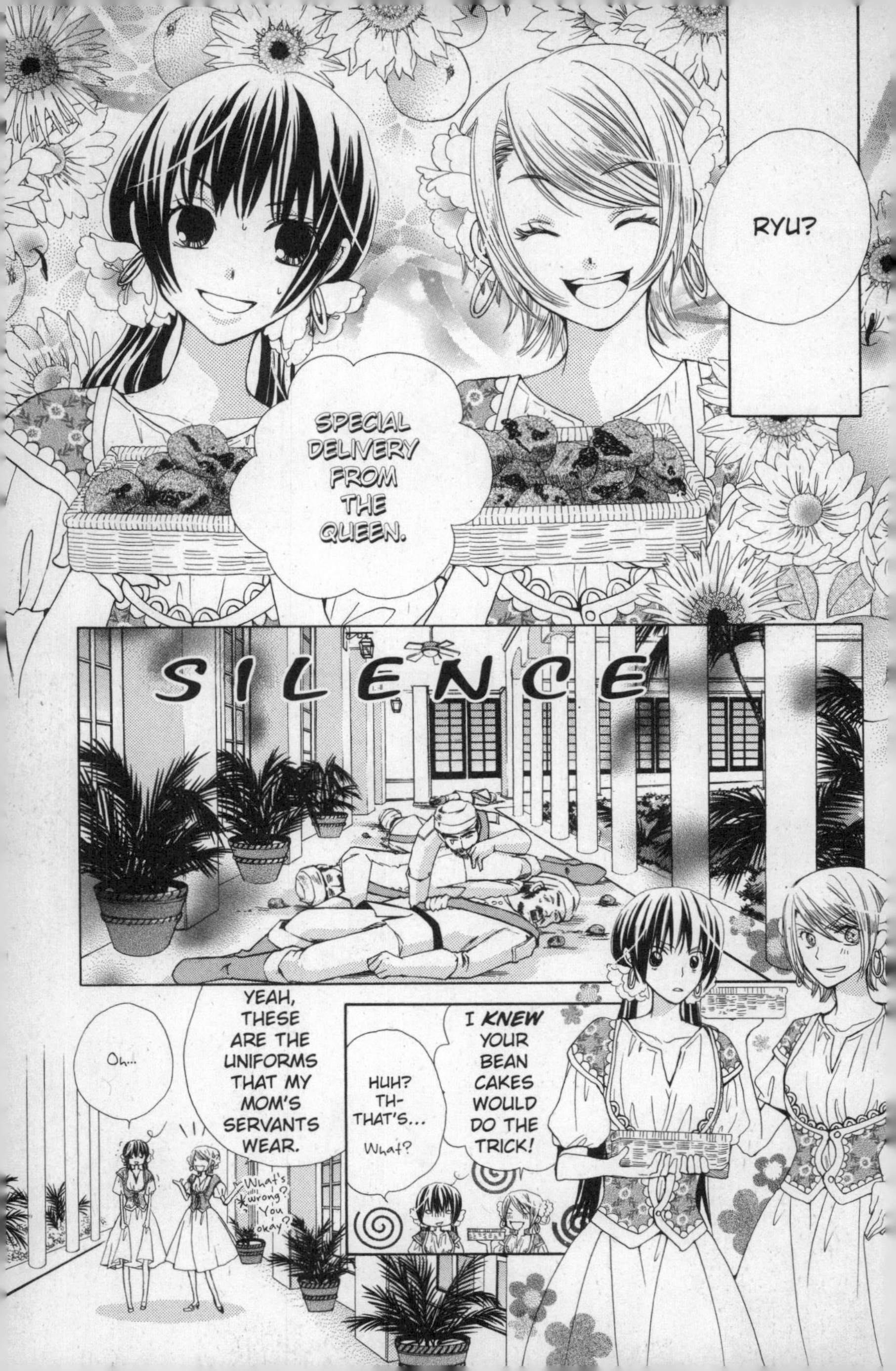
RYU?
SPECIAL DELIVERY FROM THE QUEEN.
SILENCE
I KNEW YOUR BEAN CAKES WOULD DO THE TRICK!
HUH? TH-THAT'S...
What?
YEAH, THESE ARE THE UNIFORMS THAT MY MOM'S SERVANTS WEAR.
What's wrong? You okay?
Oh...

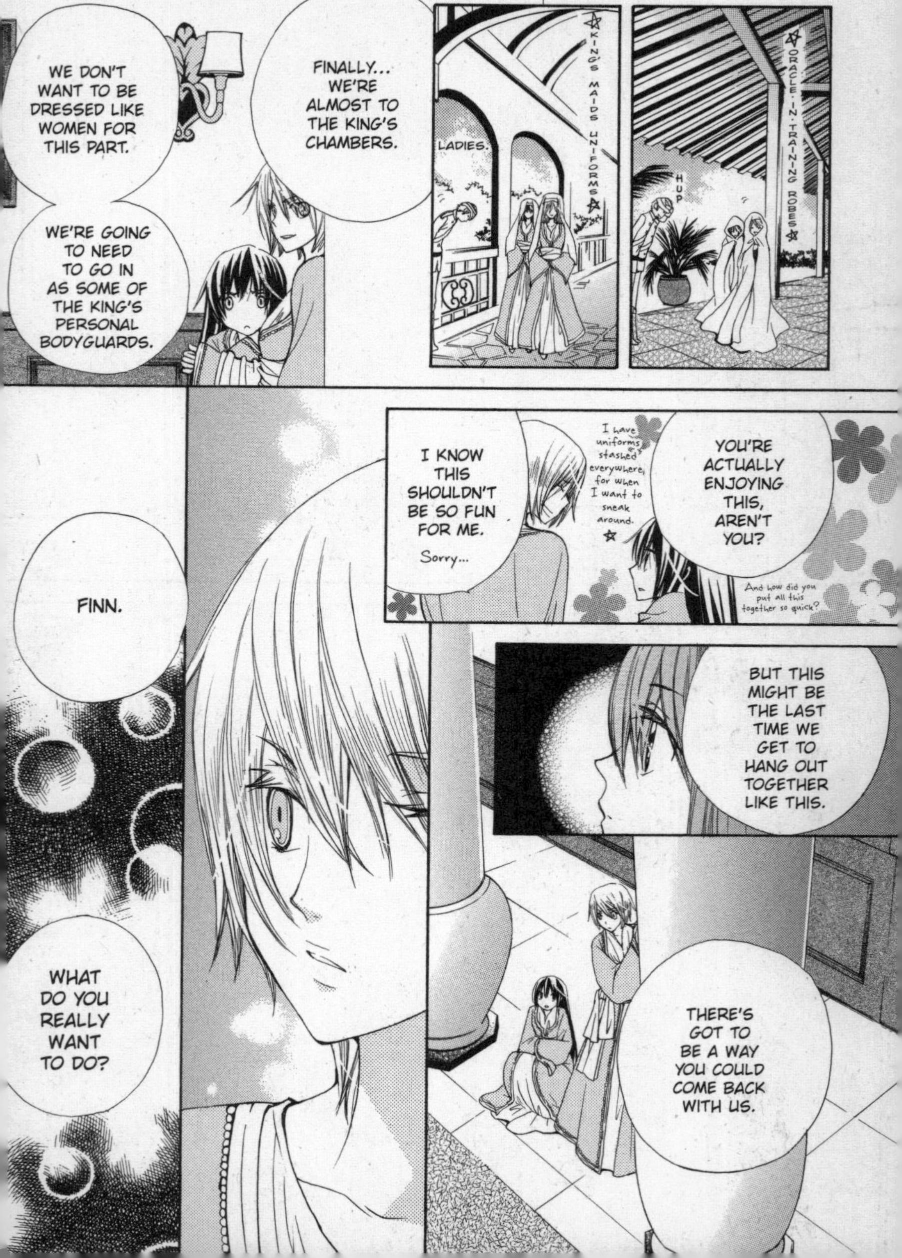

ORACLE-IN-TRAINING ROBES
HUP
KING'S MAIDS UNIFORMS
LADIES.
FINALLY... WE'RE ALMOST TO THE KING'S CHAMBERS.
WE DON'T WANT TO BE DRESSED LIKE WOMEN FOR THIS PART.
WE'RE GOING TO NEED TO GO IN AS SOME OF THE KING'S PERSONAL BODYGUARDS.
YOU'RE ACTUALLY ENJOYING THIS, AREN'T YOU?
And how did you put all this together so quick?
I have uniforms stashed everywhere, for when I want to sneak around.
I KNOW THIS SHOULDN'T BE SO FUN FOR ME.
Sorry...
BUT THIS MIGHT BE THE LAST TIME WE GET TO HANG OUT TOGETHER LIKE THIS.
THERE'S GOT TO BE A WAY YOU COULD COME BACK WITH US.
FINN.
WHAT DO YOU REALLY WANT TO DO?

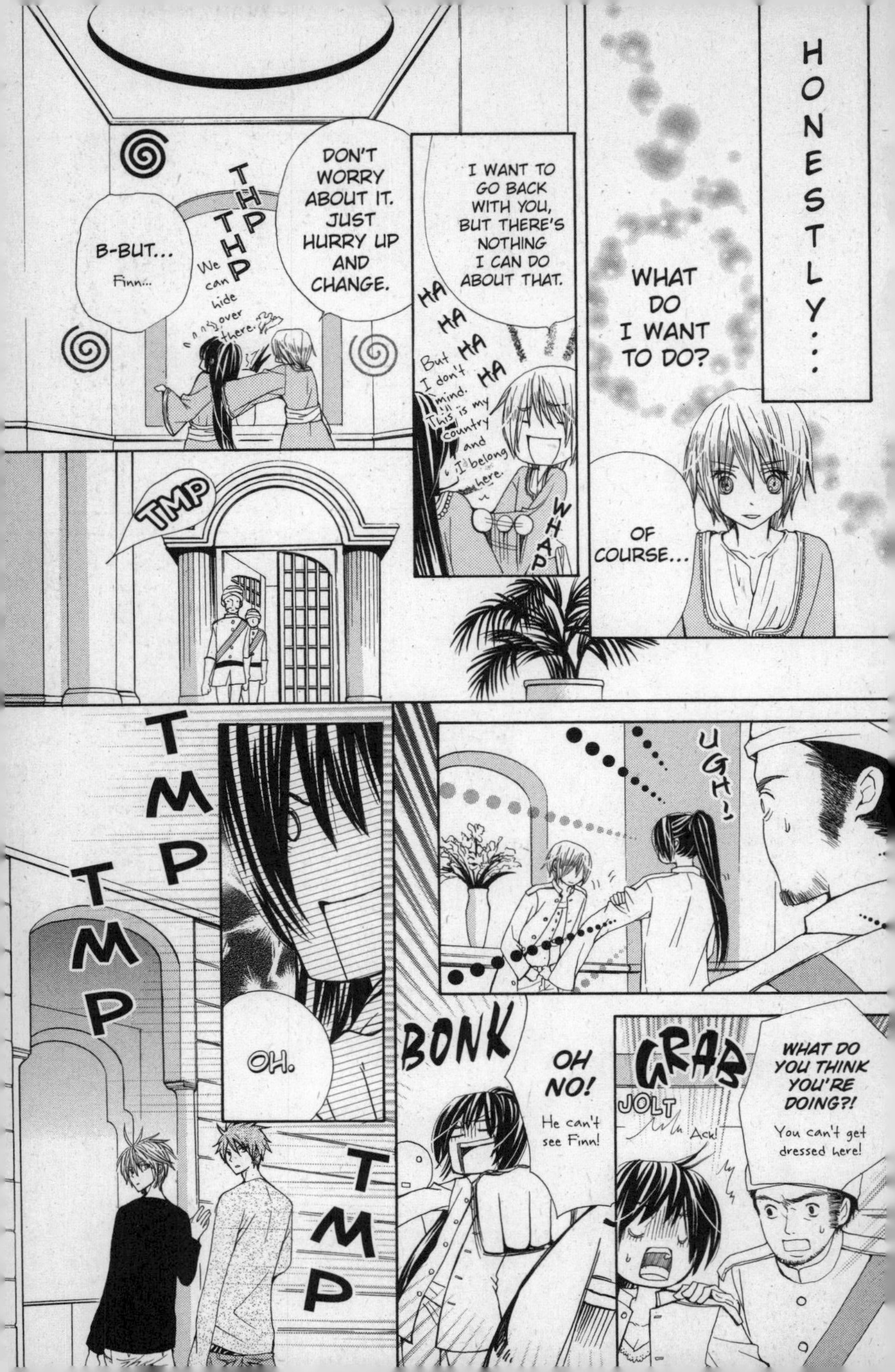
HONESTLY...
WHAT DO I WANT TO DO?
OF COURSE...
I WANT TO GO BACK WITH YOU, BUT THERE'S NOTHING I CAN DO ABOUT THAT.
HA HA HA HA
But I don't mind. This is my country and I belong here.
WHAP
DON'T WORRY ABOUT IT. JUST HURRY UP AND CHANGE.
THP THP
B-BUT...
Finn...
We can hide over there.
TMP
UGH!
BONK
OH NO!
He can't see Finn!
WHAT DO YOU THINK YOU'RE DOING?!
You can't get dressed here!
GRAB
JOLT
Ack!
OH.
TMP TMP
TMP TMP
TMP

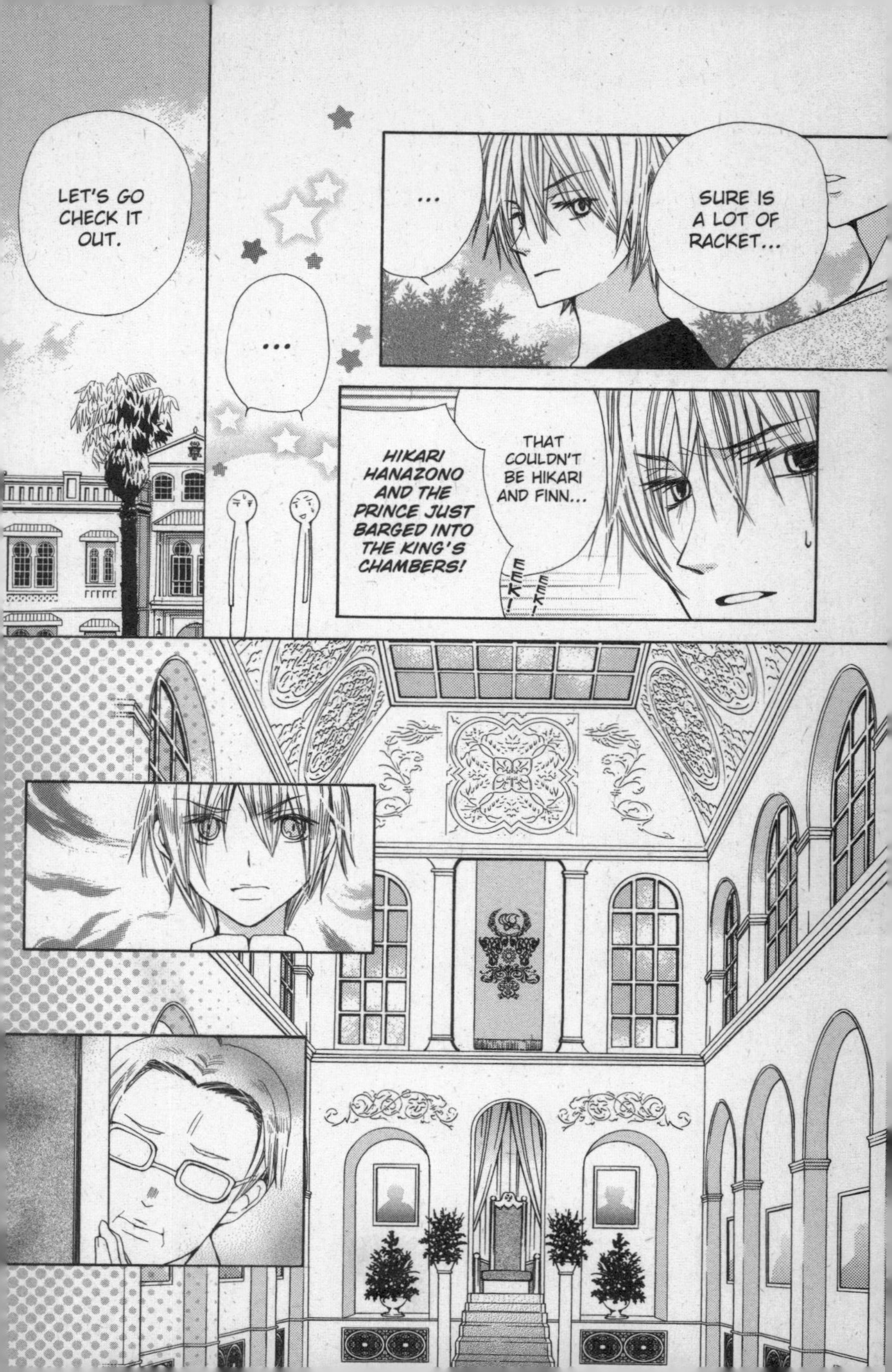
SURE IS A LOT OF RACKET...
...
THAT COULDN'T BE HIKARI AND FINN...
HIKARI HANAZONO AND THE PRINCE JUST BARGED INTO THE KING'S CHAMBERS!
EEK!
EEK!
...
LET'S GO CHECK IT OUT.

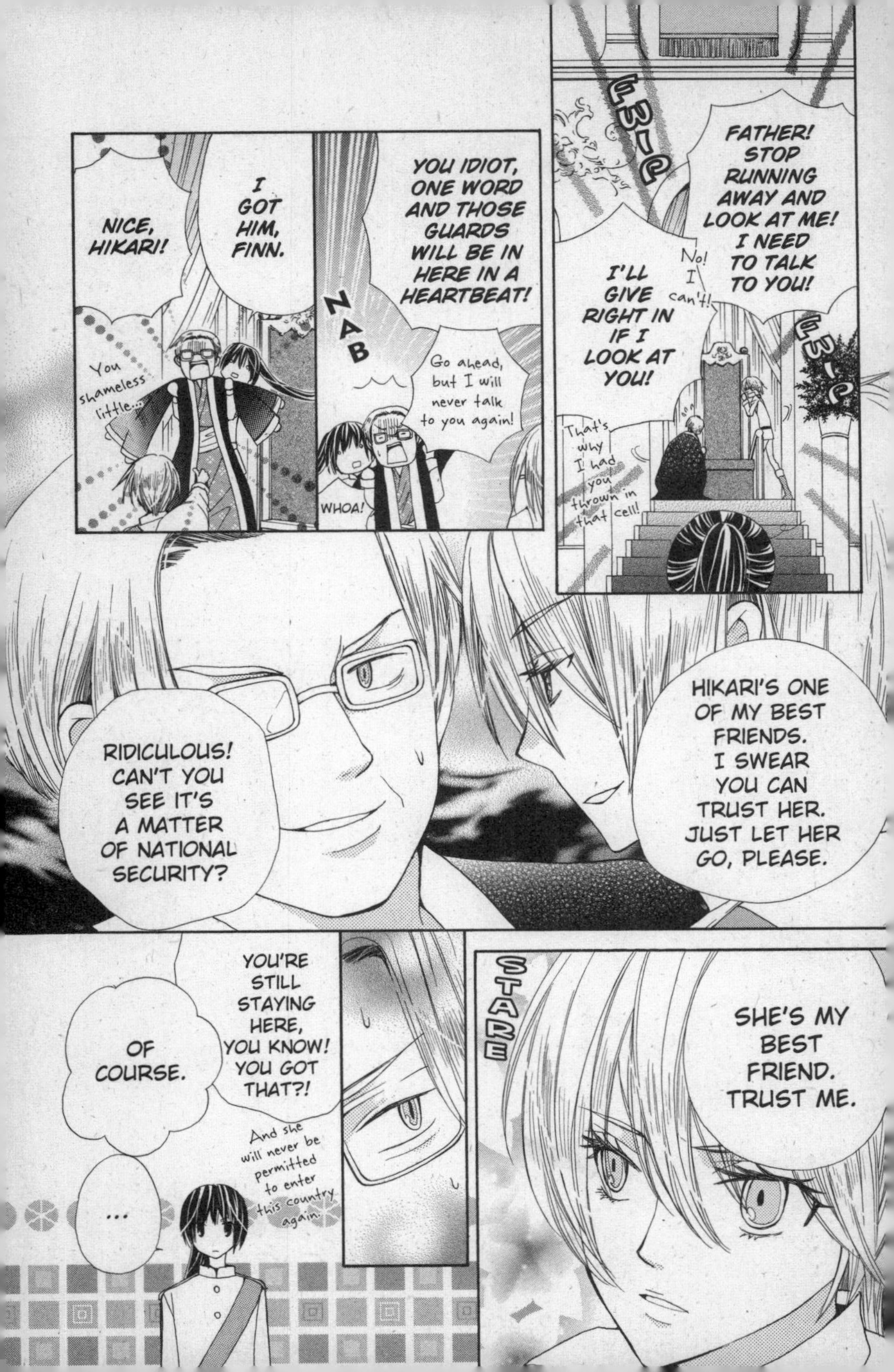
FWIP
FATHER! STOP RUNNING AWAY AND LOOK AT ME! I NEED TO TALK TO YOU!
No! I can't!
I'LL GIVE RIGHT IN IF I LOOK AT YOU!
FWIP
That's why I had you thrown in that cell!
YOU IDIOT, ONE WORD AND THOSE GUARDS WILL BE IN HERE IN A HEARTBEAT!
NAB
Go ahead, but I will never talk to you again!
WHOA!
I GOT HIM, FINN.
NICE, HIKARI!
You shameless little...
HIKARI'S ONE OF MY BEST FRIENDS. I SWEAR YOU CAN TRUST HER. JUST LET HER GO, PLEASE.
RIDICULOUS! CAN'T YOU SEE IT'S A MATTER OF NATIONAL SECURITY?
STARE
SHE'S MY BEST FRIEND. TRUST ME.
YOU'RE STILL STAYING HERE, YOU KNOW! YOU GOT THAT?!
And she will never be permitted to enter this country again.
OF COURSE.
...

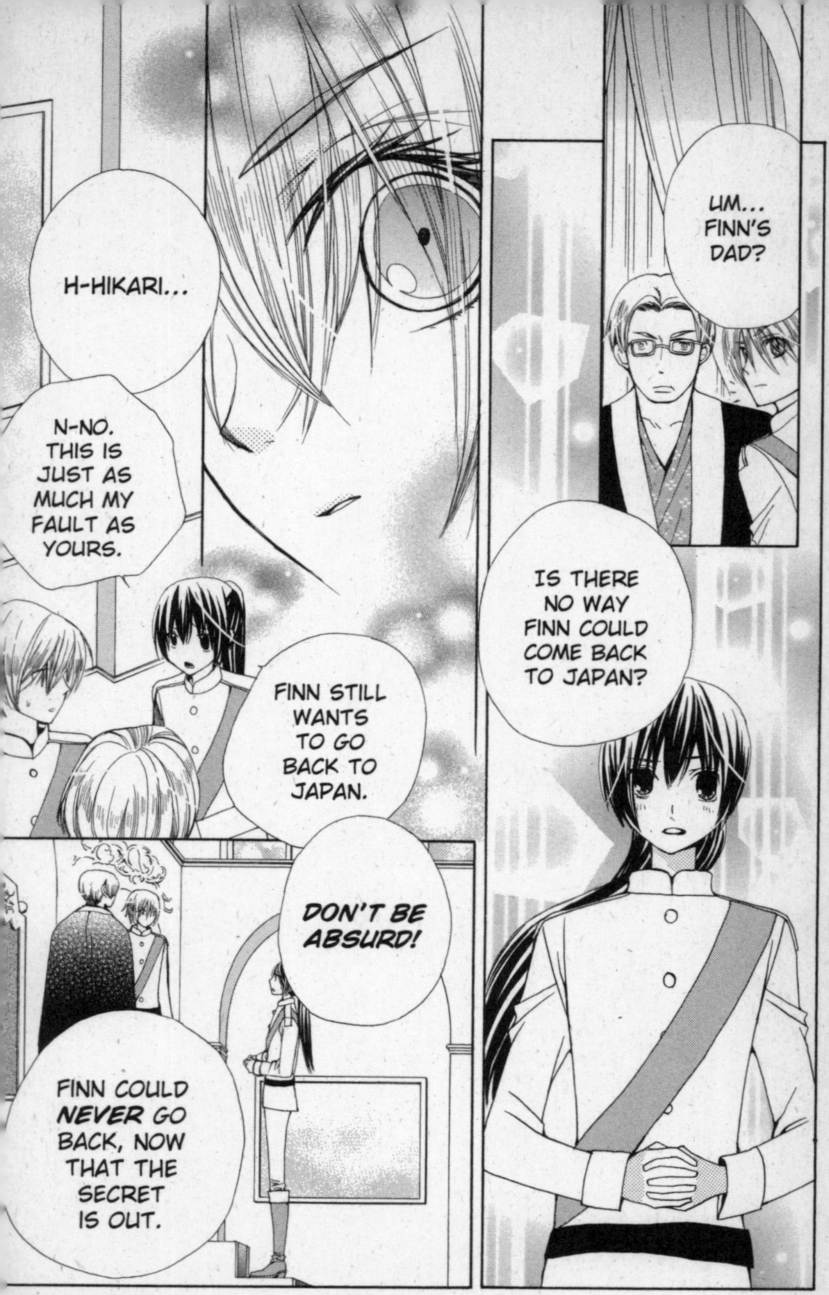
UM... FINN'S DAD?
IS THERE NO WAY FINN COULD COME BACK TO JAPAN?
H-HIKARI...
N-NO. THIS IS JUST AS MUCH MY FAULT AS YOURS.
FINN STILL WANTS TO GO BACK TO JAPAN.
DON'T BE ABSURD!
FINN COULD NEVER GO BACK, NOW THAT THE SECRET IS OUT.

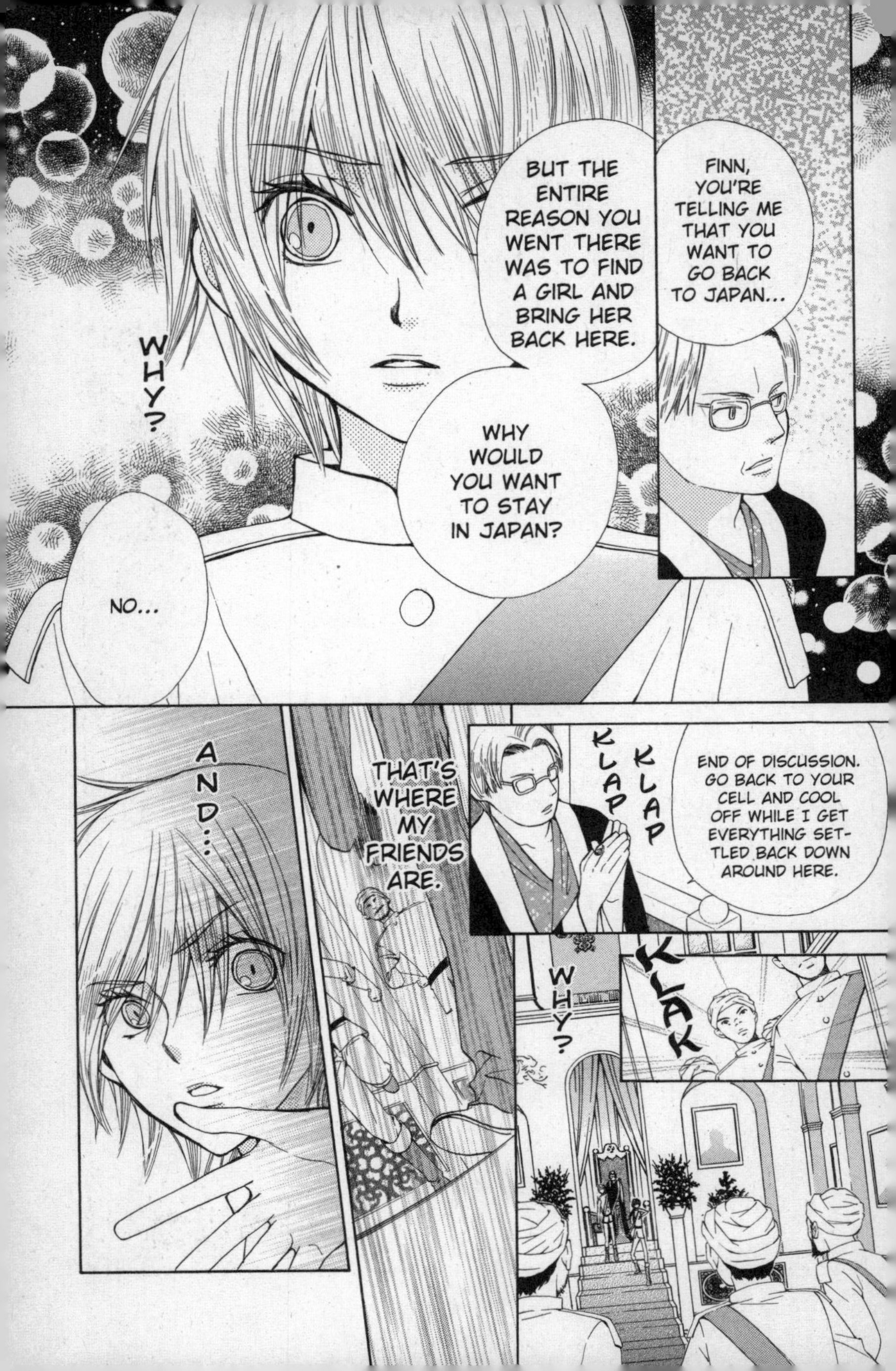
FINN, YOU'RE TELLING ME THAT YOU WANT TO GO BACK TO JAPAN...
BUT THE ENTIRE REASON YOU WENT THERE WAS TO FIND A GIRL AND BRING HER BACK HERE.
WHY WOULD YOU WANT TO STAY IN JAPAN?
WHY?
NO...
END OF DISCUSSION. GO BACK TO YOUR CELL AND COOL OFF WHILE I GET EVERYTHING SET-TLED BACK DOWN AROUND HERE.
KLAP
KLAP
KLAK
WHY?
THAT'S WHERE MY FRIENDS ARE.
AND...

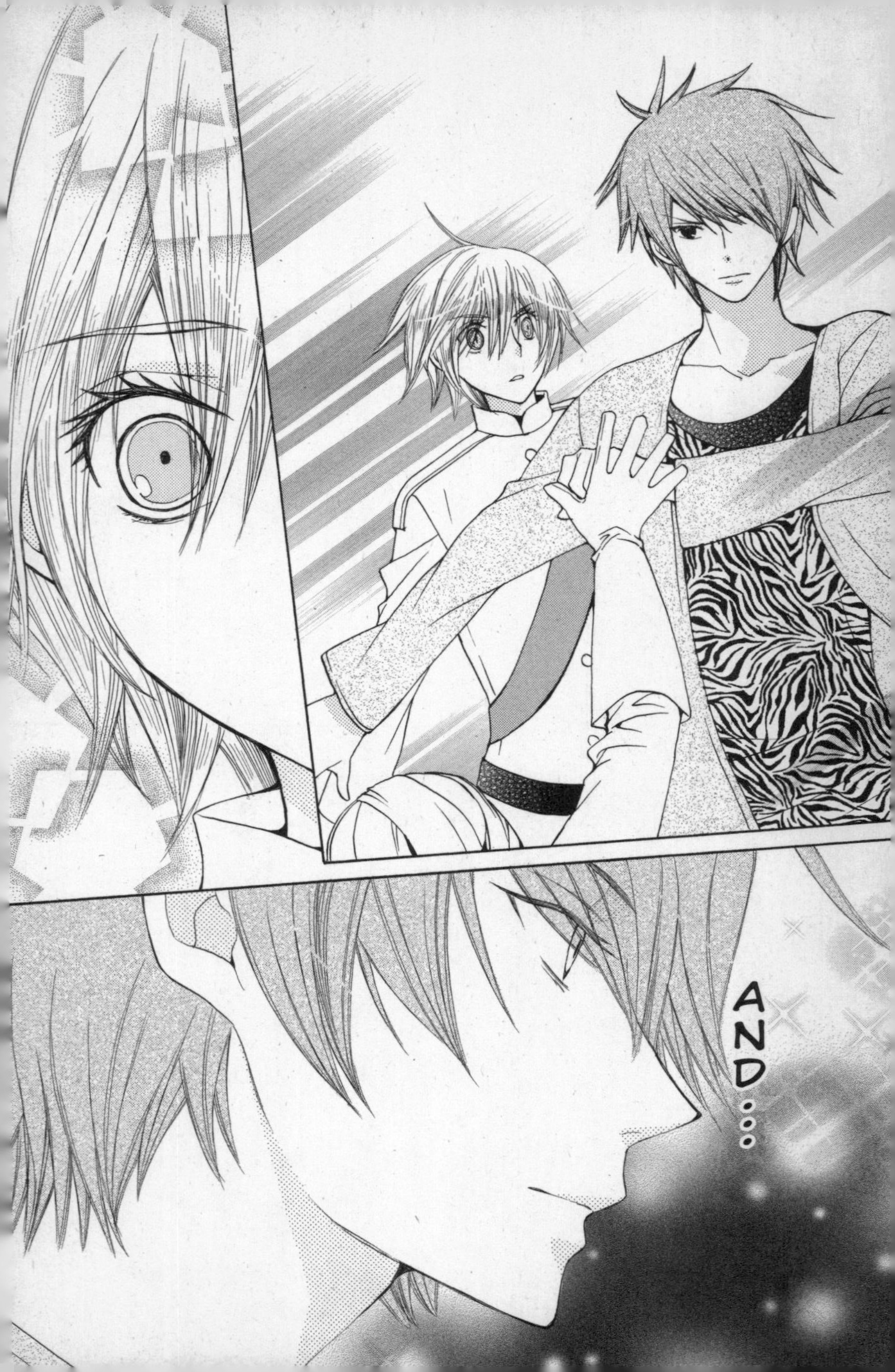
AND...

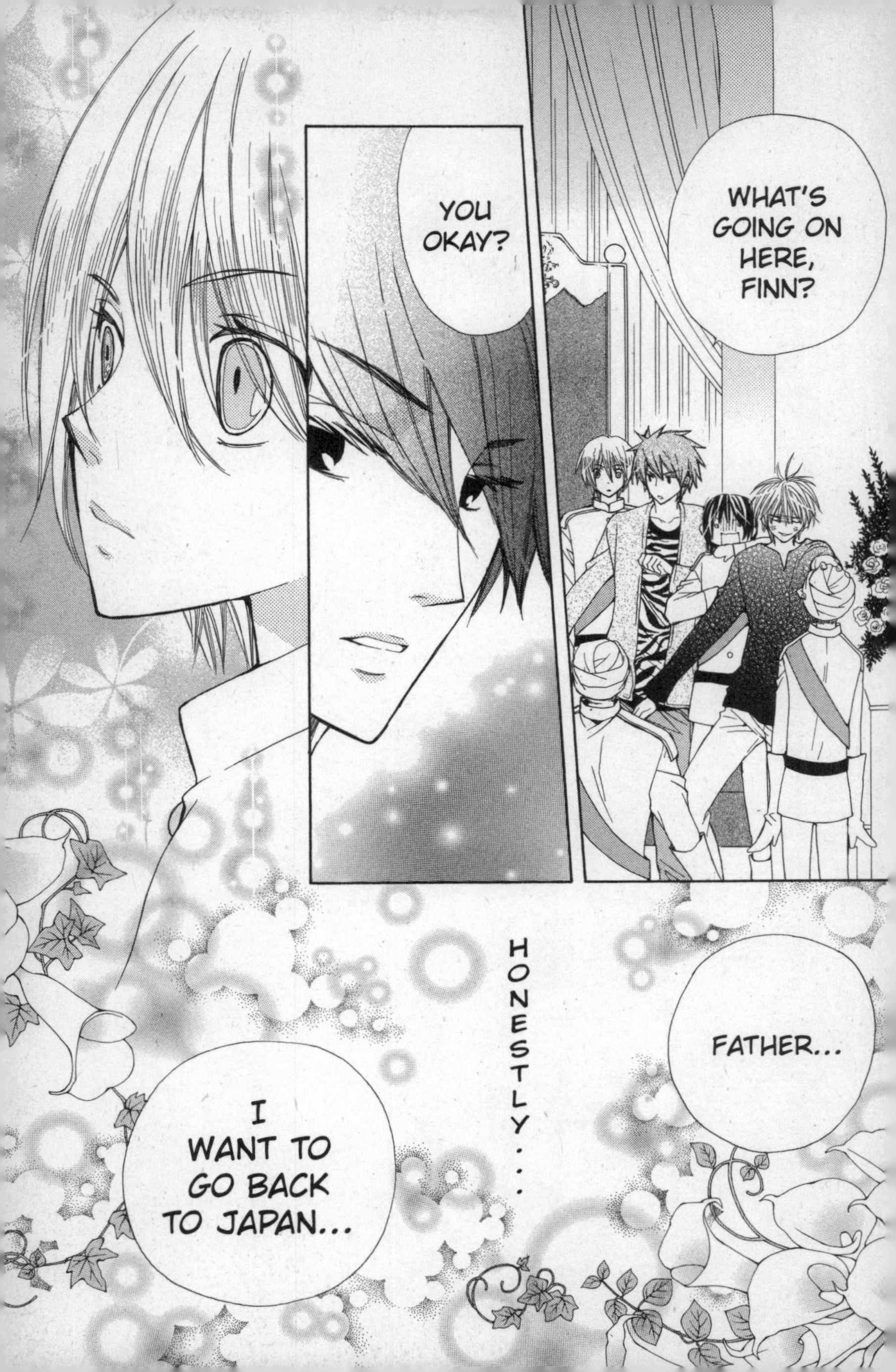
WHAT'S GOING ON HERE, FINN?
YOU OKAY?
FATHER...
HONESTLY...
I WANT TO GO BACK TO JAPAN...

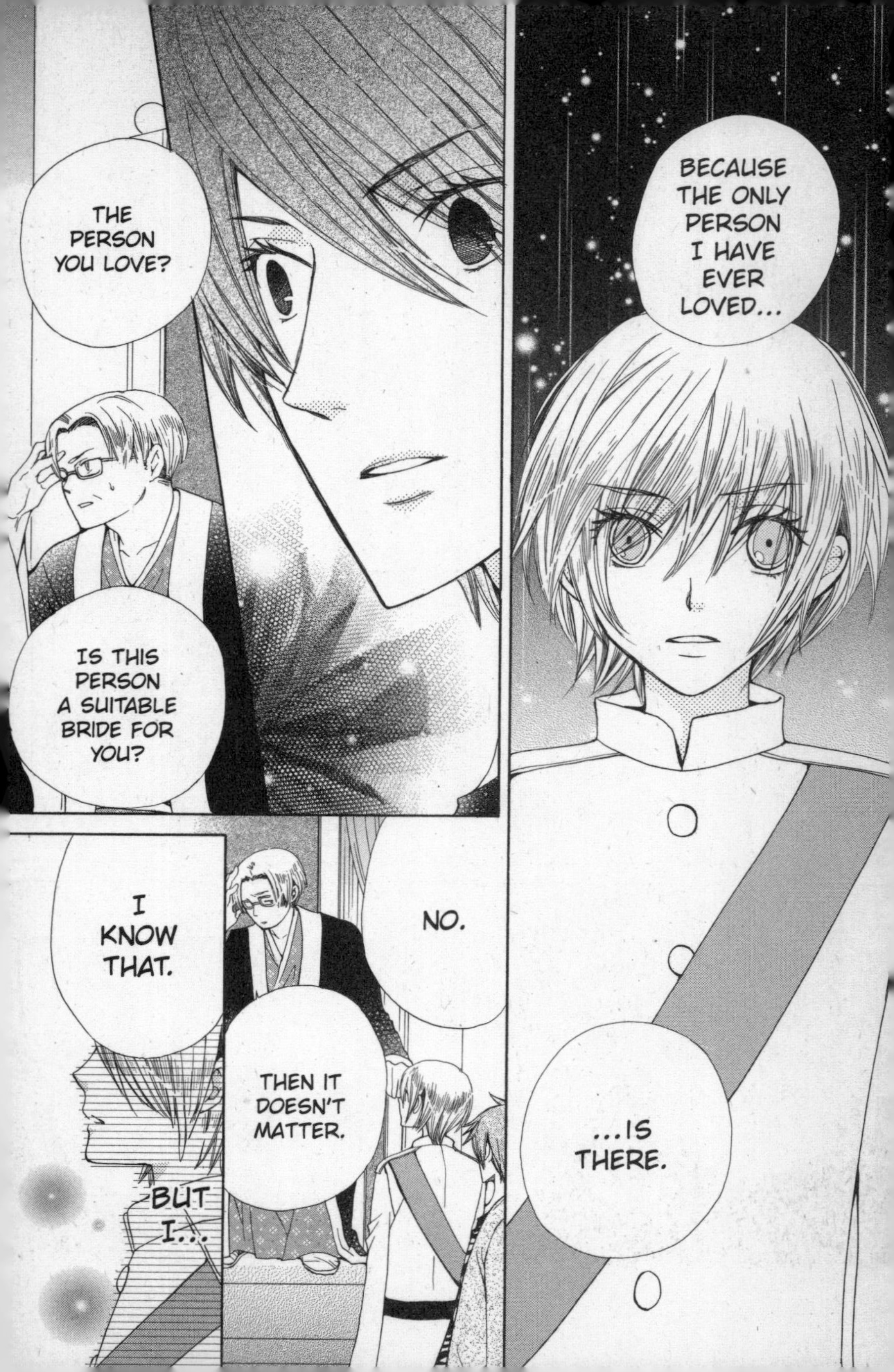
BECAUSE THE ONLY PERSON I HAVE EVER LOVED...
...IS THERE.
THE PERSON YOU LOVE?
IS THIS PERSON A SUITABLE BRIDE FOR YOU?
NO.
I KNOW THAT.
THEN IT DOESN'T MATTER.
BUT I...

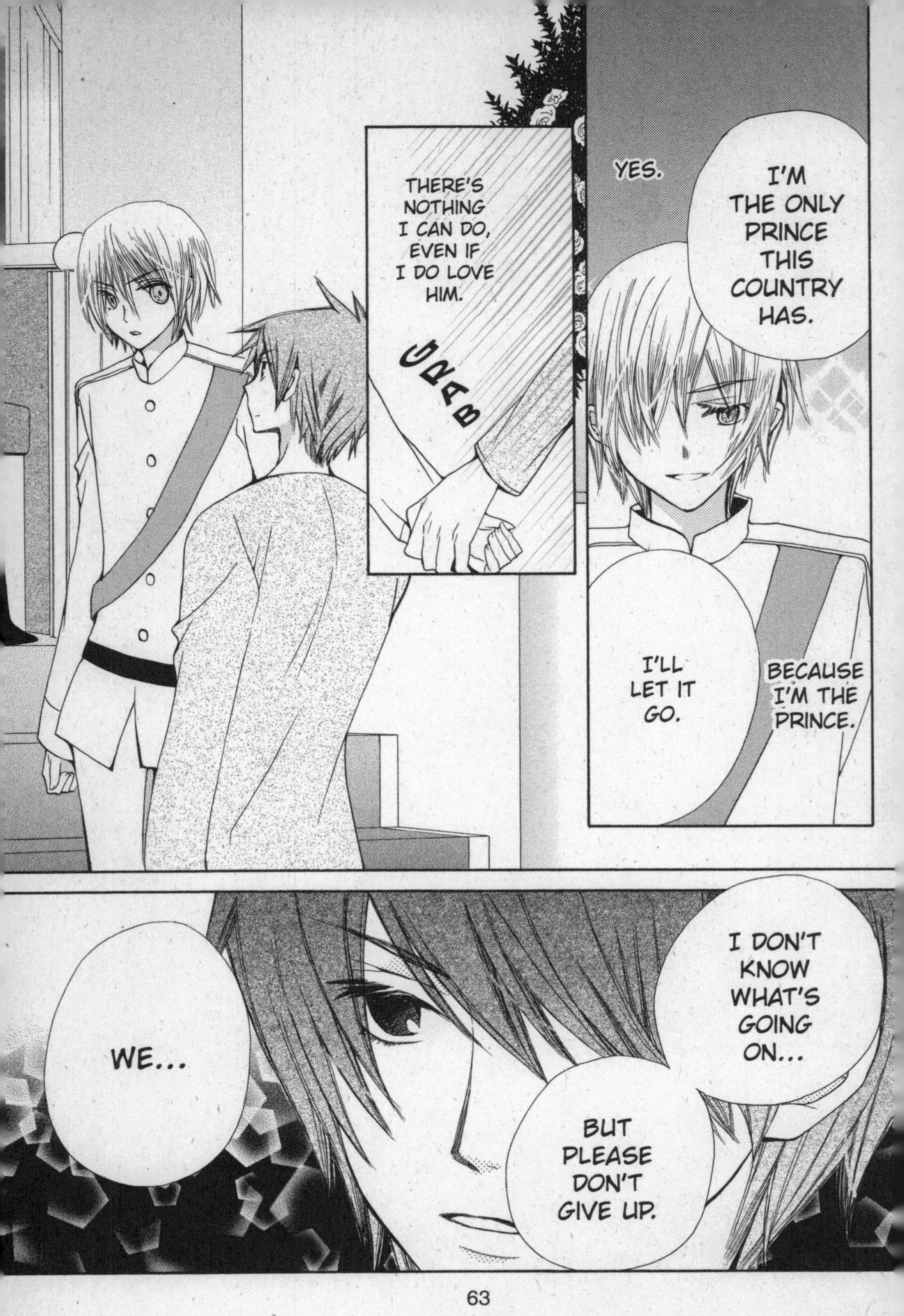
I'M THE ONLY PRINCE THIS COUNTRY HAS.
YES.
BECAUSE I'M THE PRINCE.
I'LL LET IT GO.
THERE'S NOTHING I CAN DO, EVEN IF I DO LOVE HIM.
GRAB
I DON'T KNOW WHAT'S GOING ON...
BUT PLEASE DON'T GIVE UP.
WE...

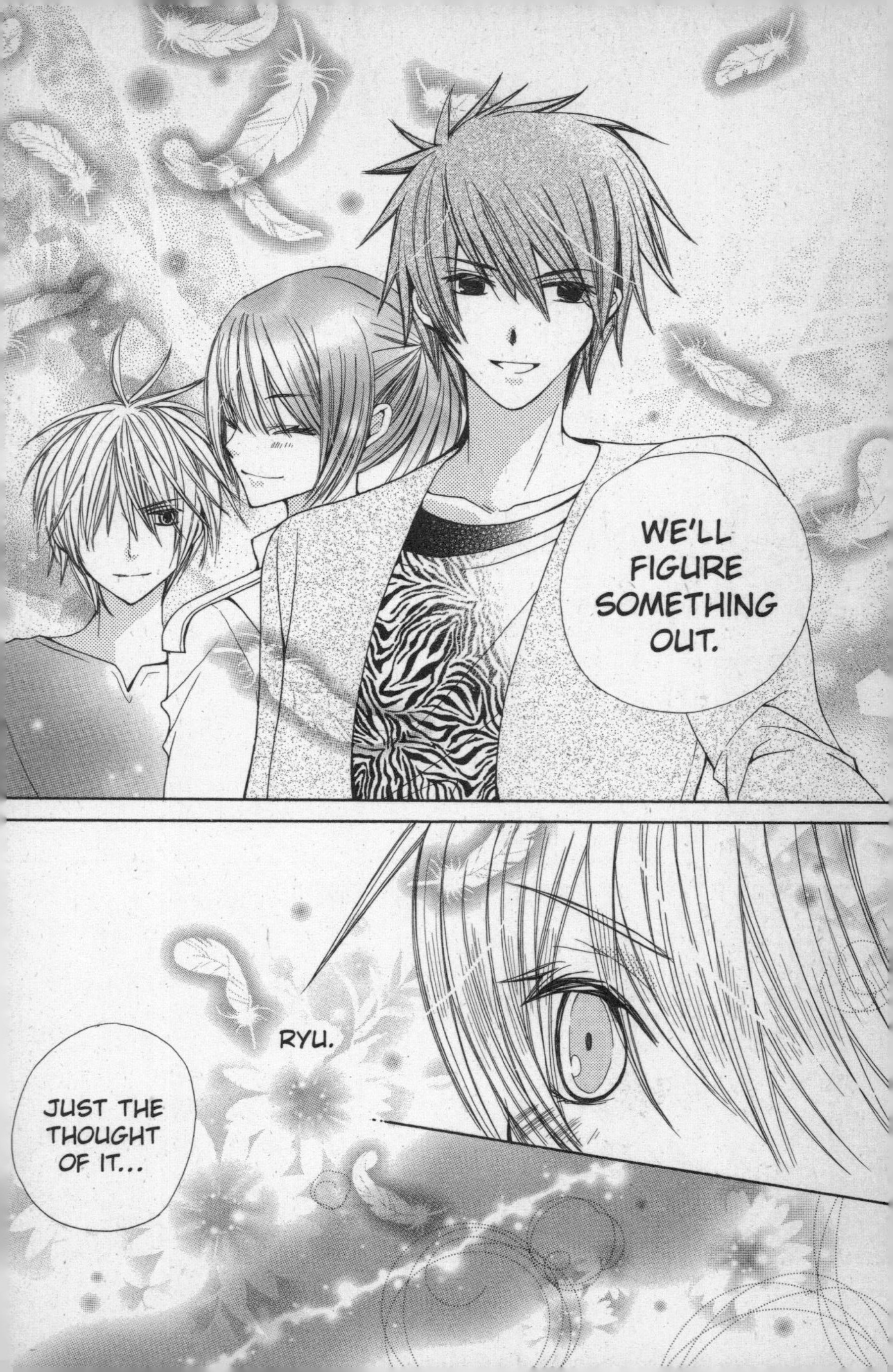
WE'LL FIGURE SOMETHING OUT.
RYU.
JUST THE THOUGHT OF IT...

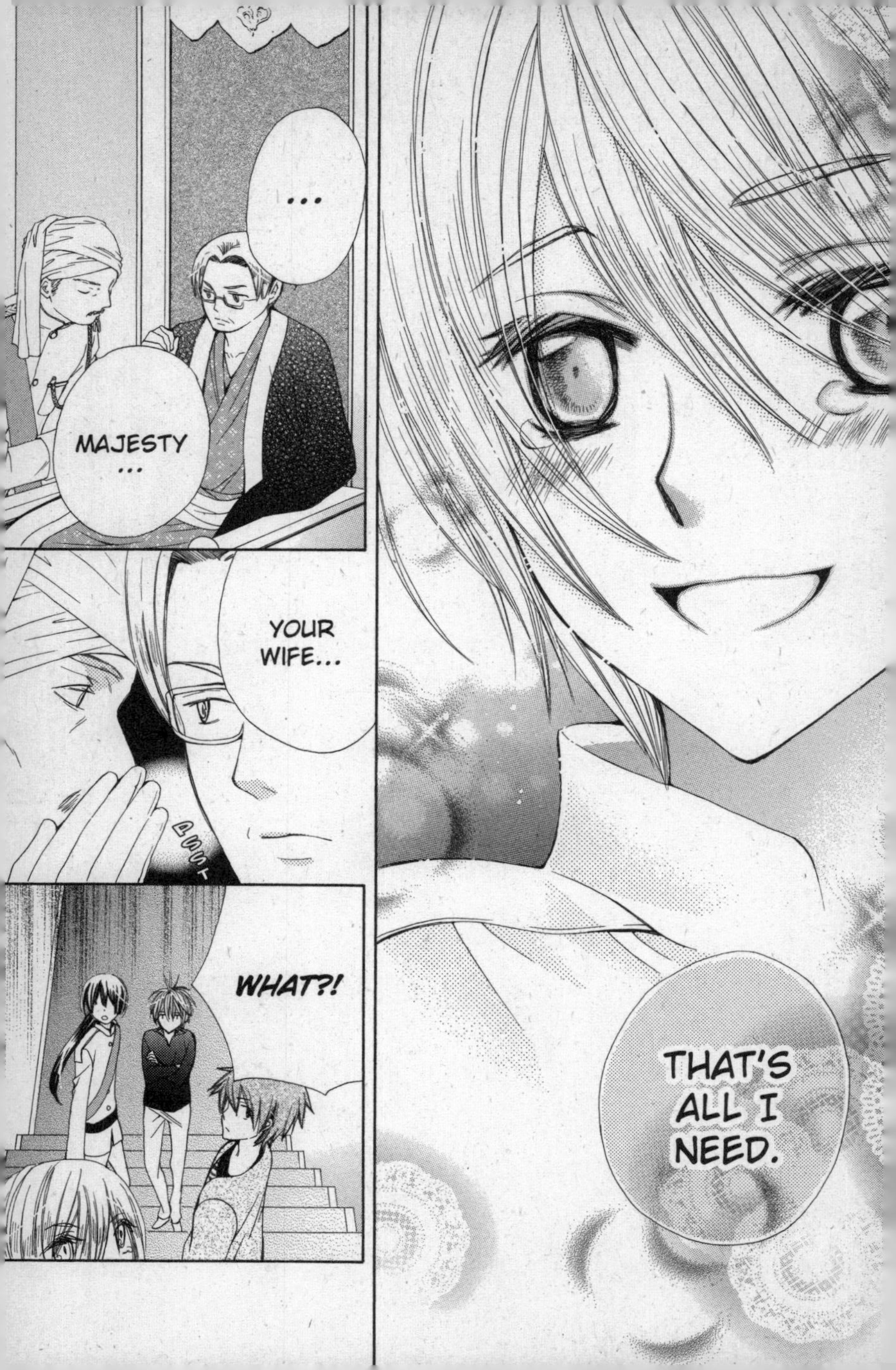
THAT'S ALL I NEED.
...
MAJESTY ...
YOUR WIFE...
PSST
WHAT?!

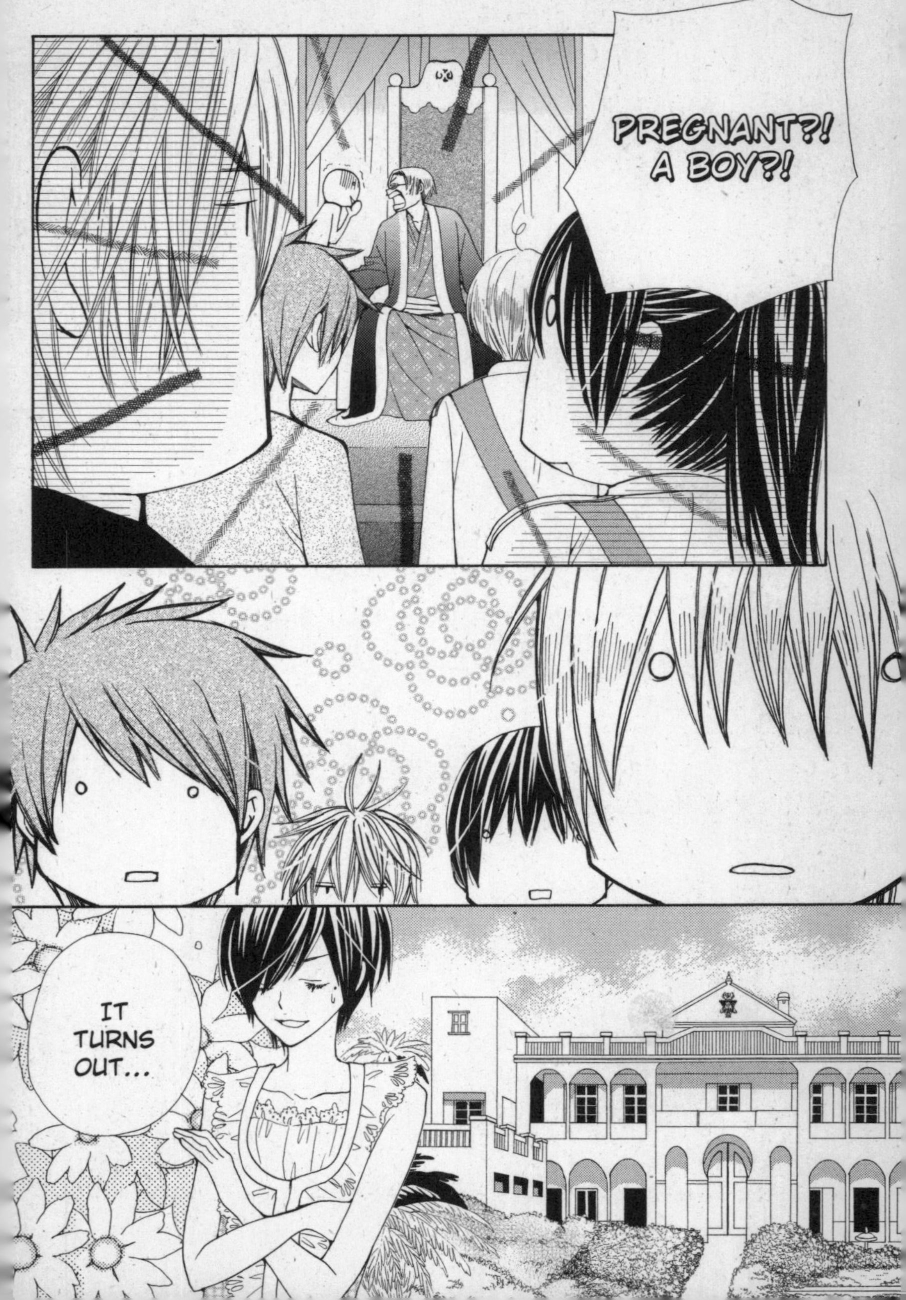
PREGNANT?! A BOY?!
IT TURNS OUT...

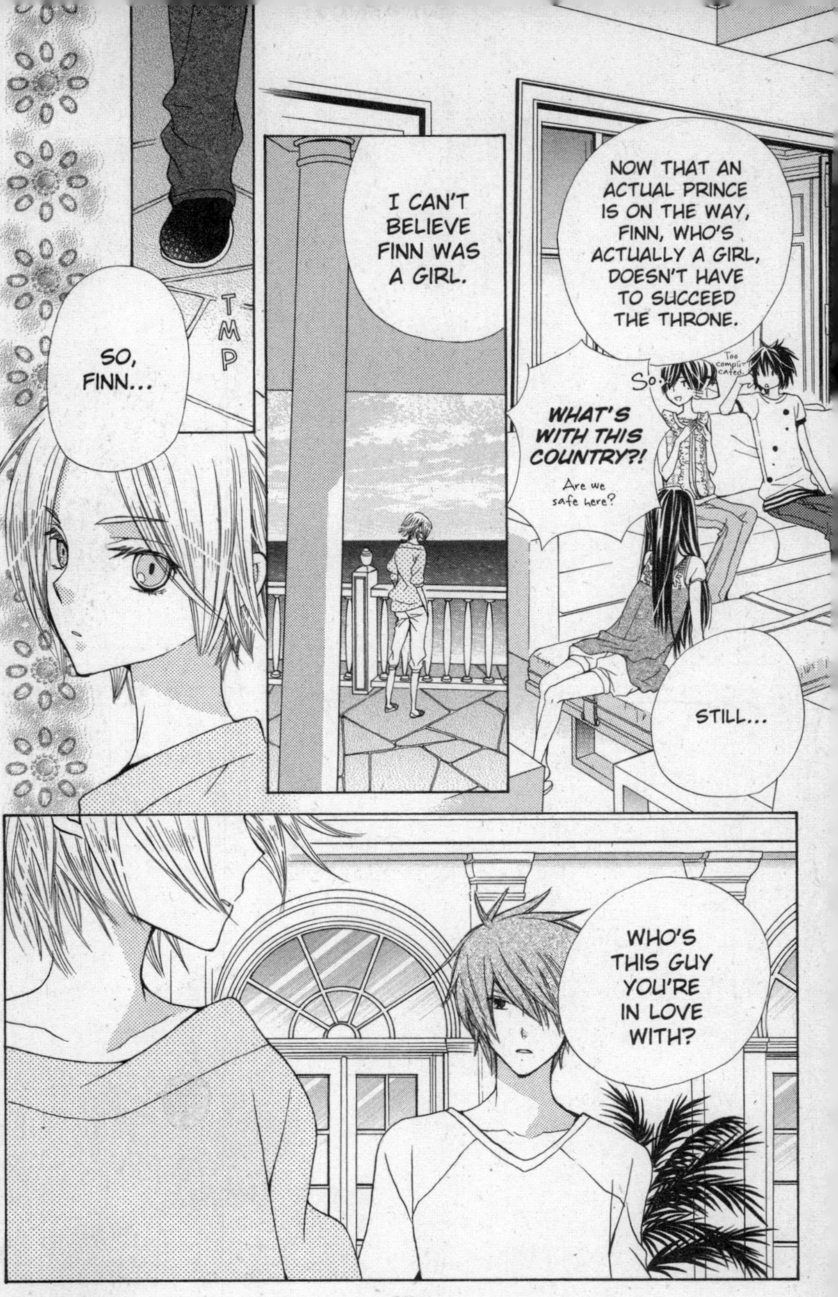
NOW THAT AN ACTUAL PRINCE IS ON THE WAY, FINN, WHO'S ACTUALLY A GIRL, DOESN'T HAVE TO SUCCEED THE THRONE.
Too compli-cated.
So...
WHAT'S WITH THIS COUNTRY?!
Are we safe here?
STILL...
I CAN'T BELIEVE FINN WAS A GIRL.
TMP
SO, FINN...
WHO'S THIS GUY YOU'RE IN LOVE WITH?

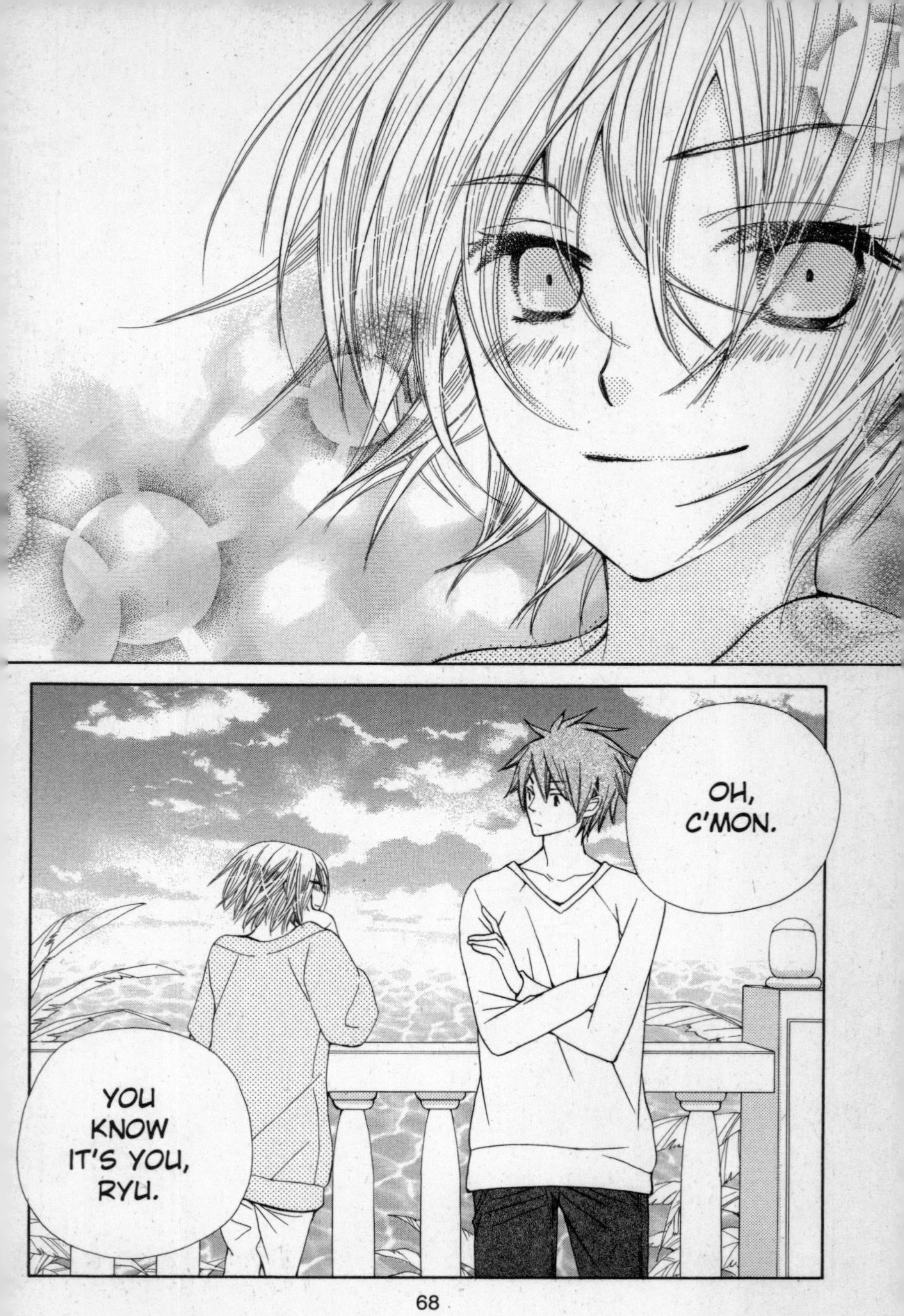
OH, C'MON.
YOU KNOW IT'S YOU, RYU.

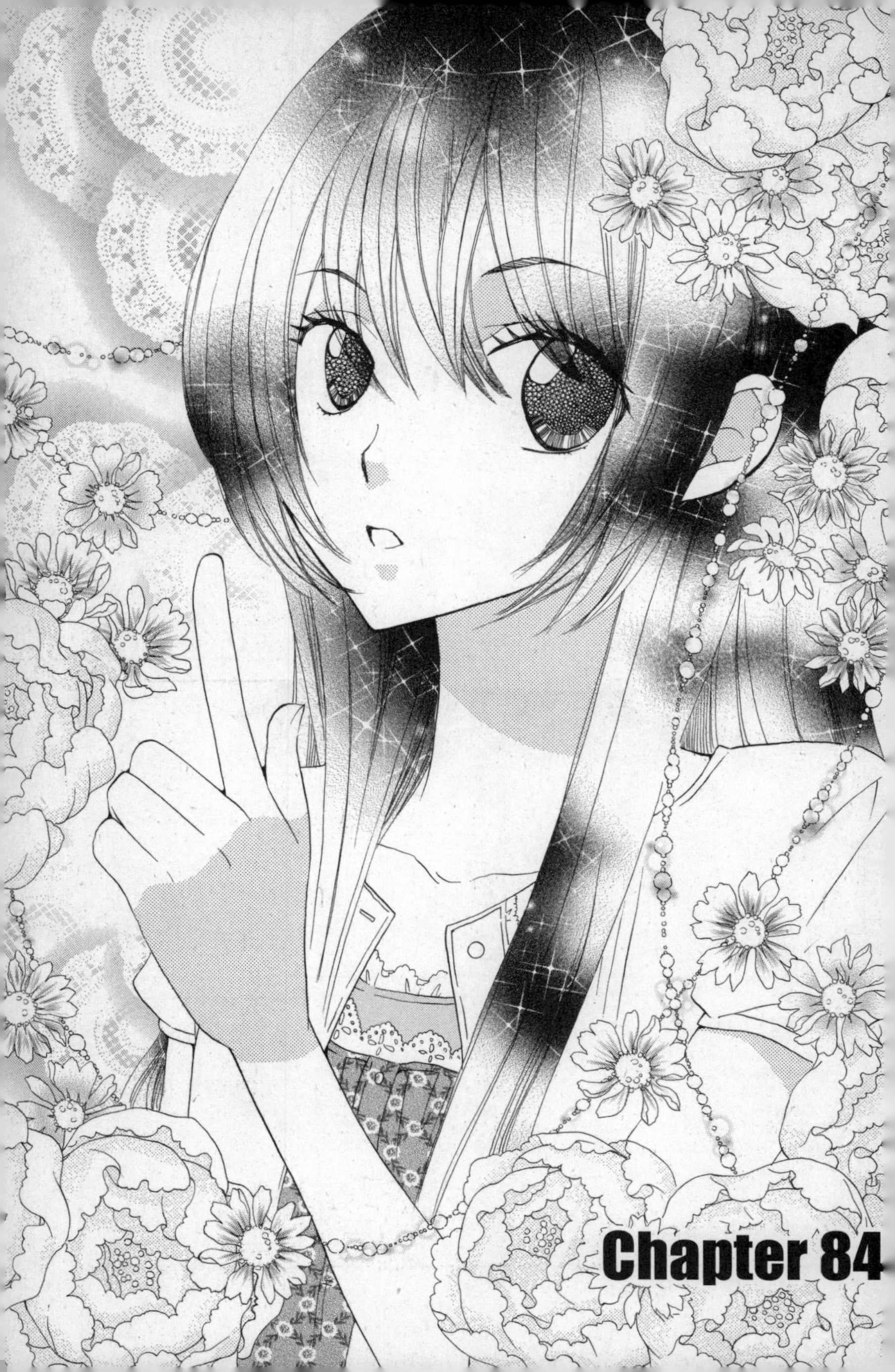
Chapter 84

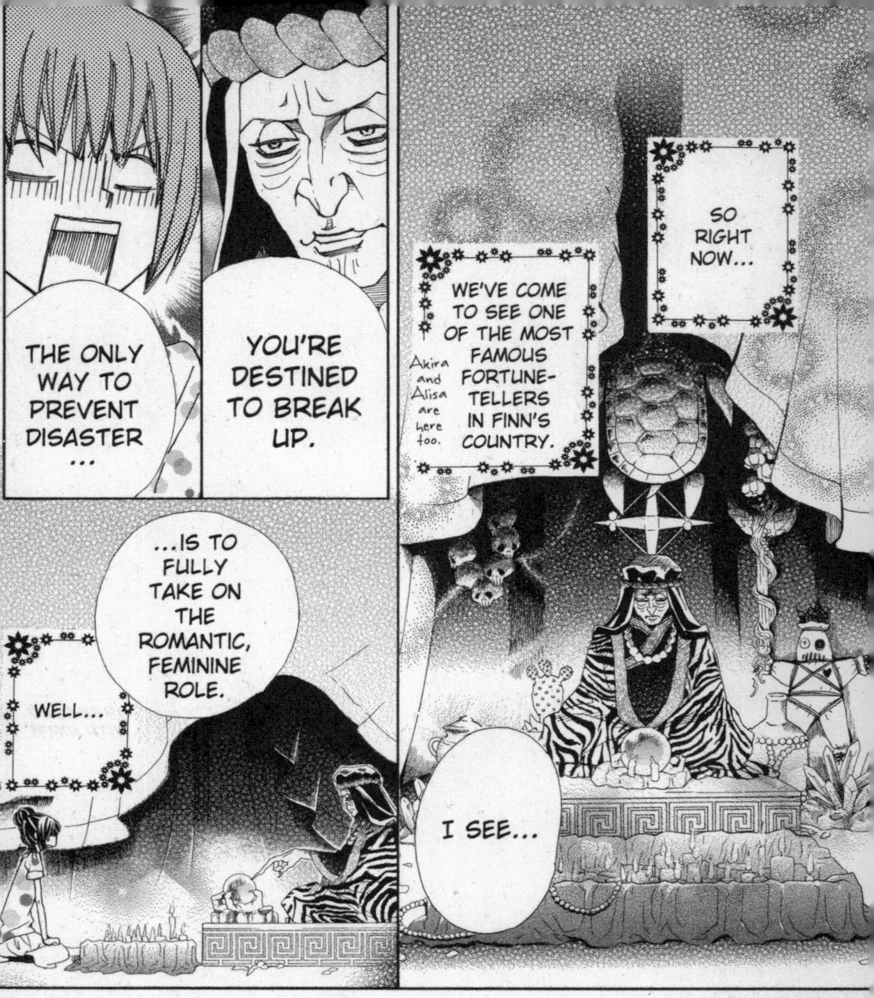

SO RIGHT NOW...
WE'VE COME TO SEE ONE OF THE MOST FAMOUS FORTUNE-TELLERS IN FINN'S COUNTRY.
Akira and Alisa are here too.
I SEE...
YOU'RE DESTINED TO BREAK UP.
THE ONLY WAY TO PREVENT DISASTER...
...IS TO FULLY TAKE ON THE ROMANTIC, FEMININE ROLE.
WELL...

•EVERY DAY•

ANY TIME I'M NOT WORKING, I LIKE TO JUST WANDER AROUND DIFFERENT PLACES.
I LOVE TO JUST WALK.
COME TO THINK OF IT, I WAS ON A DIET IN VOLUME 13, BUT I GAINED BACK ALL THE WEIGHT. I CAN'T SHAKE ALL MY HOLIDAY WEIGHT OR SOMETHING. SEEMS LIKE I'M GAINING BACK A LITTLE EXTRA TOO!

HA HA HA HA HA

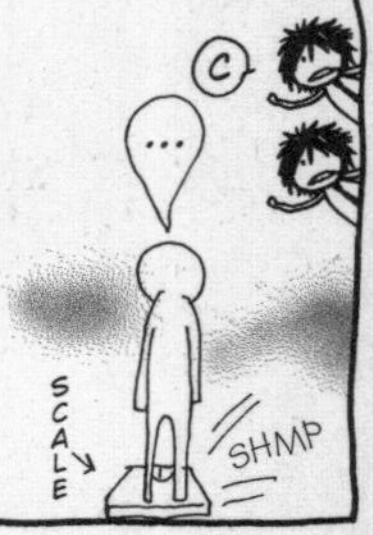

...
SCALE
SHMP

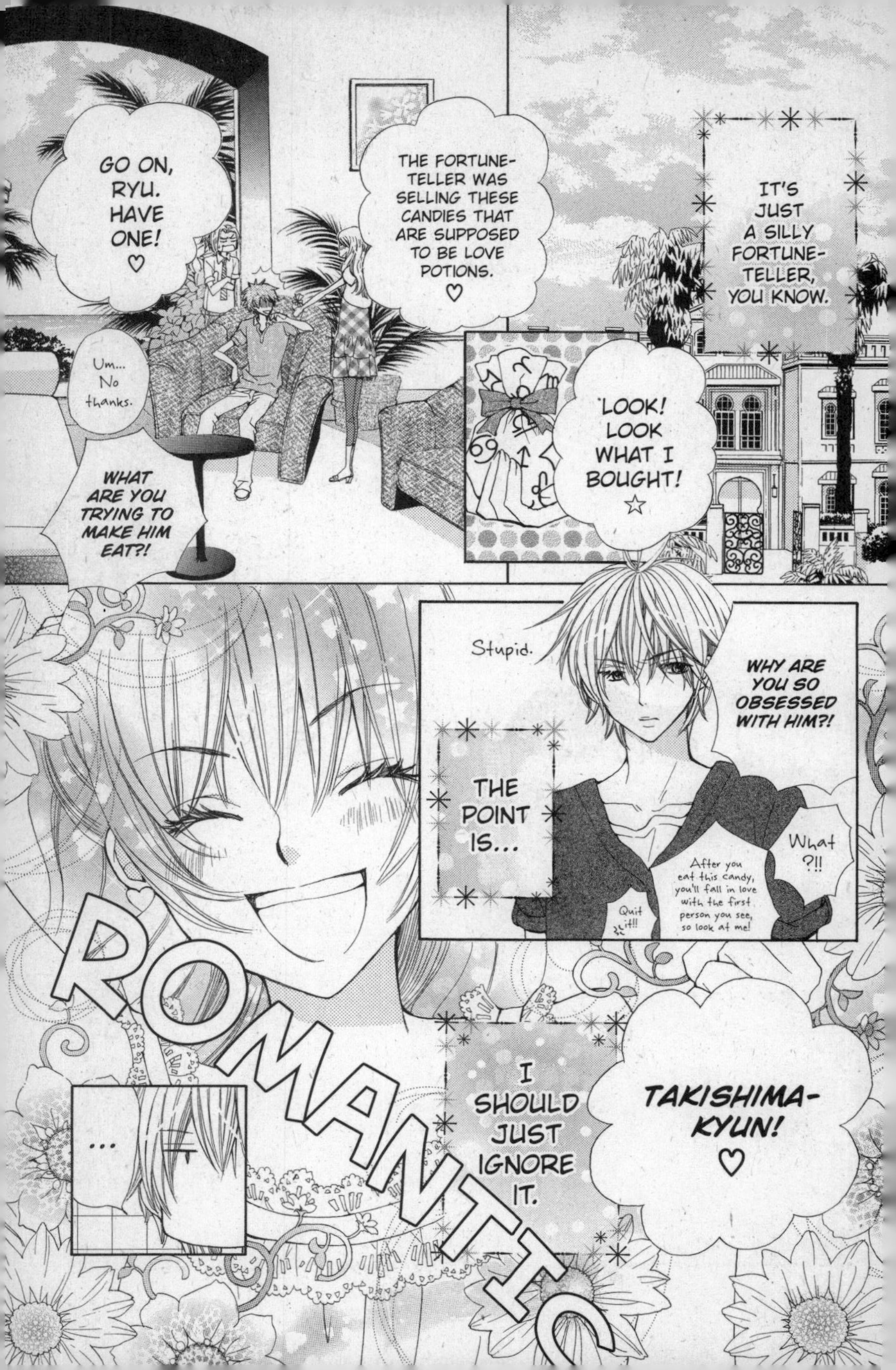

IT'S JUST A SILLY FORTUNE-TELLER, YOU KNOW.
LOOK! LOOK WHAT I BOUGHT! ☆
THE FORTUNE-TELLER WAS SELLING THESE CANDIES THAT ARE SUPPOSED TO BE LOVE POTIONS. ♡
GO ON, RYU. HAVE ONE! ♡
Um... No thanks.
WHAT ARE YOU TRYING TO MAKE HIM EAT?!
WHY ARE YOU SO OBSESSED WITH HIM?!
What?!!
After you eat this candy, you'll fall in love with the first person you see, so look at me!
Quit it!!
Stupid.
THE POINT IS...
TAKISHIMA-KYUN! ♡
I SHOULD JUST IGNORE IT.
ROMANTIC
...

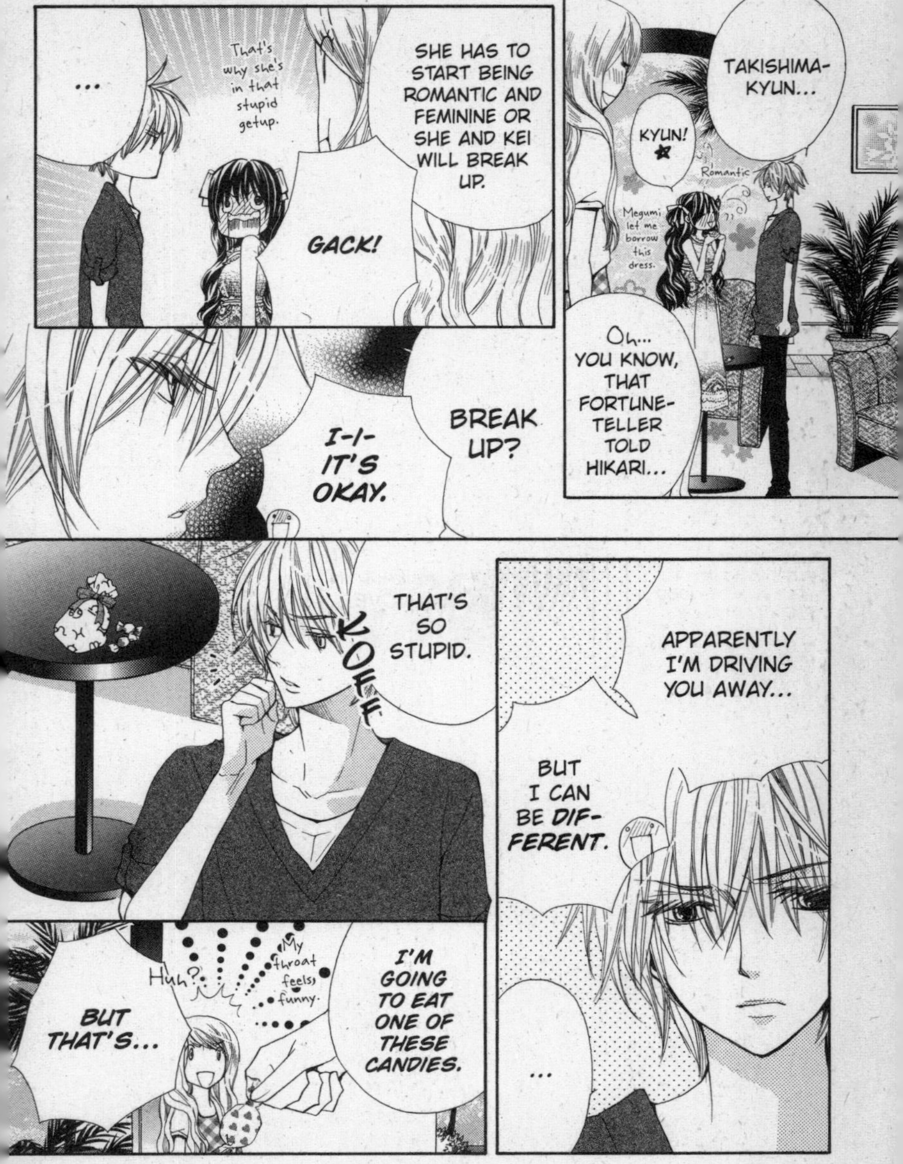
TAKISHIMA-KYUN...
KYUN! ★
Romantic
Megumi let me borrow this dress.
Oh... YOU KNOW, THAT FORTUNE-TELLER TOLD HIKARI...
SHE HAS TO START BEING ROMANTIC AND FEMININE OR SHE AND KEI WILL BREAK UP.
That's why she's in that stupid getup.
...
GACK!
BREAK UP?
I-I-IT'S OKAY.
APPARENTLY I'M DRIVING YOU AWAY...
BUT I CAN BE DIF-FERENT.
...
THAT'S SO STUPID.
KOFF
I'M GOING TO EAT ONE OF THESE CANDIES.
My throat feels funny.
Huh?
BUT THAT'S...

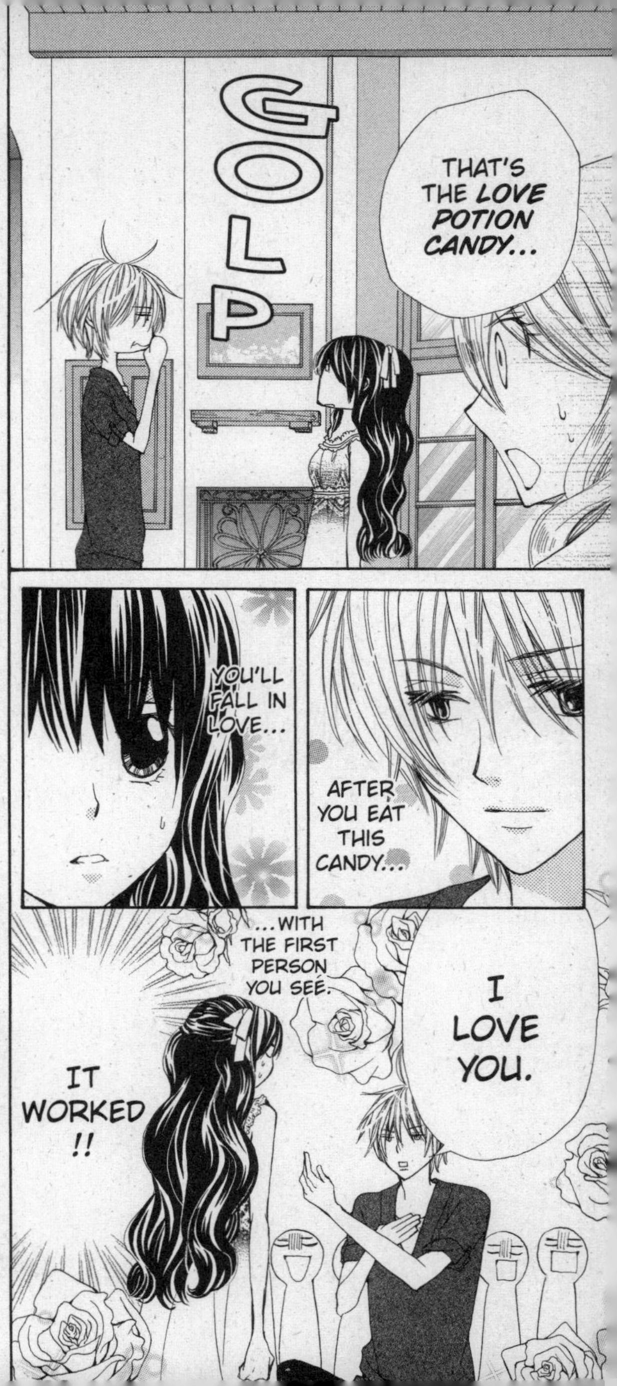
THAT'S THE LOVE POTION CANDY...
GOLP
YOU'LL FALL IN LOVE...
AFTER YOU EAT THIS CANDY...
I LOVE YOU.
...WITH THE FIRST PERSON YOU SEE.
IT WORKED !!

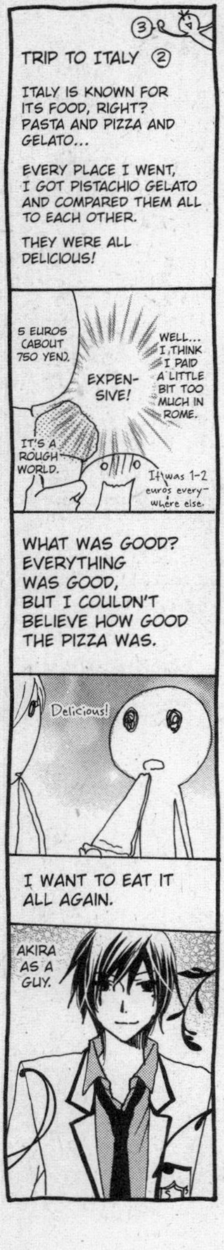
③
TRIP TO ITALY ②
ITALY IS KNOWN FOR ITS FOOD, RIGHT? PASTA AND PIZZA AND GELATO...
EVERY PLACE I WENT, I GOT PISTACHIO GELATO AND COMPARED THEM ALL TO EACH OTHER.
THEY WERE ALL DELICIOUS!
5 EUROS (ABOUT 750 YEN).
EXPEN-SIVE!
WELL... I THINK I PAID A LITTLE BIT TOO MUCH IN ROME.
IT'S A ROUGH WORLD.
It was 1-2 euros every-where else.
WHAT WAS GOOD? EVERYTHING WAS GOOD, BUT I COULDN'T BELIEVE HOW GOOD THE PIZZA WAS.
Delicious!
I WANT TO EAT IT ALL AGAIN.
AKIRA AS A GUY.

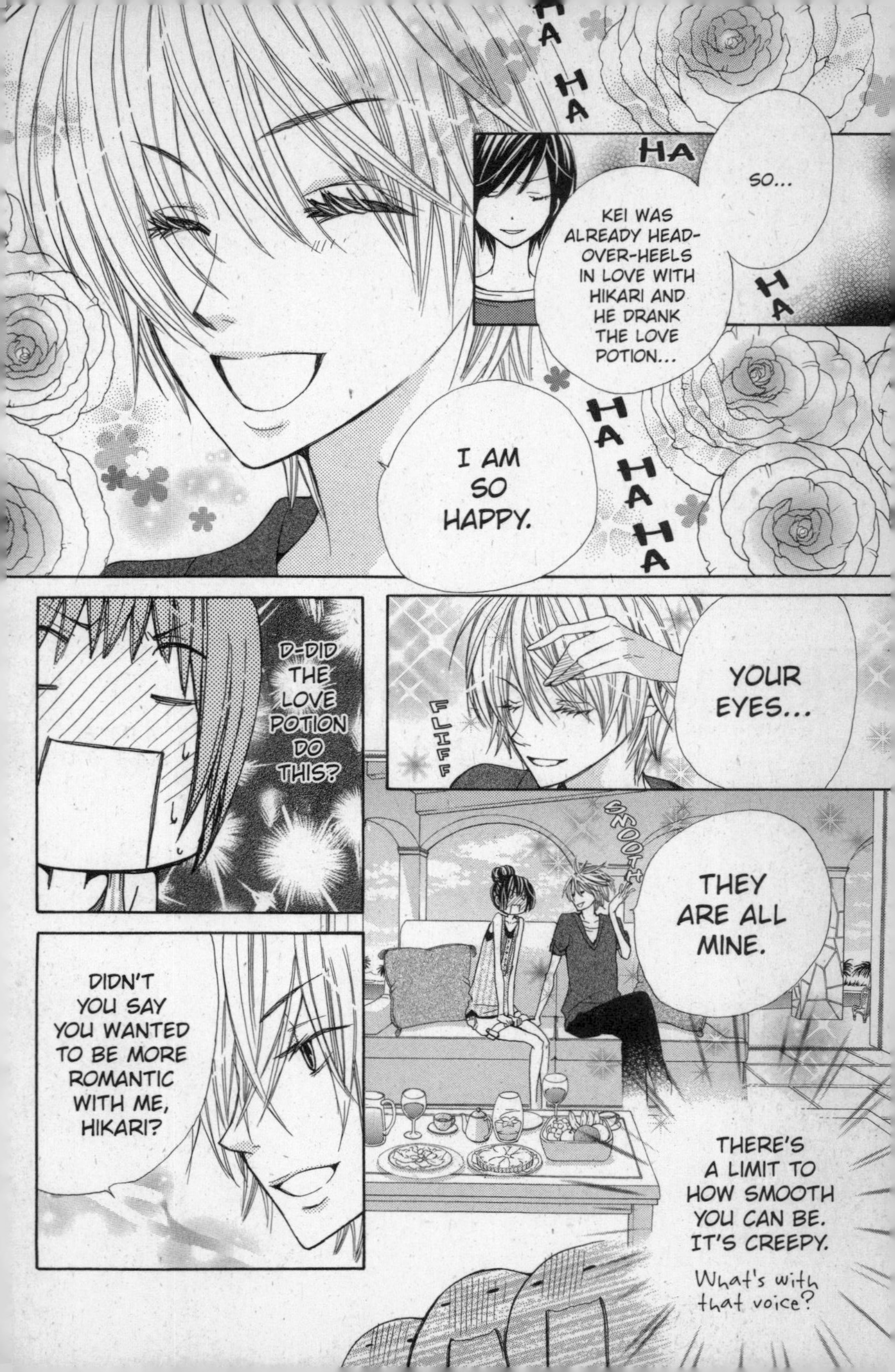
HA
HA
HA
HA
SO...
KEI WAS ALREADY HEAD-OVER-HEELS IN LOVE WITH HIKARI AND HE DRANK THE LOVE POTION...
HA
HA
I AM SO HAPPY.
HA
HA
HA
HA
HA
YOUR EYES...
FLIFF
SMOOTH
THEY ARE ALL MINE.
D-DID THE LOVE POTION DO THIS?
DIDN'T YOU SAY YOU WANTED TO BE MORE ROMANTIC WITH ME, HIKARI?
THERE'S A LIMIT TO HOW SMOOTH YOU CAN BE. IT'S CREEPY.
What's with that voice?

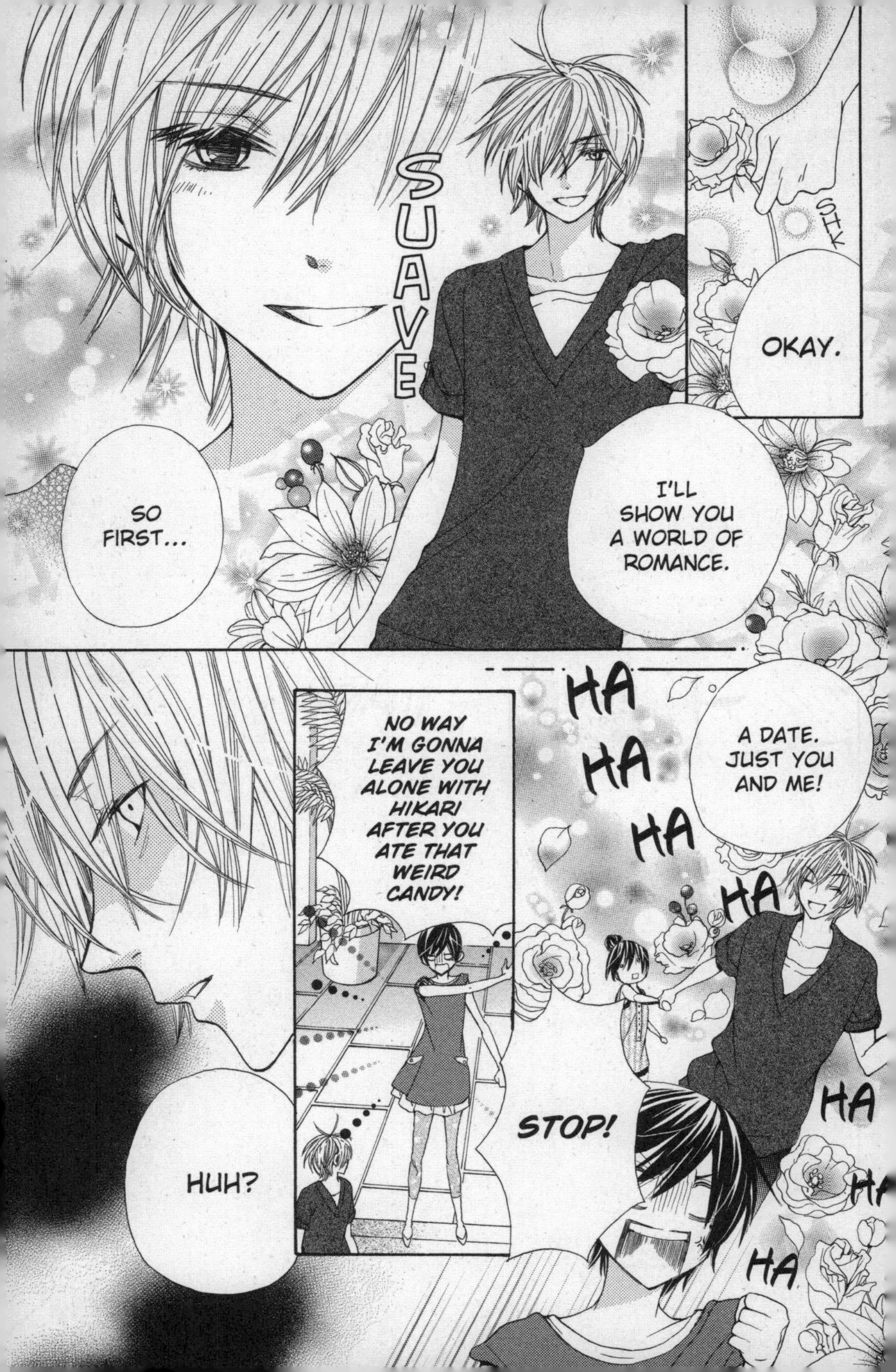
SHK
OKAY.
I'LL SHOW YOU A WORLD OF ROMANCE.
SUAVE
SO FIRST...
A DATE. JUST YOU AND ME!
HA HA HA HA HA HA HA
STOP!
NO WAY I'M GONNA LEAVE YOU ALONE WITH HIKARI AFTER YOU ATE THAT WEIRD CANDY!
HUH?

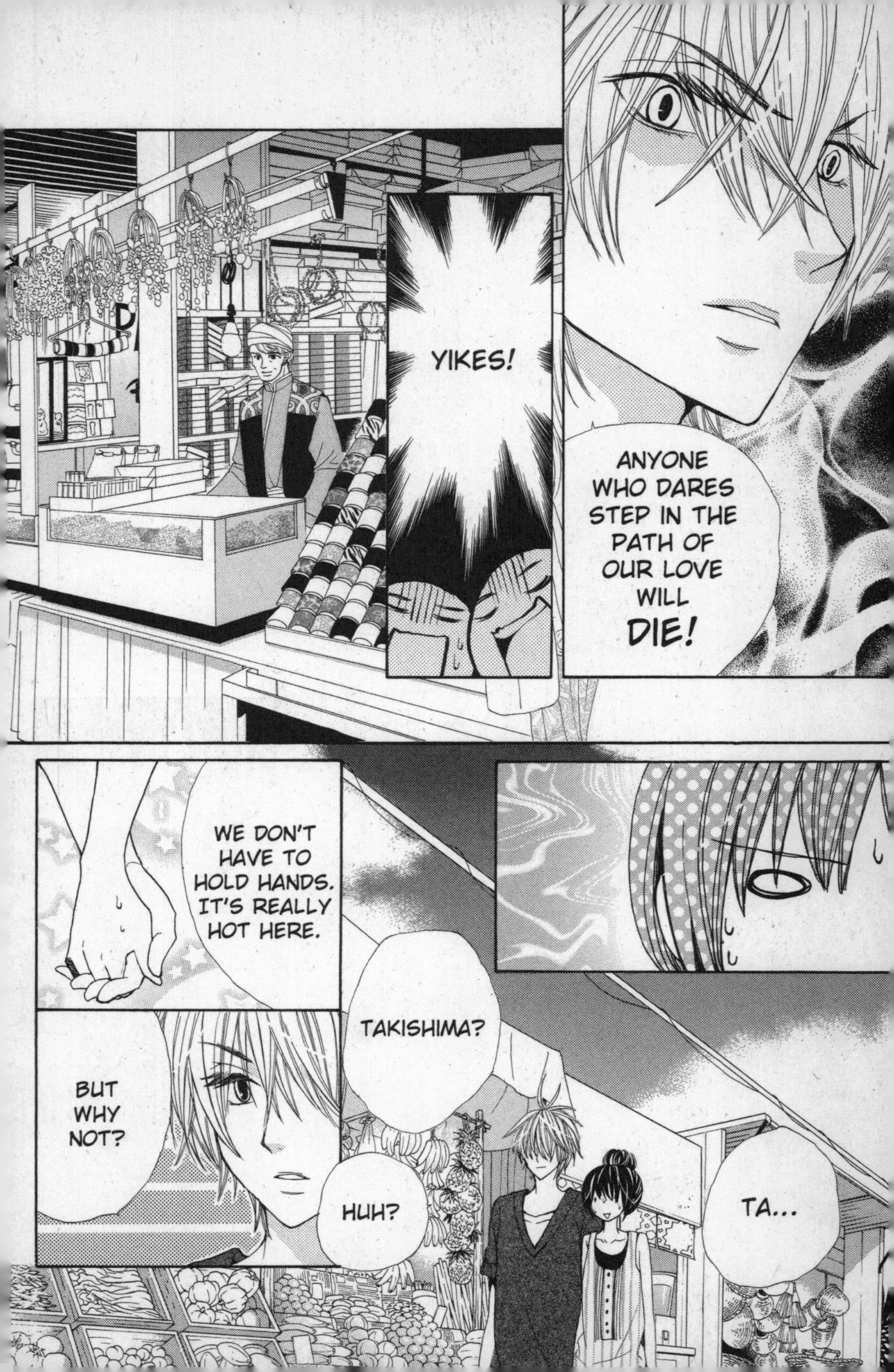
ANYONE WHO DARES STEP IN THE PATH OF OUR LOVE WILL DIE!
YIKES!
WE DON'T HAVE TO HOLD HANDS. IT'S REALLY HOT HERE.
TA...
TAKISHIMA?
HUH?
BUT WHY NOT?

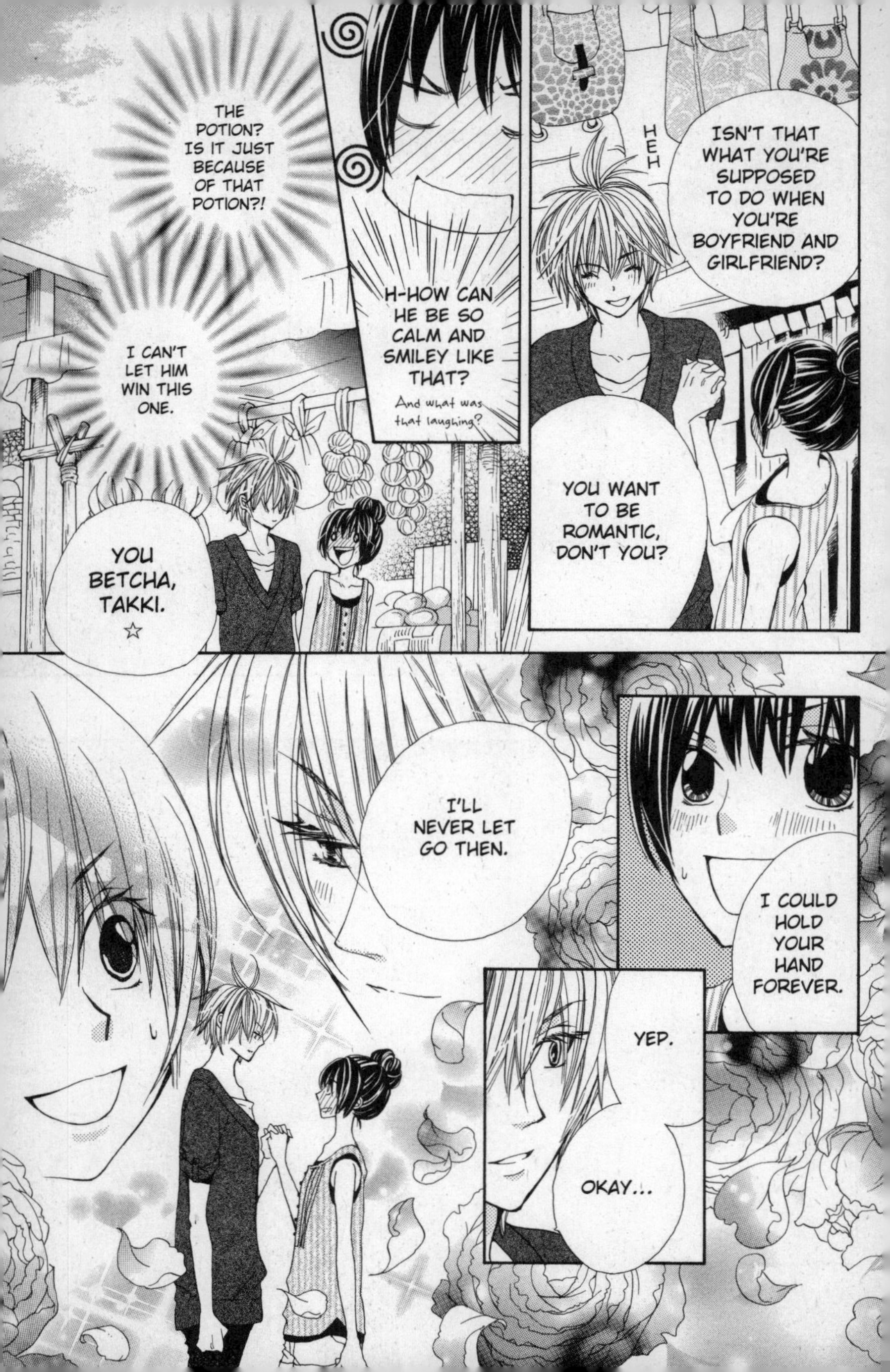

HEH
ISN'T THAT WHAT YOU'RE SUPPOSED TO DO WHEN YOU'RE BOYFRIEND AND GIRLFRIEND?
YOU WANT TO BE ROMANTIC, DON'T YOU?
H-HOW CAN HE BE SO CALM AND SMILEY LIKE THAT?
And what was that laughing?
THE POTION? IS IT JUST BECAUSE OF THAT POTION?!
I CAN'T LET HIM WIN THIS ONE.
YOU BETCHA, TAKKI. ☆
I COULD HOLD YOUR HAND FOREVER.
YEP.
OKAY...
I'LL NEVER LET GO THEN.

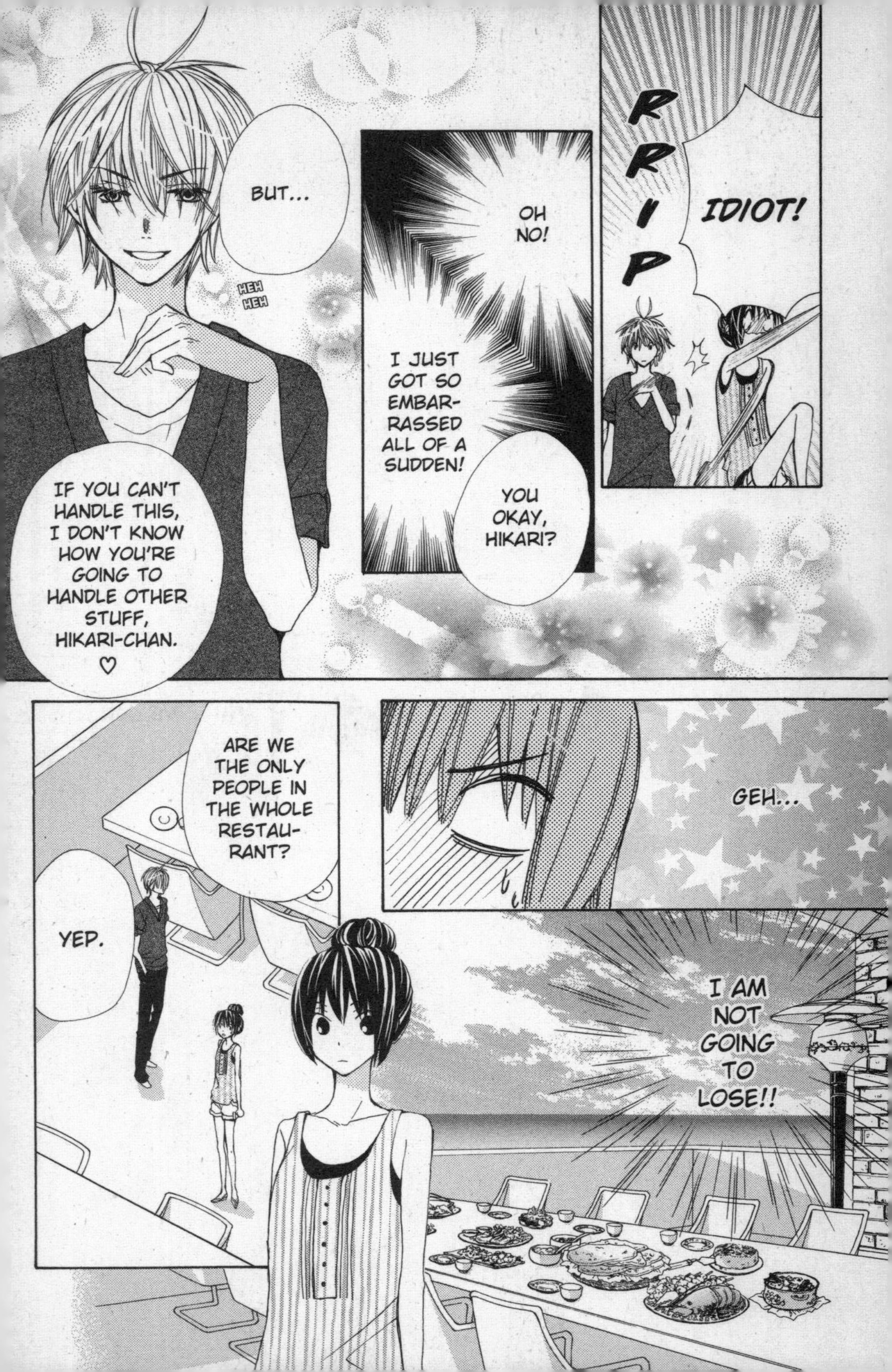
RRIP
IDIOT!
OH NO!
I JUST GOT SO EMBARRASSED ALL OF A SUDDEN!
YOU OKAY, HIKARI?
BUT...
HEH HEH
IF YOU CAN'T HANDLE THIS, I DON'T KNOW HOW YOU'RE GOING TO HANDLE OTHER STUFF, HIKARI-CHAN. ♡
GEH...
ARE WE THE ONLY PEOPLE IN THE WHOLE RESTAURANT?
YEP.
I AM NOT GOING TO LOSE!!

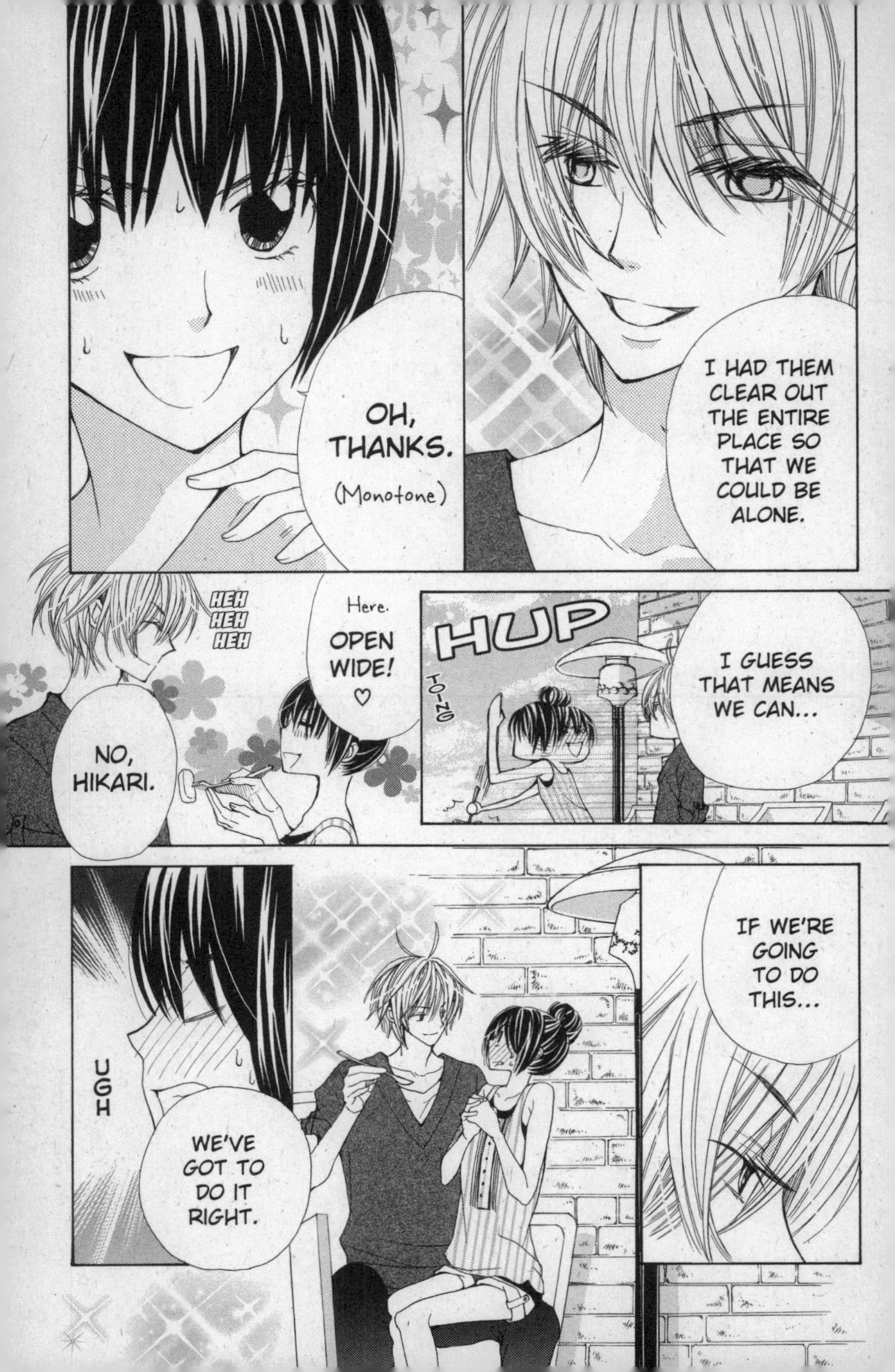
I HAD THEM CLEAR OUT THE ENTIRE PLACE SO THAT WE COULD BE ALONE.
OH, THANKS.
(Monotone)
I GUESS THAT MEANS WE CAN...
HUP
TO-ING
Here.
OPEN WIDE! ♡
HEH HEH HEH
NO, HIKARI.
IF WE'RE GOING TO DO THIS...
WE'VE GOT TO DO IT RIGHT.
UGH

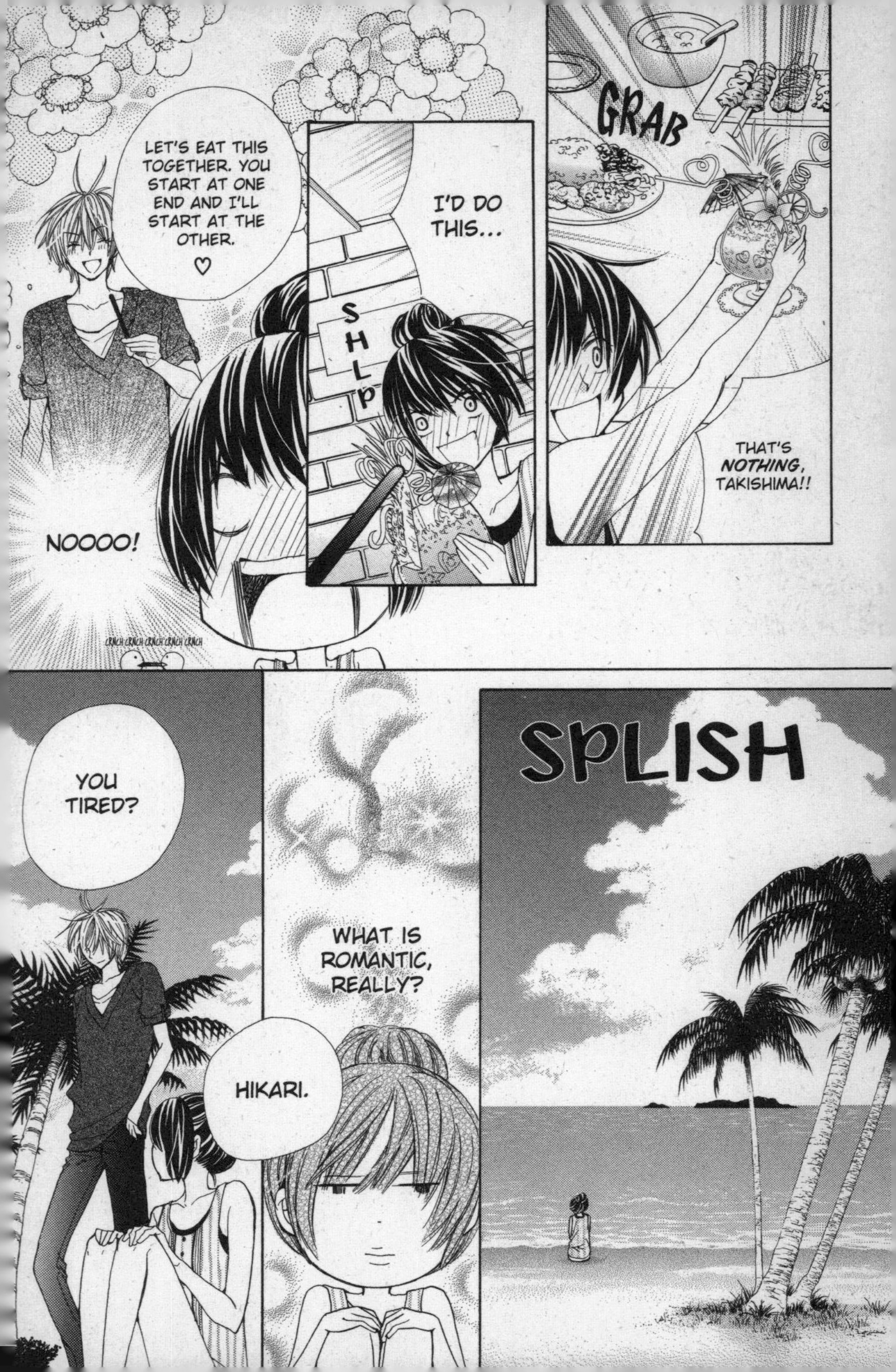
GRAB
THAT'S *NOTHING*, TAKISHIMA!!
I'D DO THIS...
SHLP
LET'S EAT THIS TOGETHER. YOU START AT ONE END AND I'LL START AT THE OTHER. ♡
NOOOO!
CRNCH CRNCH CRNCH CRNCH CRNCH
SPLISH
WHAT IS ROMANTIC, REALLY?
HIKARI.
YOU TIRED?

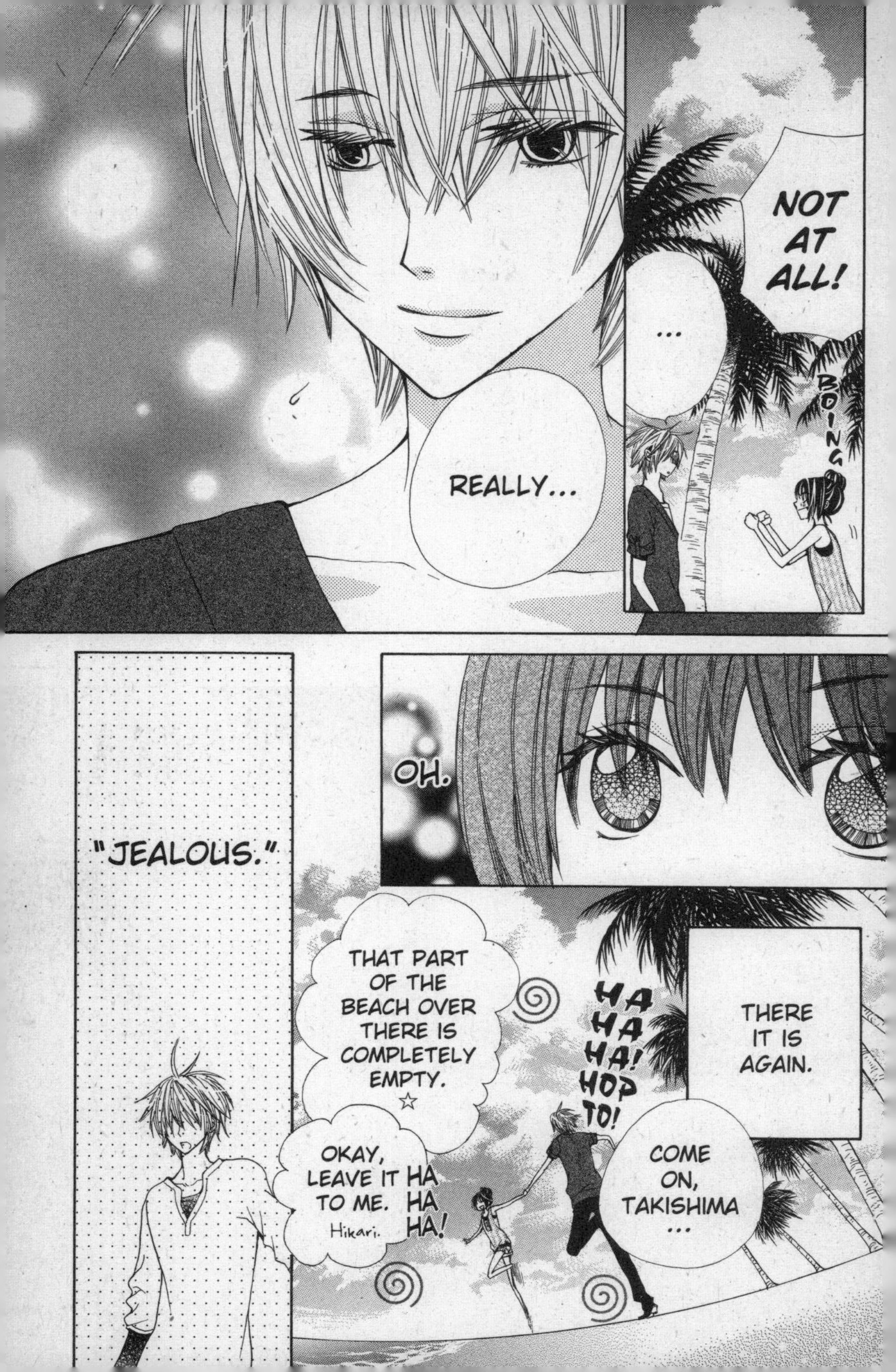
NOT AT ALL!
BOING
...
REALLY...
OH.
THERE IT IS AGAIN.
HA HA HA! HOP TO!
COME ON, TAKISHIMA...
THAT PART OF THE BEACH OVER THERE IS COMPLETELY EMPTY. ☆
OKAY, LEAVE IT TO ME.
HA HA HA!
Hikari.
"JEALOUS."

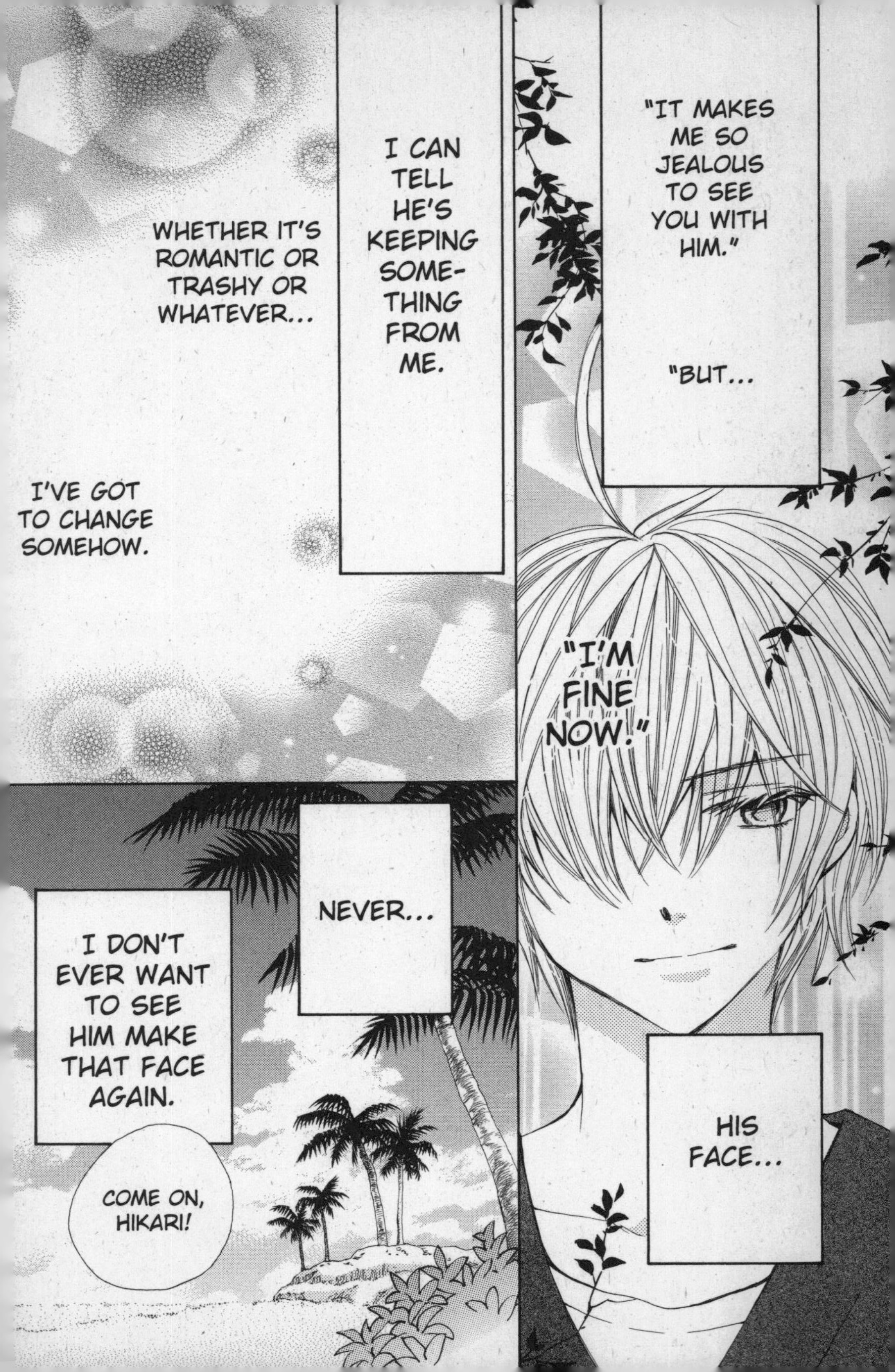
"IT MAKES ME SO JEALOUS TO SEE YOU WITH HIM."
"BUT...
"I'M FINE NOW."
HIS FACE...
I CAN TELL HE'S KEEPING SOME-THING FROM ME.
WHETHER IT'S ROMANTIC OR TRASHY OR WHATEVER...
I'VE GOT TO CHANGE SOMEHOW.
NEVER...
I DON'T EVER WANT TO SEE HIM MAKE THAT FACE AGAIN.
COME ON, HIKARI!

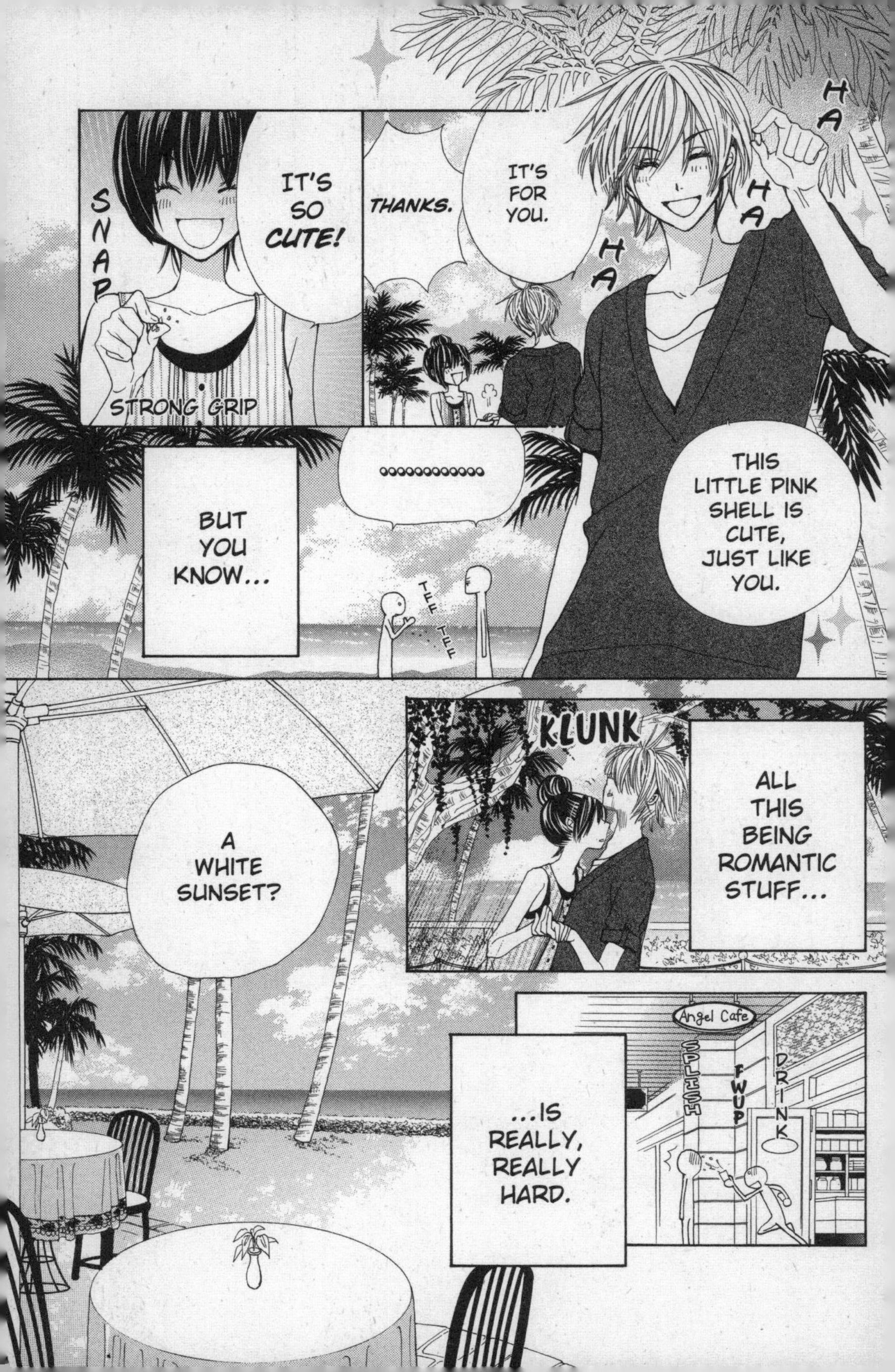
HA HA HA HA
IT'S FOR YOU.
THANKS.
IT'S SO CUTE!
SNAP
STRONG GRIP
THIS LITTLE PINK SHELL IS CUTE, JUST LIKE YOU.
....
TFF TFF
BUT YOU KNOW...
ALL THIS BEING ROMANTIC STUFF...
KLUNK
A WHITE SUNSET?
Angel Cafe
DRINK
FWUP
SPLISH
...IS REALLY, REALLY HARD.

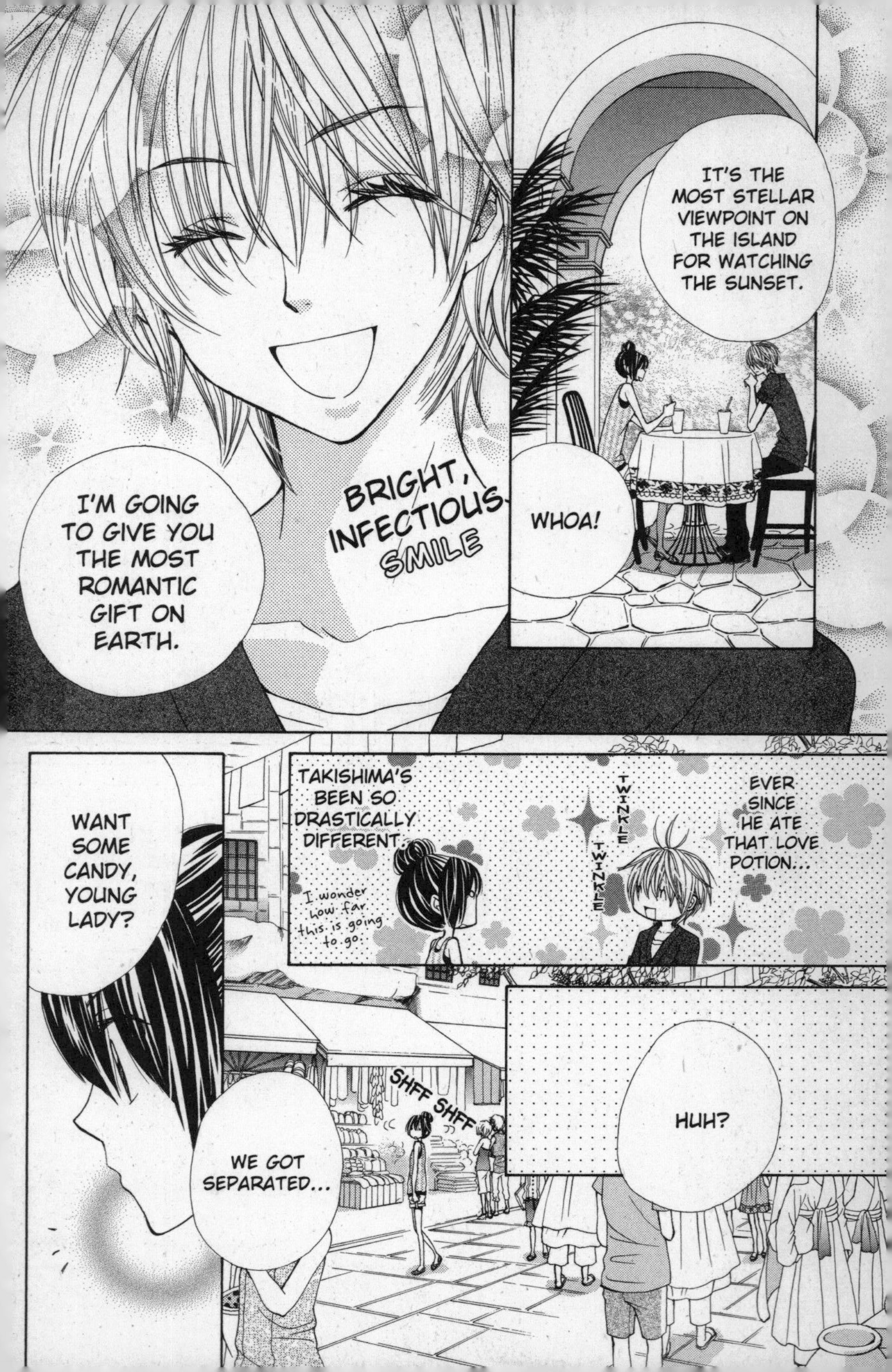
IT'S THE MOST STELLAR VIEWPOINT ON THE ISLAND FOR WATCHING THE SUNSET.
WHOA!
I'M GOING TO GIVE YOU THE MOST ROMANTIC GIFT ON EARTH.
BRIGHT, INFECTIOUS SMILE
TAKISHIMA'S BEEN SO DRASTICALLY DIFFERENT...
EVER SINCE HE ATE THAT LOVE POTION...
TWINKLE
TWINKLE
I wonder how far this is going to go.
HUH?
SHFF SHFF
WE GOT SEPARATED...
WANT SOME CANDY, YOUNG LADY?

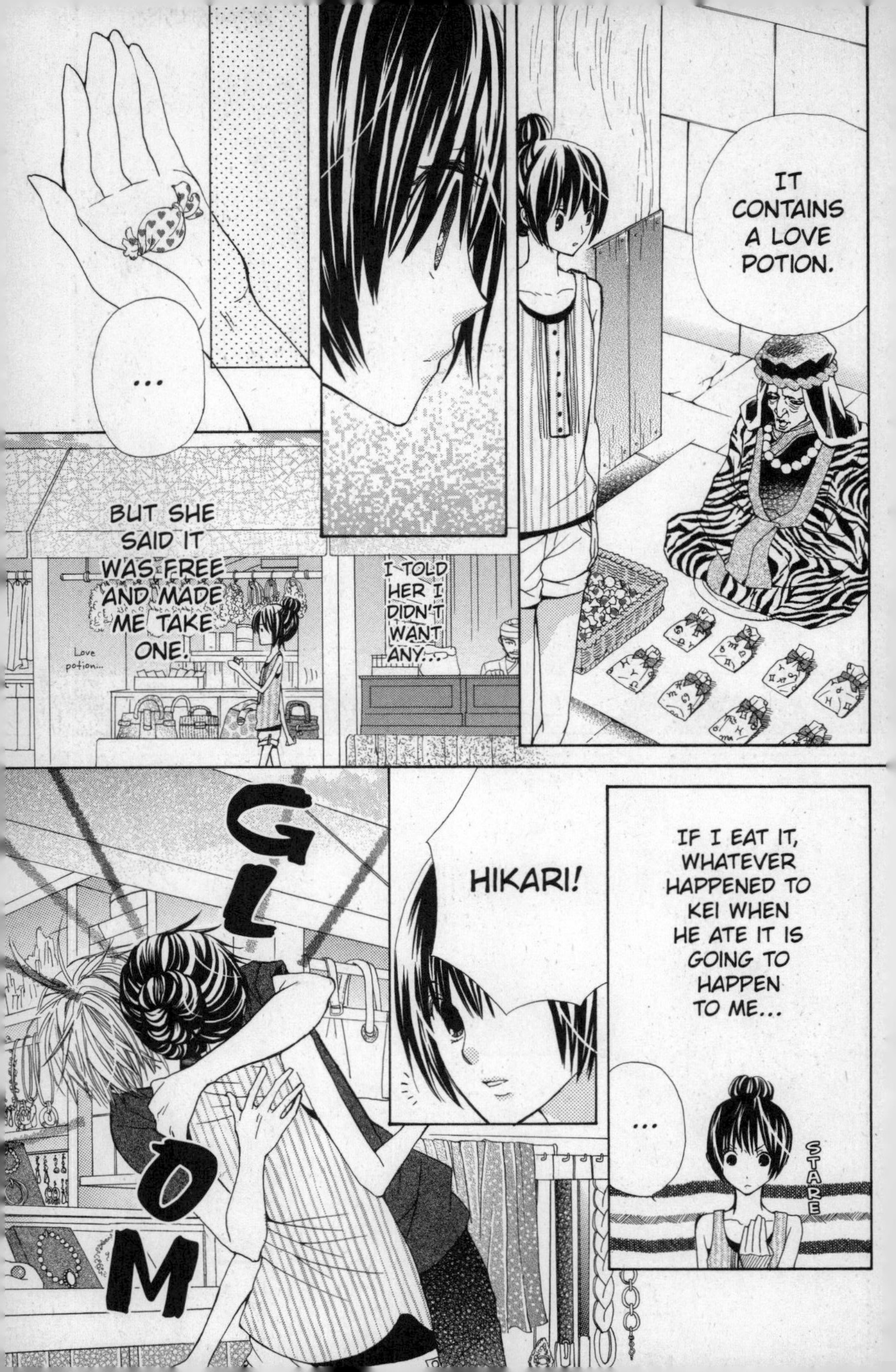
IT CONTAINS A LOVE POTION.
...
I TOLD HER I DIDN'T WANT ANY...
BUT SHE SAID IT WAS FREE AND MADE ME TAKE ONE.
Love potion...
IF I EAT IT, WHATEVER HAPPENED TO KEI WHEN HE ATE IT IS GOING TO HAPPEN TO ME...
STARE
...
HIKARI!
GLOM

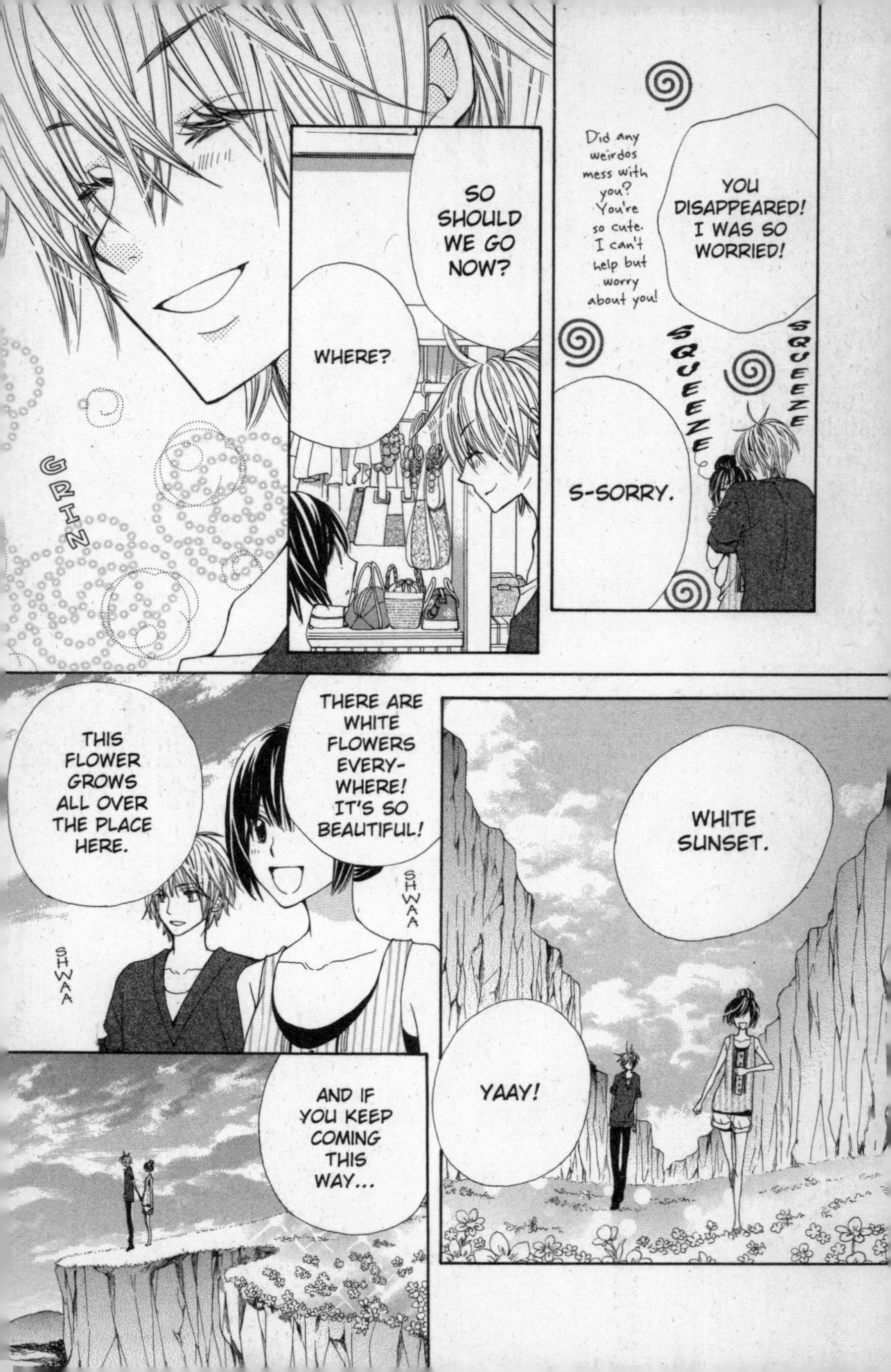
YOU DISAPPEARED! I WAS SO WORRIED!
Did any weirdos mess with you? You're so cute. I can't help but worry about you!
SQUEEZE
SQUEEZE
S-SORRY.
SO SHOULD WE GO NOW?
WHERE?
GRIN
WHITE SUNSET.
YAAY!
THERE ARE WHITE FLOWERS EVERY-WHERE! IT'S SO BEAUTIFUL!
SHWAA
THIS FLOWER GROWS ALL OVER THE PLACE HERE.
SHWAA
AND IF YOU KEEP COMING THIS WAY...

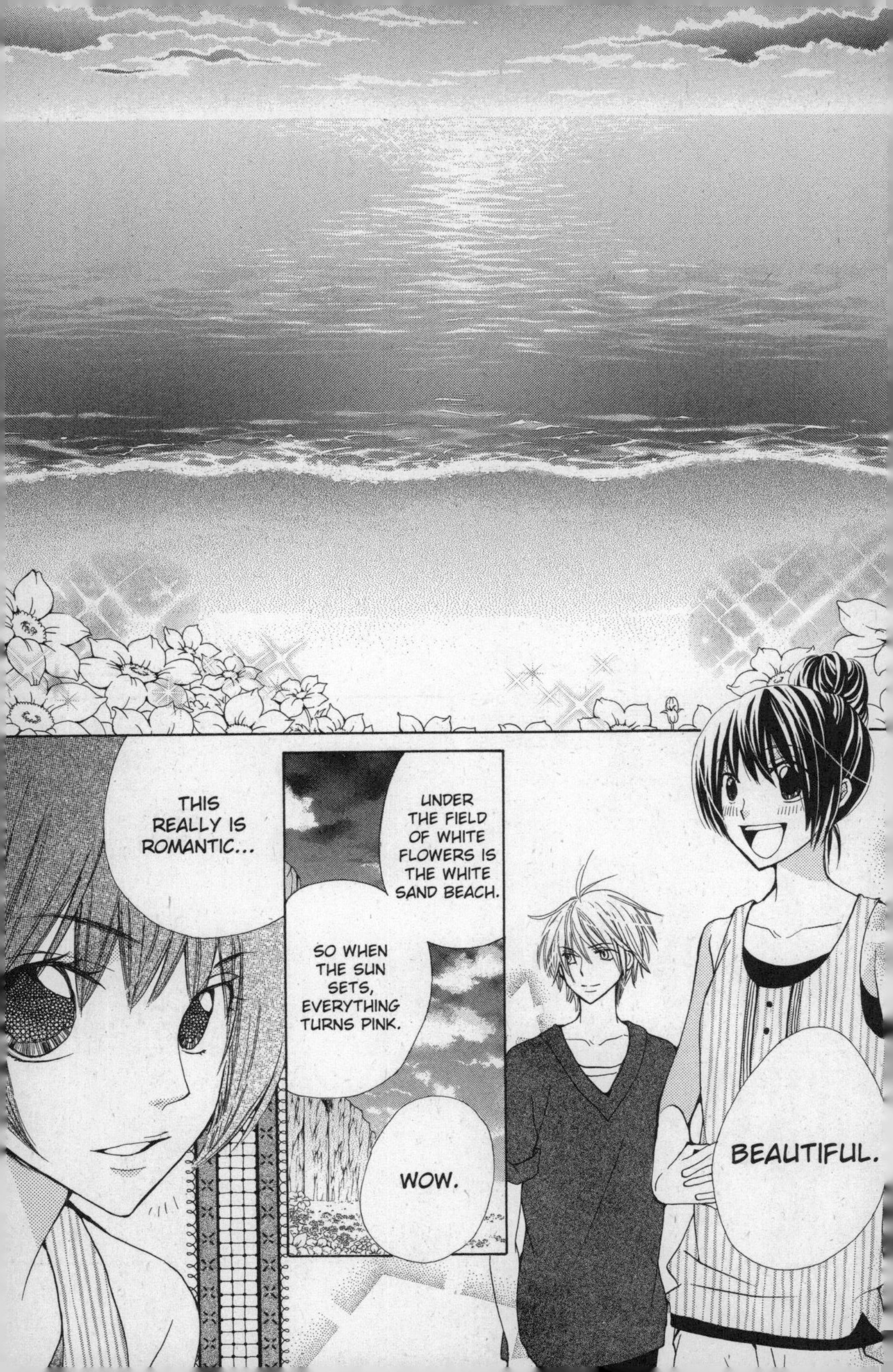
BEAUTIFUL.
WOW.
UNDER THE FIELD OF WHITE FLOWERS IS THE WHITE SAND BEACH.
SO WHEN THE SUN SETS, EVERYTHING TURNS PINK.
THIS REALLY IS ROMANTIC...

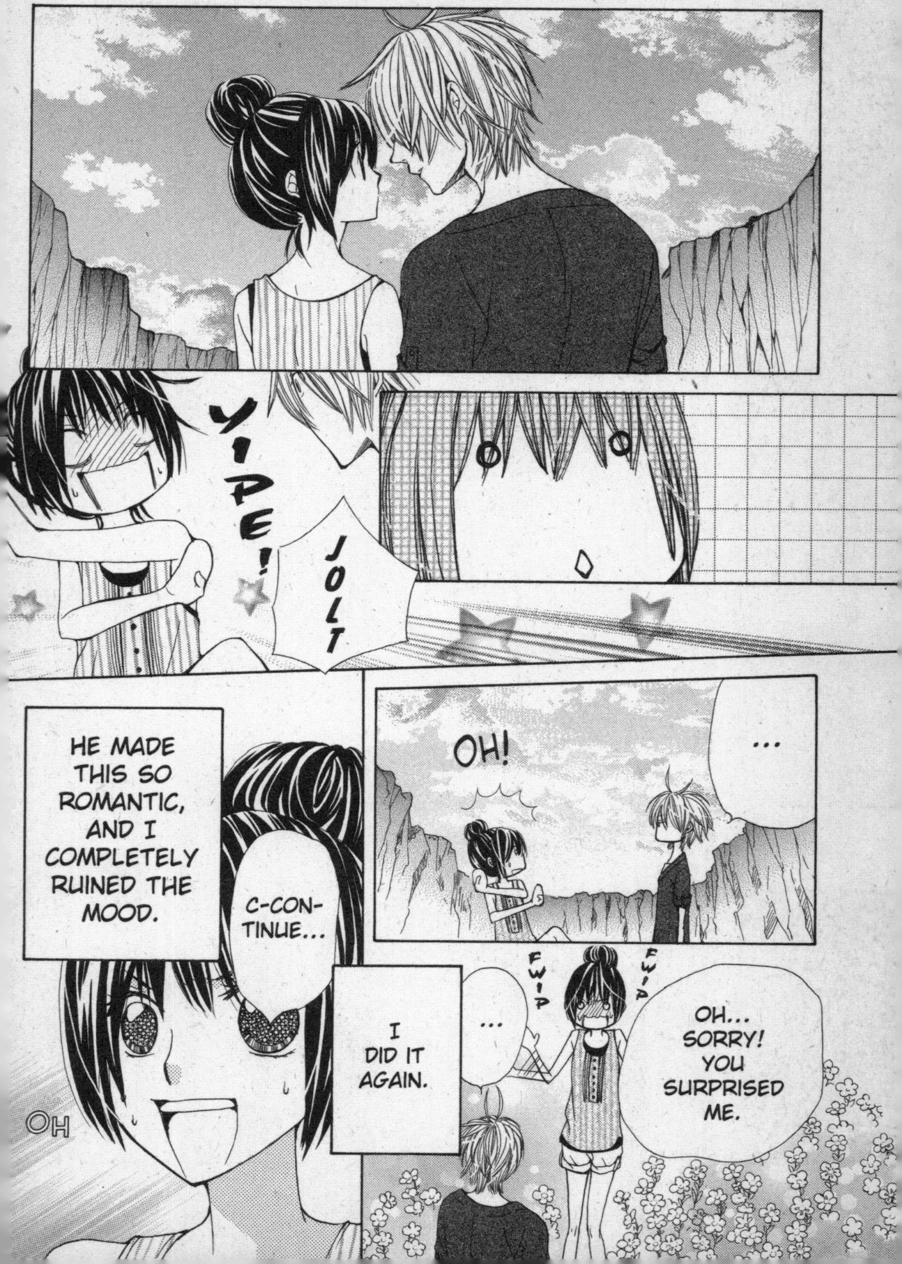
YIPE!
JOLT
...
OH!
FWIP FWIP
OH... SORRY! YOU SURPRISED ME.
...
I DID IT AGAIN.
HE MADE THIS SO ROMANTIC, AND I COMPLETELY RUINED THE MOOD.
C-CONTINUE...
OH

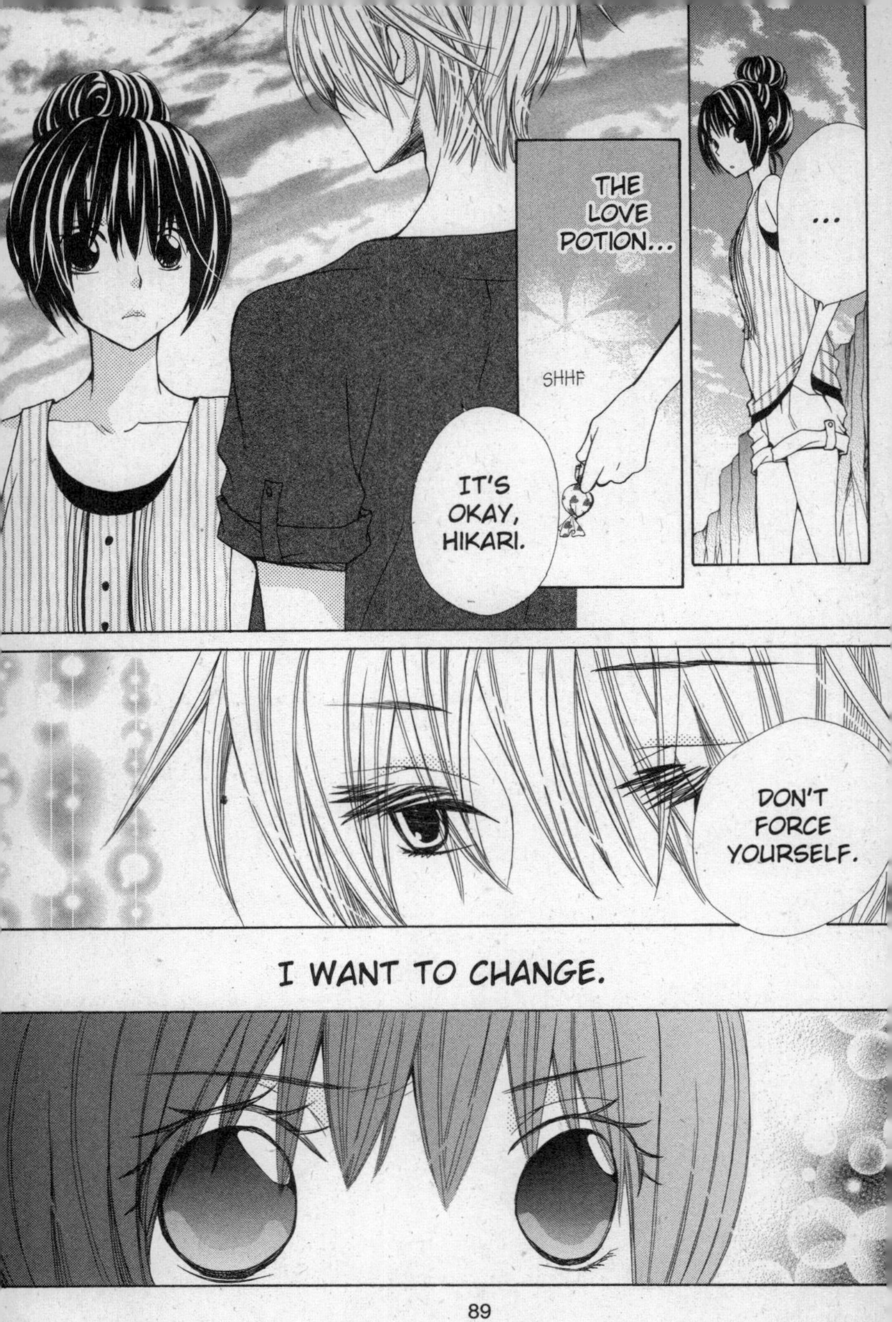
...
THE LOVE POTION...
SHHF
IT'S OKAY, HIKARI.
DON'T FORCE YOURSELF.
I WANT TO CHANGE.

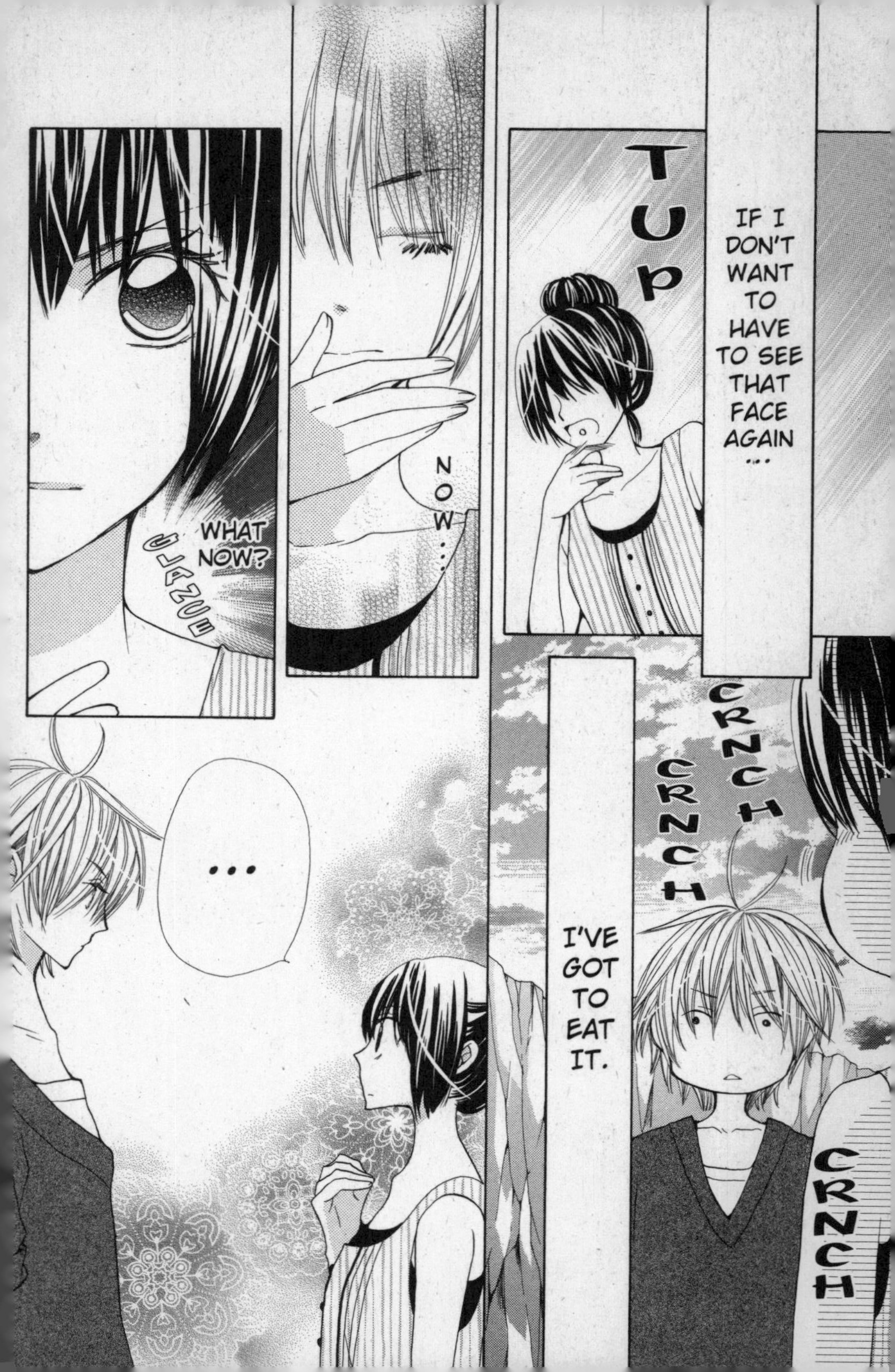
IF I DON'T WANT TO HAVE TO SEE THAT FACE AGAIN...
TUP
NOW...
WHAT NOW?
GLANCE
CRNCH
CRNCH
CRNCH
I'VE GOT TO EAT IT.
...

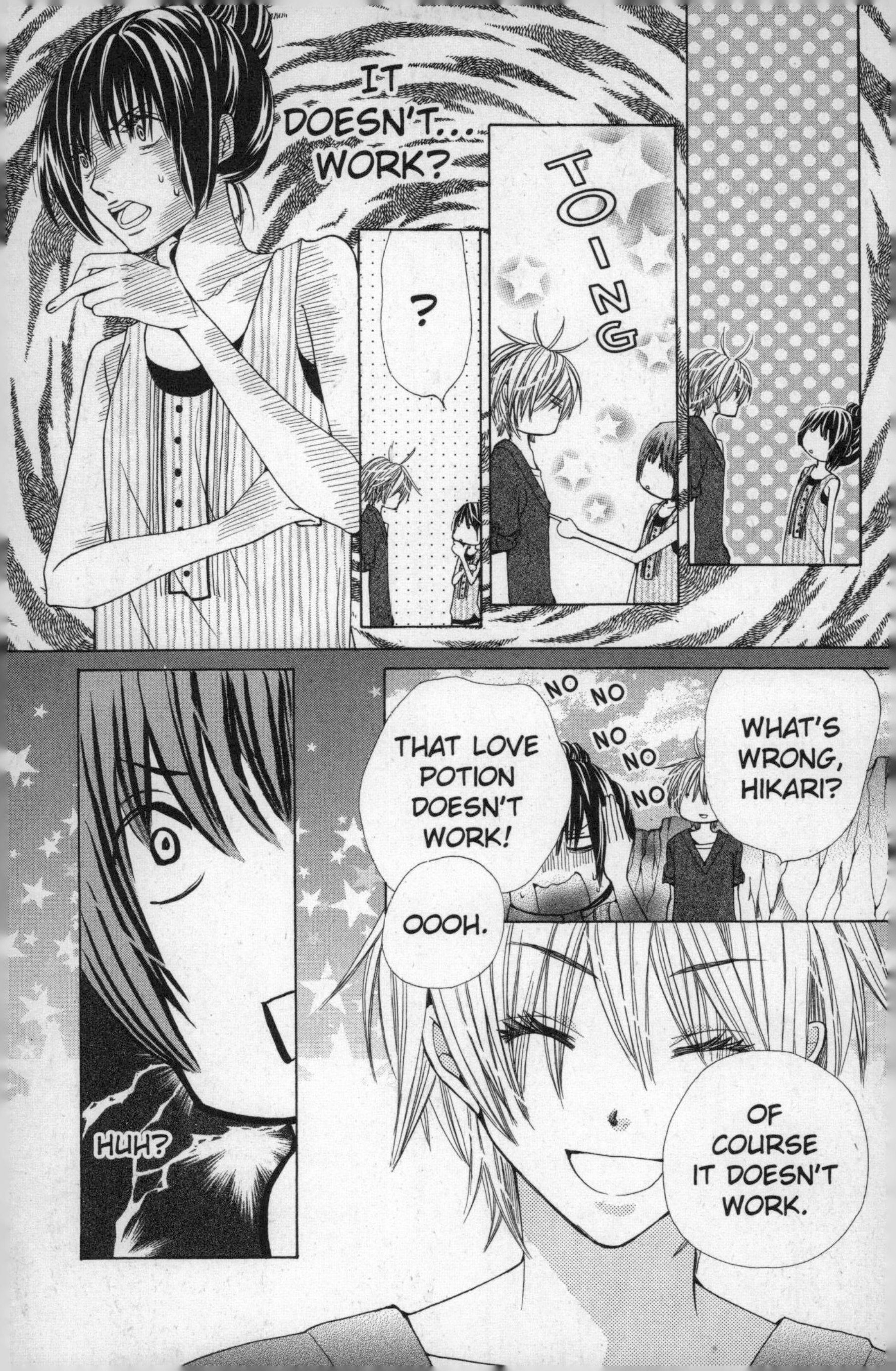
TOING
?
IT DOESN'T... WORK?
WHAT'S WRONG, HIKARI?
NO NO NO NO NO
THAT LOVE POTION DOESN'T WORK!
OOOH.
OF COURSE IT DOESN'T WORK.
HUH?

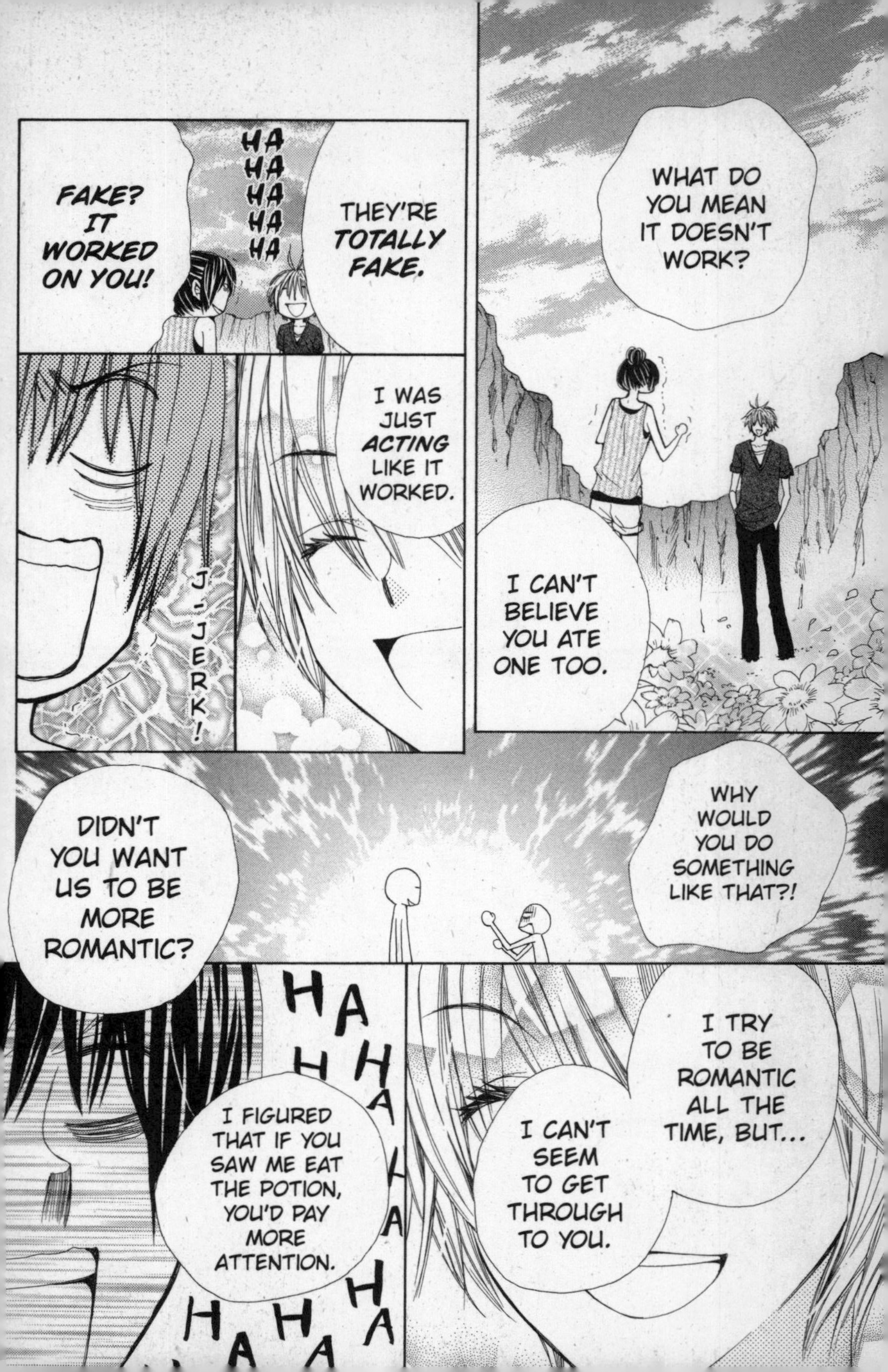
WHAT DO YOU MEAN IT DOESN'T WORK?
I CAN'T BELIEVE YOU ATE ONE TOO.
THEY'RE *TOTALLY* FAKE.
HA HA HA HA HA
FAKE? IT WORKED ON YOU!
I WAS JUST *ACTING* LIKE IT WORKED.
J-JERK!
WHY WOULD YOU DO SOMETHING LIKE THAT?!
DIDN'T YOU WANT US TO BE MORE ROMANTIC?
I TRY TO BE ROMANTIC ALL THE TIME, BUT...
I CAN'T SEEM TO GET THROUGH TO YOU.
I FIGURED THAT IF YOU SAW ME EAT THE POTION, YOU'D PAY MORE ATTENTION.
HA HA HA HA HA HA

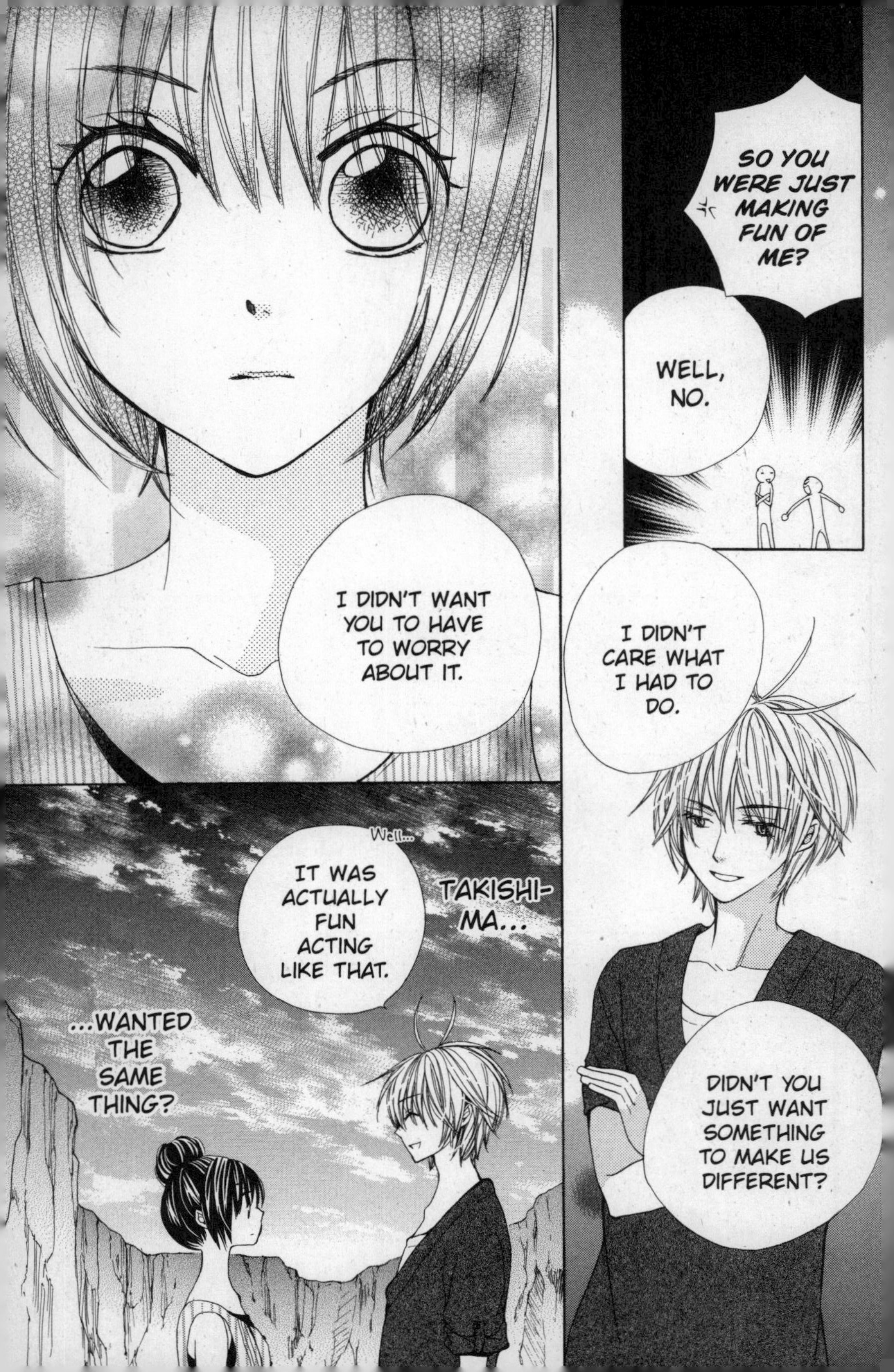
SO YOU WERE JUST MAKING FUN OF ME?
WELL, NO.
I DIDN'T CARE WHAT I HAD TO DO.
I DIDN'T WANT YOU TO HAVE TO WORRY ABOUT IT.
Well...
IT WAS ACTUALLY FUN ACTING LIKE THAT.
TAKISHIMA...
...WANTED THE SAME THING?
DIDN'T YOU JUST WANT SOMETHING TO MAKE US DIFFERENT?

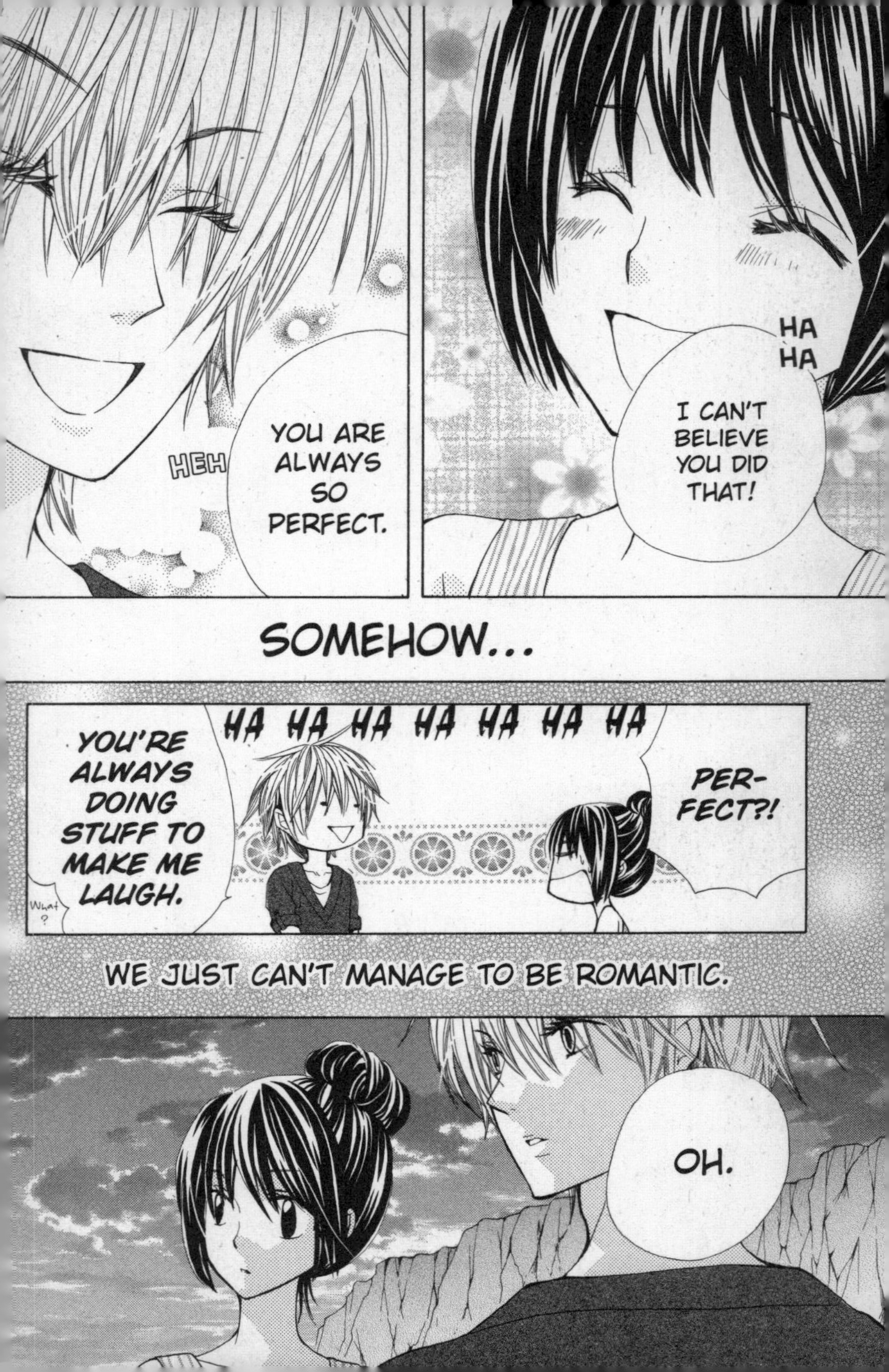
HA HA
I CAN'T BELIEVE YOU DID THAT!
HEH
YOU ARE ALWAYS SO PERFECT.
SOMEHOW...
PER-FECT?!
HA HA HA HA HA HA HA
YOU'RE ALWAYS DOING STUFF TO MAKE ME LAUGH.
What?
WE JUST CAN'T MANAGE TO BE ROMANTIC.
OH.

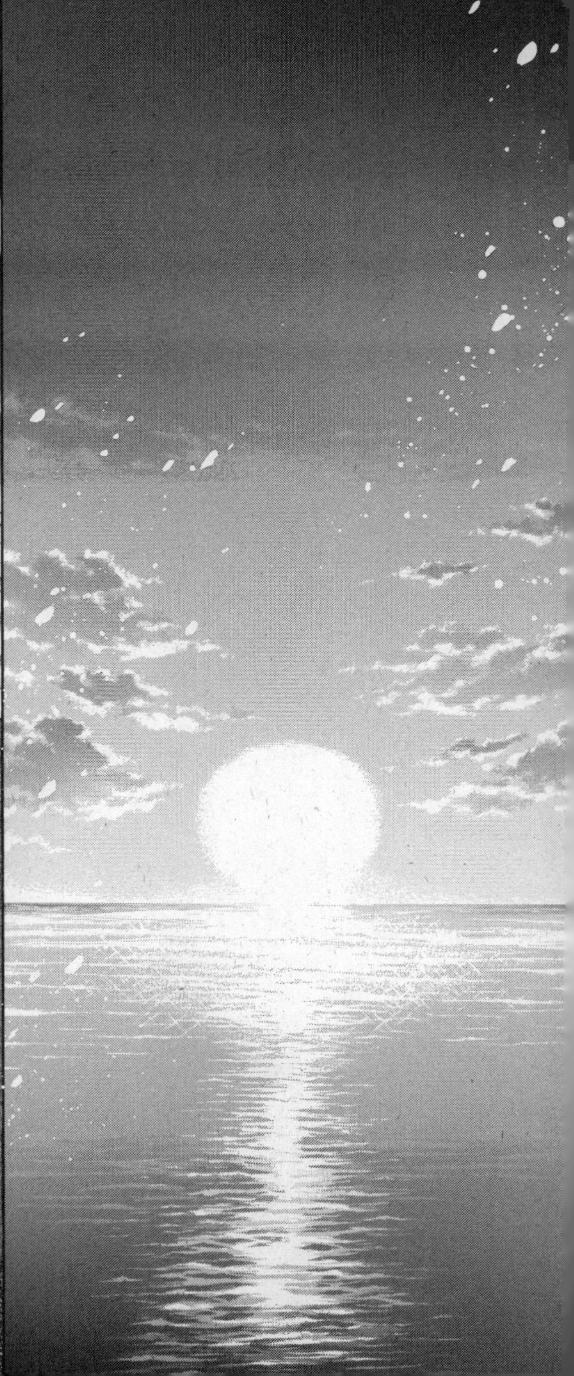

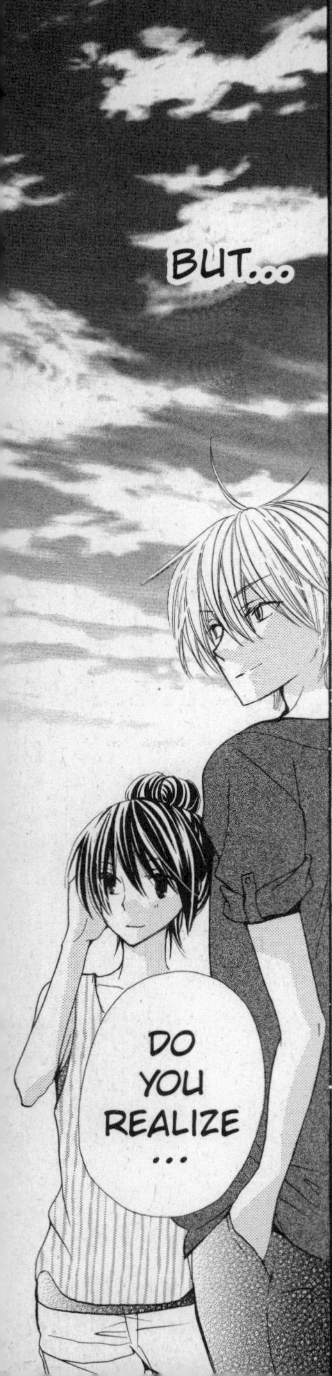
BUT...
DO YOU REALIZE ...

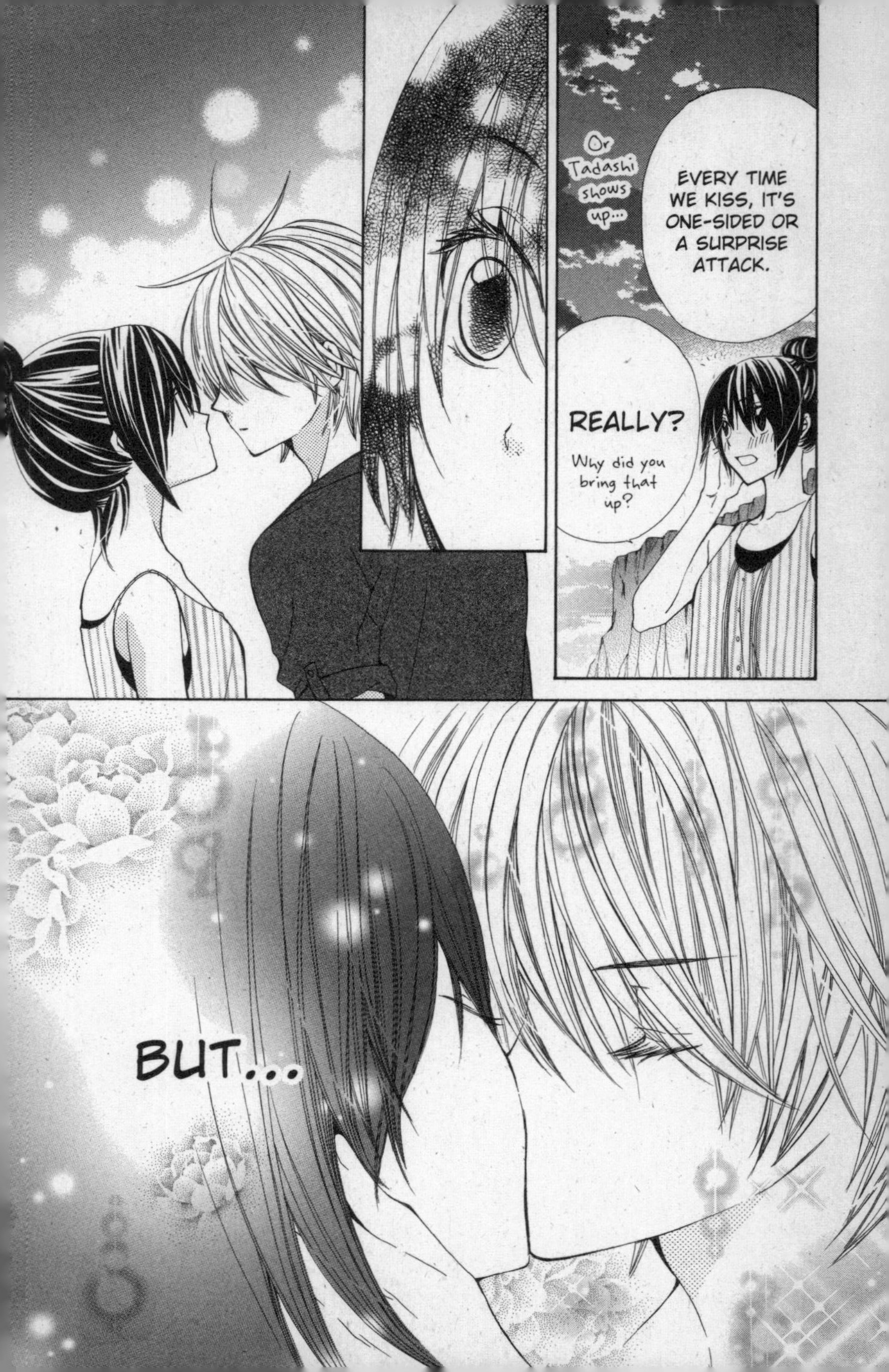
EVERY TIME WE KISS, IT'S ONE-SIDED OR A SURPRISE ATTACK.
Or Tadashi shows up...
REALLY?
Why did you bring that up?
BUT...

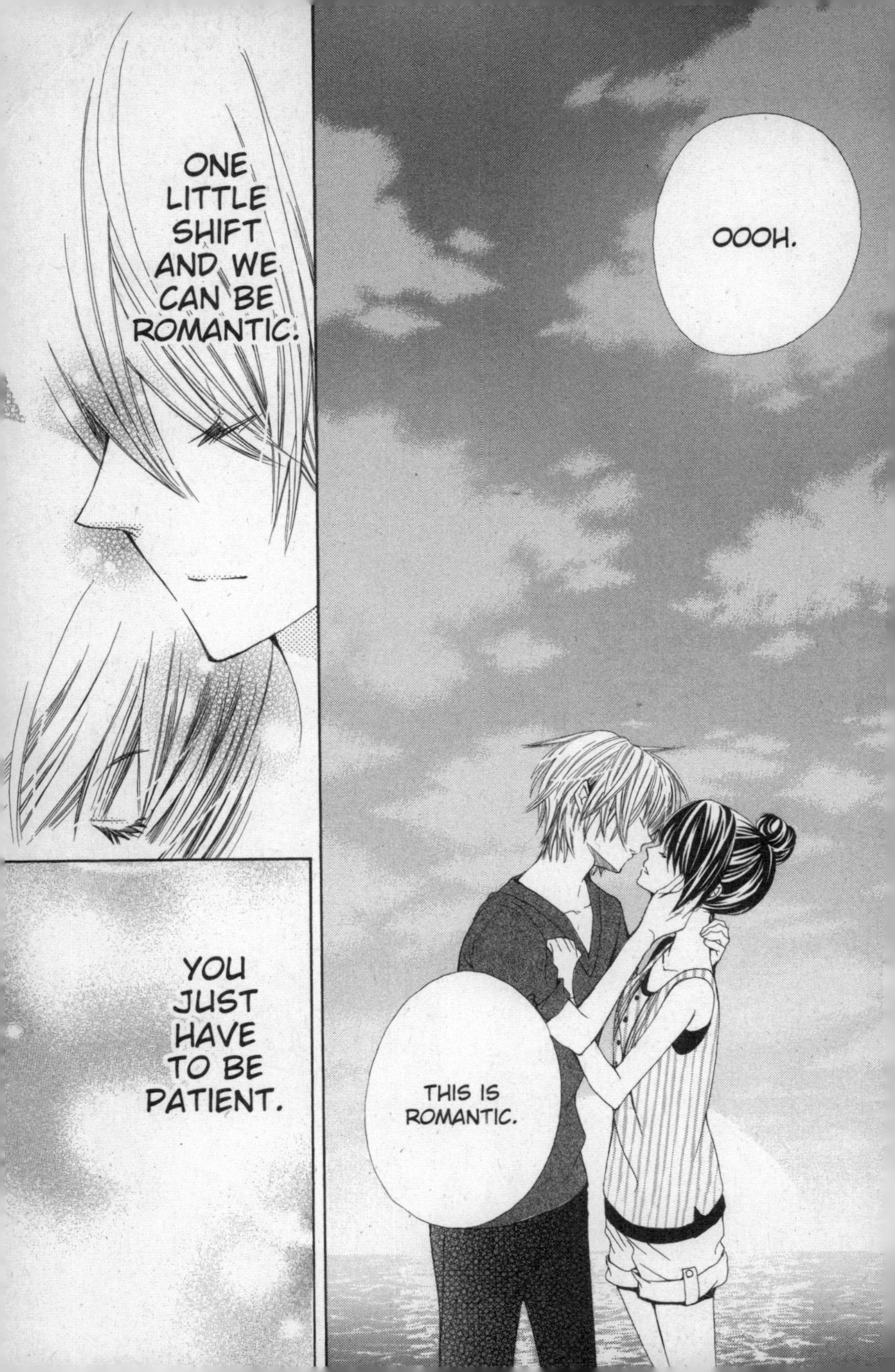
OOOH.
THIS IS ROMANTIC.
ONE LITTLE SHIFT AND WE CAN BE ROMANTIC.
YOU JUST HAVE TO BE PATIENT.

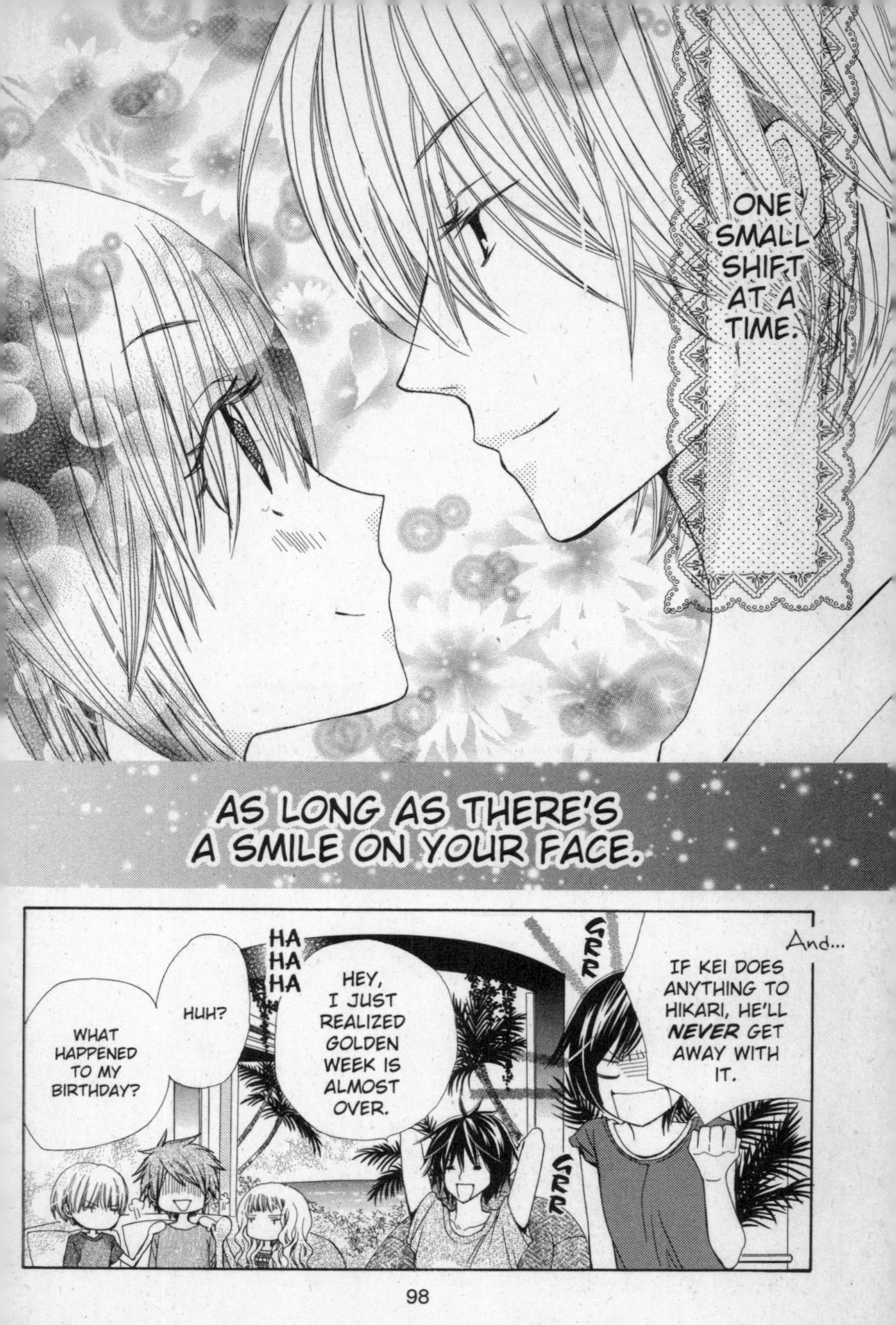
ONE SMALL SHIFT AT A TIME.
AS LONG AS THERE'S A SMILE ON YOUR FACE.
And...
IF KEI DOES ANYTHING TO HIKARI, HE'LL *NEVER* GET AWAY WITH IT.
GRR
GRR
HEY, I JUST REALIZED GOLDEN WEEK IS ALMOST OVER.
HA HA HA
HUH?
WHAT HAPPENED TO MY BIRTHDAY?

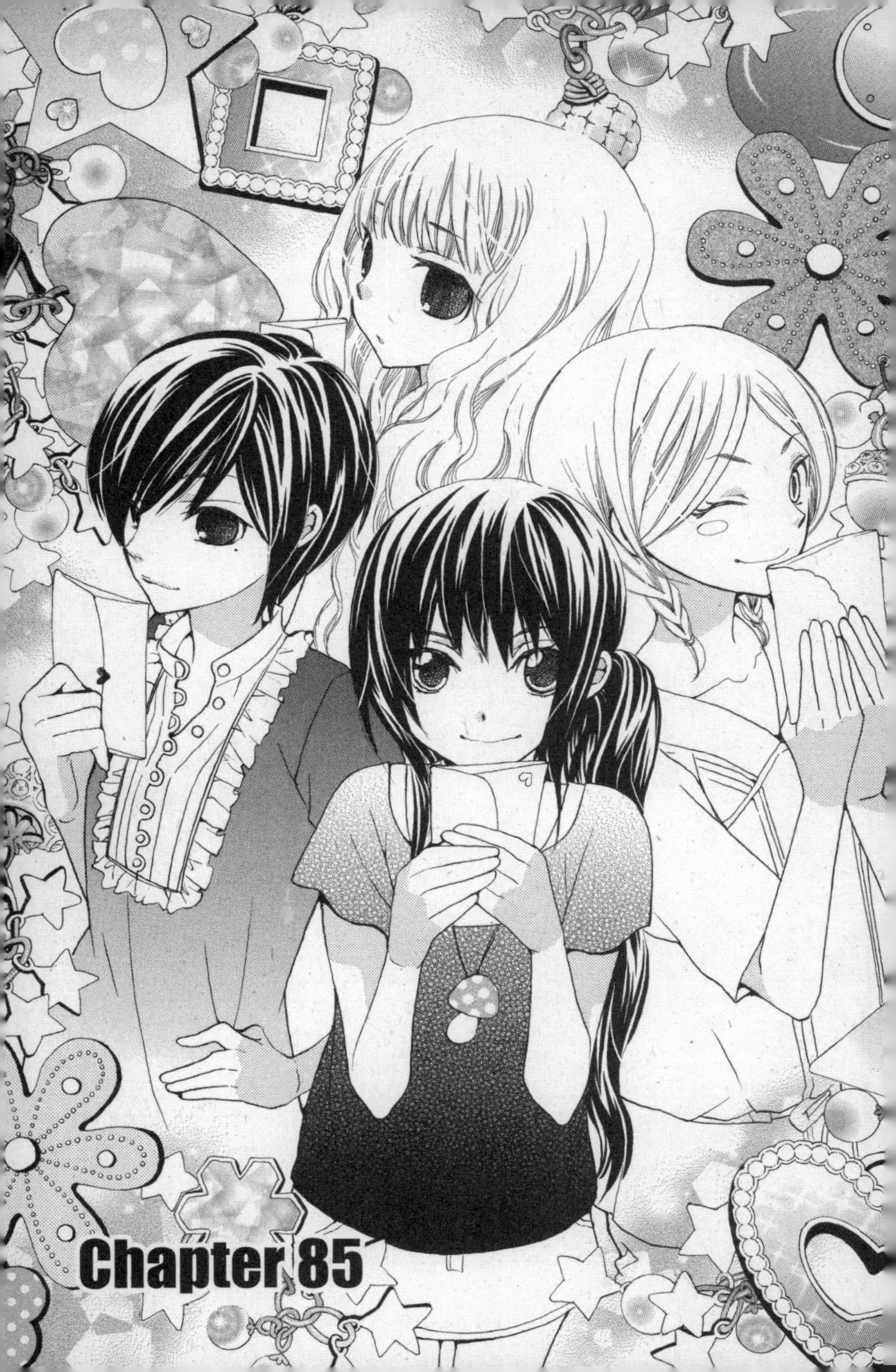
Chapter 85

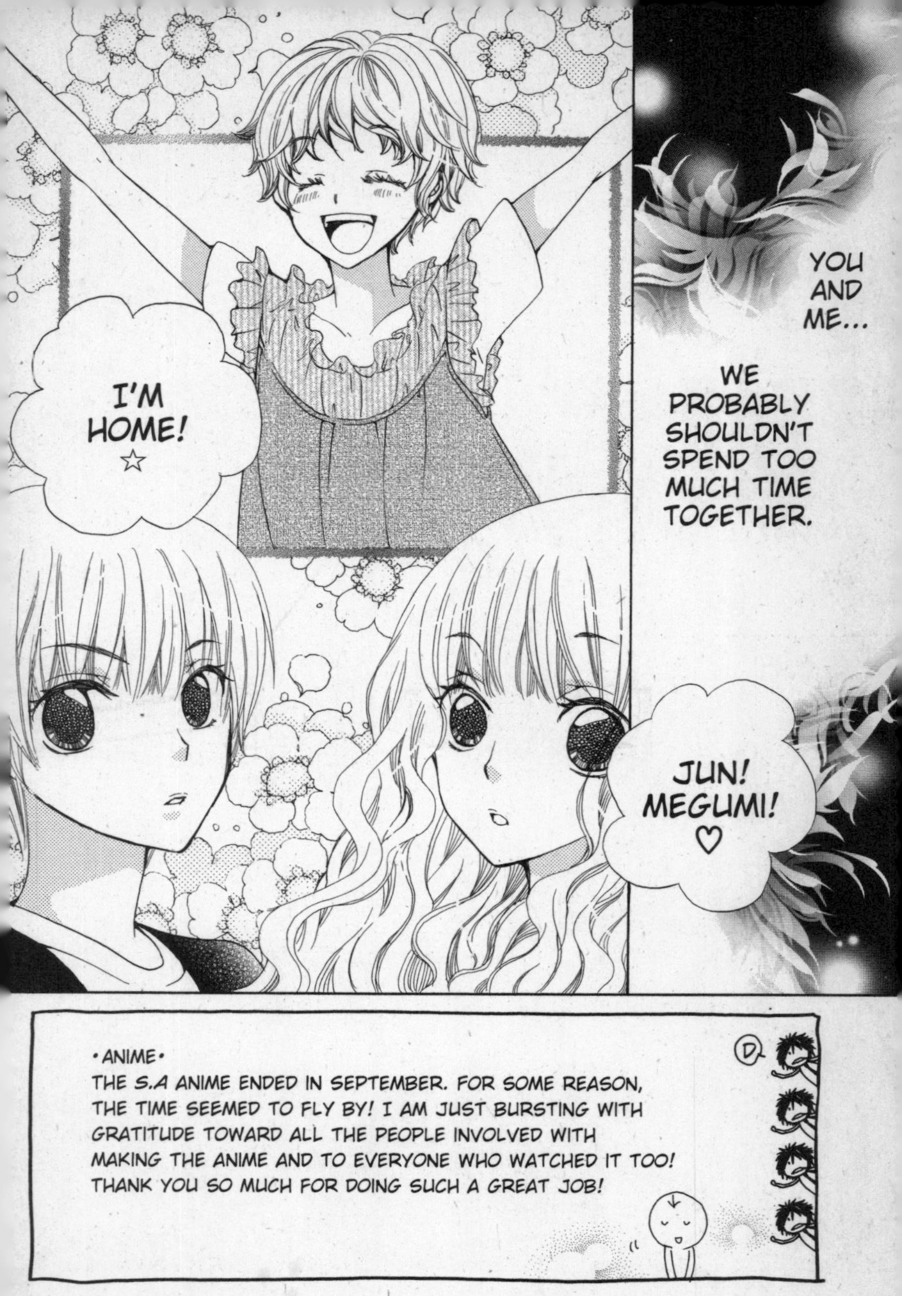
YOU AND ME...
WE PROBABLY SHOULDN'T SPEND TOO MUCH TIME TOGETHER.
JUN! MEGUMI! ♡
I'M HOME! ☆

•ANIME•

THE S.A ANIME ENDED IN SEPTEMBER. FOR SOME REASON, THE TIME SEEMED TO FLY BY! I AM JUST BURSTING WITH GRATITUDE TOWARD ALL THE PEOPLE INVOLVED WITH MAKING THE ANIME AND TO EVERYONE WHO WATCHED IT TOO! THANK YOU SO MUCH FOR DOING SUCH A GREAT JOB!

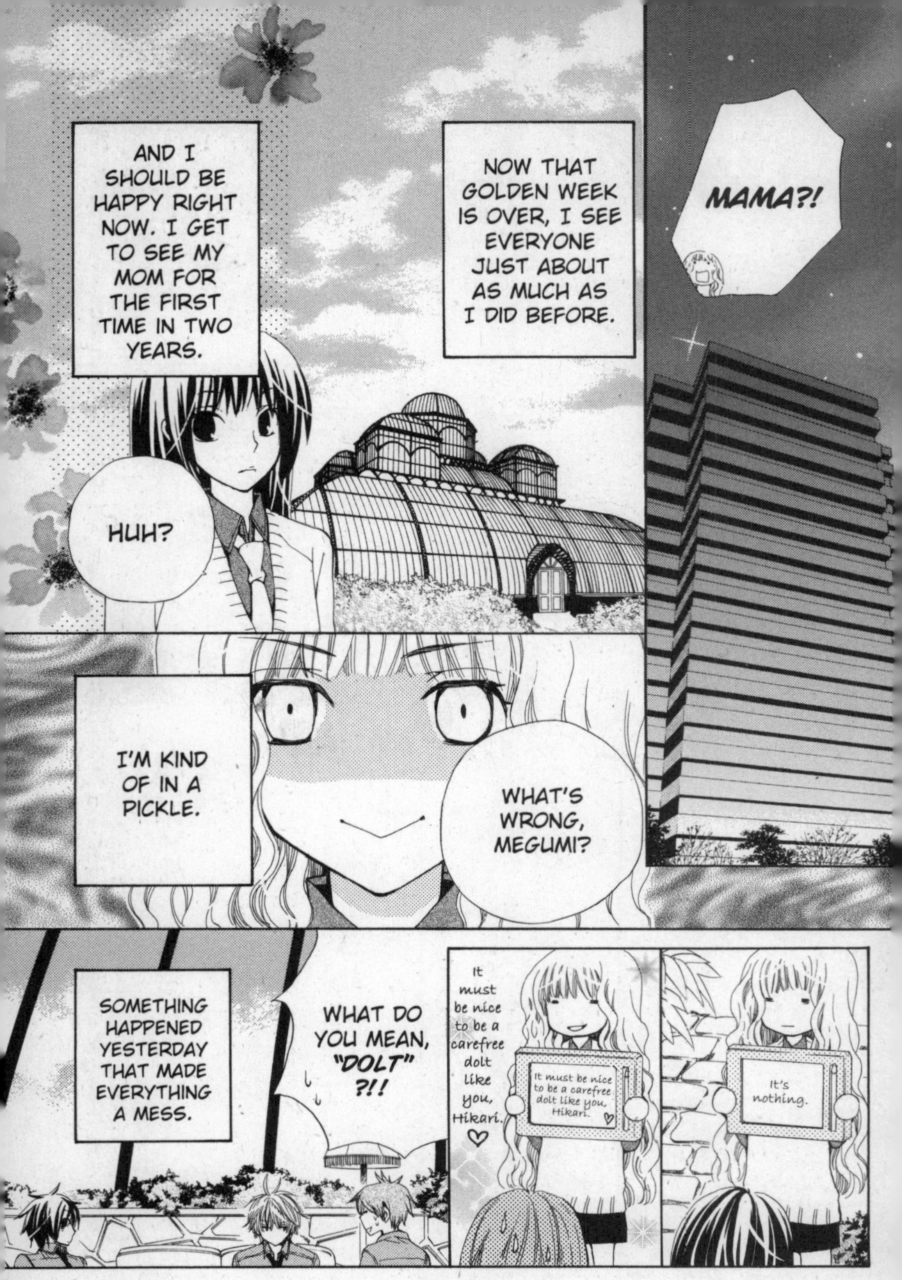
MAMA?!
NOW THAT GOLDEN WEEK IS OVER, I SEE EVERYONE JUST ABOUT AS MUCH AS I DID BEFORE.
AND I SHOULD BE HAPPY RIGHT NOW. I GET TO SEE MY MOM FOR THE FIRST TIME IN TWO YEARS.
HUH?
WHAT'S WRONG, MEGUMI?
I'M KIND OF IN A PICKLE.
It's nothing.
It must be nice to be a carefree dolt like you, Hikari. ♡
It must be nice to be a carefree dolt like you, Hikari. ♡
WHAT DO YOU MEAN, "DOLT"?!!
SOMETHING HAPPENED YESTERDAY THAT MADE EVERYTHING A MESS.

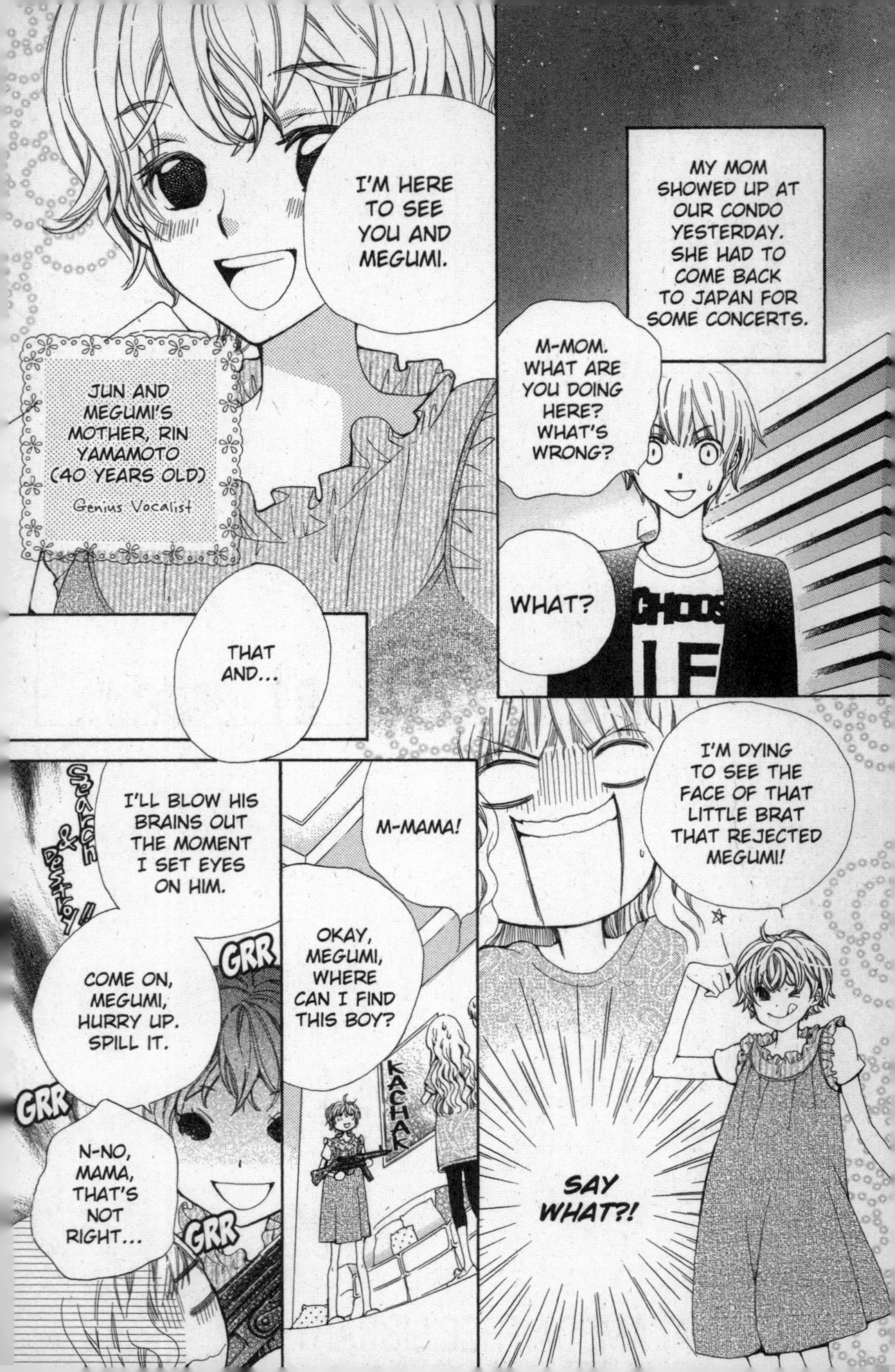
MY MOM SHOWED UP AT OUR CONDO YESTERDAY. SHE HAD TO COME BACK TO JAPAN FOR SOME CONCERTS.
M-MOM. WHAT ARE YOU DOING HERE? WHAT'S WRONG?
WHAT?
I'M HERE TO SEE YOU AND MEGUMI.
JUN AND MEGUMI'S MOTHER, RIN YAMAMOTO (40 YEARS OLD)
Genius Vocalist
THAT AND...
I'M DYING TO SEE THE FACE OF THAT LITTLE BRAT THAT REJECTED MEGUMI!
SAY WHAT?!
M-MAMA!
OKAY, MEGUMI, WHERE CAN I FIND THIS BOY?
KACHAK
I'LL BLOW HIS BRAINS OUT THE MOMENT I SET EYES ON HIM.
Search & Destroy!!
GRR
COME ON, MEGUMI, HURRY UP. SPILL IT.
GRR
N-NO, MAMA, THAT'S NOT RIGHT...
GRR

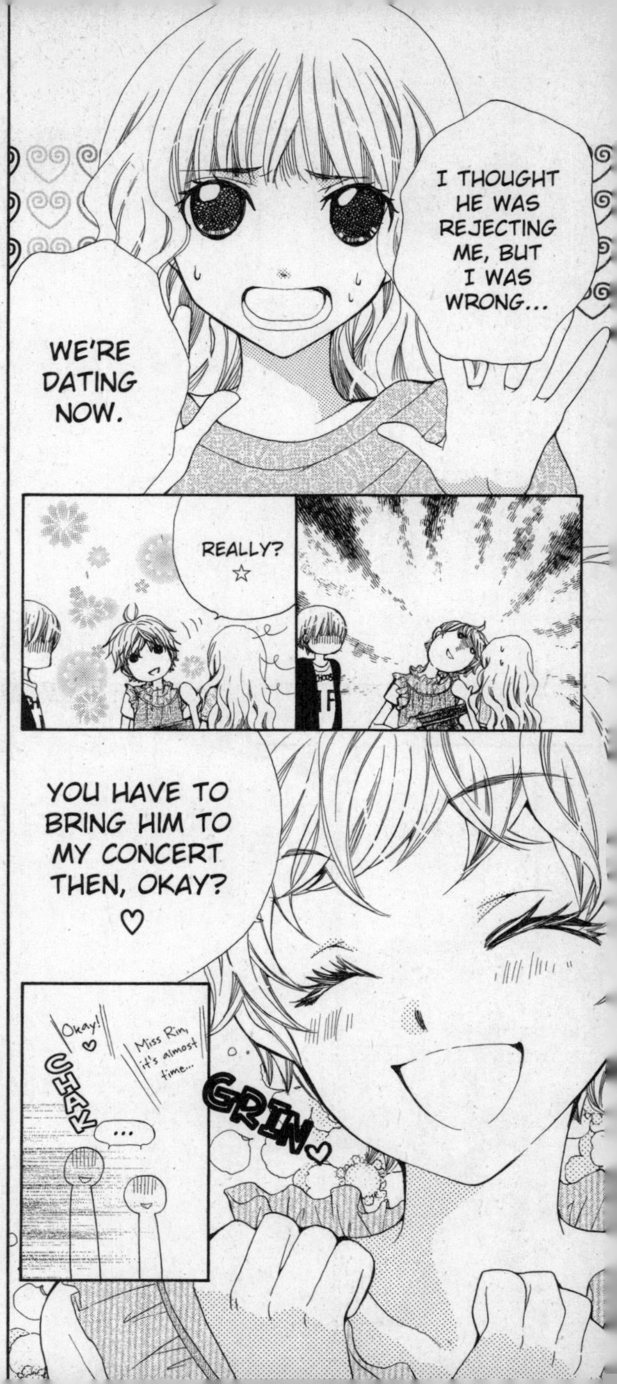
I THOUGHT HE WAS REJECTING ME, BUT I WAS WRONG...
WE'RE DATING NOW.
REALLY? ☆
YOU HAVE TO BRING HIM TO MY CONCERT THEN, OKAY? ♡
GRIN♡
Miss Rin, it's almost time...
Okay! ♡
CHAY
...
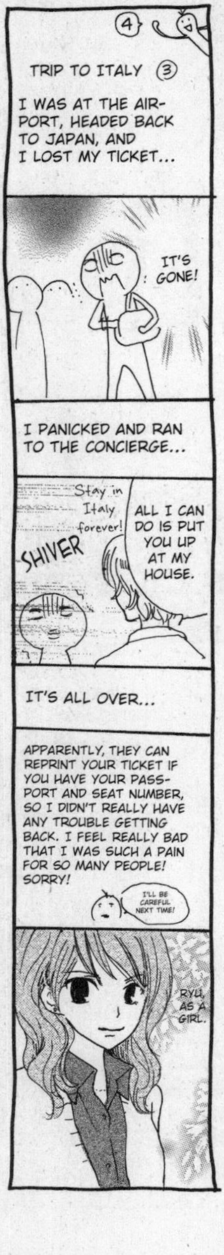
④
TRIP TO ITALY ③
I WAS AT THE AIRPORT, HEADED BACK TO JAPAN, AND I LOST MY TICKET...
IT'S GONE!
I PANICKED AND RAN TO THE CONCIERGE...
ALL I CAN DO IS PUT YOU UP AT MY HOUSE.
Stay in Italy forever!
SHIVER
IT'S ALL OVER...
APPARENTLY, THEY CAN REPRINT YOUR TICKET IF YOU HAVE YOUR PASSPORT AND SEAT NUMBER, SO I DIDN'T REALLY HAVE ANY TROUBLE GETTING BACK. I FEEL REALLY BAD THAT I WAS SUCH A PAIN FOR SO MANY PEOPLE! SORRY!
I'LL BE CAREFUL NEXT TIME!
RYU, AS A GIRL.

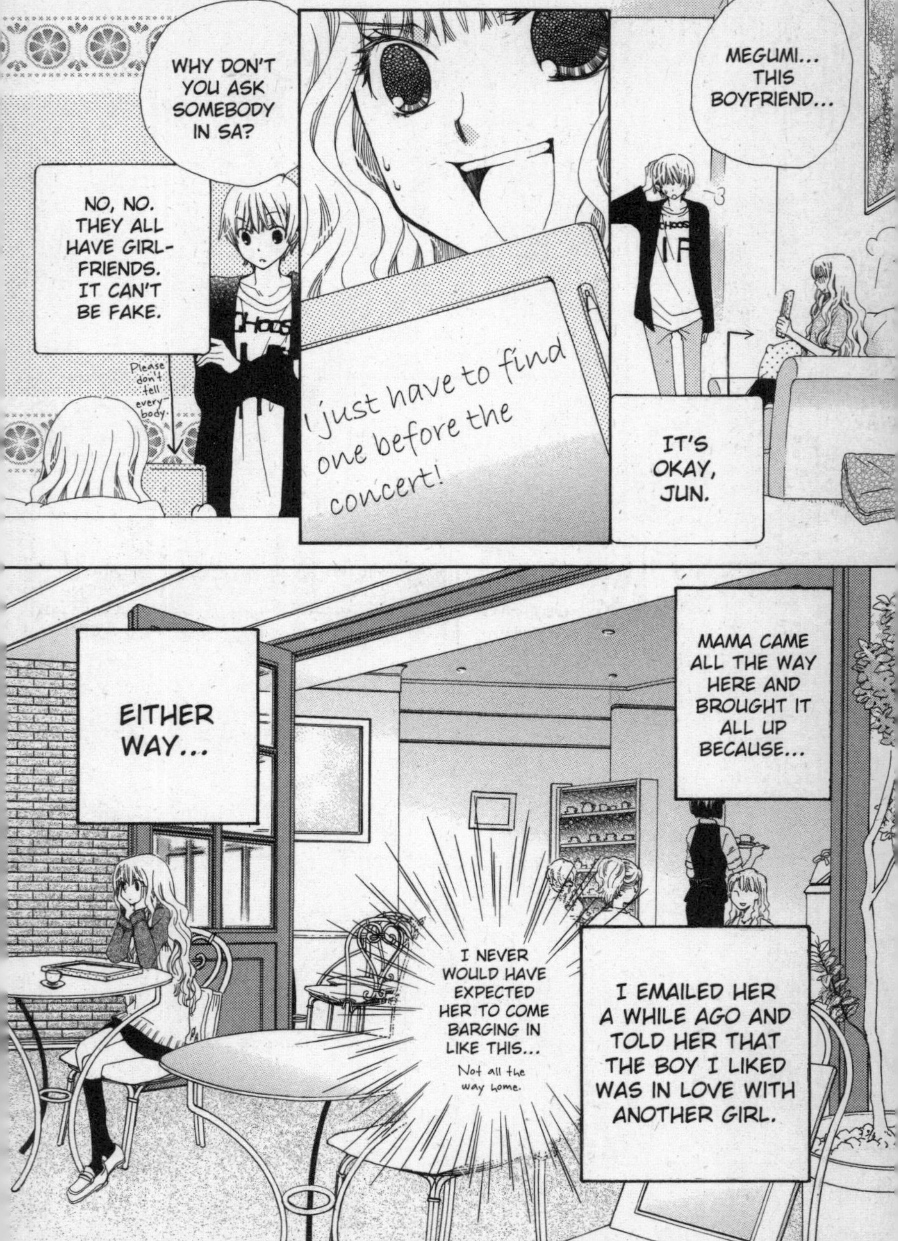
MEGUMI... THIS BOYFRIEND...
IT'S OKAY, JUN.
I just have to find one before the concert!
WHY DON'T YOU ASK SOMEBODY IN SA?
NO, NO. THEY ALL HAVE GIRL-FRIENDS. IT CAN'T BE FAKE.
Please don't tell every-body.
MAMA CAME ALL THE WAY HERE AND BROUGHT IT ALL UP BECAUSE...
I EMAILED HER A WHILE AGO AND TOLD HER THAT THE BOY I LIKED WAS IN LOVE WITH ANOTHER GIRL.
EITHER WAY...
I NEVER WOULD HAVE EXPECTED HER TO COME BARGING IN LIKE THIS...
Not all the way home.

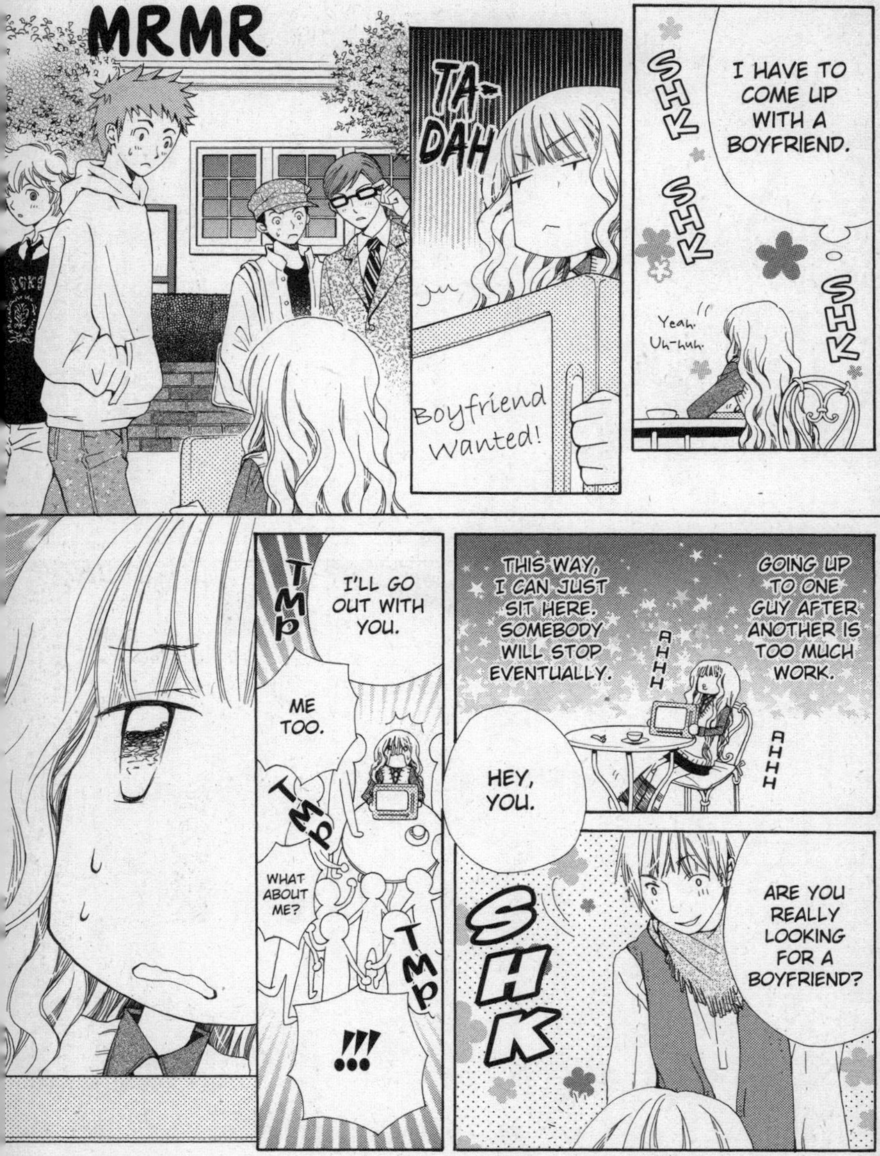
I HAVE TO COME UP WITH A BOYFRIEND.
SHK SHK SHK
Yeah. Uh-huh.
TA-DAH
Boyfriend Wanted!
MRMR
GOING UP TO ONE GUY AFTER ANOTHER IS TOO MUCH WORK.
THIS WAY, I CAN JUST SIT HERE. SOMEBODY WILL STOP EVENTUALLY.
AHHH
AHHH
HEY, YOU.
ARE YOU REALLY LOOKING FOR A BOYFRIEND?
SHK
TMP
I'LL GO OUT WITH YOU.
ME TOO.
TMP
WHAT ABOUT ME?
TMP
!!!

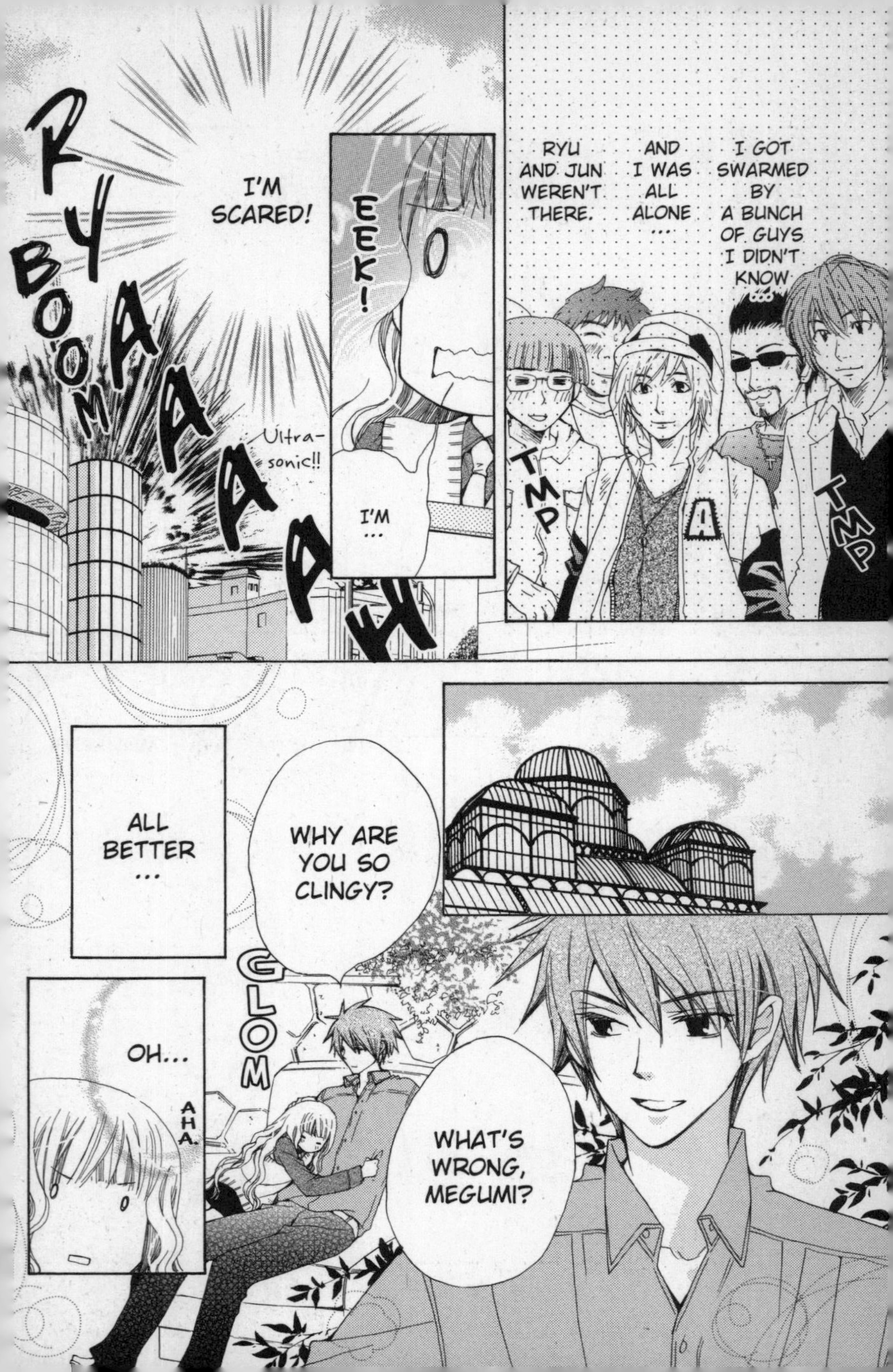
I GOT SWARMED BY A BUNCH OF GUYS I DIDN'T KNOW
AND I WAS ALL ALONE...
RYU AND JUN WEREN'T THERE.
TMP
A
TMP
EEK!
I'M...
I'M SCARED!
RYAAAAH
BOOM
Ultra-sonic!!
WHAT'S WRONG, MEGUMI?
WHY ARE YOU SO CLINGY?
GLOM
ALL BETTER...
OH...
AHA.

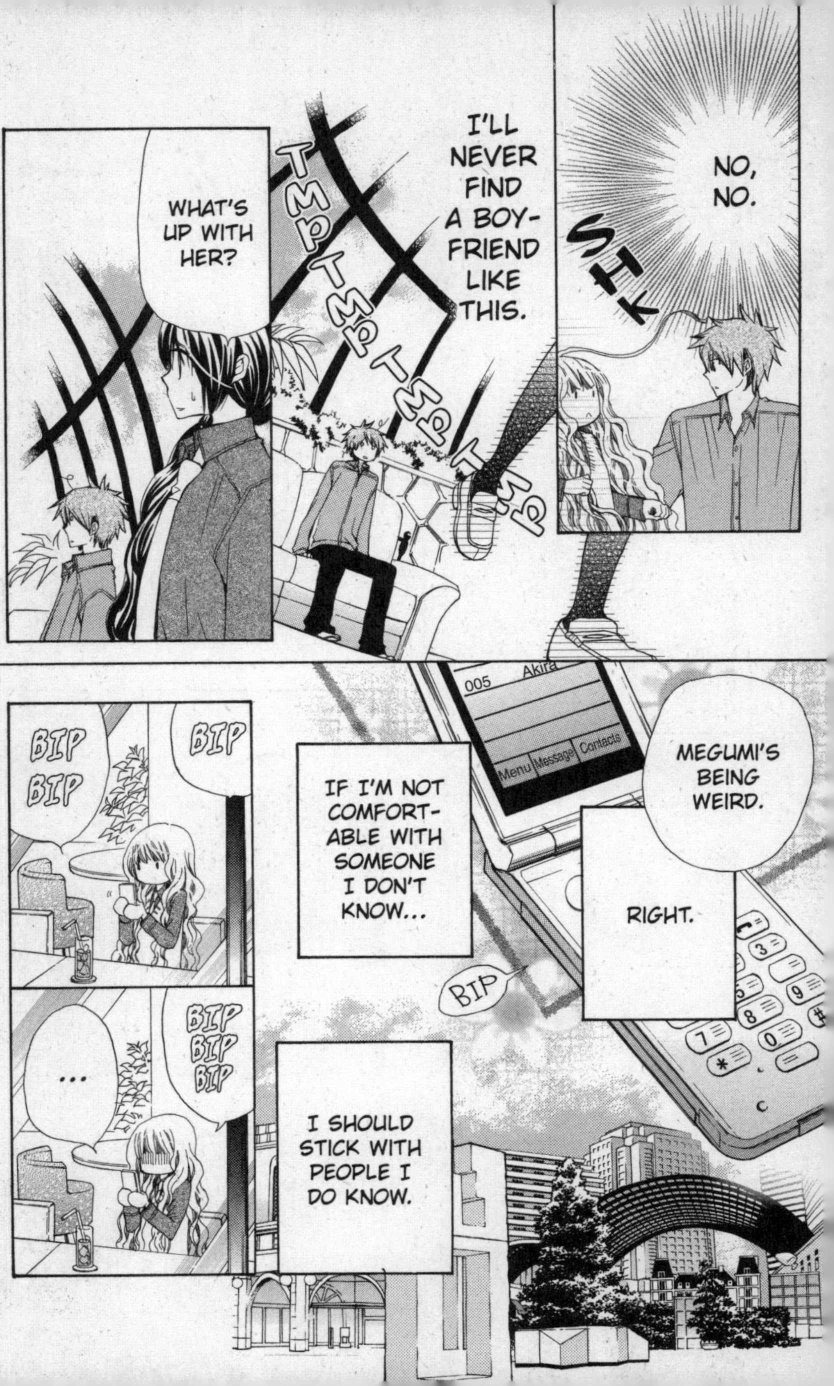
NO, NO.
SHK
I'LL NEVER FIND A BOY-FRIEND LIKE THIS.
TMP TMP TMP TMP TMP
WHAT'S UP WITH HER?
MEGUMI'S BEING WEIRD.
RIGHT.
Akira
005
Menu
Message
Contacts
BIP
IF I'M NOT COMFORT-ABLE WITH SOMEONE I DON'T KNOW...
I SHOULD STICK WITH PEOPLE I DO KNOW.
BIP
BIP BIP
BIP BIP BIP
...

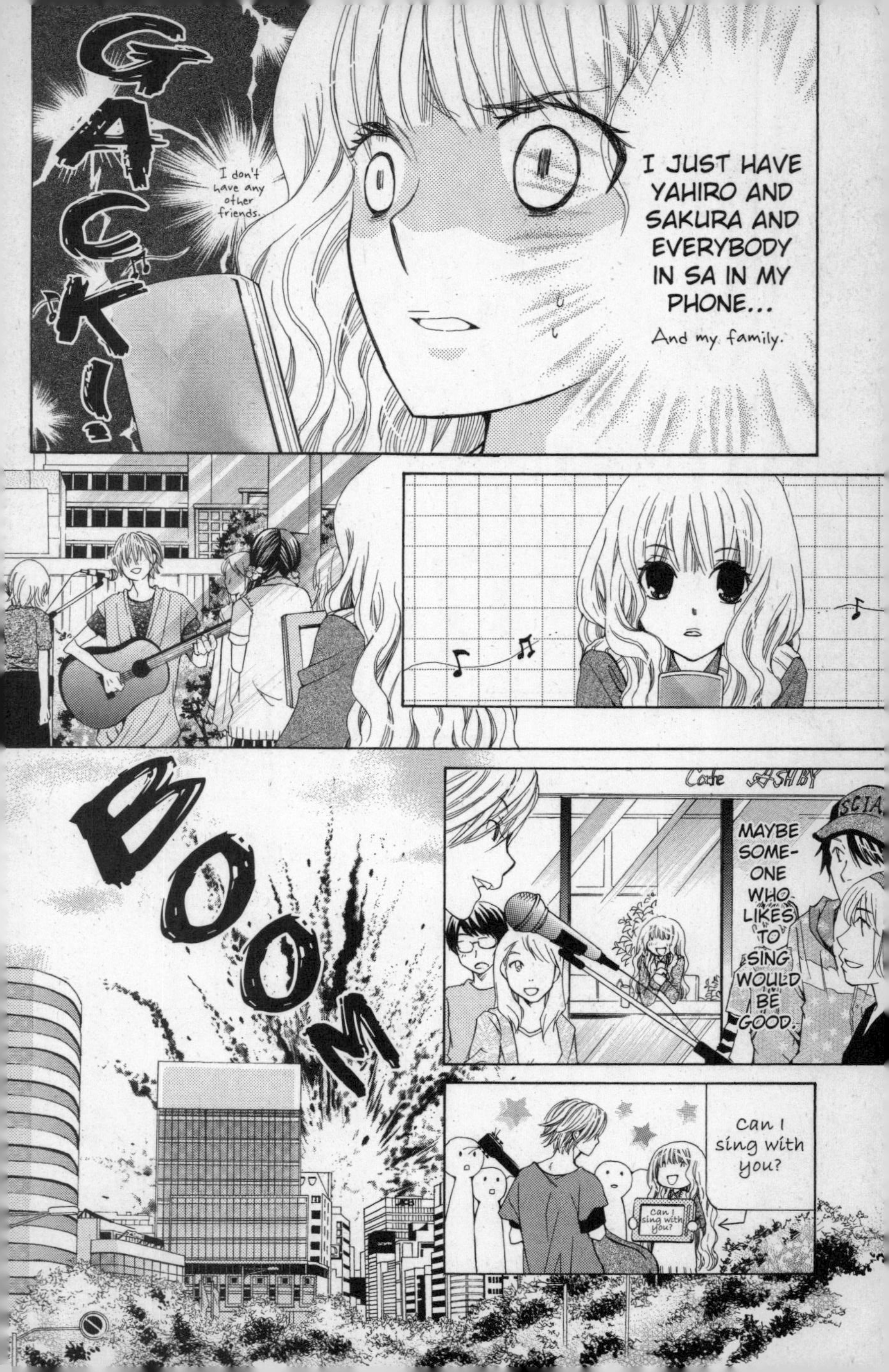
I JUST HAVE YAHIRO AND SAKURA AND EVERYBODY IN SA IN MY PHONE...
And my family.
I don't have any other friends.
GACK!!
MAYBE SOME-ONE WHO LIKES TO SING WOULD BE GOOD.
Cafe ASHBY
BOOM
Can I sing with you?
Can I sing with you?

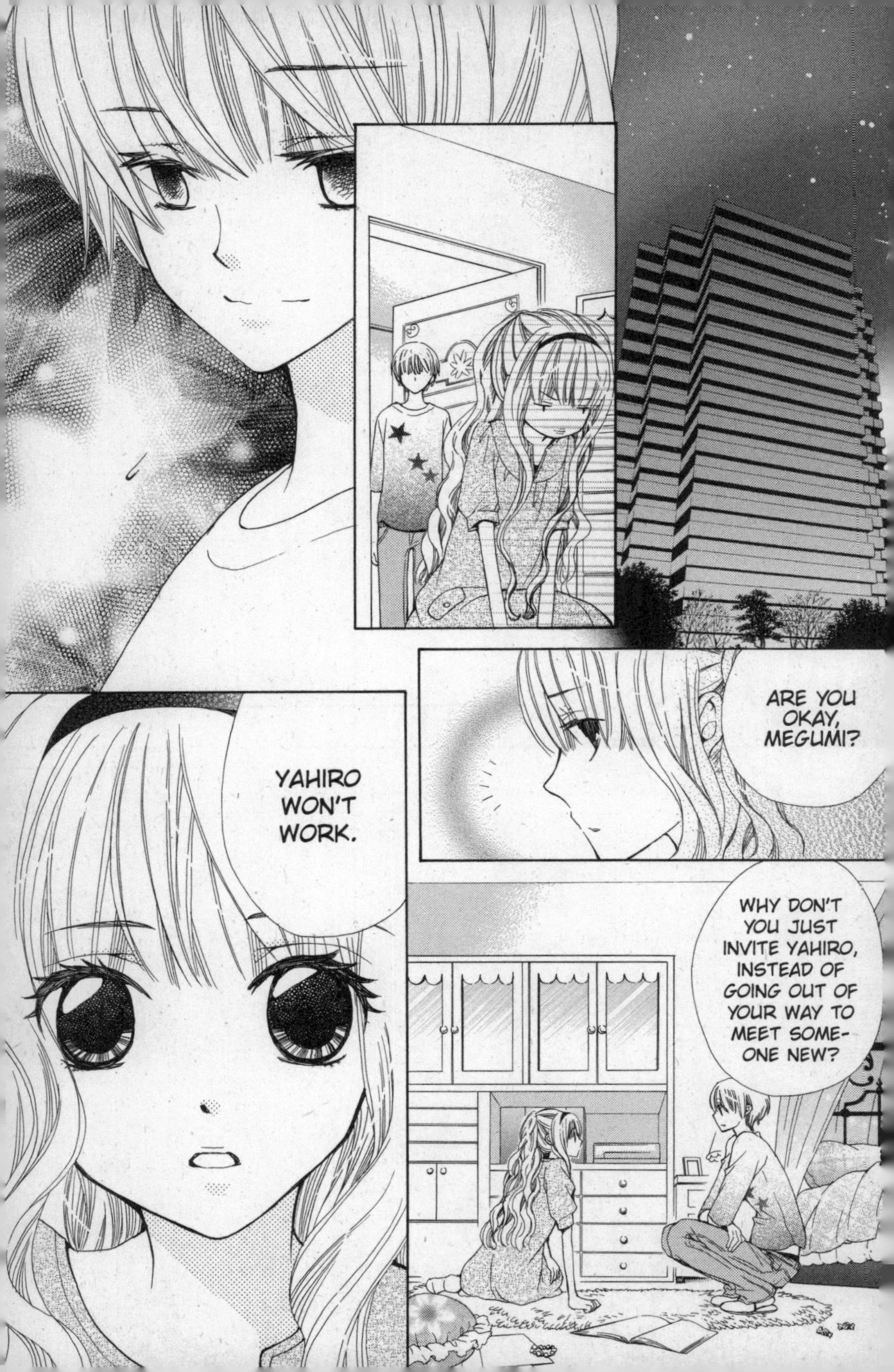
ARE YOU OKAY, MEGUMI?
WHY DON'T YOU JUST INVITE YAHIRO, INSTEAD OF GOING OUT OF YOUR WAY TO MEET SOME-ONE NEW?
YAHIRO WON'T WORK.

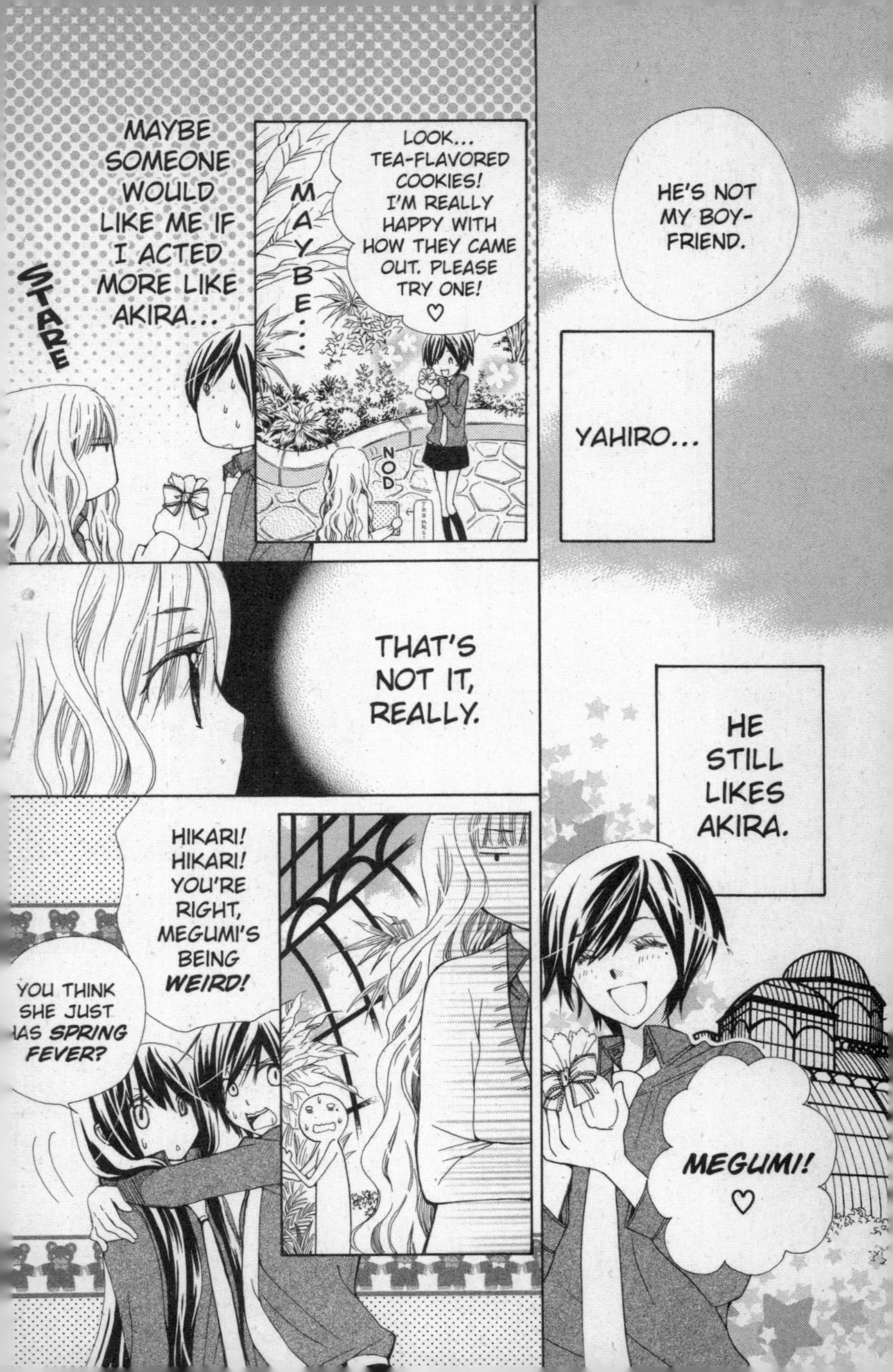
HE'S NOT MY BOY-FRIEND.
YAHIRO...
HE STILL LIKES AKIRA.
MEGUMI! ♡
LOOK... TEA-FLAVORED COOKIES! I'M REALLY HAPPY WITH HOW THEY CAME OUT. PLEASE TRY ONE! ♡
MAYBE...
NOD
MAYBE SOMEONE WOULD LIKE ME IF I ACTED MORE LIKE AKIRA...
STARE
THAT'S NOT IT, REALLY.
HIKARI! HIKARI! YOU'RE RIGHT, MEGUMI'S BEING *WEIRD!*
YOU THINK SHE JUST HAS *SPRING FEVER?*

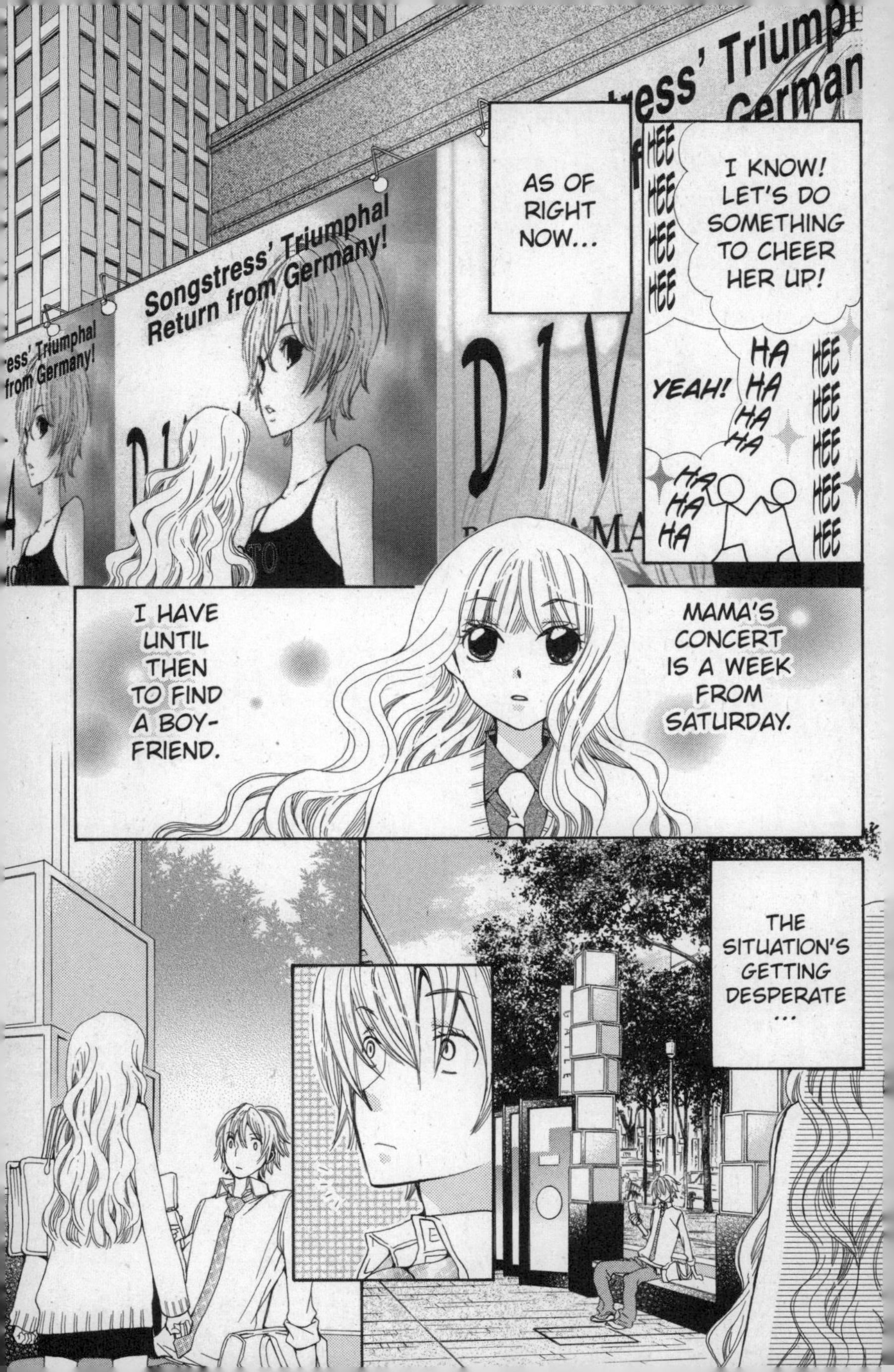
I KNOW! LET'S DO SOMETHING TO CHEER HER UP!
HEE HEE HEE HEE
YEAH!
HA HA HA HA
HA HA HA
HEE HEE HEE HEE HEE HEE HEE
AS OF RIGHT NOW...
Songstress' Triumphal Return from Germany!
MAMA'S CONCERT IS A WEEK FROM SATURDAY.
I HAVE UNTIL THEN TO FIND A BOY-FRIEND.
THE SITUATION'S GETTING DESPERATE...

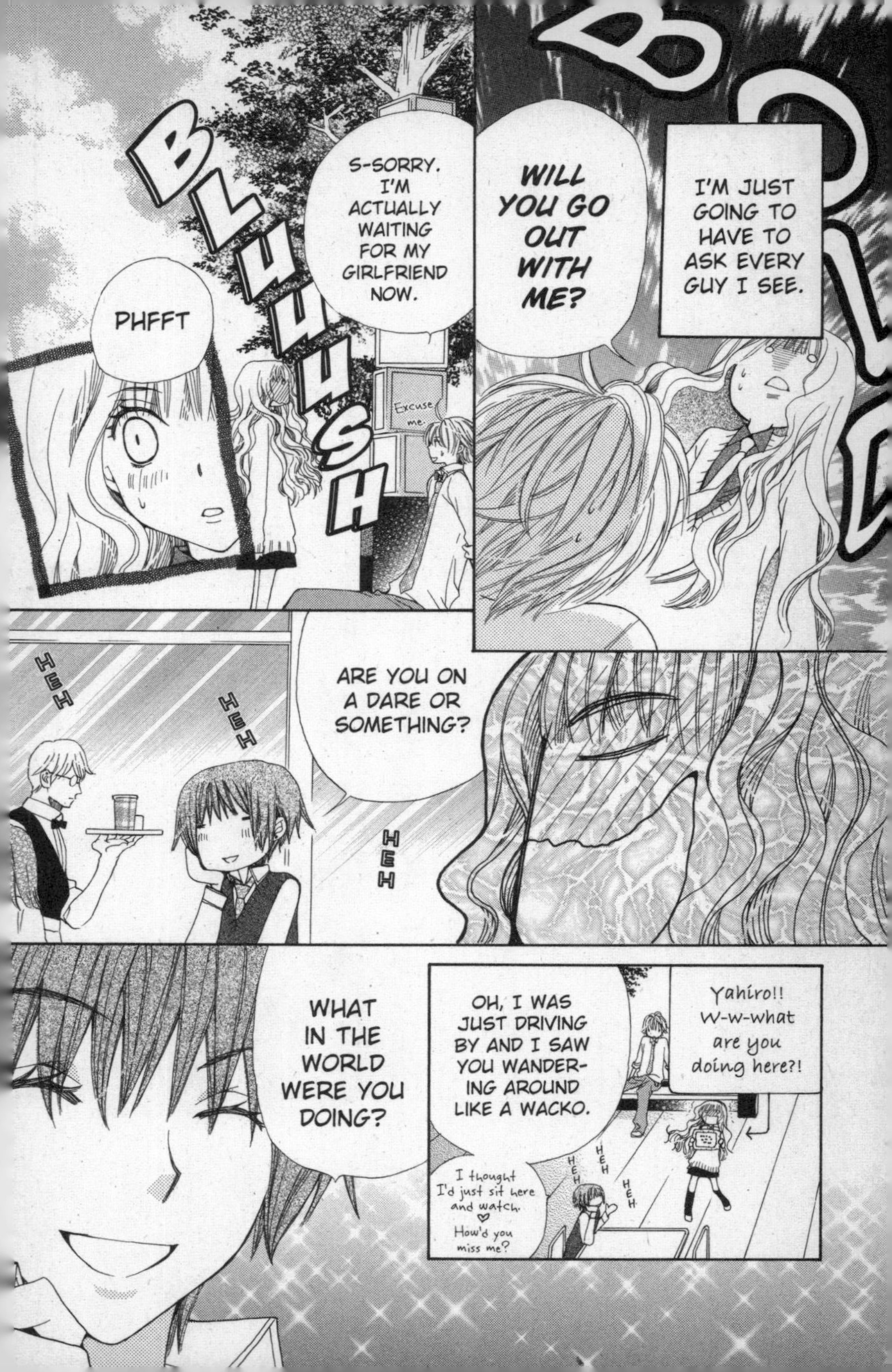
I'M JUST GOING TO HAVE TO ASK EVERY GUY I SEE.
WILL YOU GO OUT WITH ME?
S-SORRY. I'M ACTUALLY WAITING FOR MY GIRLFRIEND NOW.
Excuse me.
BLUUUSH
PHFFT
ARE YOU ON A DARE OR SOMETHING?
HEH HEH
HEH HEH
HEH HEH
Yahiro!! W-w-what are you doing here?!
OH, I WAS JUST DRIVING BY AND I SAW YOU WANDERING AROUND LIKE A WACKO.
HEH HEH HEH HEH HEH HEH
I thought I'd just sit here and watch. ♥ How'd you miss me?
WHAT IN THE WORLD WERE YOU DOING?

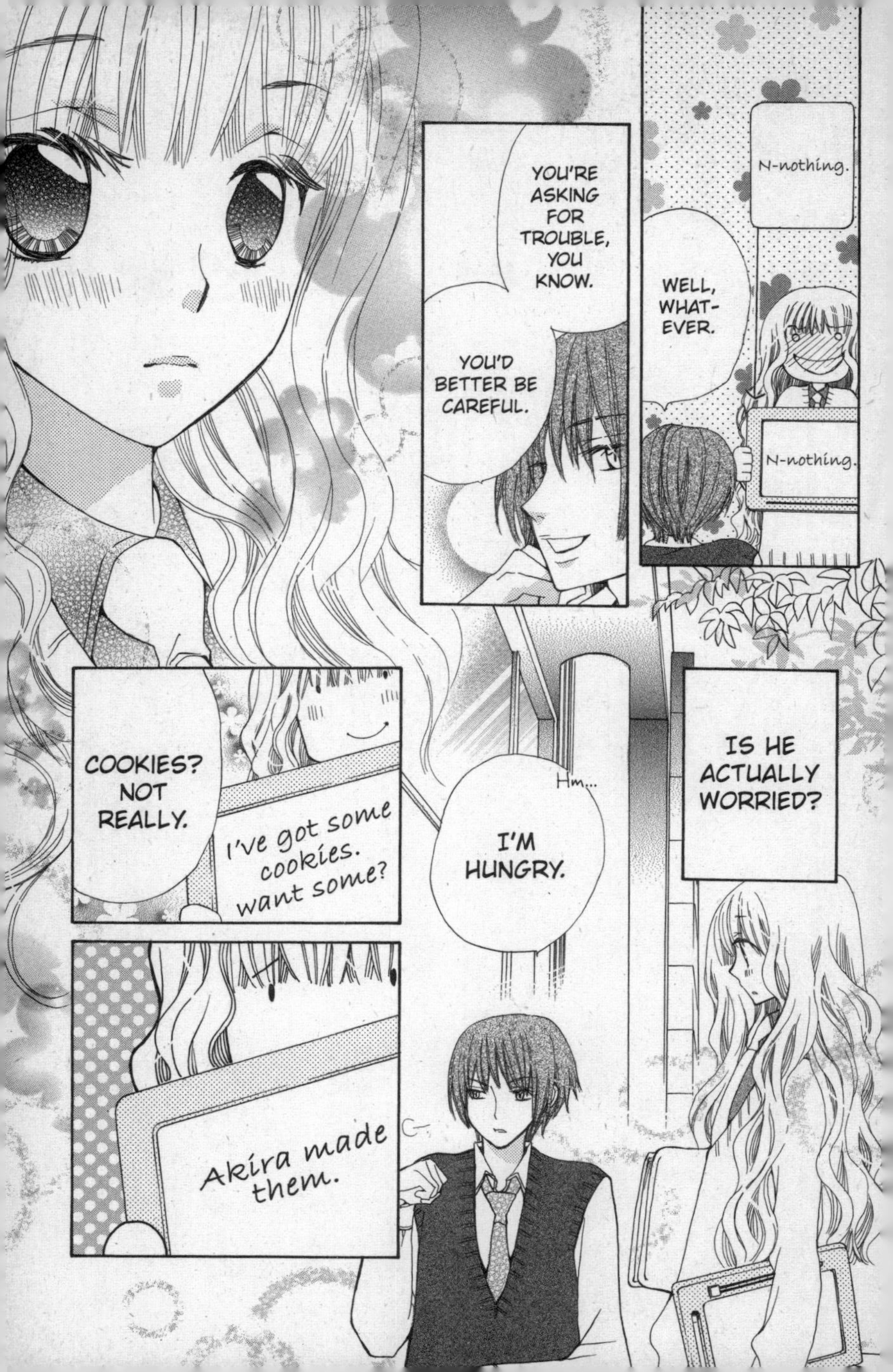
N-nothing.
WELL, WHAT-EVER.
N-nothing.
YOU'RE ASKING FOR TROUBLE, YOU KNOW.
YOU'D BETTER BE CAREFUL.
IS HE ACTUALLY WORRIED?
Hm...
I'M HUNGRY.
COOKIES? NOT REALLY.
I've got some cookies. want some?
Akira made them.

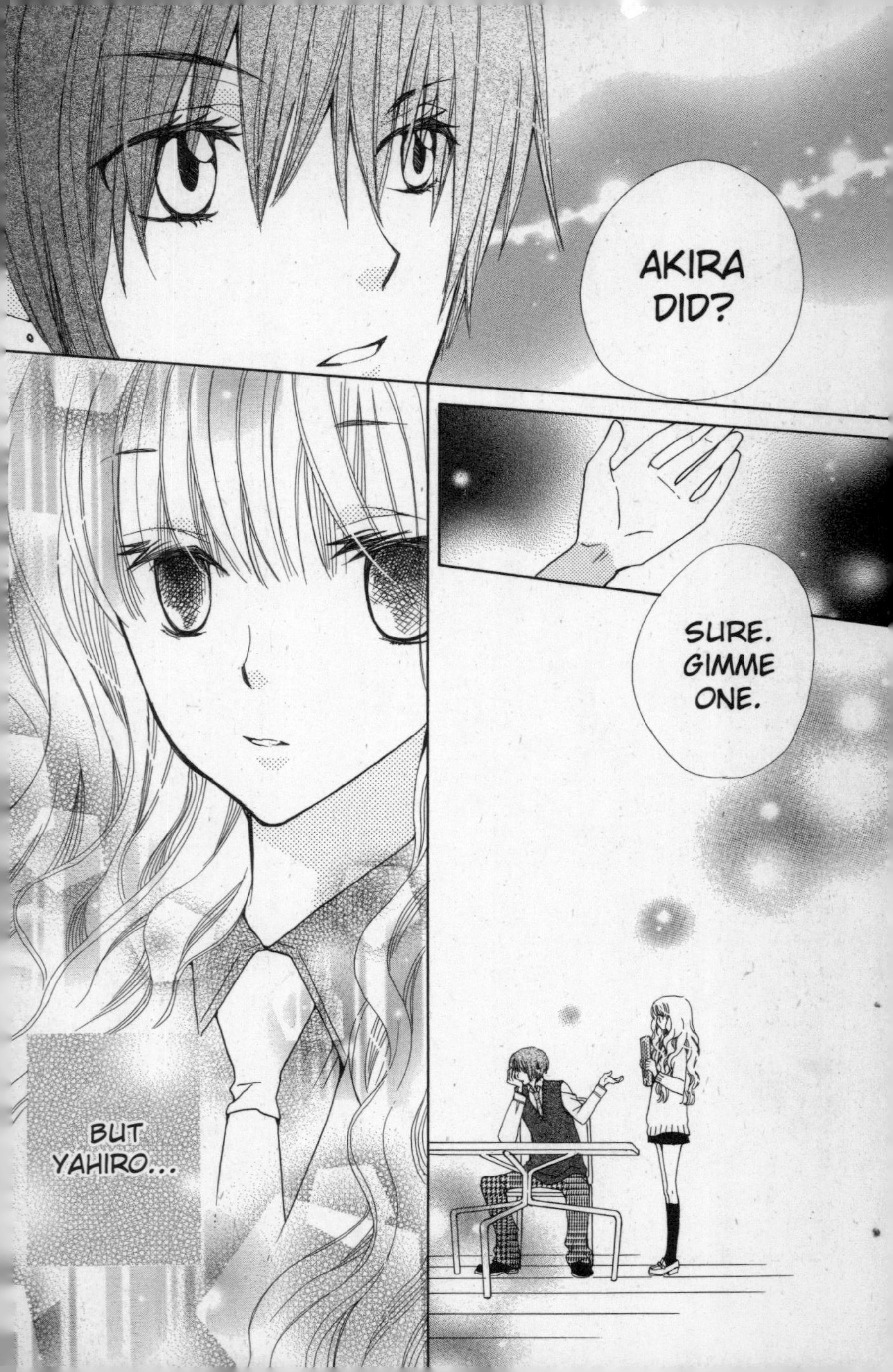
AKIRA DID?
SURE. GIMME ONE.
BUT YAHIRO...

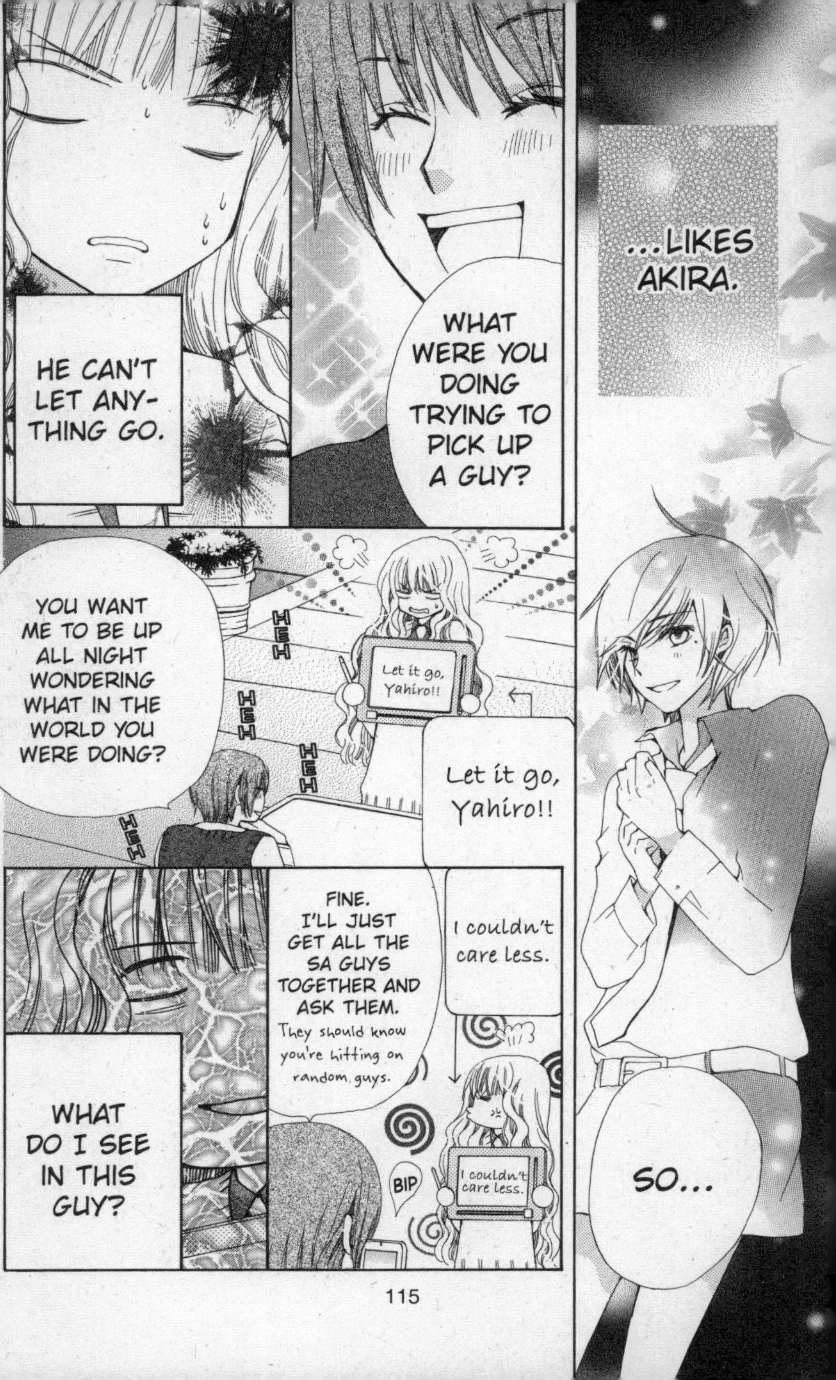
...LIKES AKIRA.
SO...
WHAT WERE YOU DOING TRYING TO PICK UP A GUY?
HE CAN'T LET ANY-THING GO.
Let it go, Yahiro!!
Let it go, Yahiro!!
HEH HEH HEH HEH
YOU WANT ME TO BE UP ALL NIGHT WONDERING WHAT IN THE WORLD YOU WERE DOING?
I couldn't care less.
FINE. I'LL JUST GET ALL THE SA GUYS TOGETHER AND ASK THEM.
They should know you're hitting on random guys.
I couldn't care less.
BIP
WHAT DO I SEE IN THIS GUY?

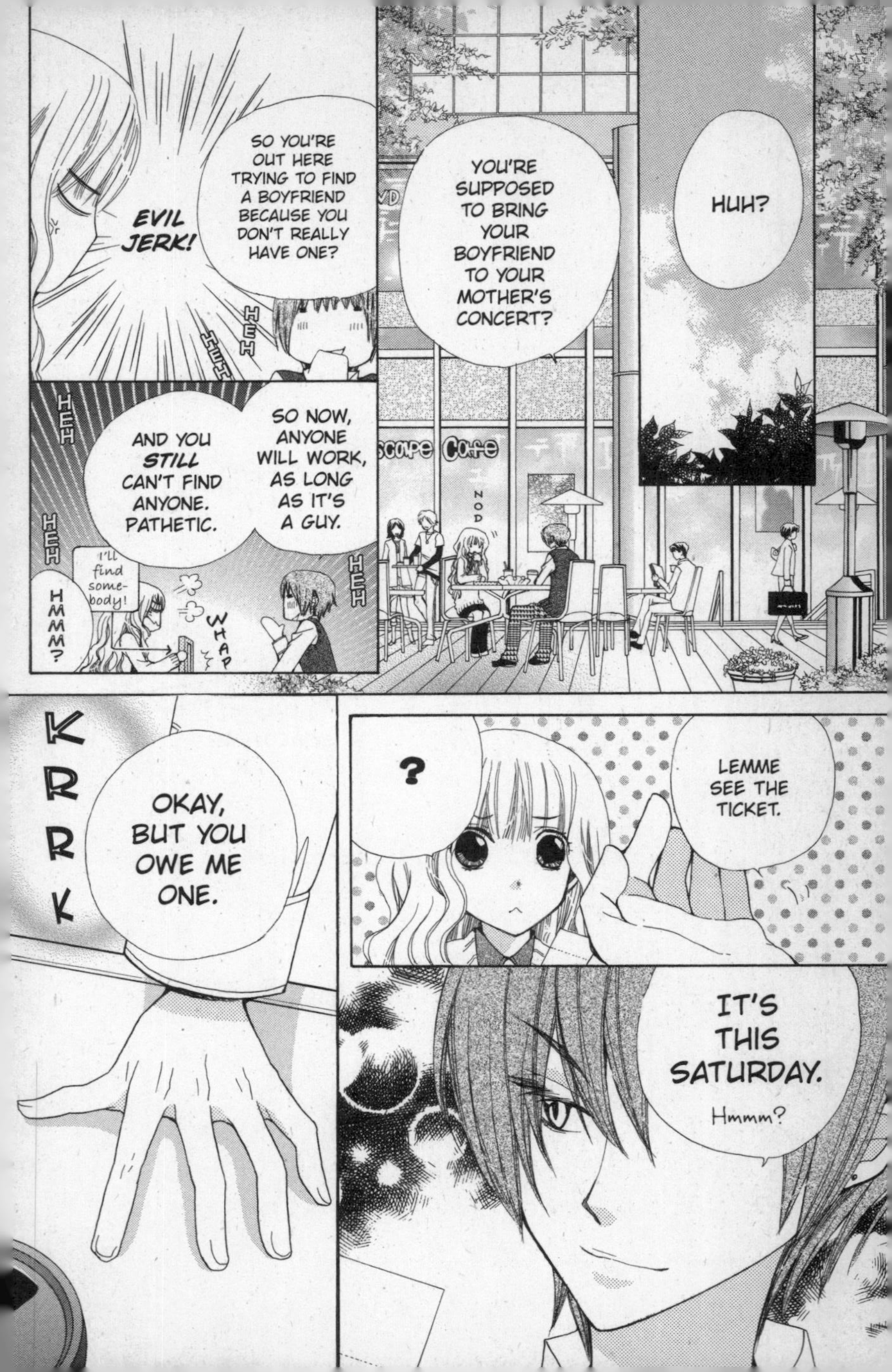
HUH?
YOU'RE SUPPOSED TO BRING YOUR BOYFRIEND TO YOUR MOTHER'S CONCERT?
NOD
SO YOU'RE OUT HERE TRYING TO FIND A BOYFRIEND BECAUSE YOU DON'T REALLY HAVE ONE?
EVIL JERK!
HEH HEH
SO NOW, ANYONE WILL WORK, AS LONG AS IT'S A GUY.
AND YOU STILL CAN'T FIND ANYONE. PATHETIC.
HEH HEH HEH
I'll find some-body!
WHAP
HMMM?
LEMME SEE THE TICKET.
?
IT'S THIS SATURDAY.
Hmmm?
KRRK
OKAY, BUT YOU OWE ME ONE.

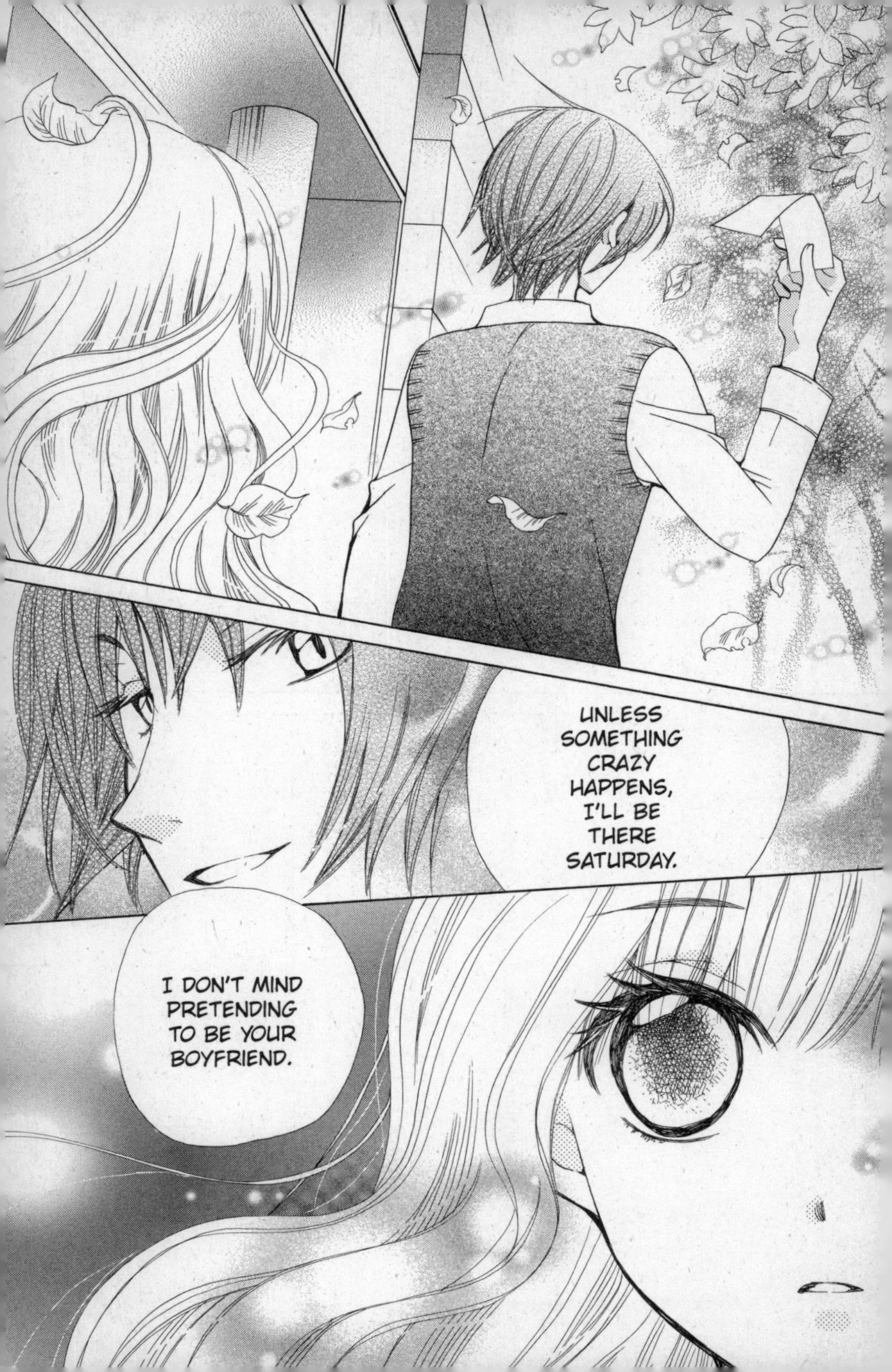
UNLESS SOMETHING CRAZY HAPPENS, I'LL BE THERE SATURDAY.
I DON'T MIND PRETENDING TO BE YOUR BOYFRIEND.

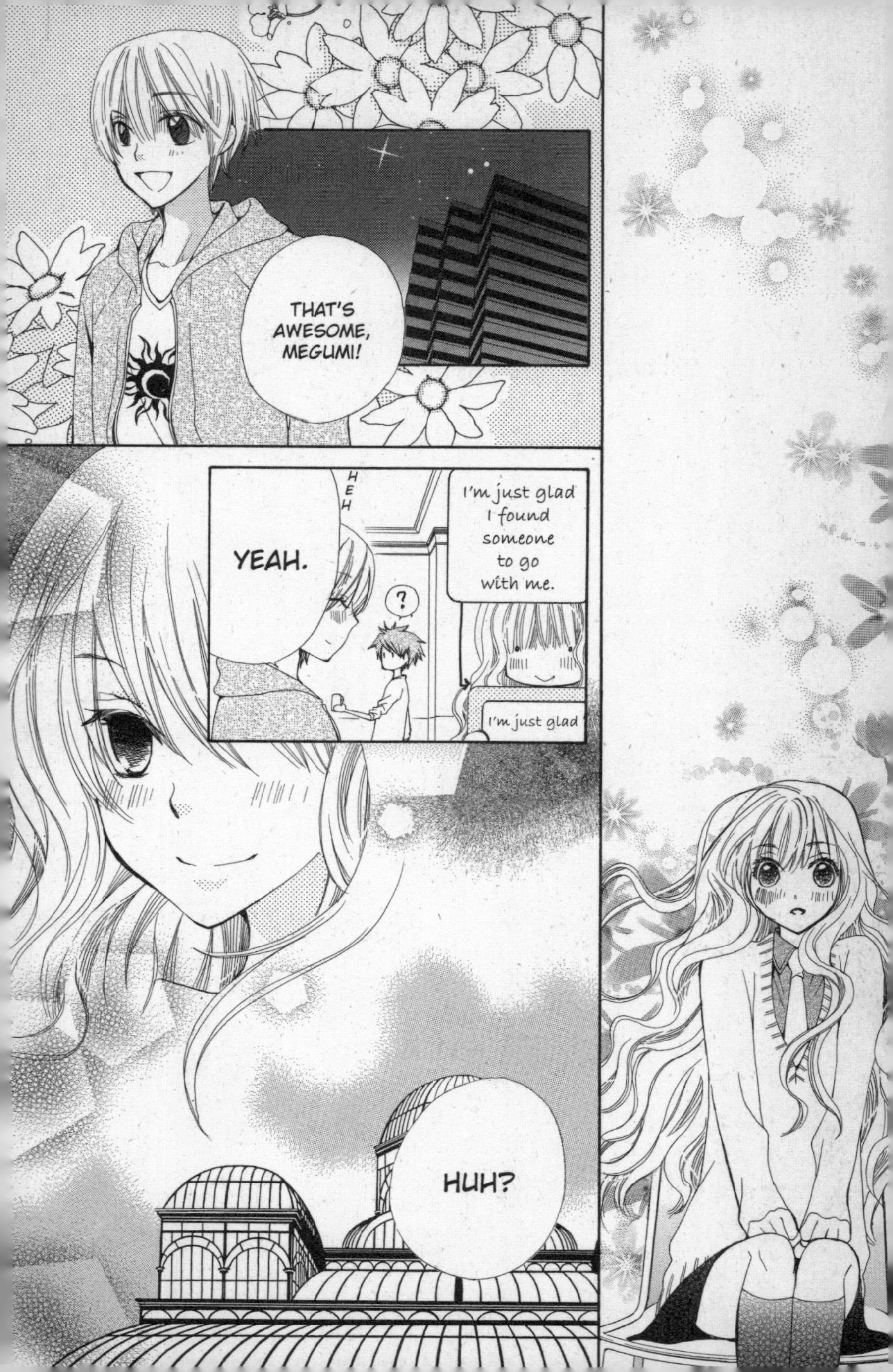
THAT'S AWESOME, MEGUMI!
I'm just glad I found someone to go with me.
I'm just glad
HEH HEH
?
YEAH.
HUH?

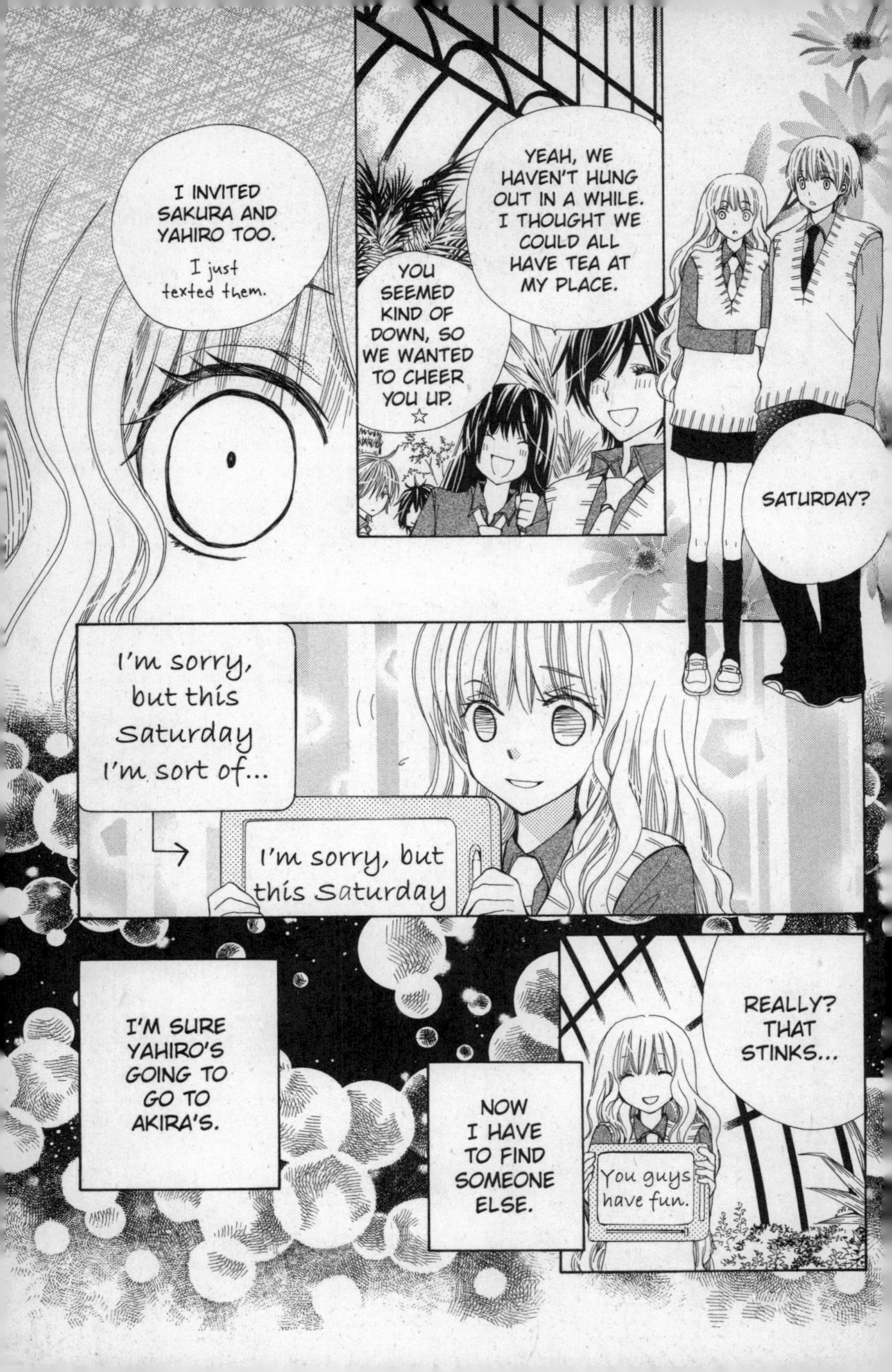
SATURDAY?
YEAH, WE HAVEN'T HUNG OUT IN A WHILE. I THOUGHT WE COULD ALL HAVE TEA AT MY PLACE.
YOU SEEMED KIND OF DOWN, SO WE WANTED TO CHEER YOU UP. ☆
I INVITED SAKURA AND YAHIRO TOO.
I just texted them.
I'm sorry, but this Saturday I'm sort of...
I'm sorry, but this Saturday
REALLY? THAT STINKS...
You guys have fun.
NOW I HAVE TO FIND SOMEONE ELSE.
I'M SURE YAHIRO'S GOING TO GO TO AKIRA'S.

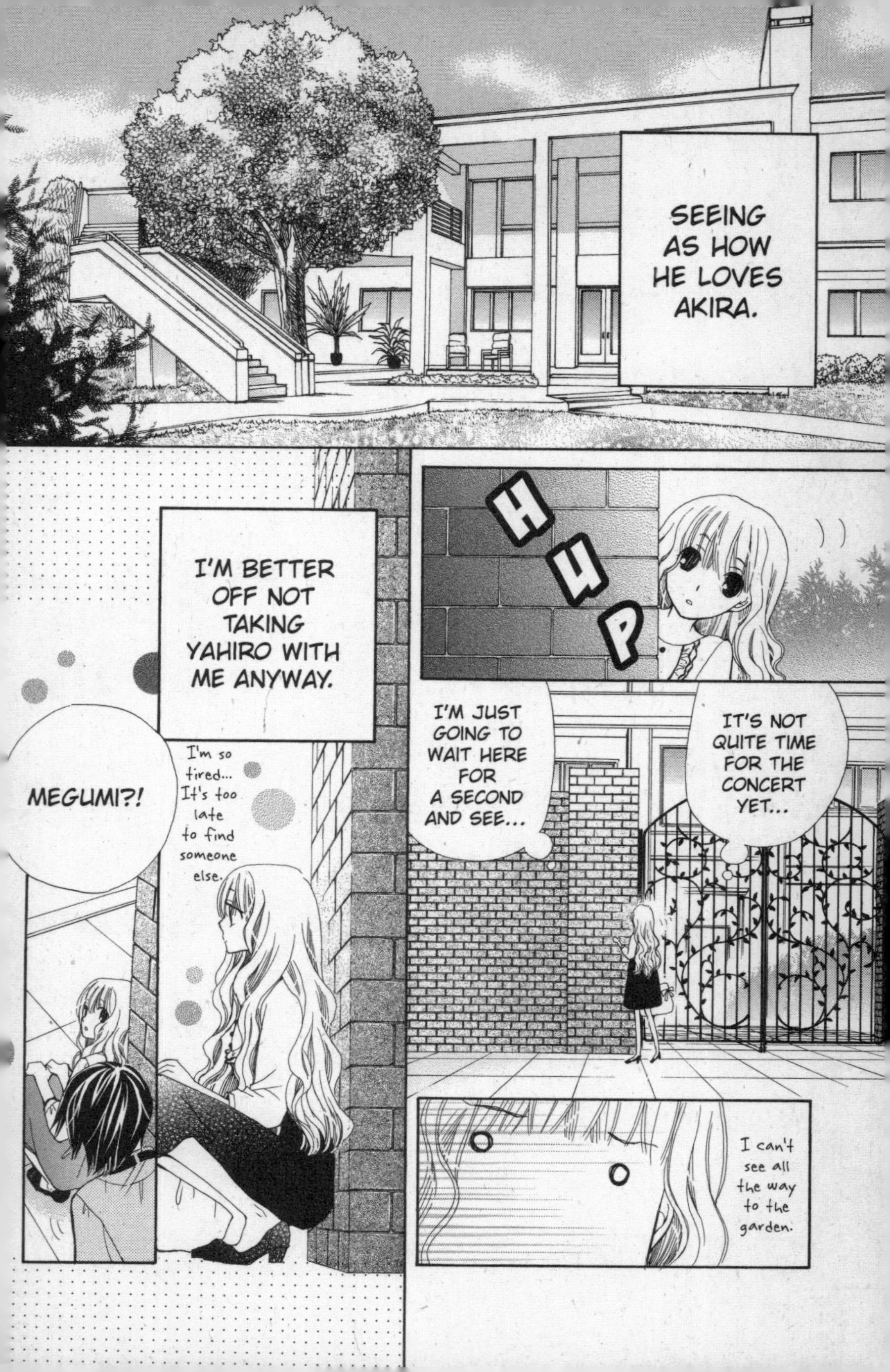
SEEING AS HOW HE LOVES AKIRA.
HUP
IT'S NOT QUITE TIME FOR THE CONCERT YET...
I'M JUST GOING TO WAIT HERE FOR A SECOND AND SEE...
I can't see all the way to the garden.
I'M BETTER OFF NOT TAKING YAHIRO WITH ME ANYWAY.
I'm so tired... It's too late to find someone else.
MEGUMI?!

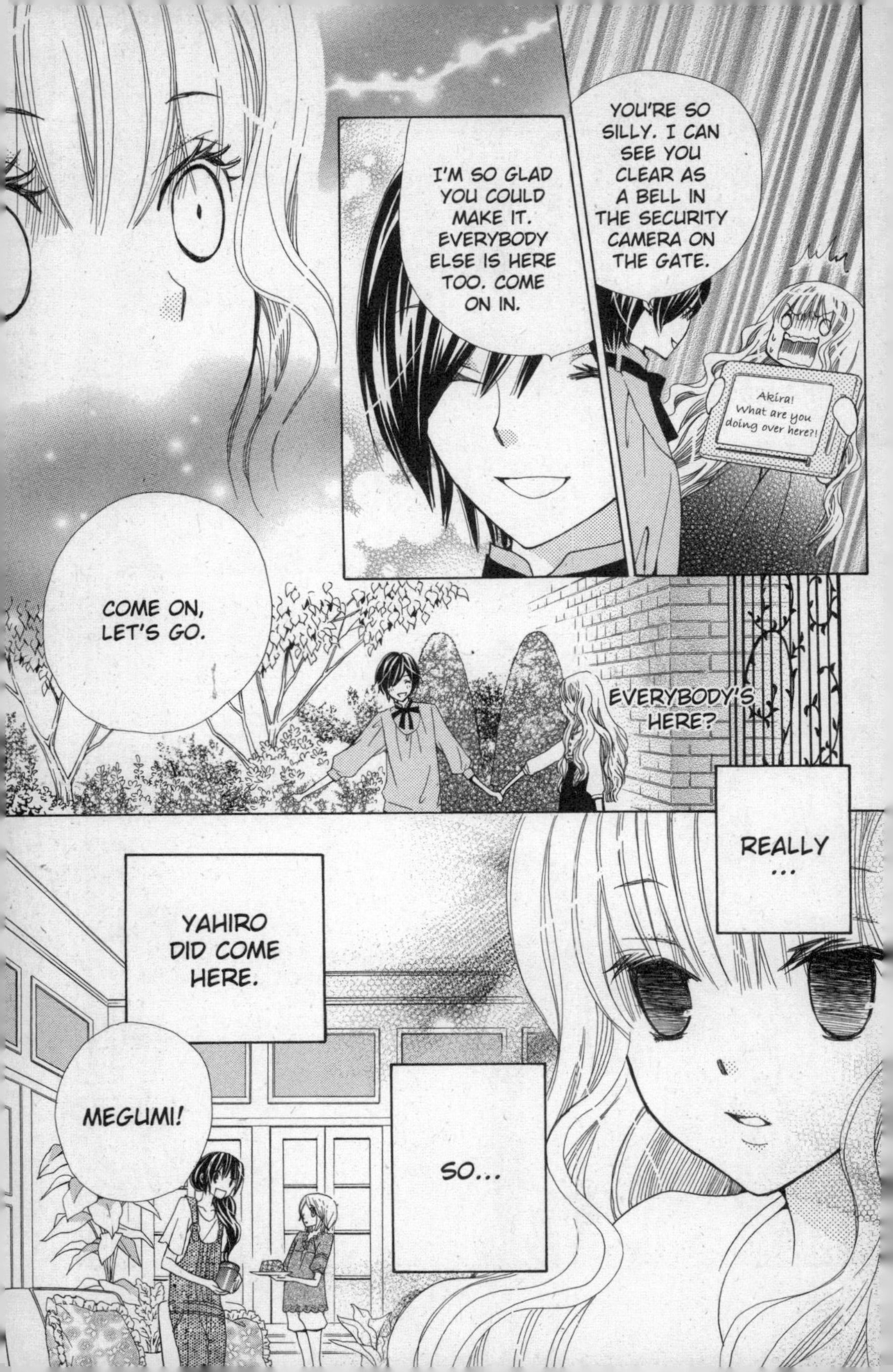
YOU'RE SO SILLY. I CAN SEE YOU CLEAR AS A BELL IN THE SECURITY CAMERA ON THE GATE.
Akira! What are you doing over here?!
I'M SO GLAD YOU COULD MAKE IT. EVERYBODY ELSE IS HERE TOO. COME ON IN.
EVERYBODY'S HERE?
COME ON, LET'S GO.
REALLY ...
YAHIRO DID COME HERE.
SO...
MEGUMI!

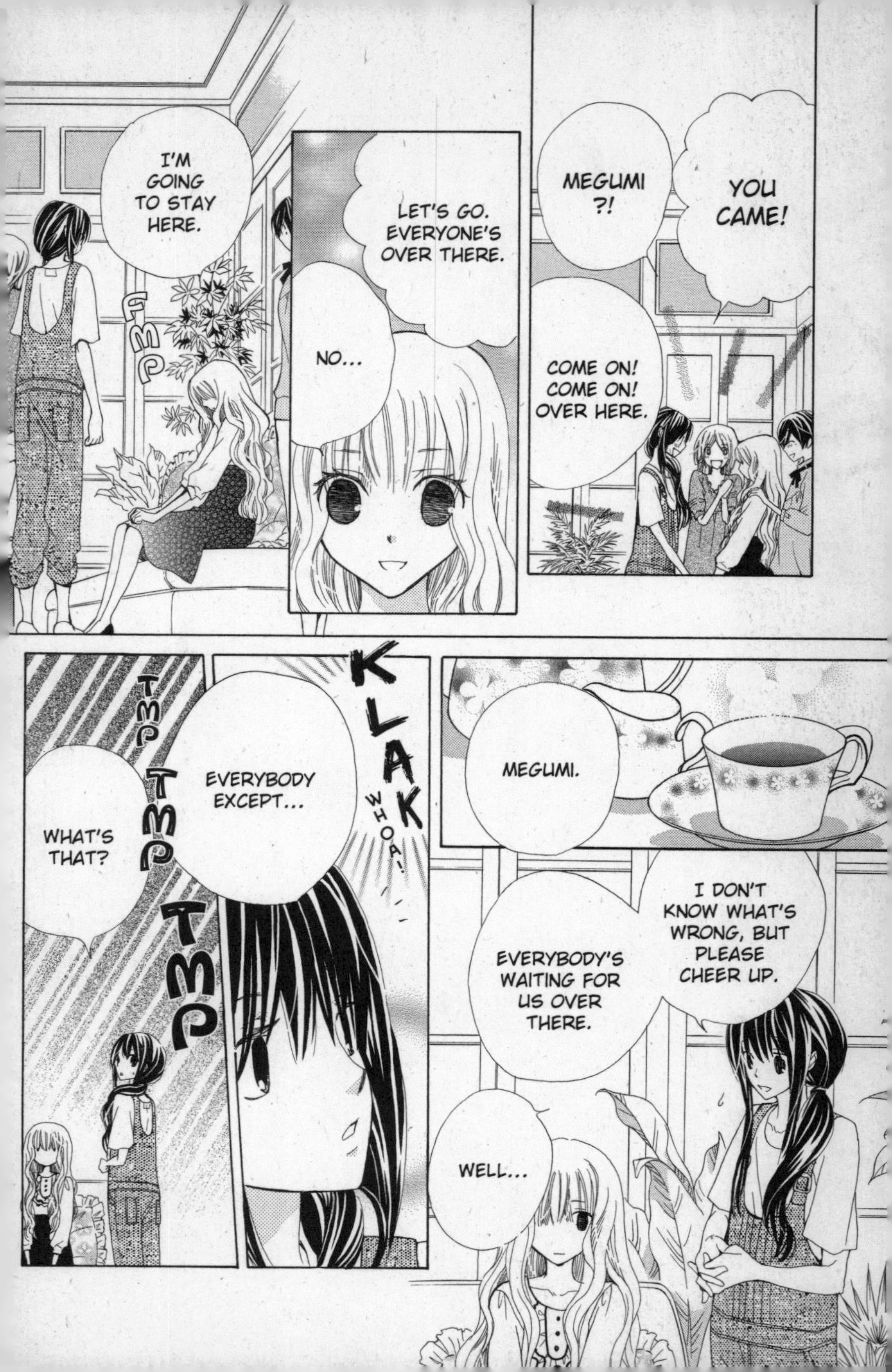
YOU CAME!
MEGUMI ?!
COME ON! COME ON! OVER HERE.
LET'S GO. EVERYONE'S OVER THERE.
NO...
I'M GOING TO STAY HERE.
FMP
MEGUMI.
I DON'T KNOW WHAT'S WRONG, BUT PLEASE CHEER UP.
EVERYBODY'S WAITING FOR US OVER THERE.
WELL...
KLAK
WHOA!
EVERYBODY EXCEPT...
TMP
TMP
TMP
WHAT'S THAT?

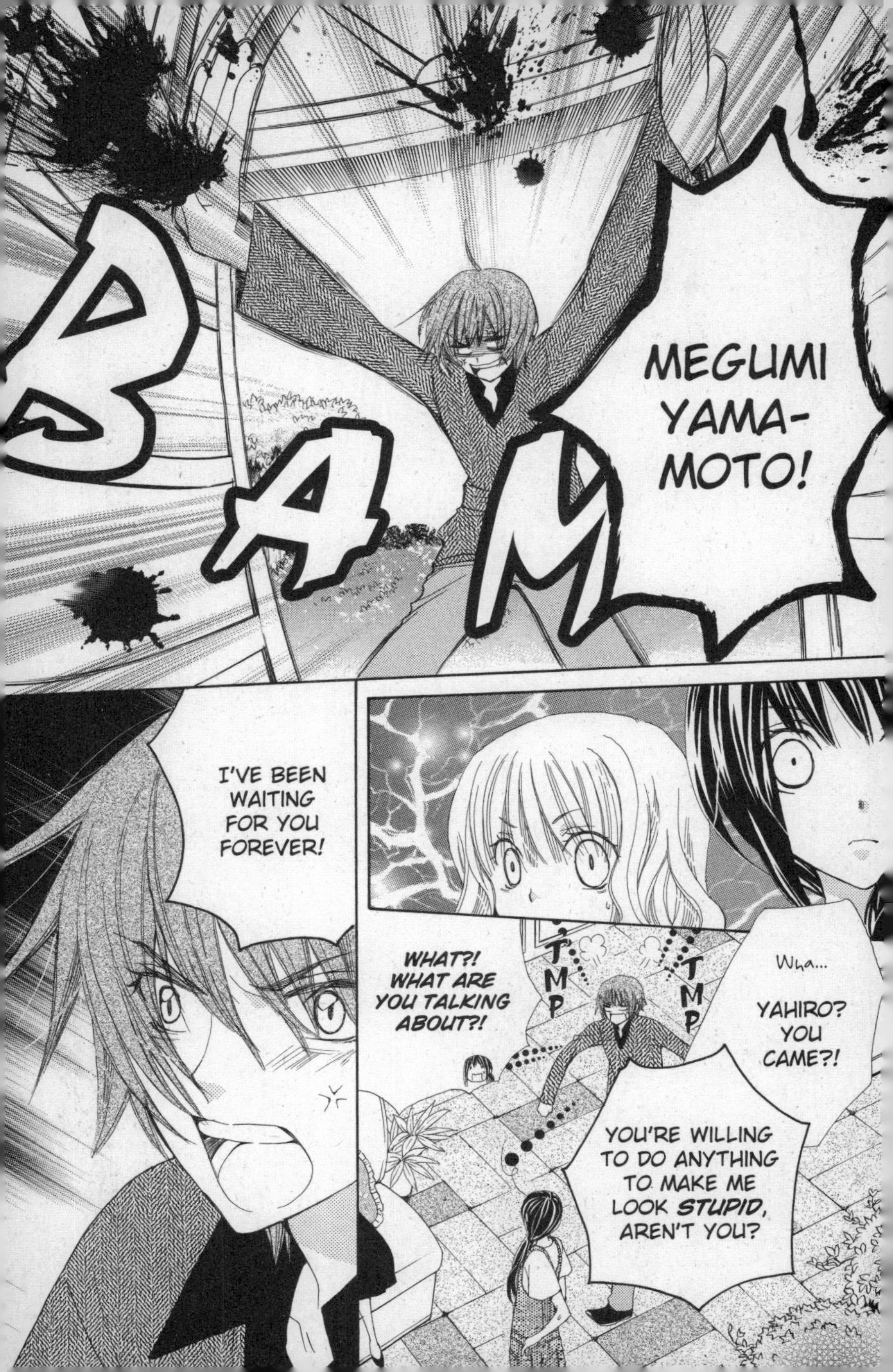
MEGUMI YAMAMOTO!
BAM
Wha...
YAHIRO? YOU CAME?!
TMP
TMP
WHAT?! WHAT ARE YOU TALKING ABOUT?!
YOU'RE WILLING TO DO ANYTHING TO MAKE ME LOOK **STUPID**, AREN'T YOU?
I'VE BEEN WAITING FOR YOU FOREVER!

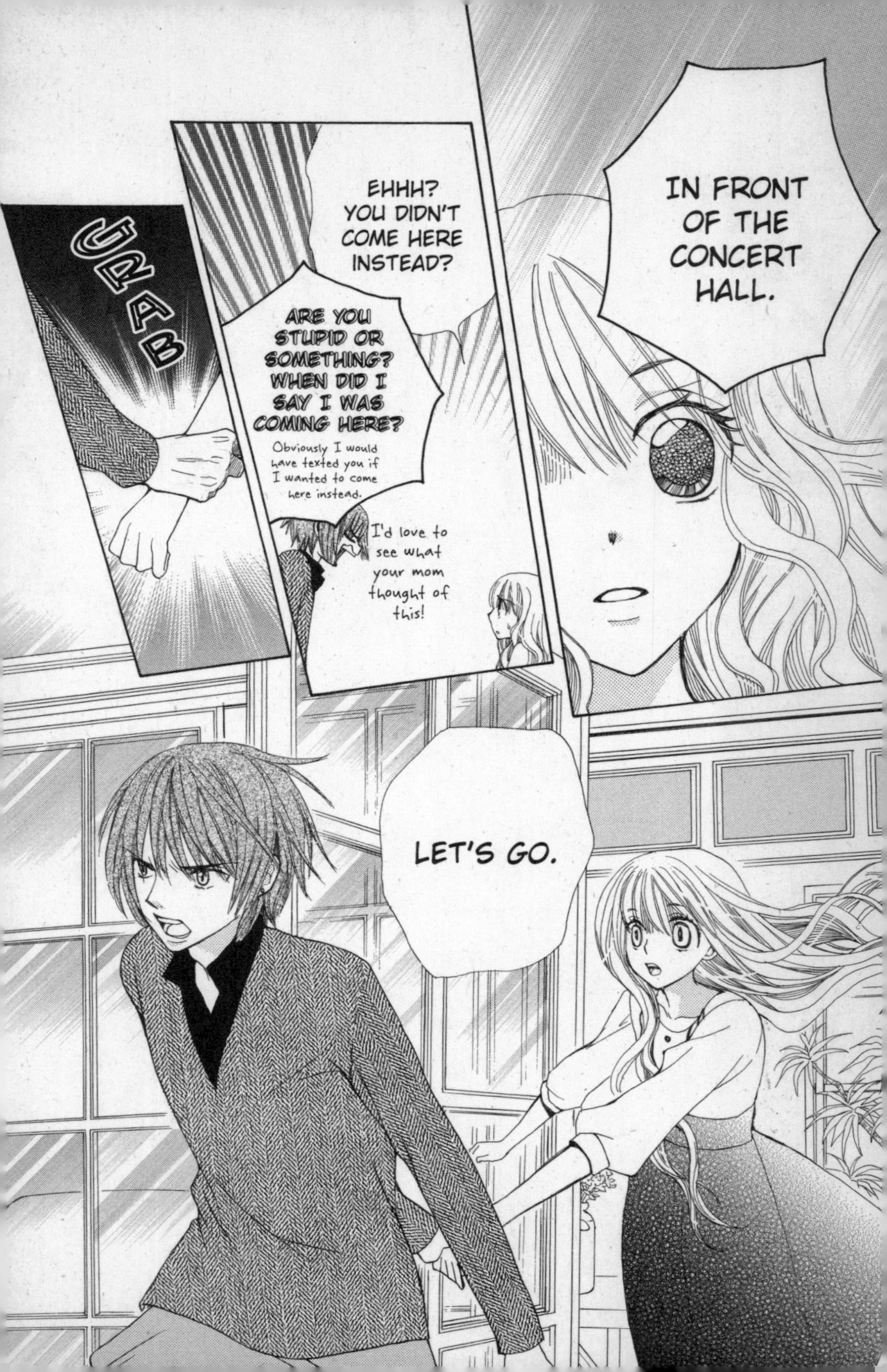
IN FRONT OF THE CONCERT HALL.
EHHH? YOU DIDN'T COME HERE INSTEAD?
ARE YOU STUPID OR SOMETHING? WHEN DID I SAY I WAS COMING HERE?
Obviously I would have texted you if I wanted to come here instead.
I'd love to see what your mom thought of this!
GRAB
LET'S GO.

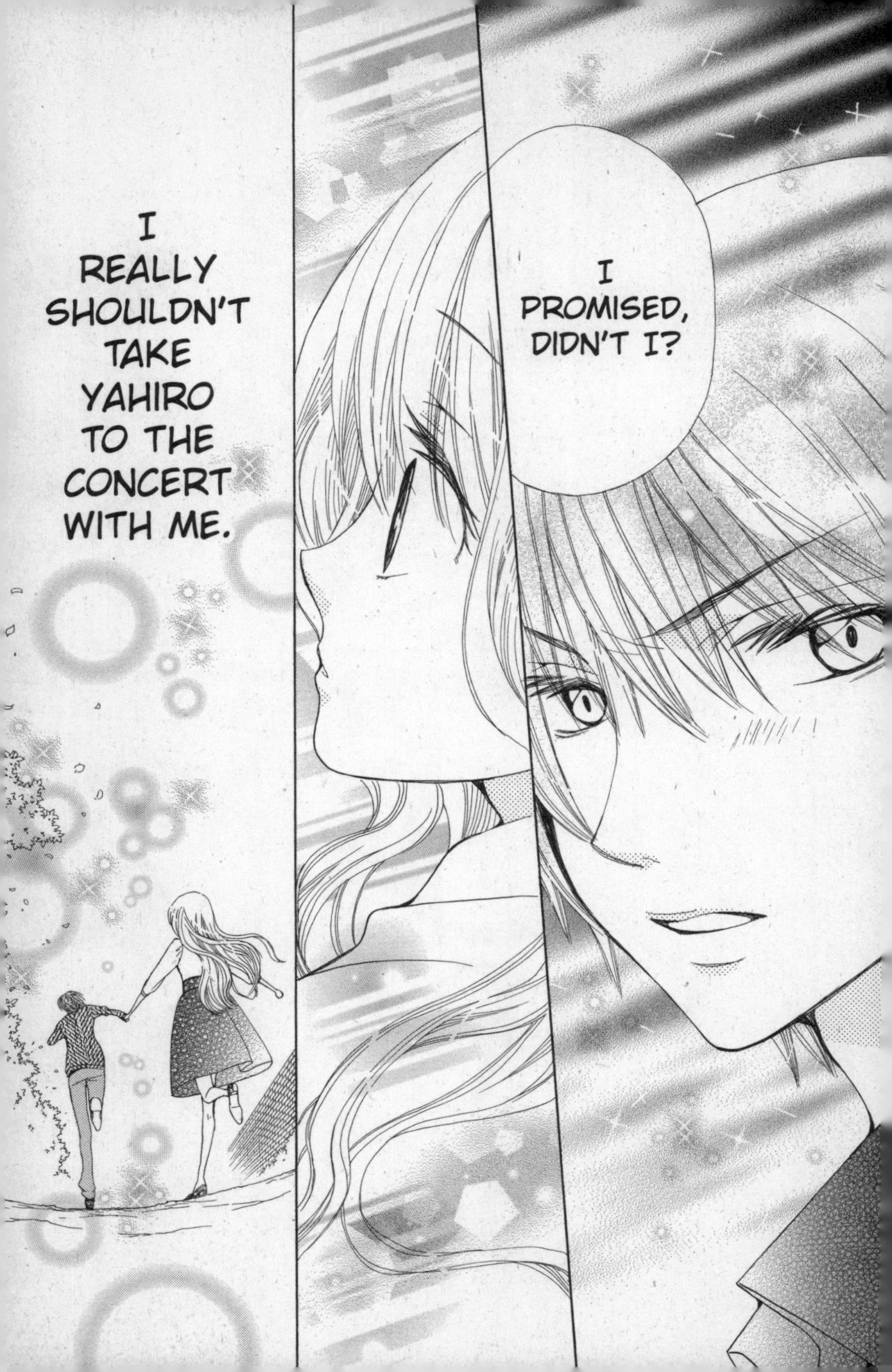
I PROMISED, DIDN'T I?
I REALLY SHOULDN'T TAKE YAHIRO TO THE CONCERT WITH ME.

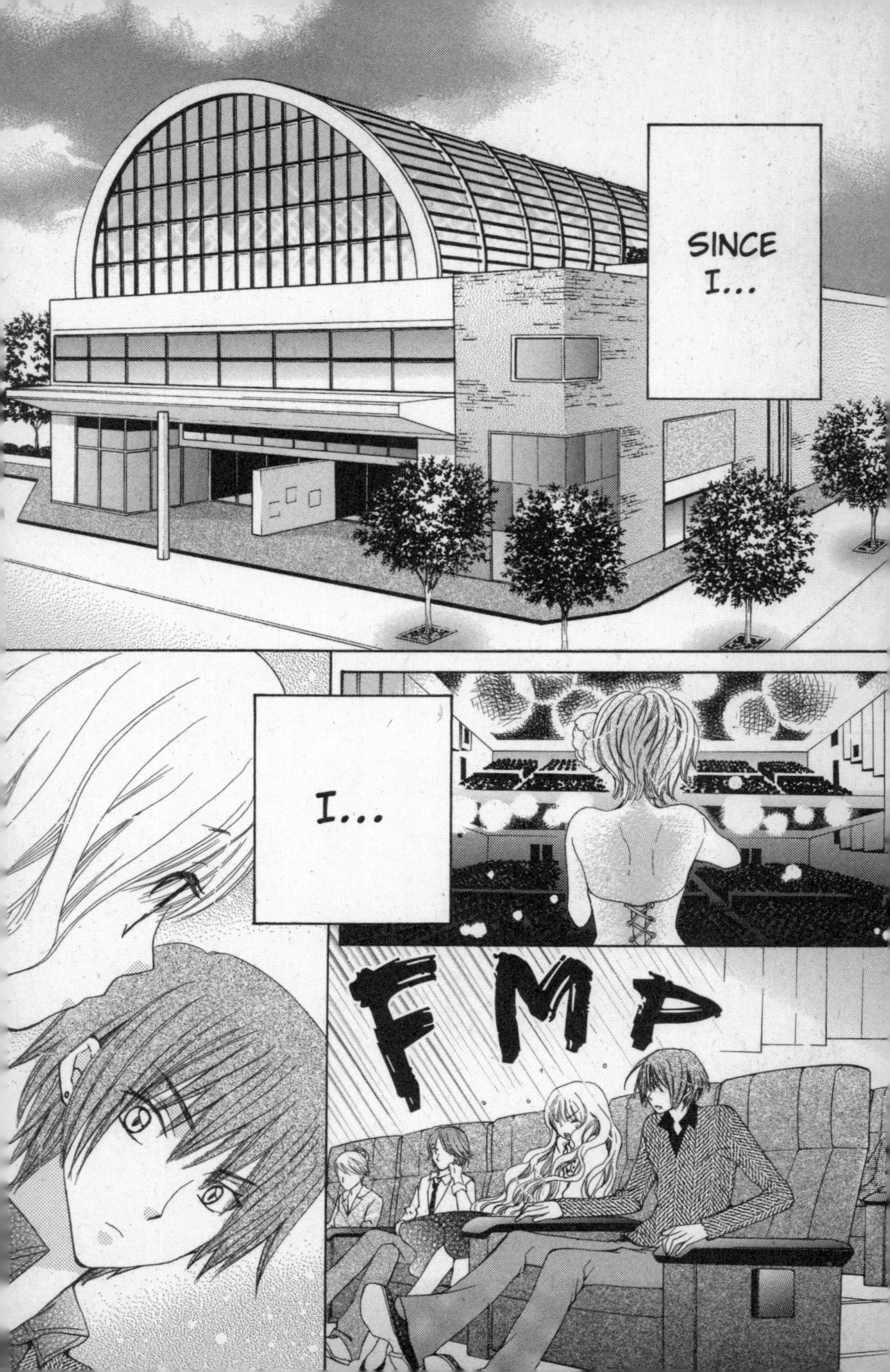
SINCE I...
I...
FMP

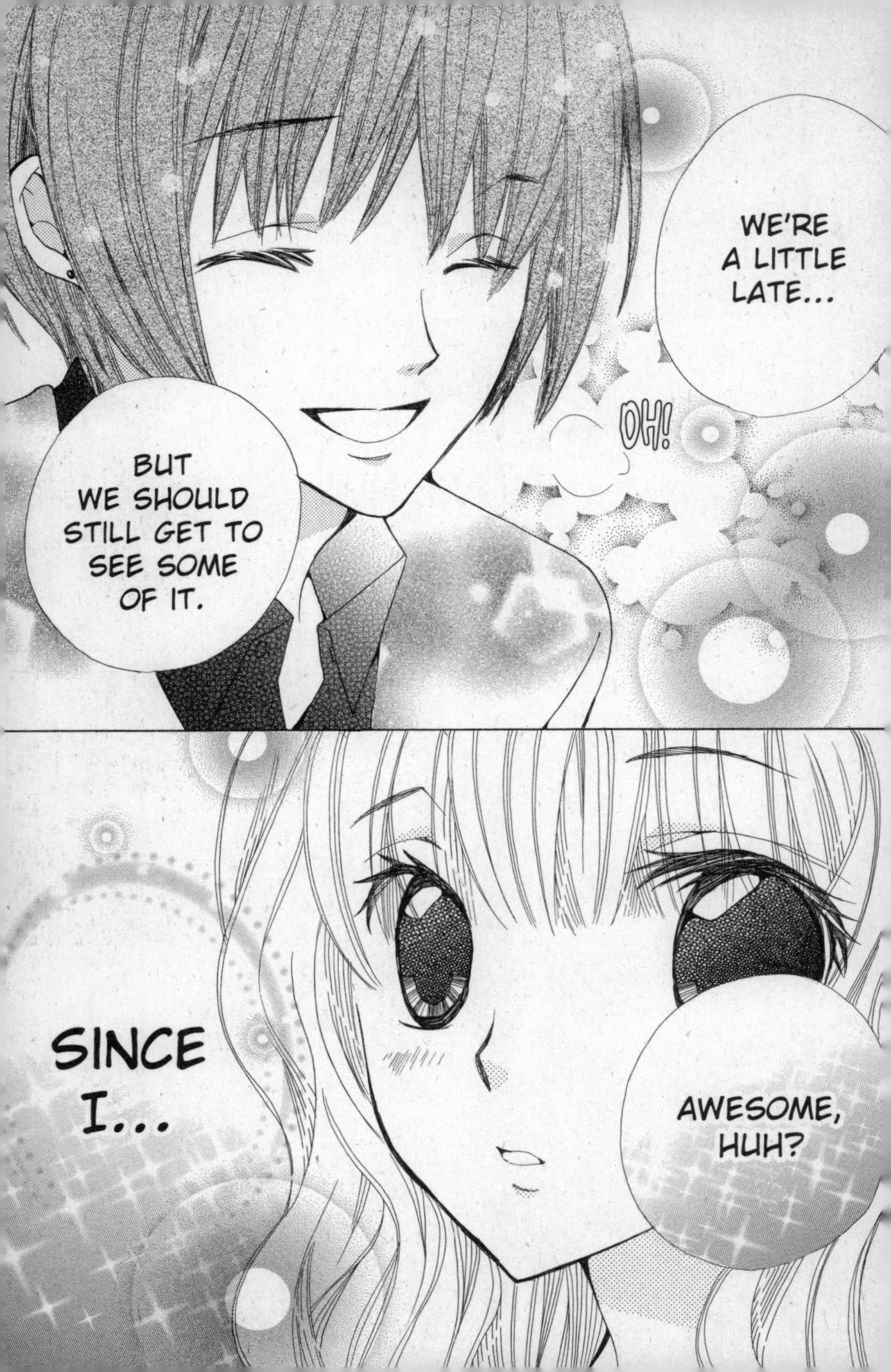
WE'RE A LITTLE LATE...
OH!
BUT WE SHOULD STILL GET TO SEE SOME OF IT.
AWESOME, HUH?
SINCE I...

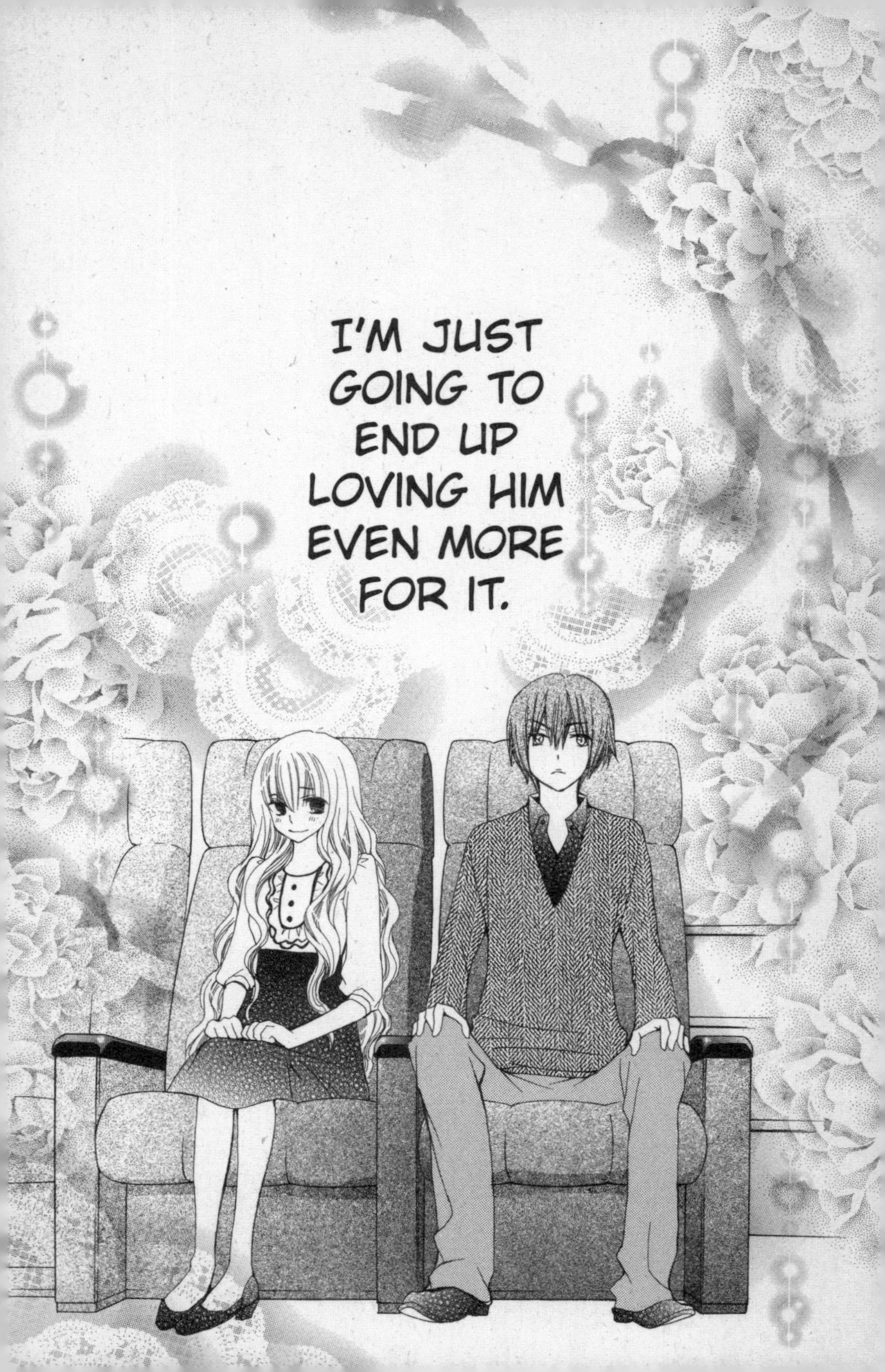
I'M JUST GOING TO END UP LOVING HIM EVEN MORE FOR IT.

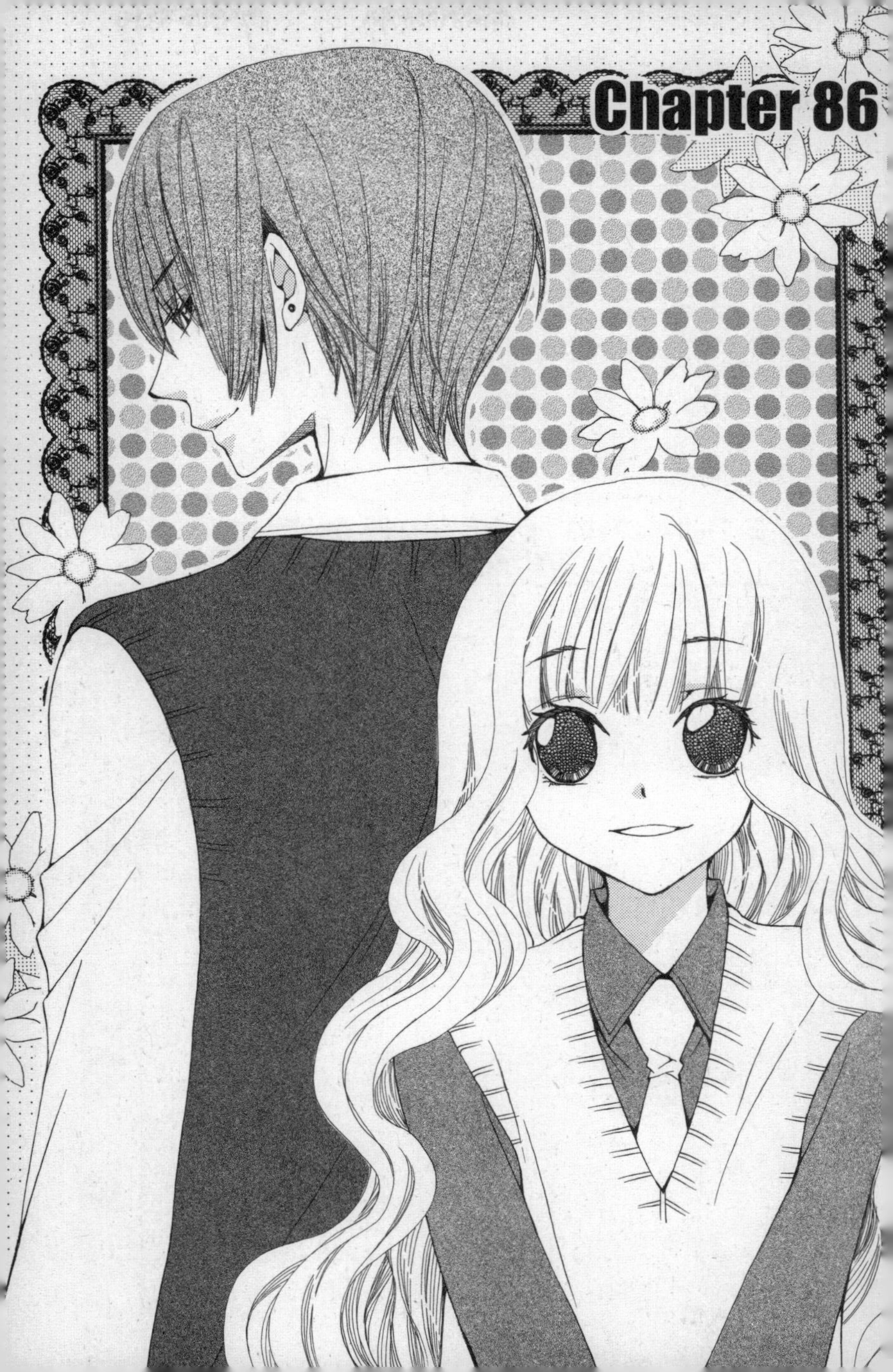
Chapter 86

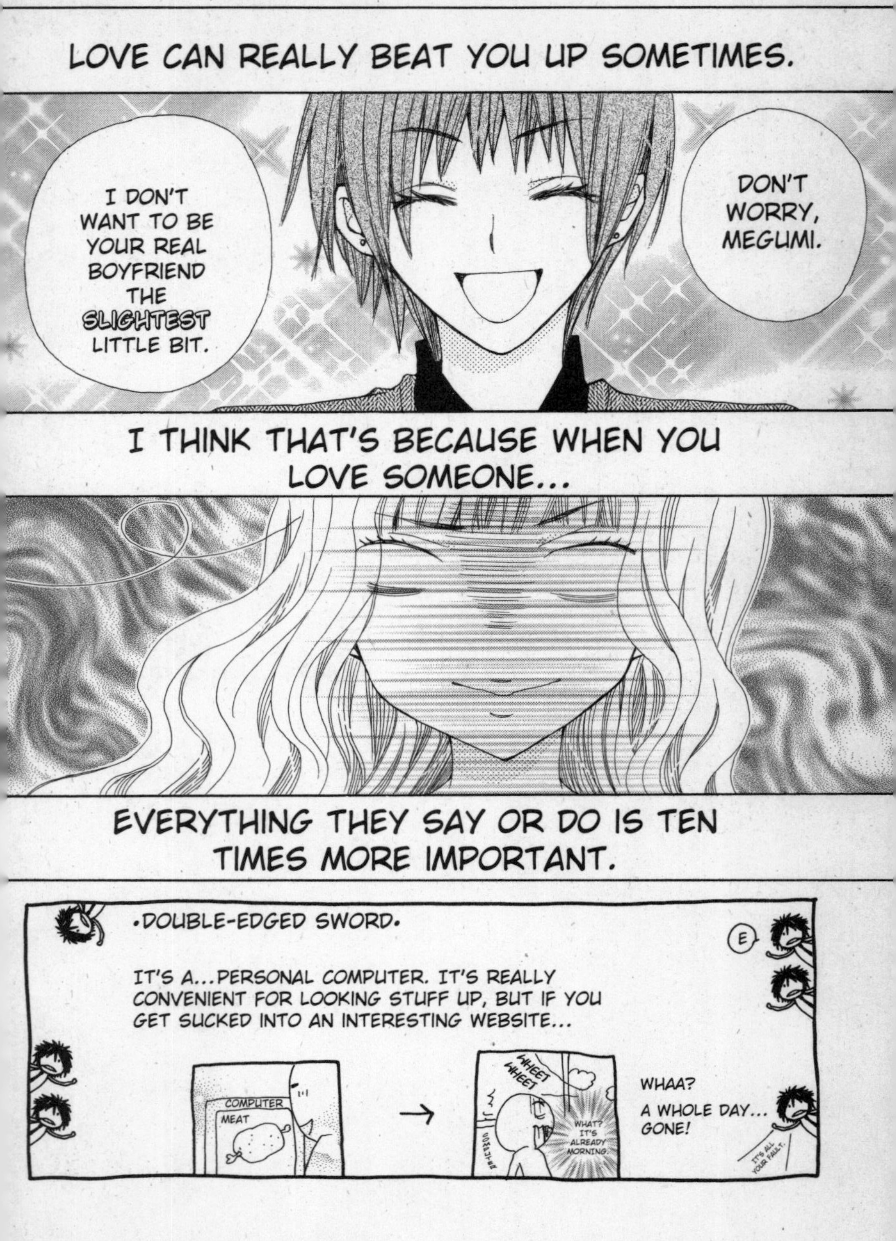
LOVE CAN REALLY BEAT YOU UP SOMETIMES.
DON'T WORRY, MEGUMI.
I DON'T WANT TO BE YOUR REAL BOYFRIEND THE SLIGHTEST LITTLE BIT.
I THINK THAT'S BECAUSE WHEN YOU LOVE SOMEONE...
EVERYTHING THEY SAY OR DO IS TEN TIMES MORE IMPORTANT.
•DOUBLE-EDGED SWORD•
E
IT'S A...PERSONAL COMPUTER. IT'S REALLY CONVENIENT FOR LOOKING STUFF UP, BUT IF YOU GET SUCKED INTO AN INTERESTING WEBSITE...
COMPUTER
MEAT
WHEET WHEET
WHAT? IT'S ALREADY MORNING.
WHAA?
A WHOLE DAY... GONE!
IT'S ALL YOUR FAULT.

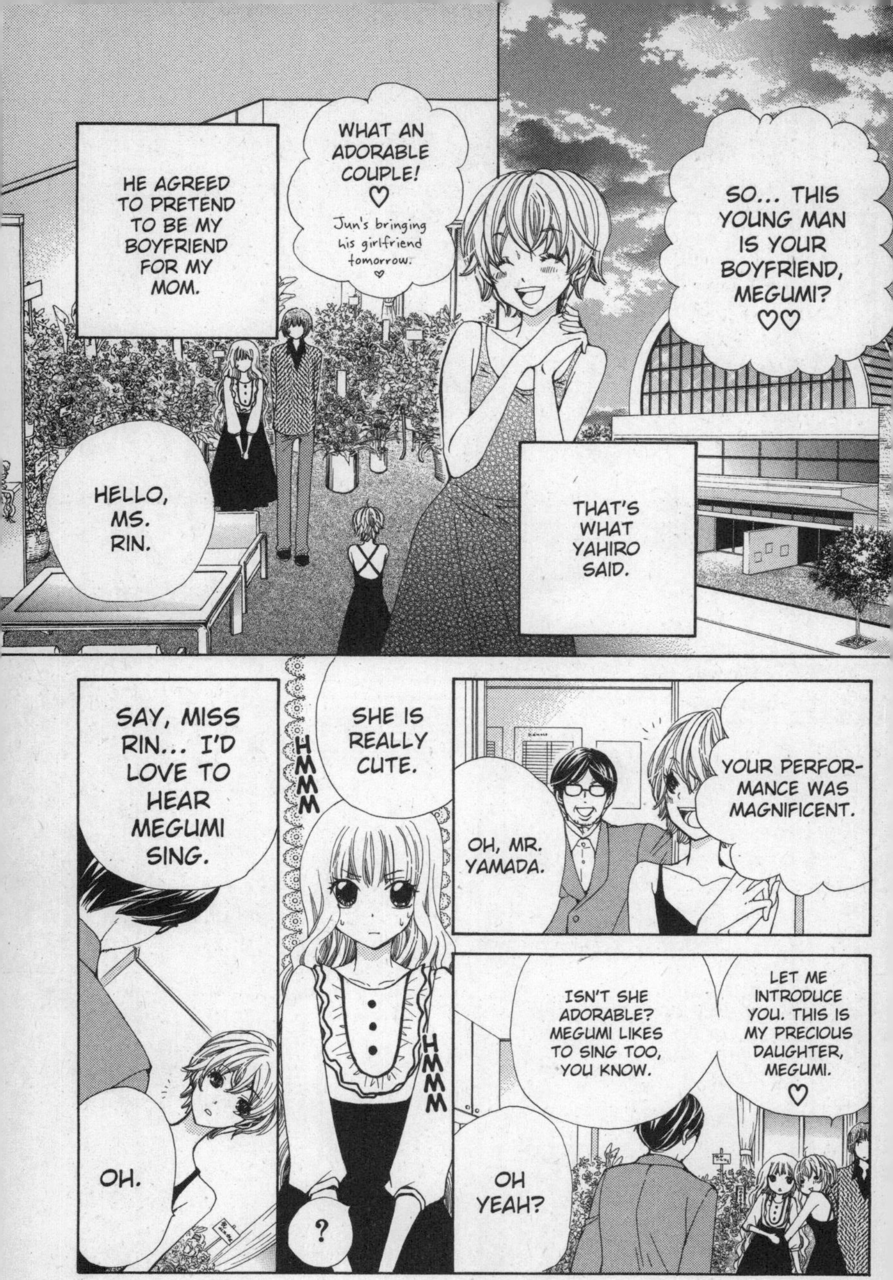

SO... THIS YOUNG MAN IS YOUR BOYFRIEND, MEGUMI? ♡♡
THAT'S WHAT YAHIRO SAID.
WHAT AN ADORABLE COUPLE! ♡
Jun's bringing his girlfriend tomorrow. ♡
HE AGREED TO PRETEND TO BE MY BOYFRIEND FOR MY MOM.
HELLO, MS. RIN.
YOUR PERFORMANCE WAS MAGNIFICENT.
OH, MR. YAMADA.
LET ME INTRODUCE YOU. THIS IS MY PRECIOUS DAUGHTER, MEGUMI. ♡
ISN'T SHE ADORABLE? MEGUMI LIKES TO SING TOO, YOU KNOW.
OH YEAH?
SHE IS REALLY CUTE.
HMMM
HMMM
?
SAY, MISS RIN... I'D LOVE TO HEAR MEGUMI SING.
OH.

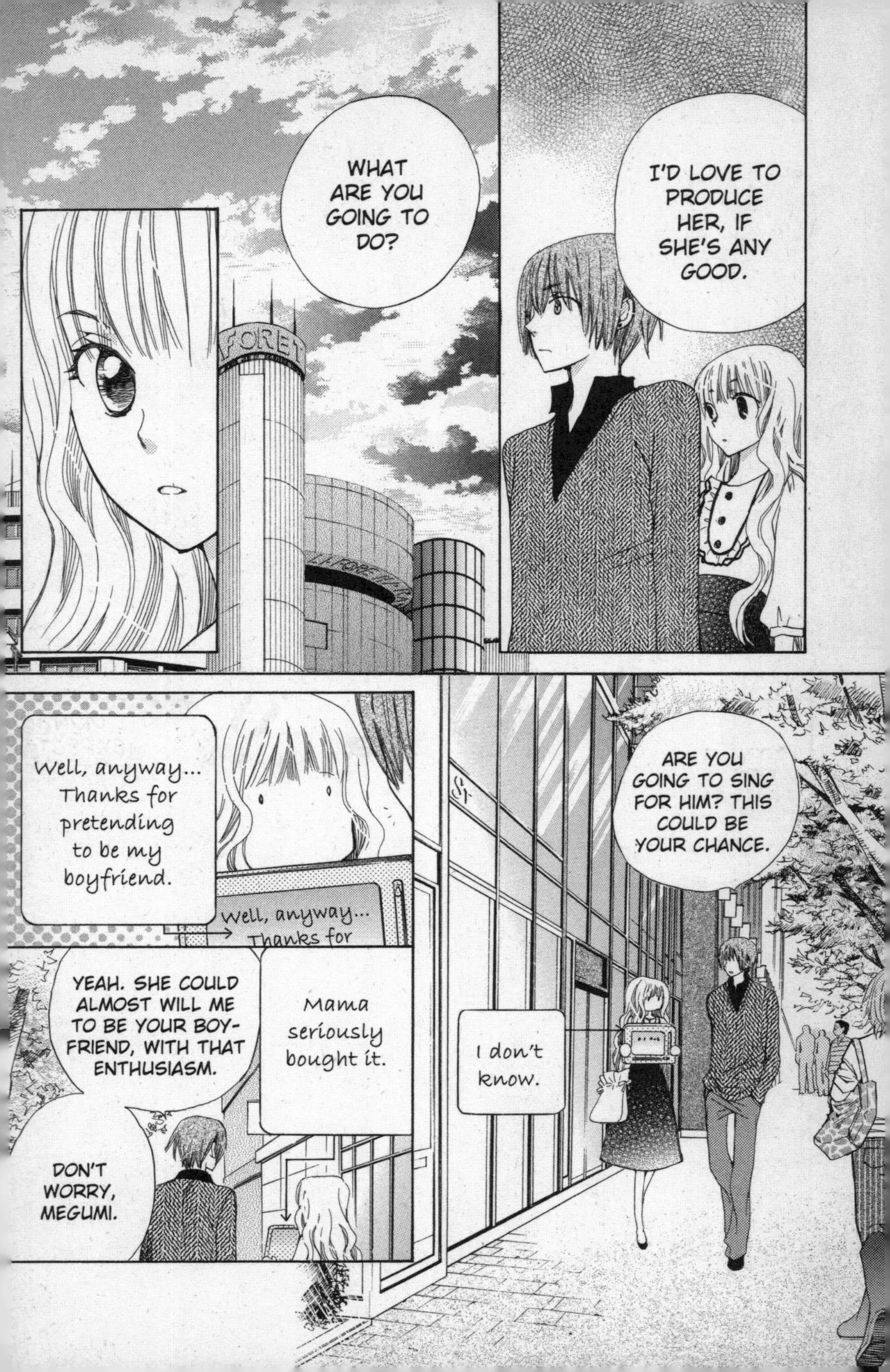

I'D LOVE TO PRODUCE HER, IF SHE'S ANY GOOD.
WHAT ARE YOU GOING TO DO?
ARE YOU GOING TO SING FOR HIM? THIS COULD BE YOUR CHANCE.
I don't know.
Well, anyway... Thanks for pretending to be my boyfriend.
Well, anyway... Thanks for
Mama seriously bought it.
YEAH. SHE COULD ALMOST WILL ME TO BE YOUR BOY-FRIEND, WITH THAT ENTHUSIASM.
DON'T WORRY, MEGUMI.

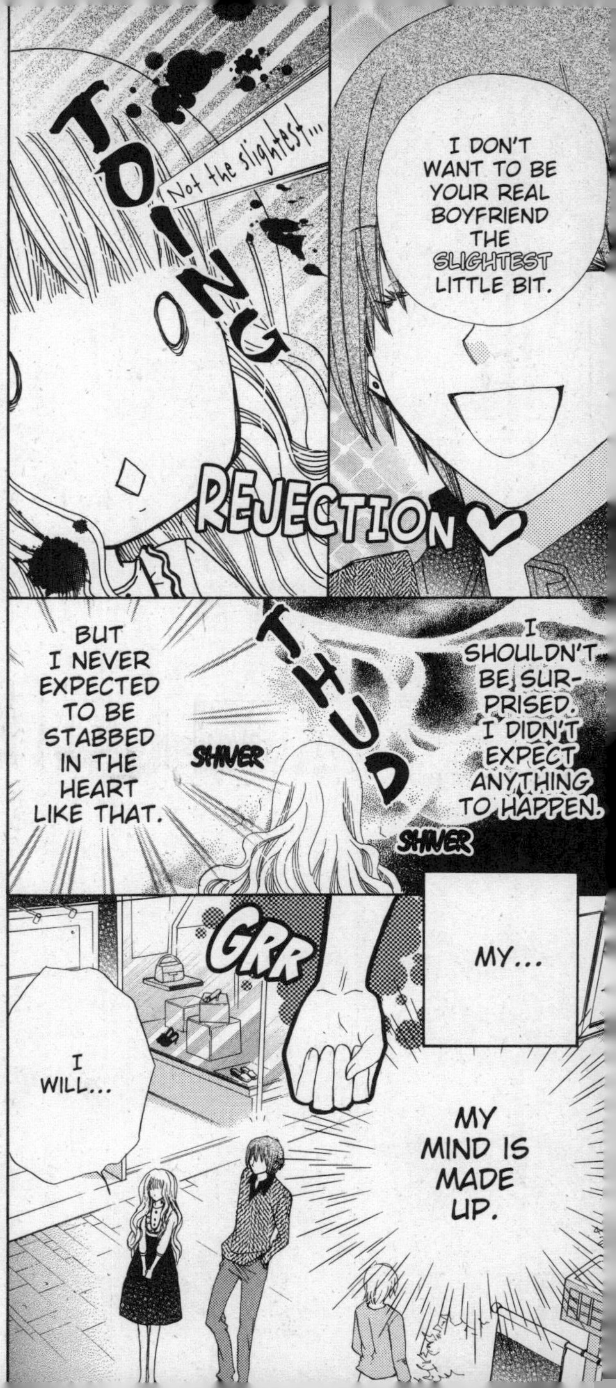
I DON'T WANT TO BE YOUR REAL BOYFRIEND THE SLIGHTEST LITTLE BIT.
REJECTION
TOING
Not the slightest...
I SHOULDN'T BE SUR-PRISED. I DIDN'T EXPECT ANYTHING TO HAPPEN.
THUD
SHIVER
SHIVER
BUT I NEVER EXPECTED TO BE STABBED IN THE HEART LIKE THAT.
MY...
GRR
MY MIND IS MADE UP.
I WILL...

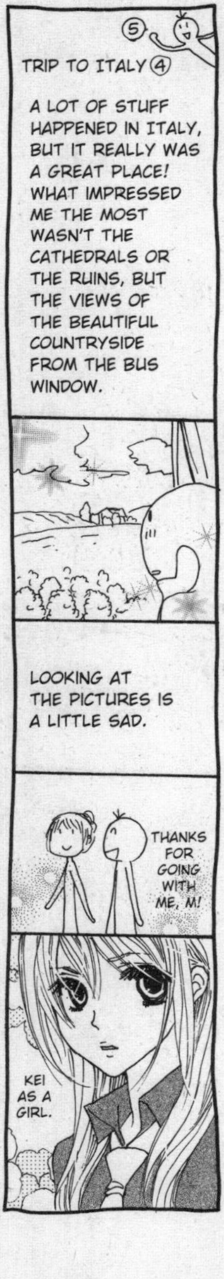
⑤
TRIP TO ITALY ④
A LOT OF STUFF HAPPENED IN ITALY, BUT IT REALLY WAS A GREAT PLACE! WHAT IMPRESSED ME THE MOST WASN'T THE CATHEDRALS OR THE RUINS, BUT THE VIEWS OF THE BEAUTIFUL COUNTRYSIDE FROM THE BUS WINDOW.
LOOKING AT THE PICTURES IS A LITTLE SAD.
THANKS FOR GOING WITH ME, M!
KEI AS A GIRL.

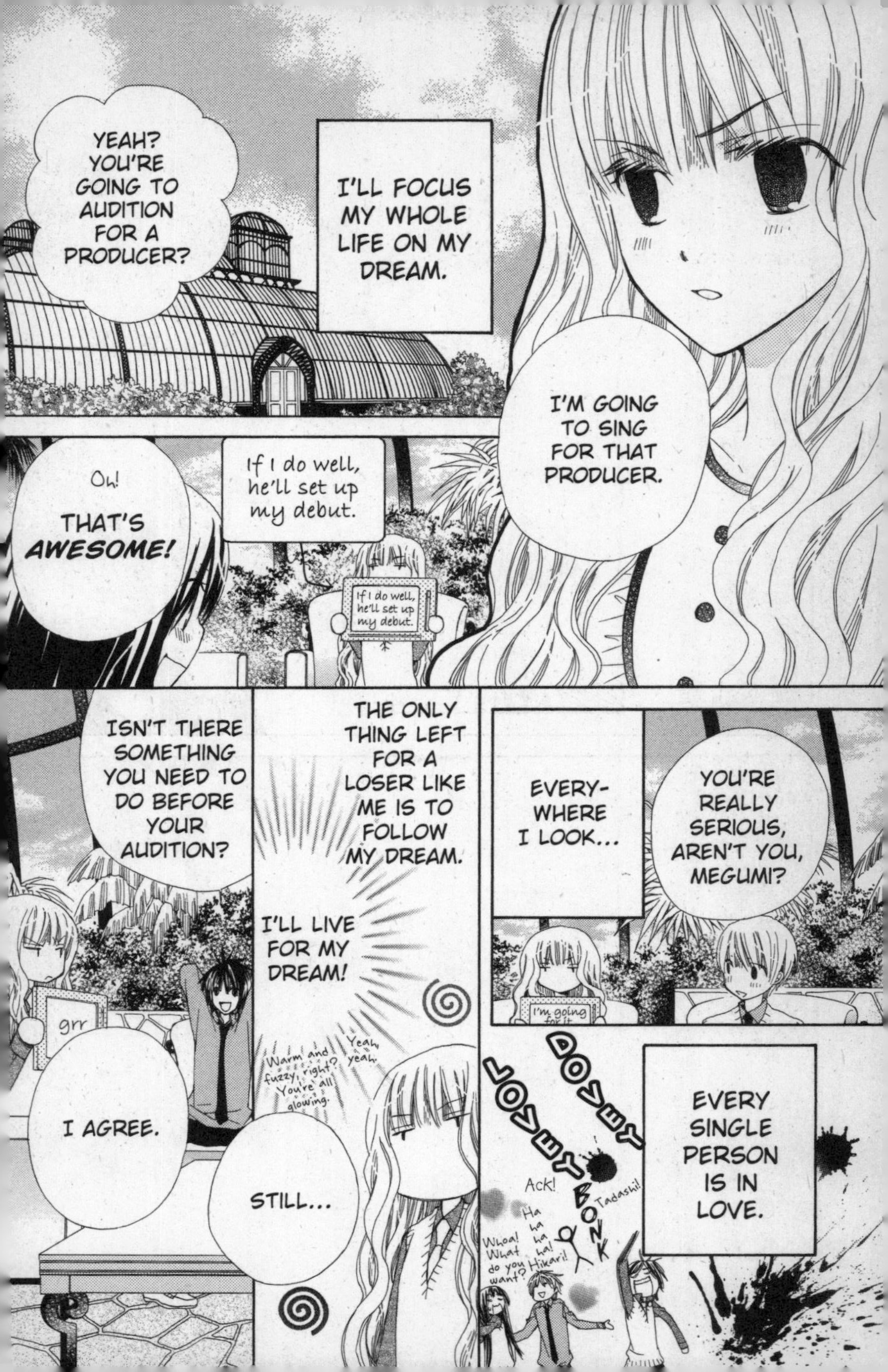
I'M GOING TO SING FOR THAT PRODUCER.
I'LL FOCUS MY WHOLE LIFE ON MY DREAM.
YEAH? YOU'RE GOING TO AUDITION FOR A PRODUCER?
If I do well, he'll set up my debut.
If I do well, he'll set up my debut.
Oh!
THAT'S *AWESOME!*
EVERY-WHERE I LOOK...
YOU'RE REALLY SERIOUS, AREN'T YOU, MEGUMI?
I'm going for it
EVERY SINGLE PERSON IS IN LOVE.
DOVEY
LOVEY
BONK
Tadashi!
Ack!
Ha ha ha ha! Hikari!
Whoa! What do you want?
THE ONLY THING LEFT FOR A LOSER LIKE ME IS TO FOLLOW MY DREAM.
I'LL LIVE FOR MY DREAM!
Yeah, yeah.
Warm and fuzzy, right? You're all glowing.
STILL...
ISN'T THERE SOMETHING YOU NEED TO DO BEFORE YOUR AUDITION?
grr
I AGREE.

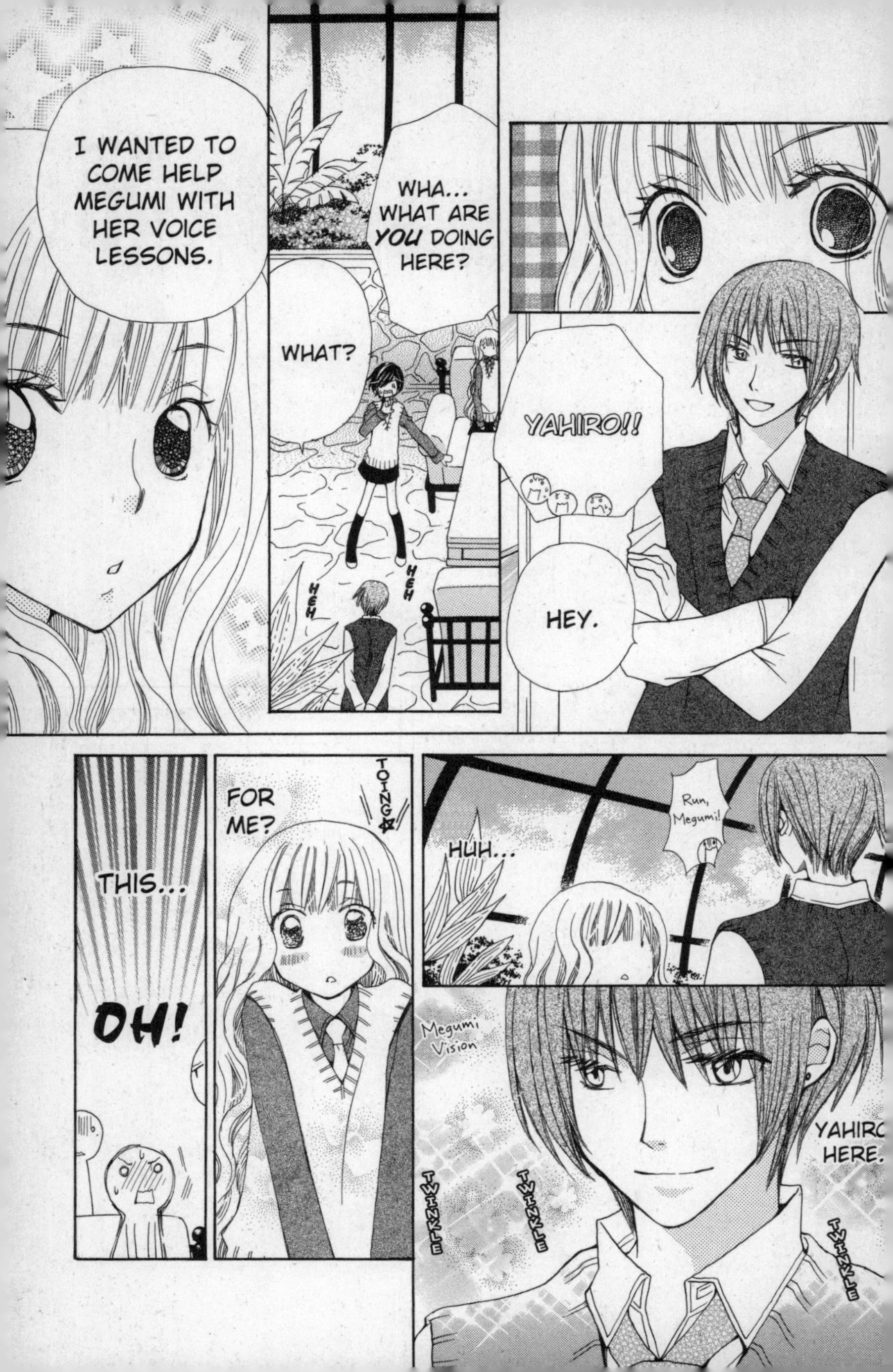
YAHIRO!!
HEY.
WHAT?
WHA... WHAT ARE YOU DOING HERE?
HEH
HEH
I WANTED TO COME HELP MEGUMI WITH HER VOICE LESSONS.
Run, Megumi!
HUH...
YAHIRO HERE.
TWINKLE
TWINKLE
TWINKLE
Megumi Vision
FOR ME?
TOING☆
THIS...
OH!

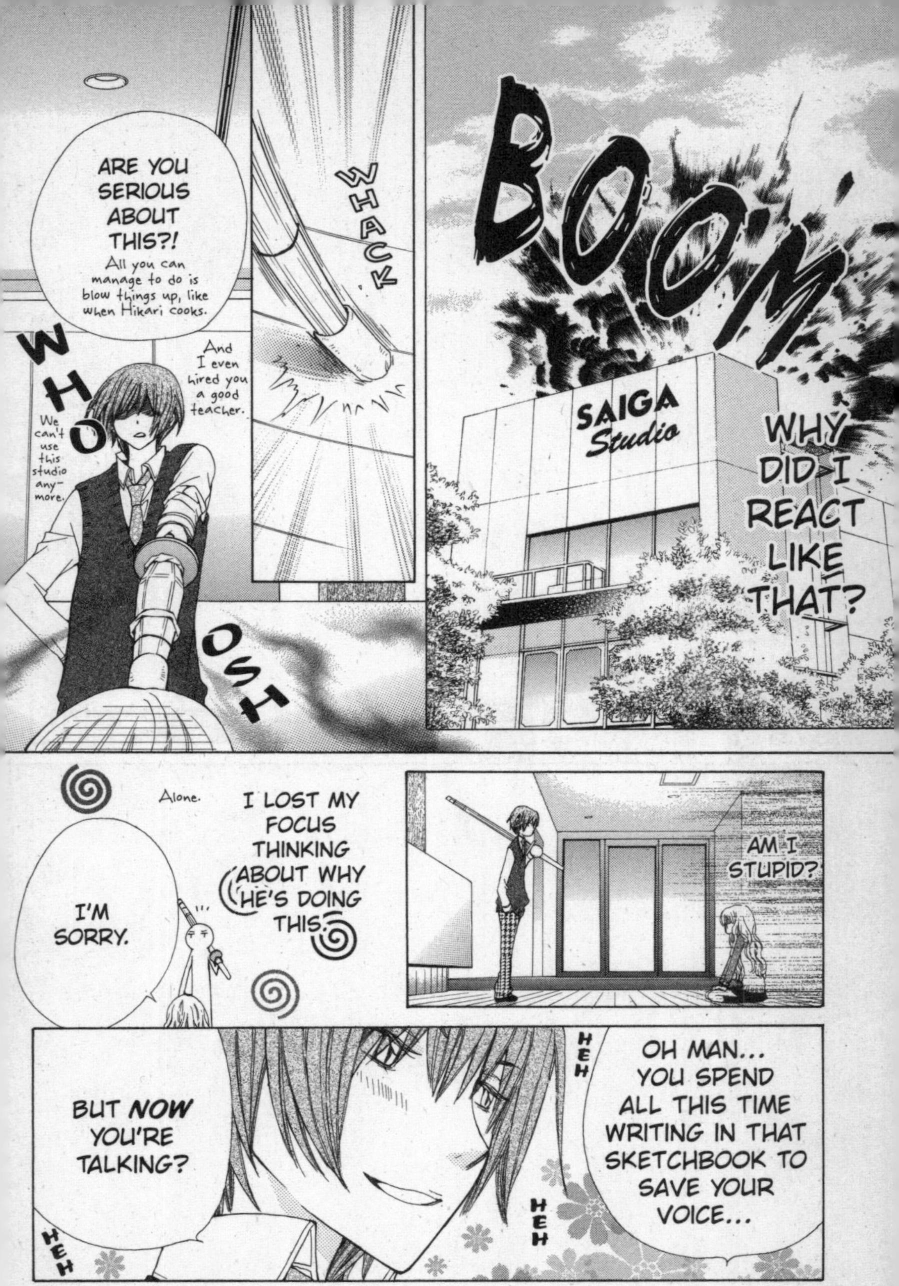
BOOM
SAIGA Studio
WHY DID I REACT LIKE THAT?
WHACK
ARE YOU SERIOUS ABOUT THIS?! All you can manage to do is blow things up, like when Hikari cooks.
And I even hired you a good teacher.
We can't use this studio anymore.
WHOOSH
AM I STUPID?
I LOST MY FOCUS THINKING ABOUT WHY HE'S DOING THIS.
Alone.
I'M SORRY.
OH MAN... YOU SPEND ALL THIS TIME WRITING IN THAT SKETCHBOOK TO SAVE YOUR VOICE...
HEH
HEH
BUT NOW YOU'RE TALKING?
HEH

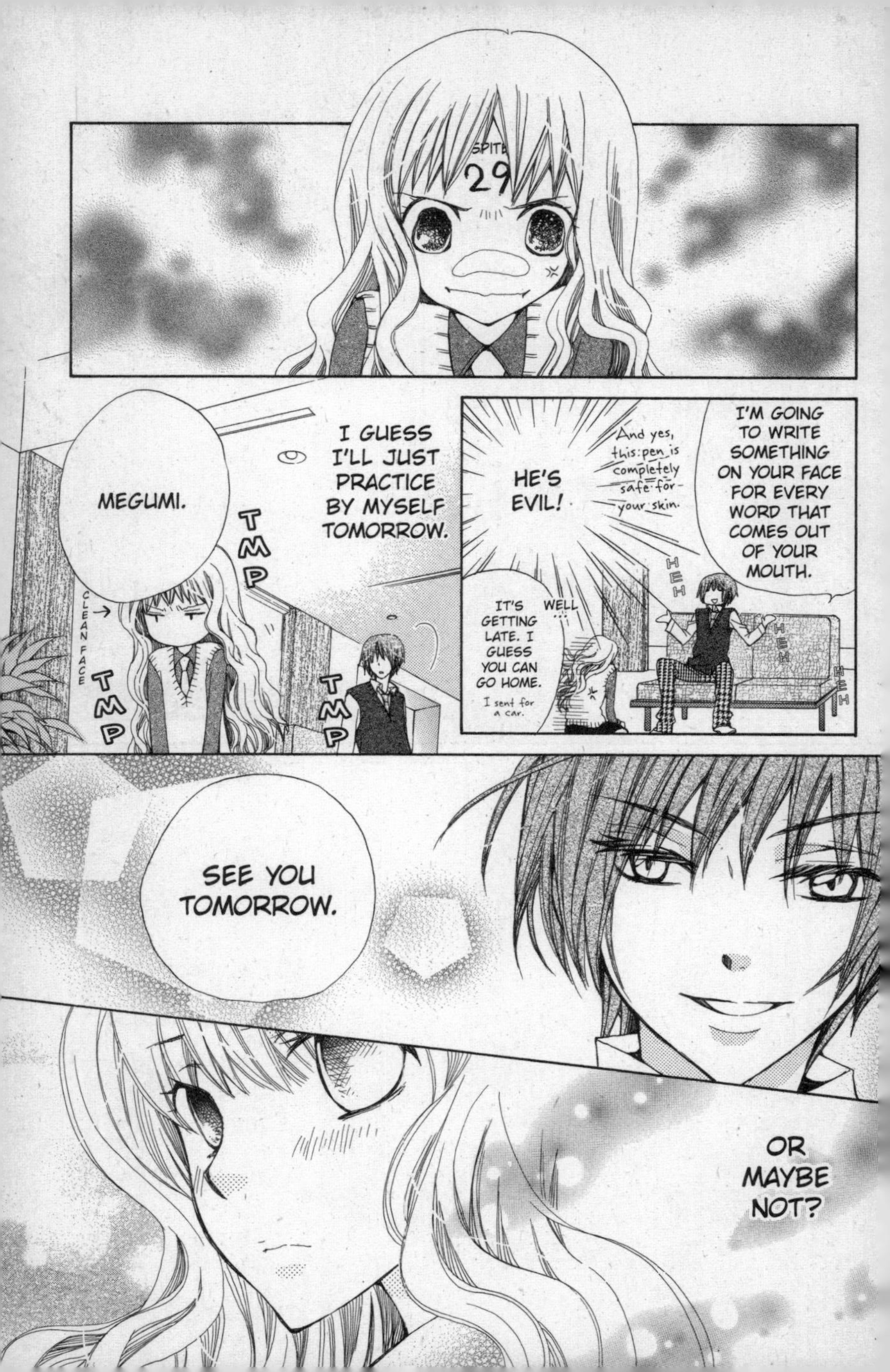
SPITE
29
I'M GOING TO WRITE SOMETHING ON YOUR FACE FOR EVERY WORD THAT COMES OUT OF YOUR MOUTH.
HEH HEH HEH
HE'S EVIL!
And yes, this pen is completely safe for your skin.
WELL...
IT'S GETTING LATE. I GUESS YOU CAN GO HOME.
I sent for a car.
I GUESS I'LL JUST PRACTICE BY MYSELF TOMORROW.
MEGUMI.
TMP TMP
CLEAN FACE
TMP
SEE YOU TOMORROW.
OR MAYBE NOT?

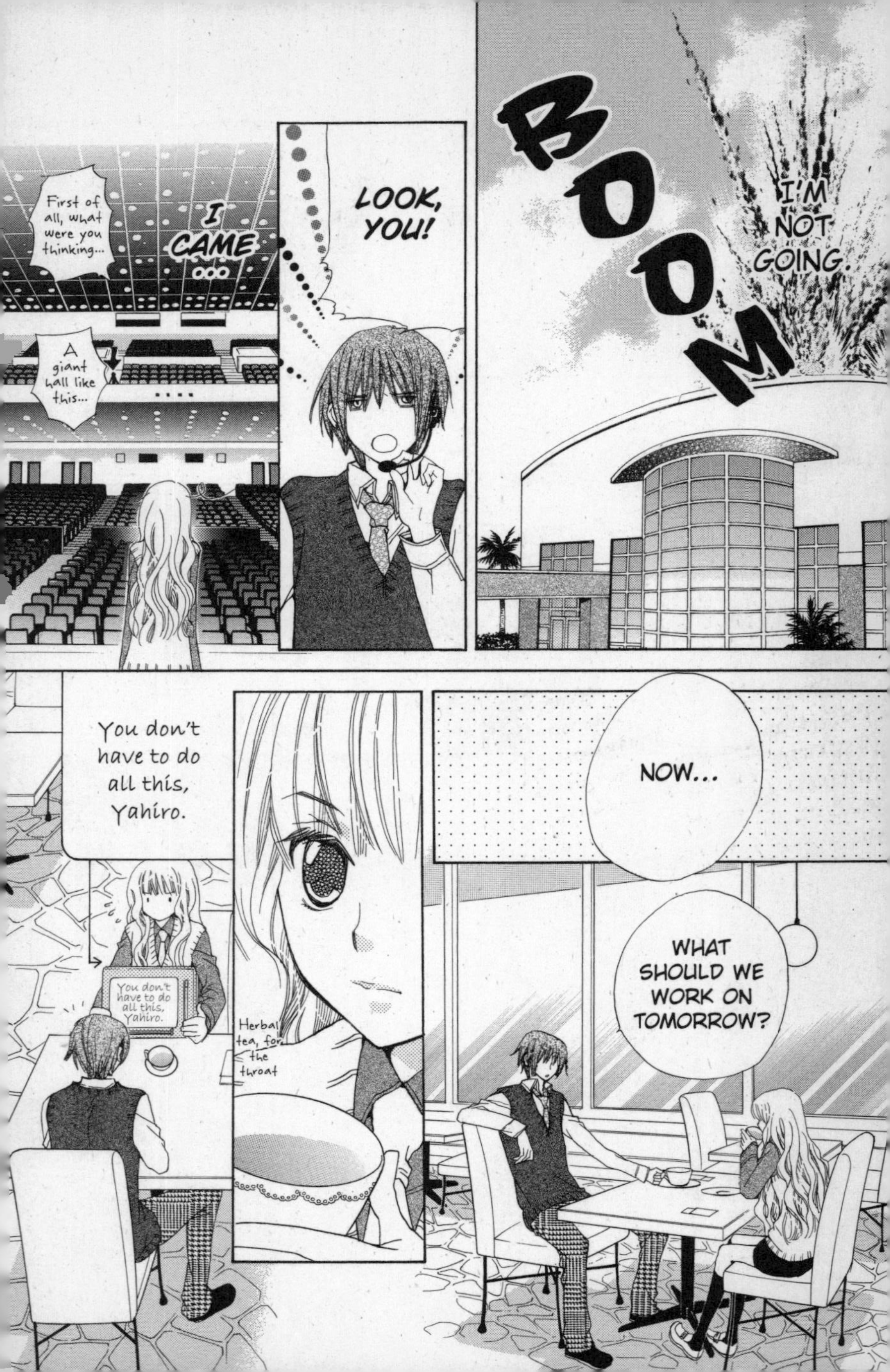
BOOM
I'M NOT GOING.
LOOK, YOU!
I CAME...
First of all, what were you thinking...
A giant hall like this...
NOW...
WHAT SHOULD WE WORK ON TOMORROW?
Herbal tea, for the throat
You don't have to do all this, Yahiro.
You don't have to do all this, Yahiro.

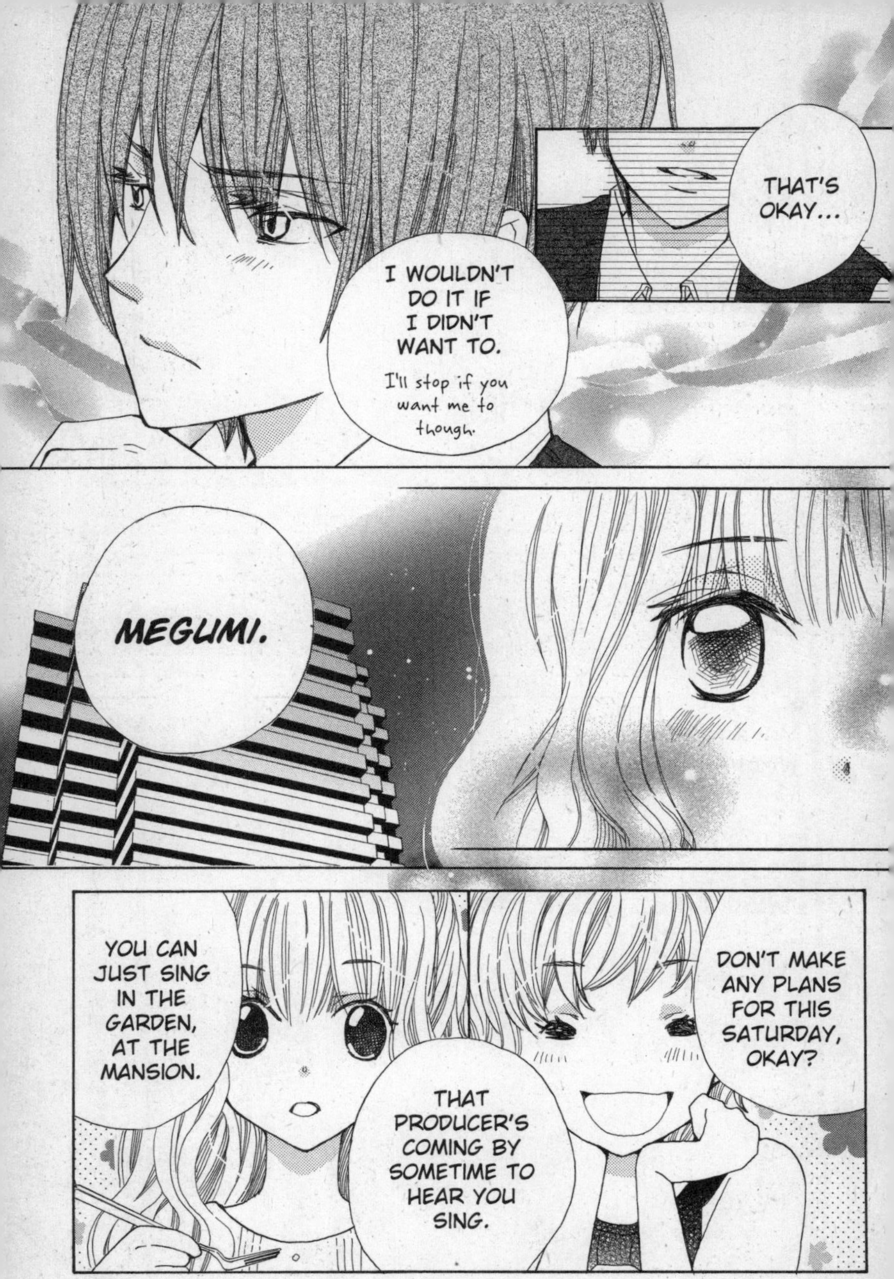
THAT'S OKAY...
I WOULDN'T DO IT IF I DIDN'T WANT TO.
I'll stop if you want me to though.
MEGUMI.
DON'T MAKE ANY PLANS FOR THIS SATURDAY, OKAY?
THAT PRODUCER'S COMING BY SOMETIME TO HEAR YOU SING.
YOU CAN JUST SING IN THE GARDEN, AT THE MANSION.

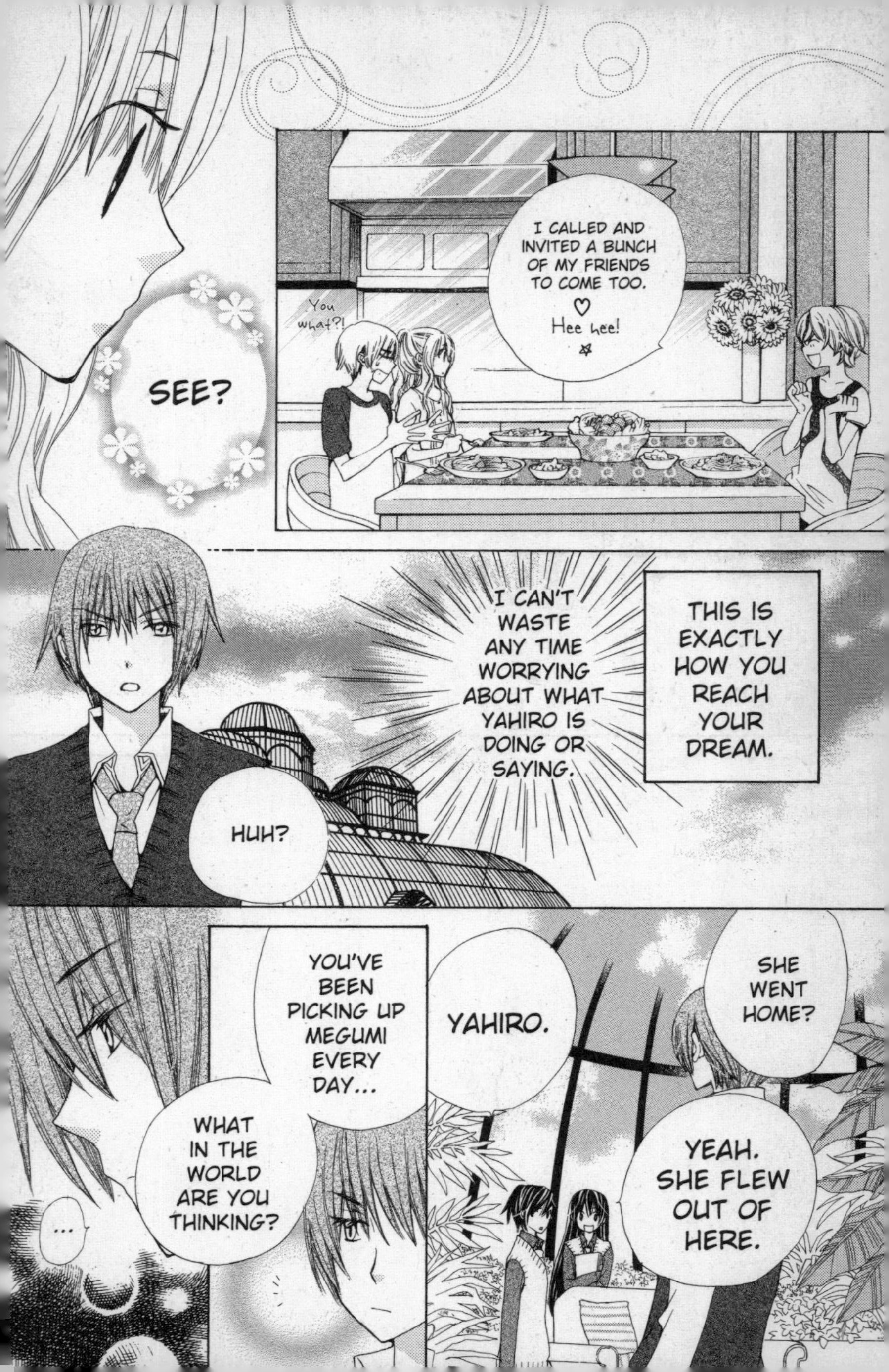
I CALLED AND INVITED A BUNCH OF MY FRIENDS TO COME TOO. ♡ Hee hee! ☆
You what?!
SEE?
THIS IS EXACTLY HOW YOU REACH YOUR DREAM.
I CAN'T WASTE ANY TIME WORRYING ABOUT WHAT YAHIRO IS DOING OR SAYING.
HUH?
SHE WENT HOME?
YEAH. SHE FLEW OUT OF HERE.
YAHIRO.
YOU'VE BEEN PICKING UP MEGUMI EVERY DAY...
WHAT IN THE WORLD ARE YOU THINKING?
...

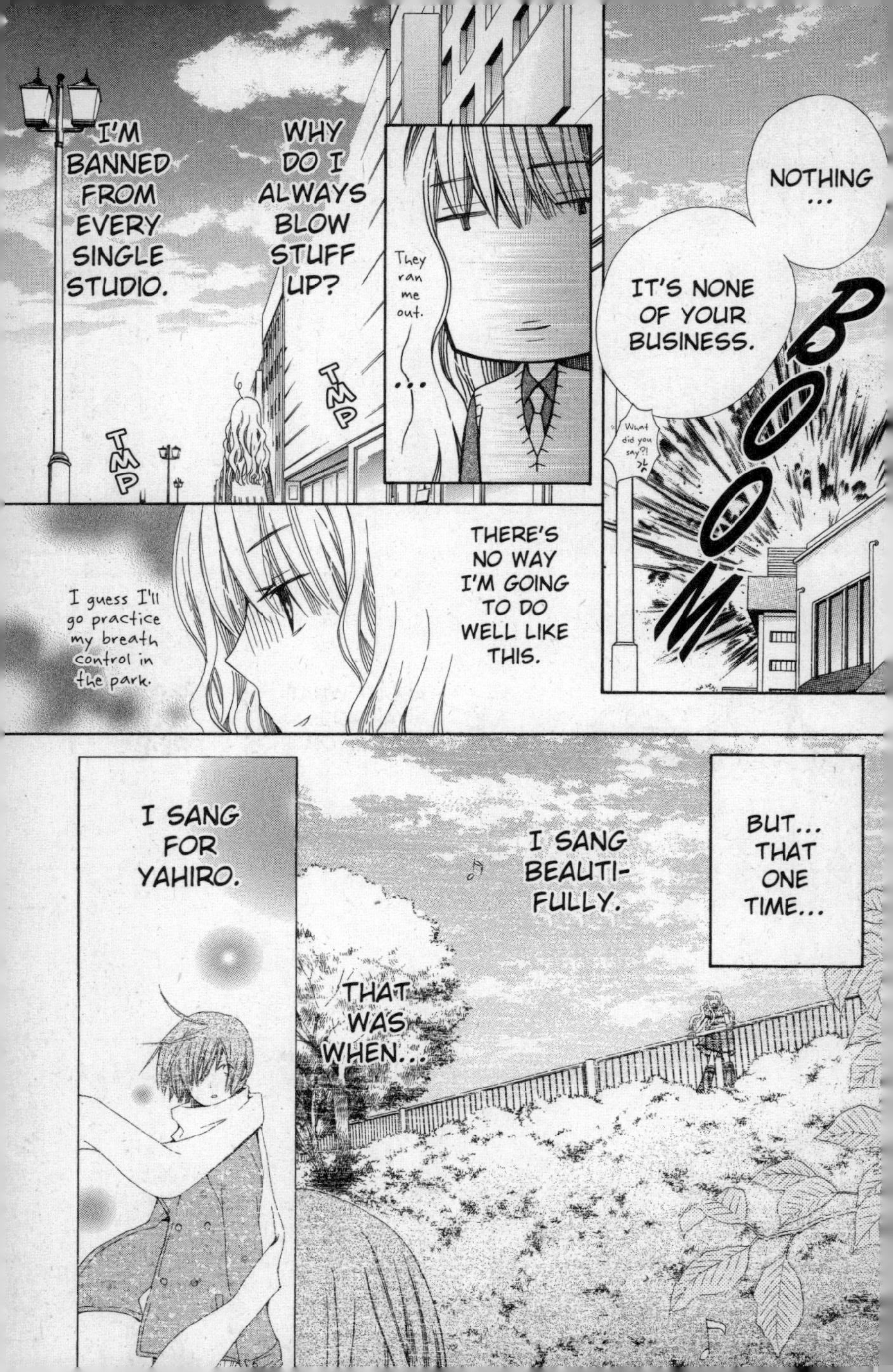
NOTHING ...
IT'S NONE OF YOUR BUSINESS.
What did you say?!
BOOM
They ran me out.
...
TMP
I'M BANNED FROM EVERY SINGLE STUDIO.
WHY DO I ALWAYS BLOW STUFF UP?
TMP
THERE'S NO WAY I'M GOING TO DO WELL LIKE THIS.
I guess I'll go practice my breath control in the park.
BUT... THAT ONE TIME...
I SANG BEAUTI-FULLY.
I SANG FOR YAHIRO.
THAT WAS WHEN...

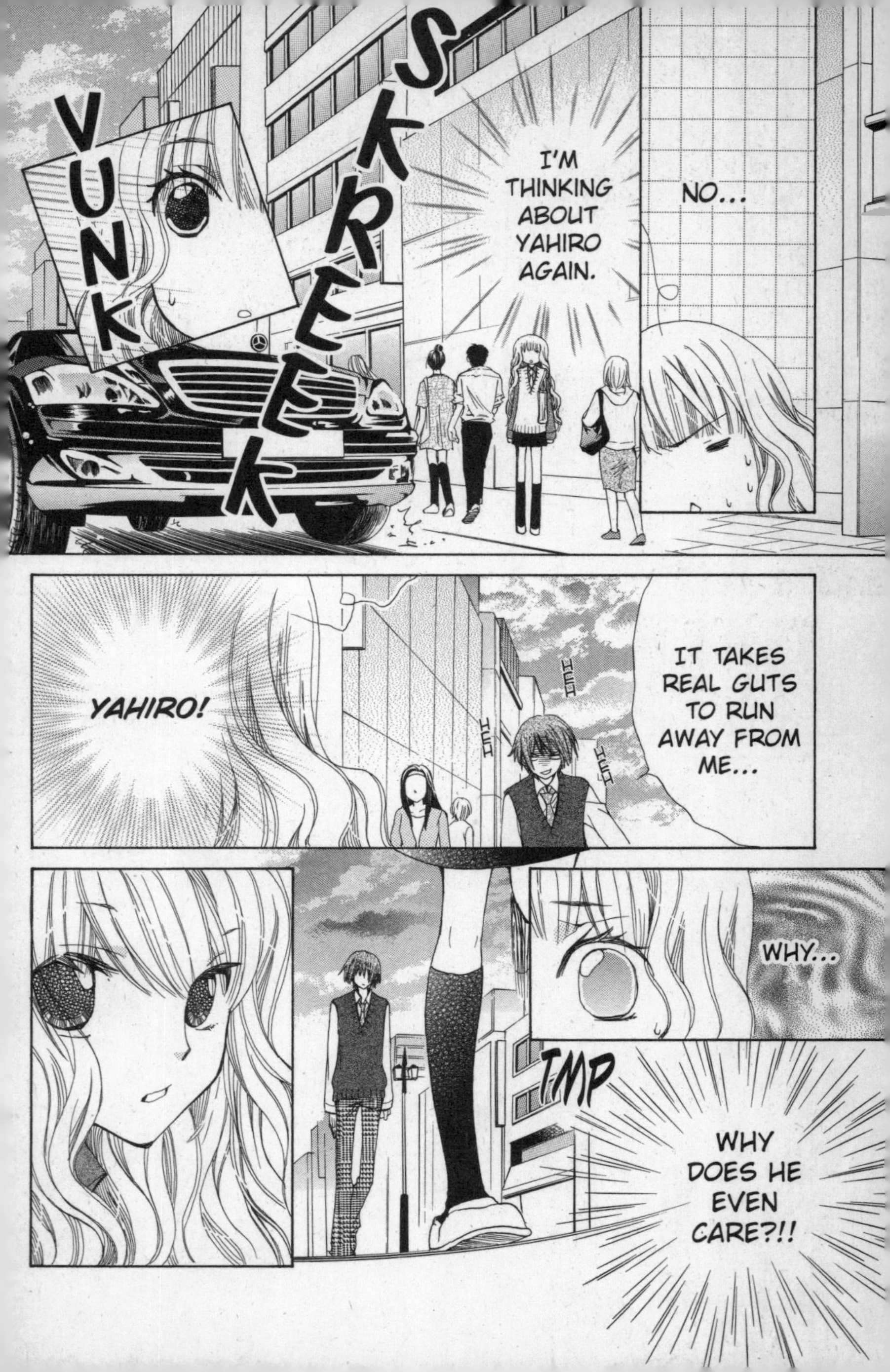
NO...
I'M THINKING ABOUT YAHIRO AGAIN.
SKREEEK
VUNK
IT TAKES REAL GUTS TO RUN AWAY FROM ME...
HEH
HEH
HEH
YAHIRO!
WHY...
TMP
WHY DOES HE EVEN CARE?!!

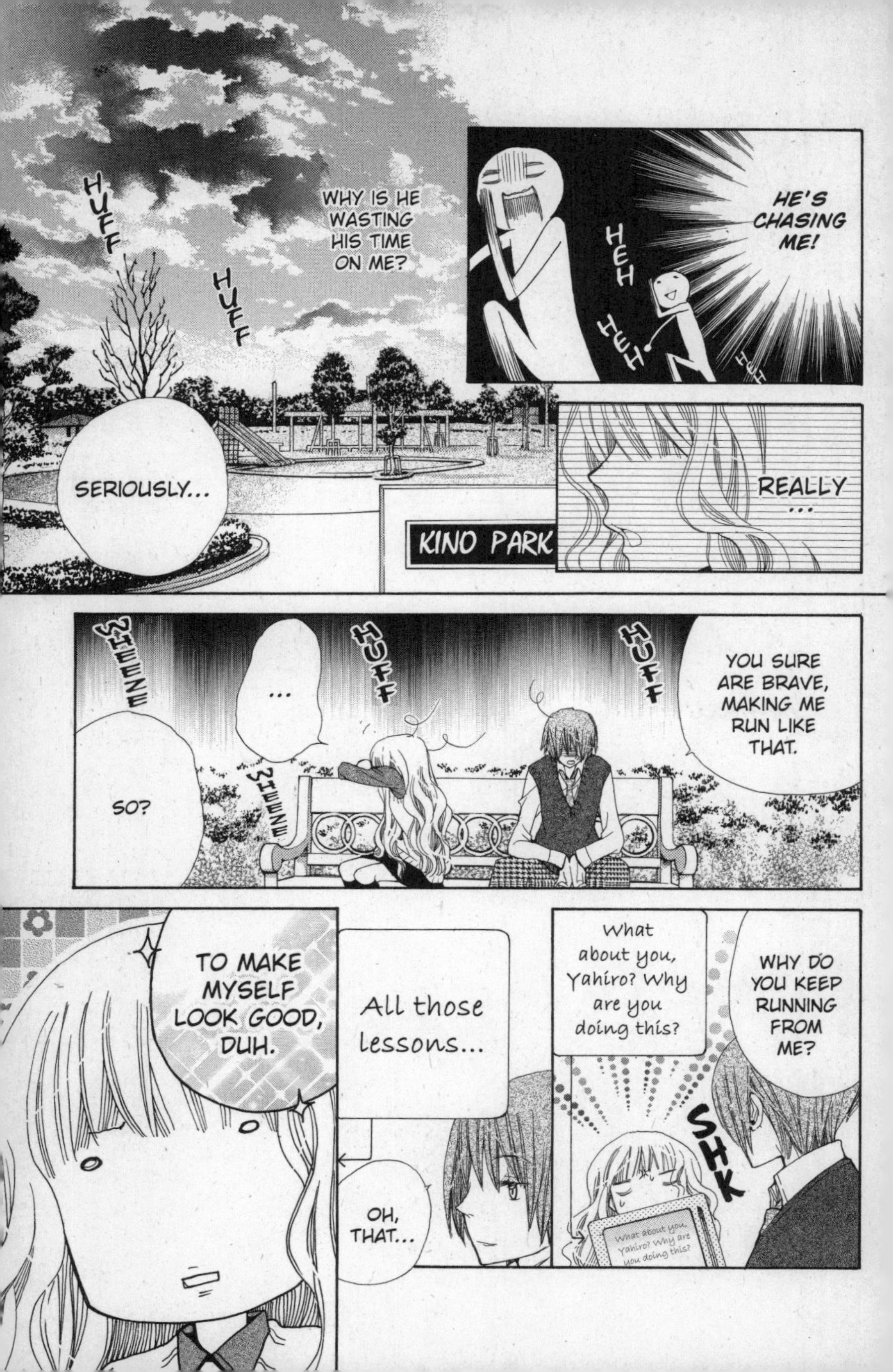
HE'S CHASING ME!
HEH HEH
HEH
WHY IS HE WASTING HIS TIME ON ME?
HUFF
HUFF
REALLY...
KINO PARK
SERIOUSLY...
YOU SURE ARE BRAVE, MAKING ME RUN LIKE THAT.
HUFF
HUFF
...
WHEEZE
WHEEZE
SO?
WHY DO YOU KEEP RUNNING FROM ME?
SHK
What about you, Yahiro? Why are you doing this?
What about you, Yahiro? Why are you doing this?
OH, THAT...
All those lessons...
TO MAKE MYSELF LOOK GOOD, DUH.

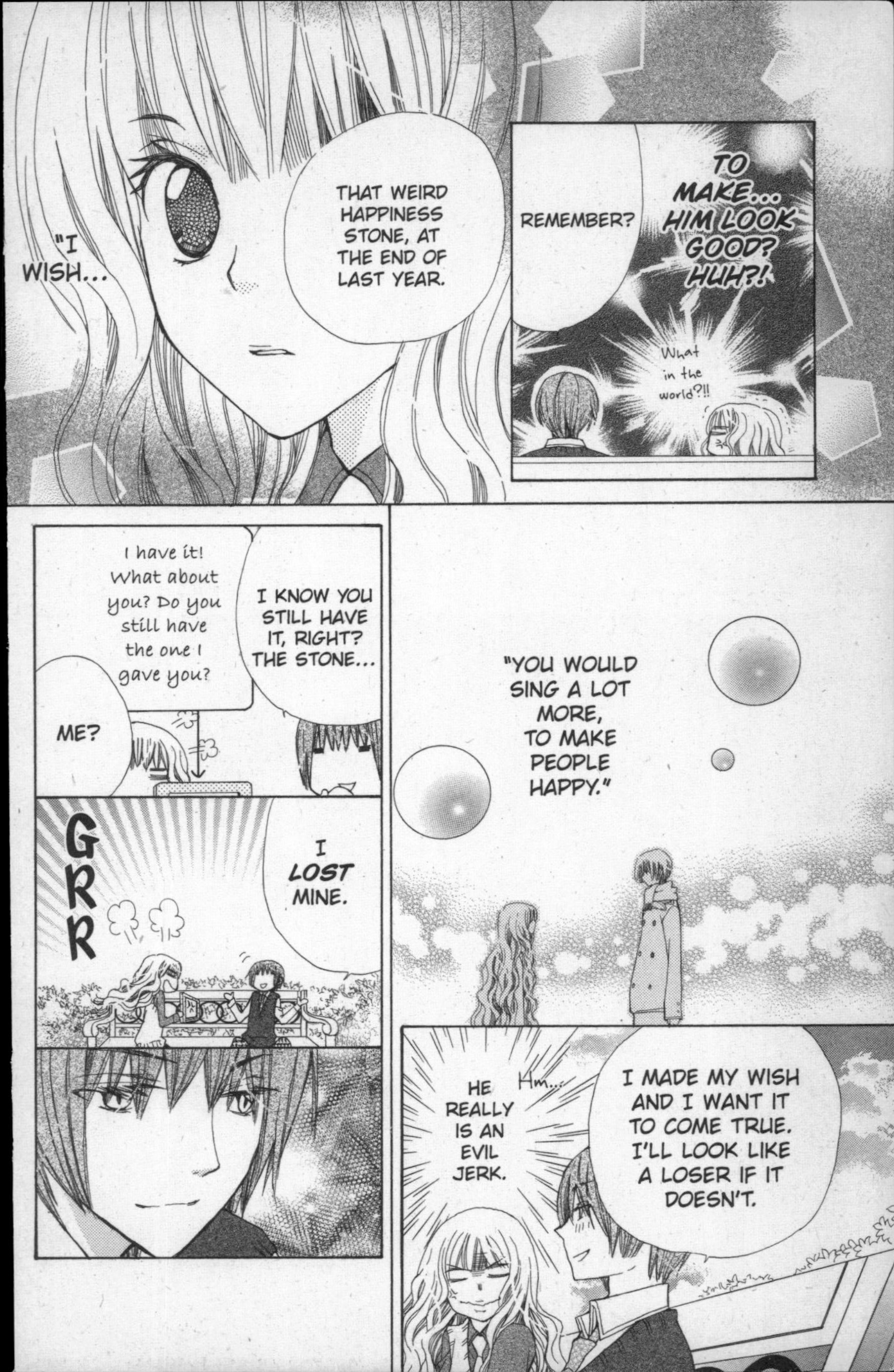
REMEMBER?
TO MAKE... HIM LOOK GOOD? HUH?!
What in the world?!!
THAT WEIRD HAPPINESS STONE, AT THE END OF LAST YEAR.
"I WISH...
"YOU WOULD SING A LOT MORE, TO MAKE PEOPLE HAPPY."
I MADE MY WISH AND I WANT IT TO COME TRUE. I'LL LOOK LIKE A LOSER IF IT DOESN'T.
Hm...
HE REALLY IS AN EVIL JERK.
I KNOW YOU STILL HAVE IT, RIGHT? THE STONE...
I have it! What about you? Do you still have the one I gave you?
ME?
I LOST MINE.
GRR

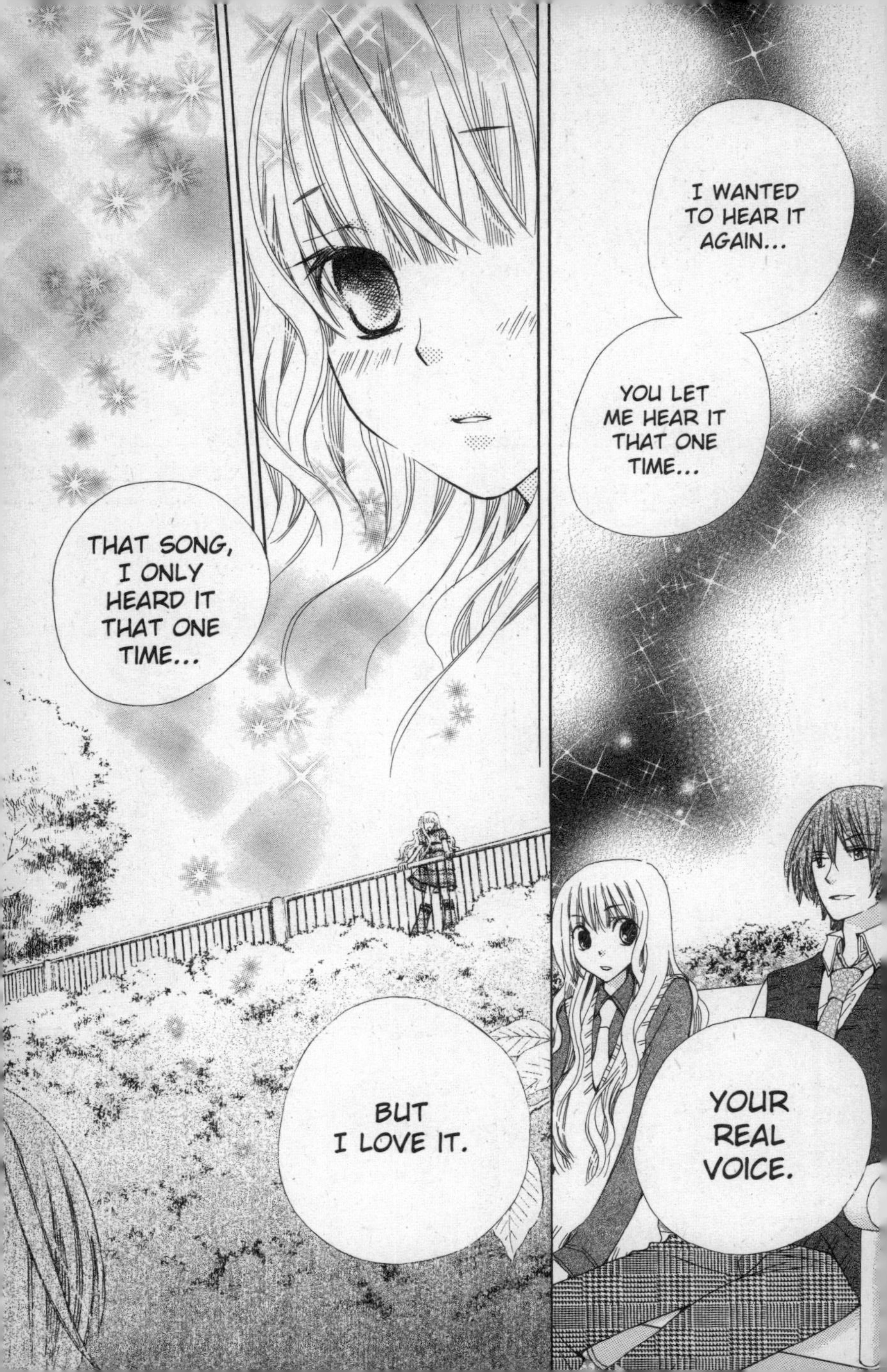
I WANTED TO HEAR IT AGAIN...
YOU LET ME HEAR IT THAT ONE TIME...
YOUR REAL VOICE.
THAT SONG, I ONLY HEARD IT THAT ONE TIME...
BUT I LOVE IT.

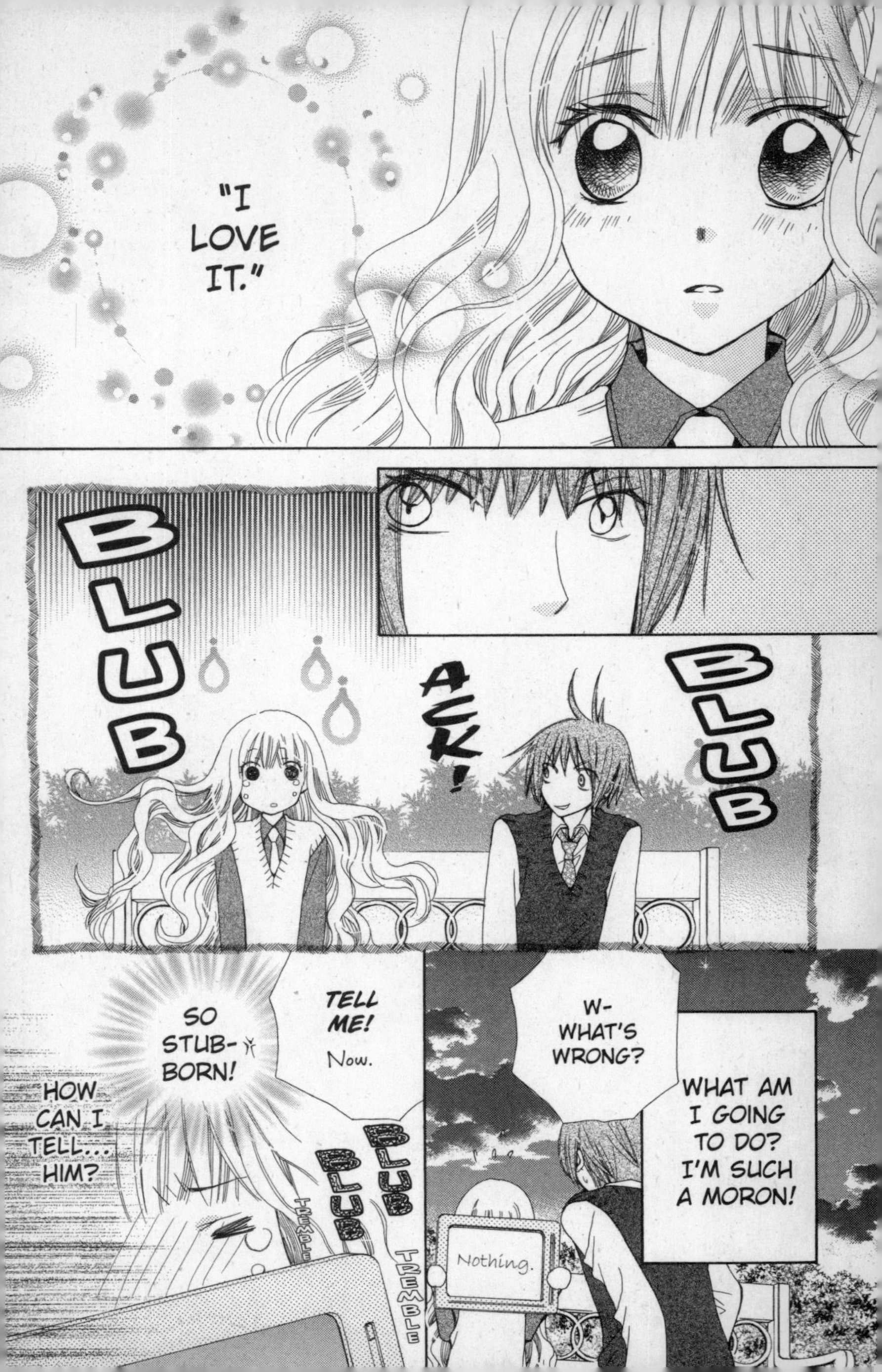
"I LOVE IT."
BLUB
ACK!
BLUB
W- WHAT'S WRONG?
WHAT AM I GOING TO DO? I'M SUCH A MORON!
Nothing.
TELL ME!
Now.
SO STUBBORN!
BLUB
BLUB
TREMBLE
TREMBLE
HOW CAN I TELL... HIM?

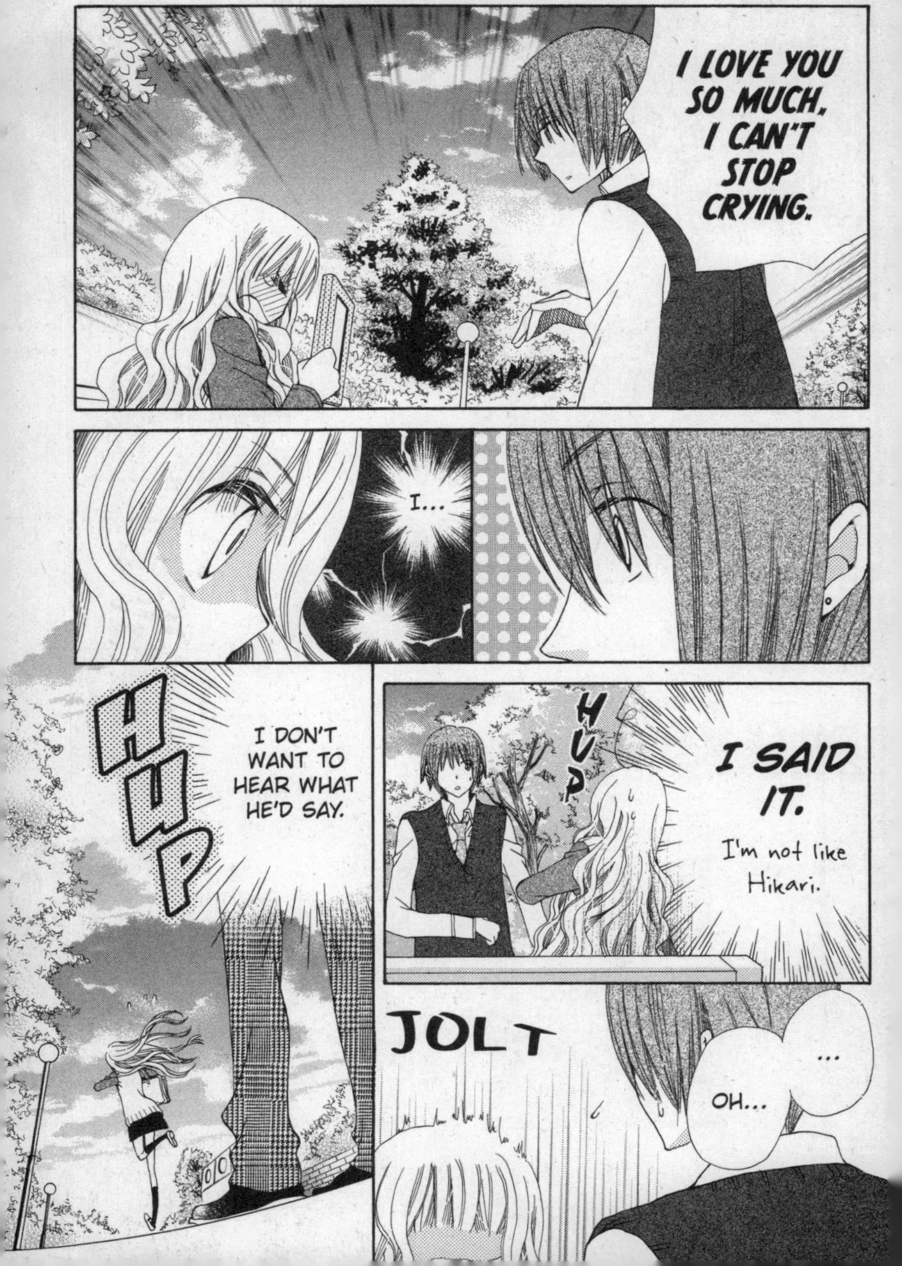
I LOVE YOU SO MUCH, I CAN'T STOP CRYING.
I...
I SAID IT.
HUP
I'm not like Hikari.
JOLT
...
OH...
HUP
I DON'T WANT TO HEAR WHAT HE'D SAY.

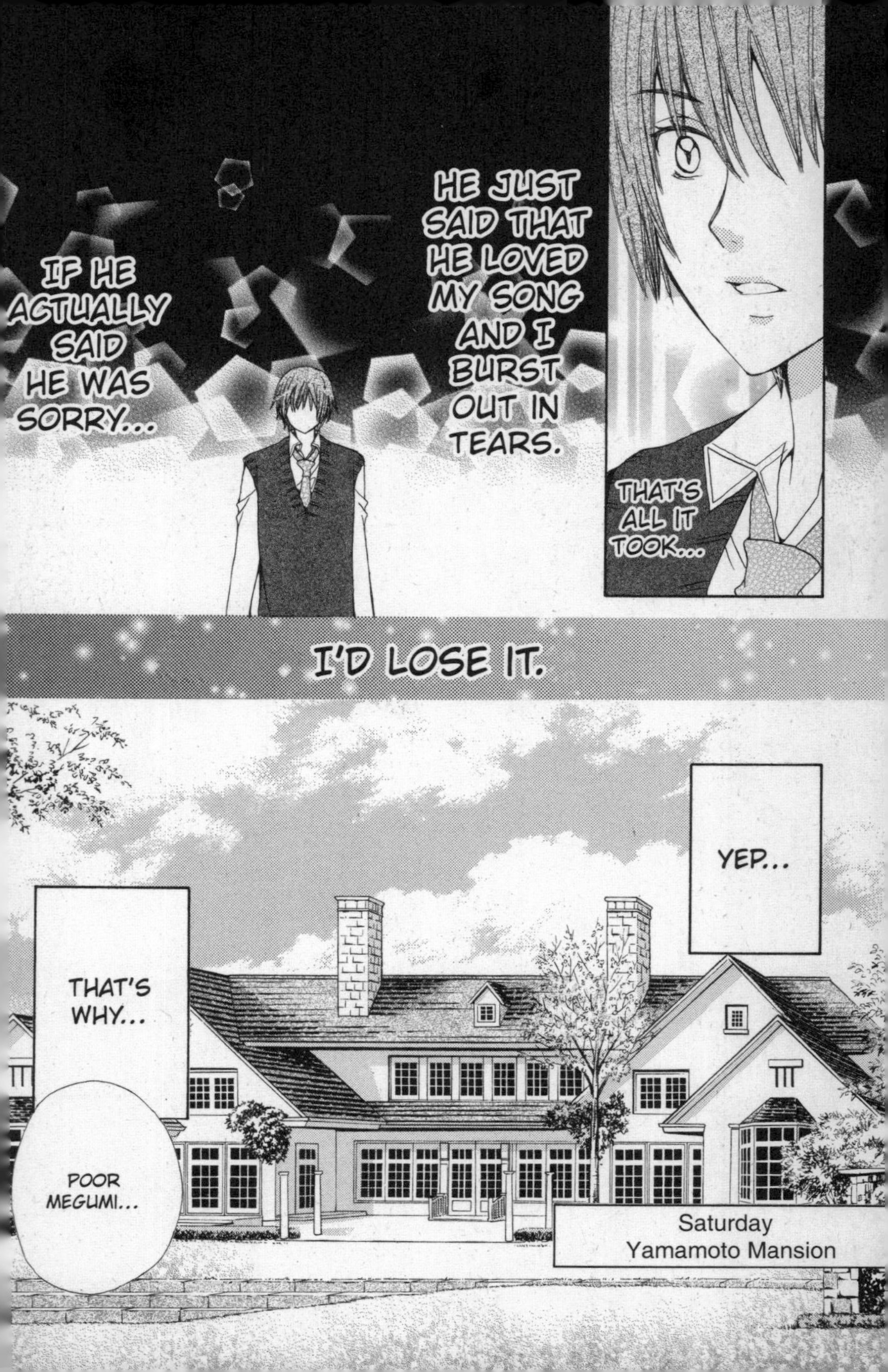
HE JUST SAID THAT HE LOVED MY SONG AND I BURST OUT IN TEARS.
THAT'S ALL IT TOOK...
IF HE ACTUALLY SAID HE WAS SORRY...
I'D LOSE IT.
YEP...
THAT'S WHY...
POOR MEGUMI...
Saturday
Yamamoto Mansion

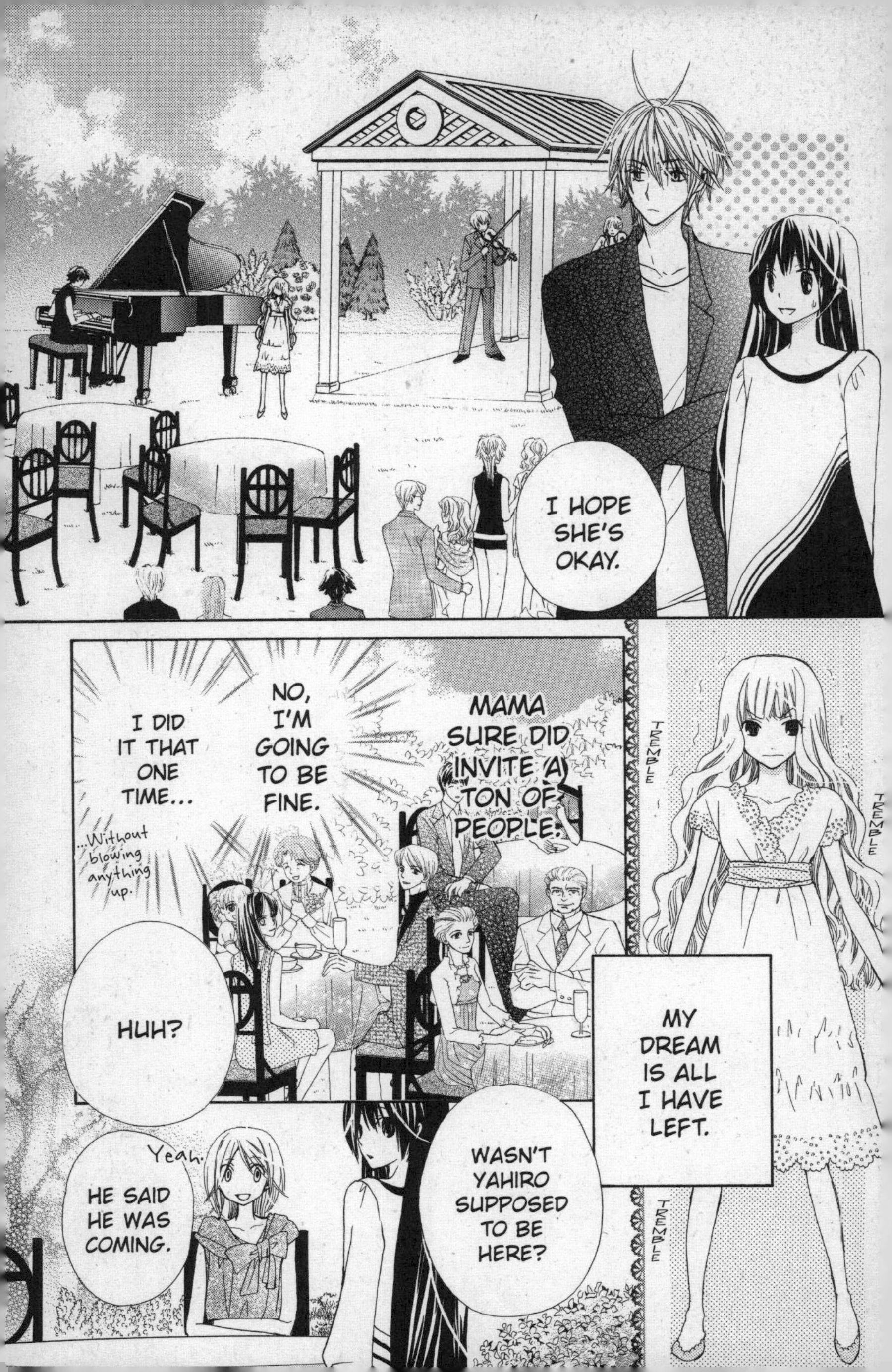
I HOPE SHE'S OKAY.
TREMBLE
TREMBLE
MY DREAM IS ALL I HAVE LEFT.
TREMBLE
MAMA SURE DID INVITE A TON OF PEOPLE.
NO, I'M GOING TO BE FINE.
I DID IT THAT ONE TIME...
...Without blowing anything up.
HUH?
WASN'T YAHIRO SUPPOSED TO BE HERE?
Yeah.
HE SAID HE WAS COMING.

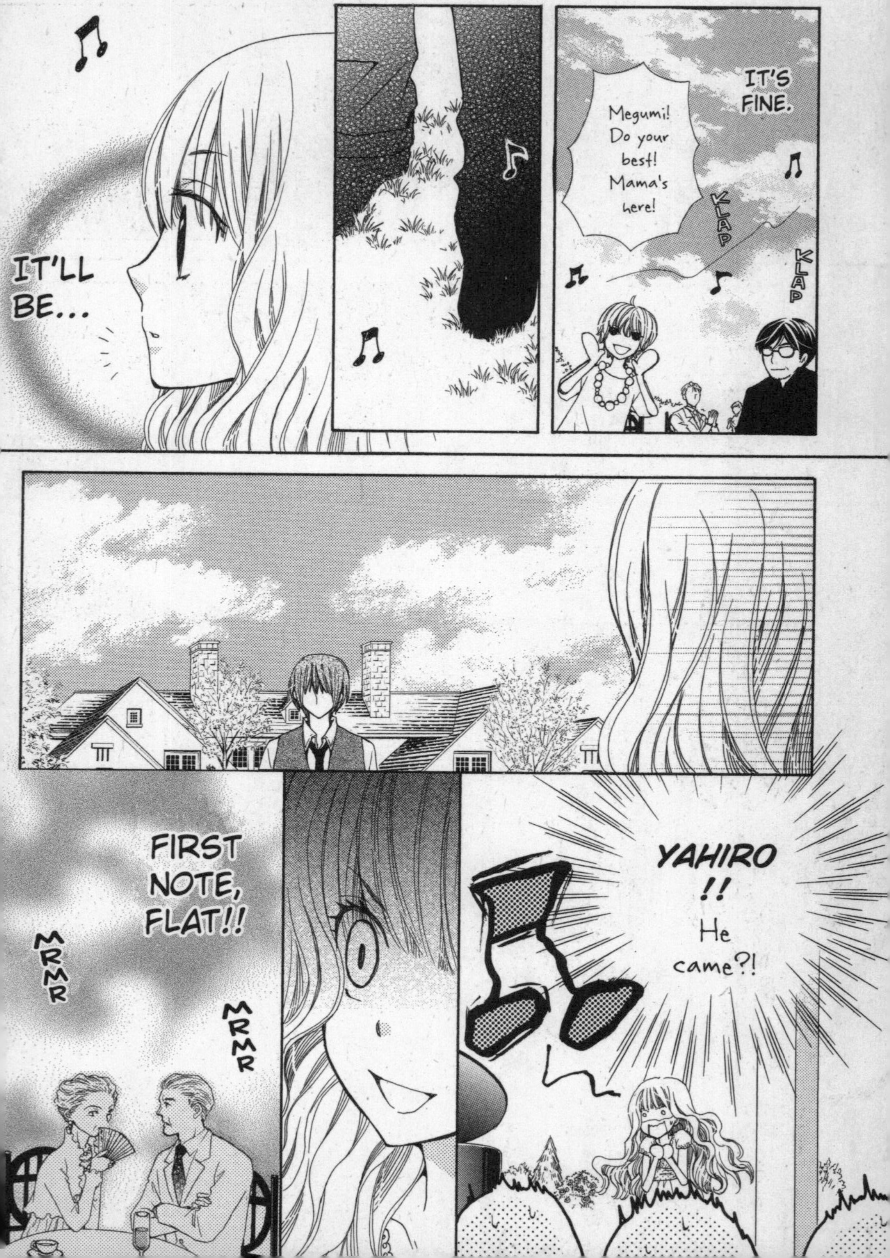
IT'S FINE.
Megumi! Do your best! Mama's here!
KLAP
KLAP
IT'LL BE...
YAHIRO!!
He came?!
FIRST NOTE, FLAT!!
MRMR
MRMR

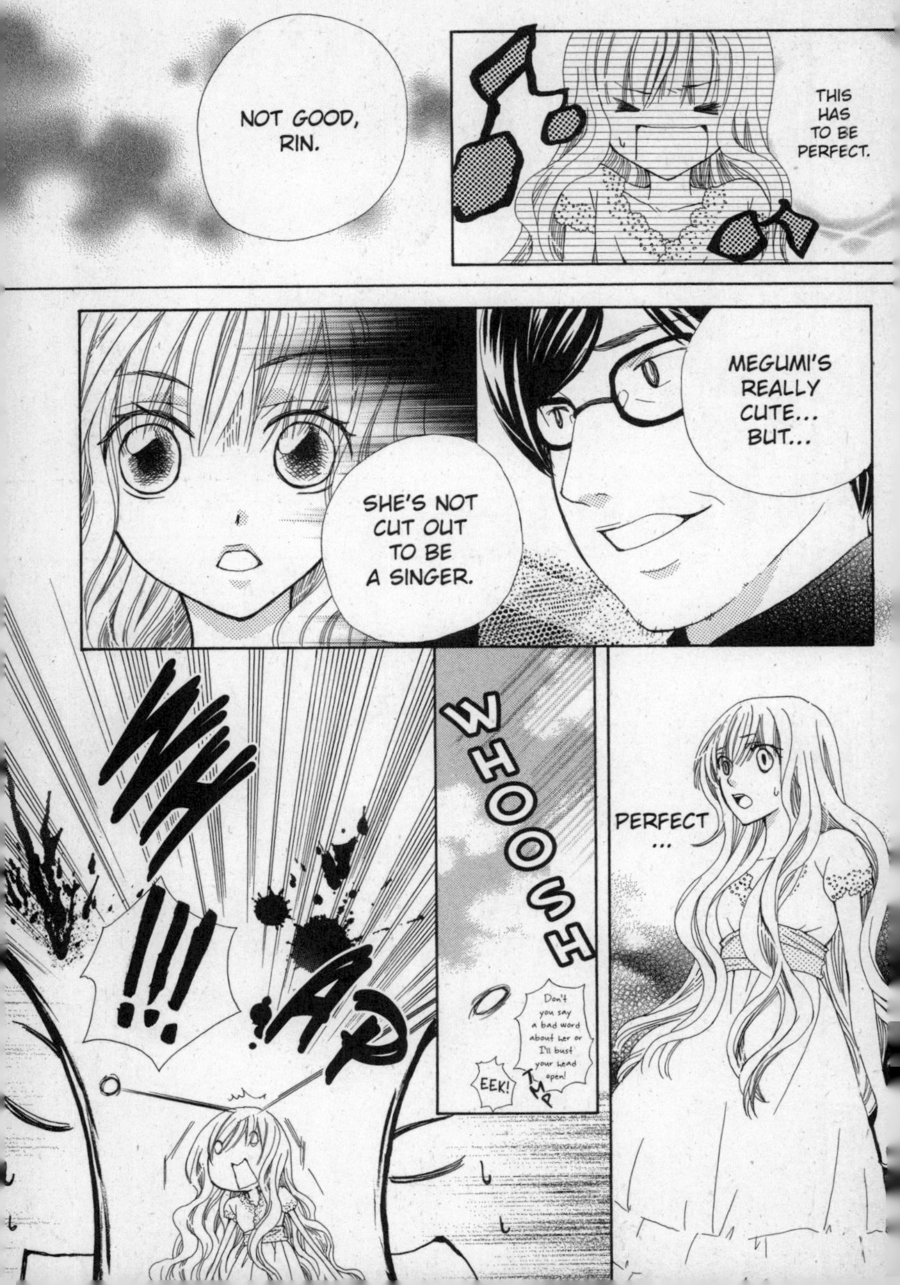
THIS HAS TO BE PERFECT.
NOT GOOD, RIN.
MEGUMI'S REALLY CUTE... BUT...
SHE'S NOT CUT OUT TO BE A SINGER.
PERFECT...
WHOOSH
Don't you say a bad word about her or I'll bust your head open!
TMP
EEK!
WHAP!!!

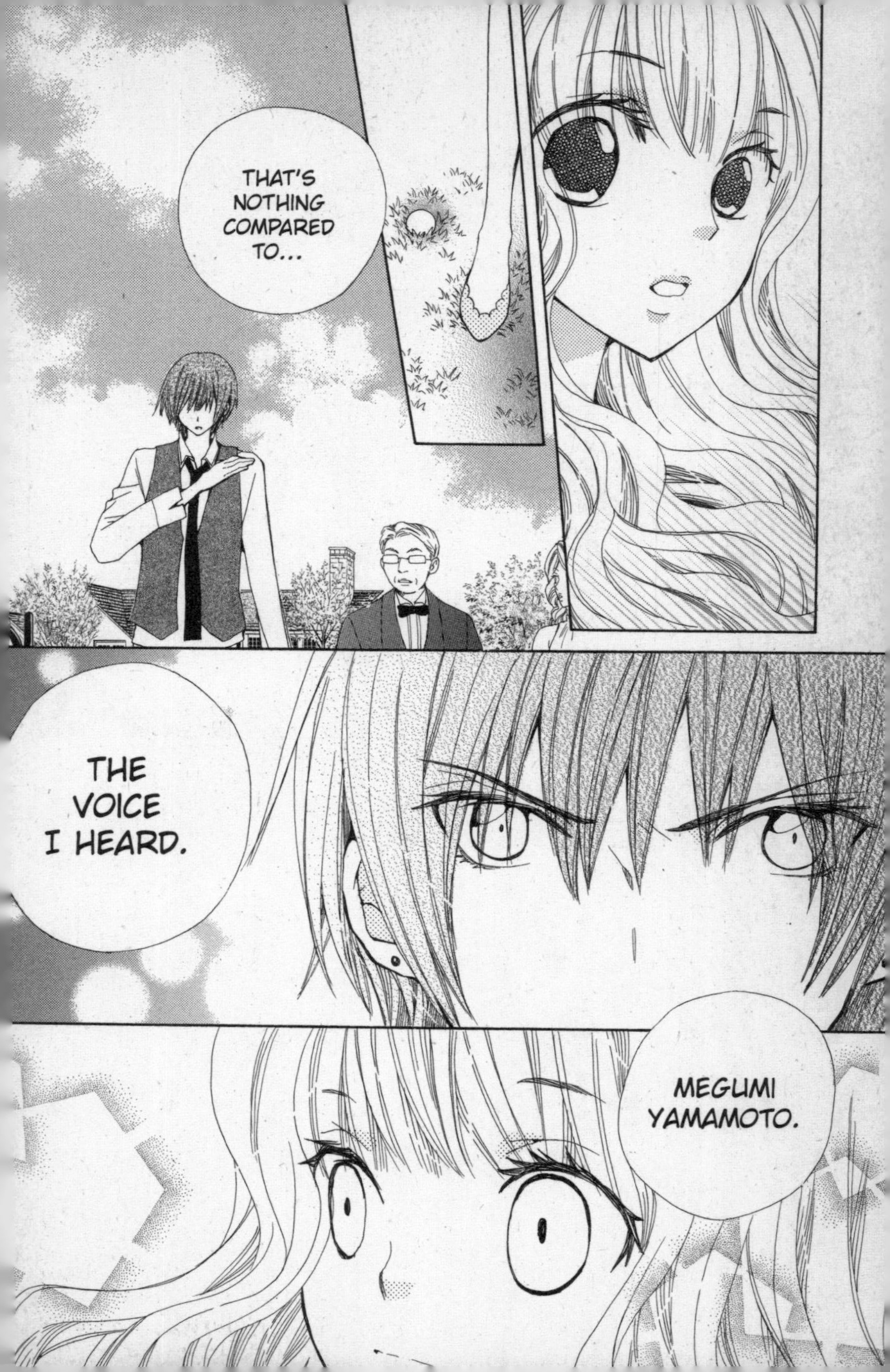
THAT'S NOTHING COMPARED TO...
THE VOICE I HEARD.
MEGUMI YAMAMOTO.

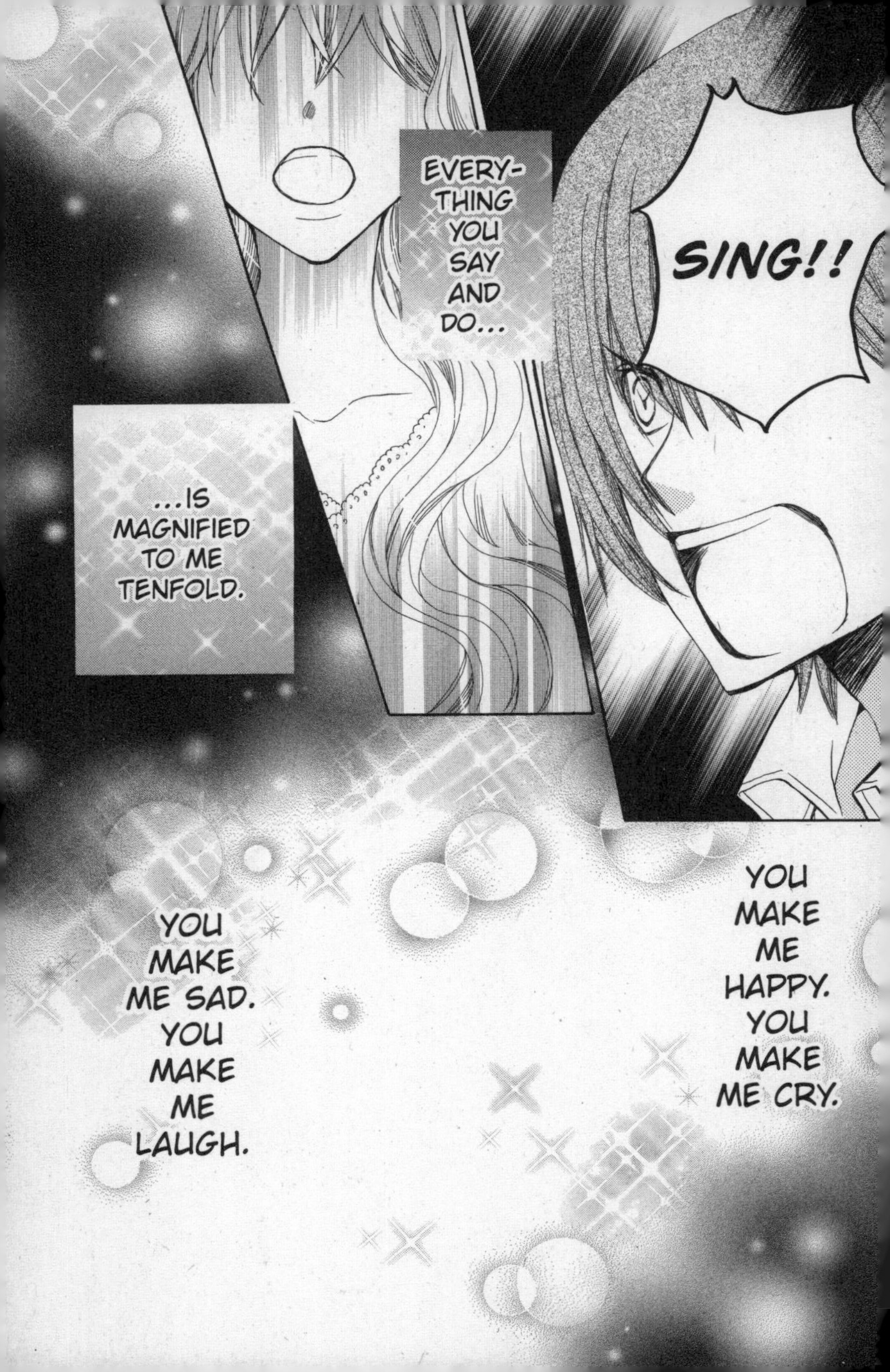
SING!!
EVERYTHING YOU SAY AND DO...
...IS MAGNIFIED TO ME TENFOLD.
YOU MAKE ME HAPPY. YOU MAKE ME CRY.
YOU MAKE ME SAD. YOU MAKE ME LAUGH.

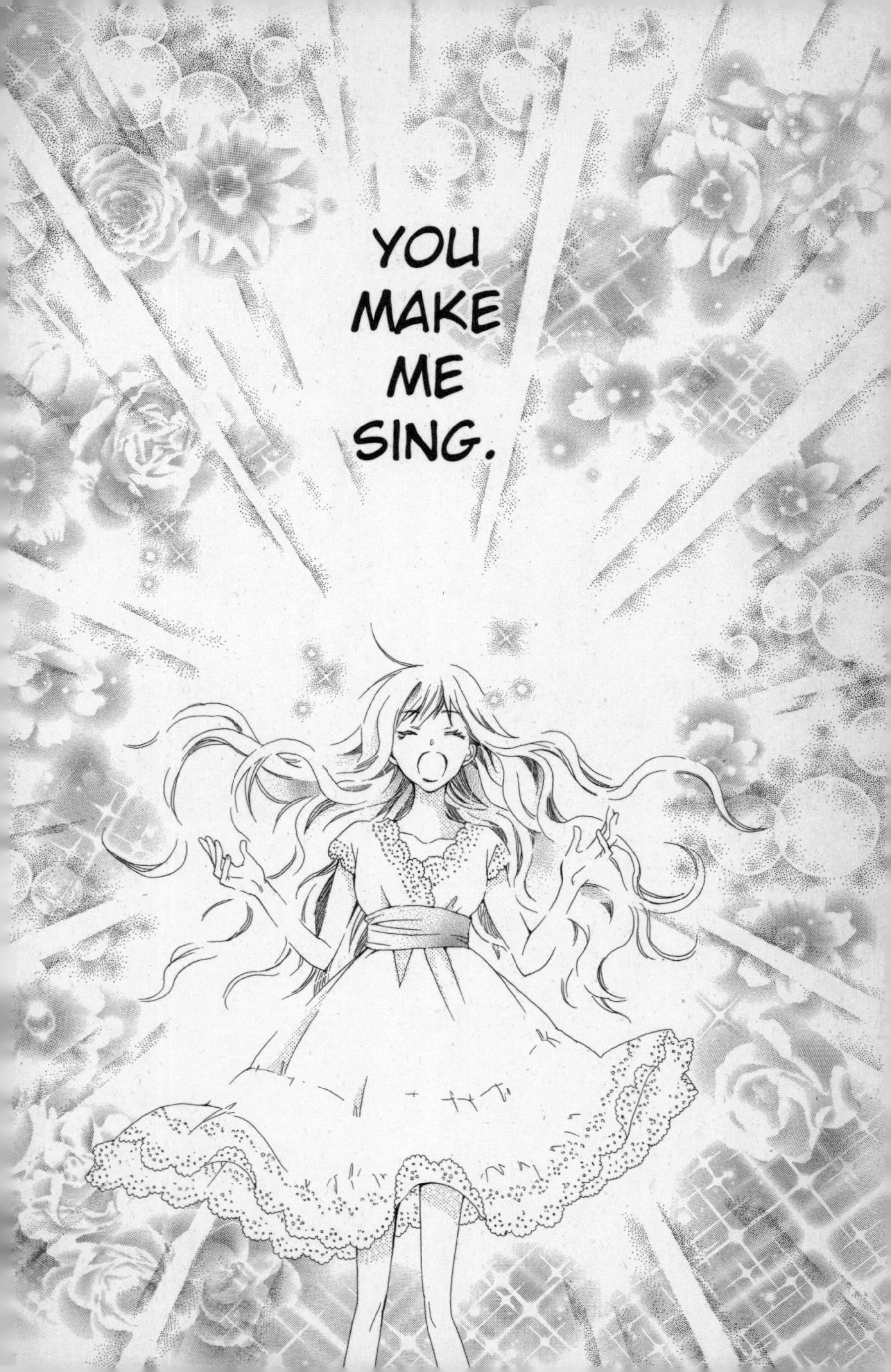
YOU MAKE ME SING.

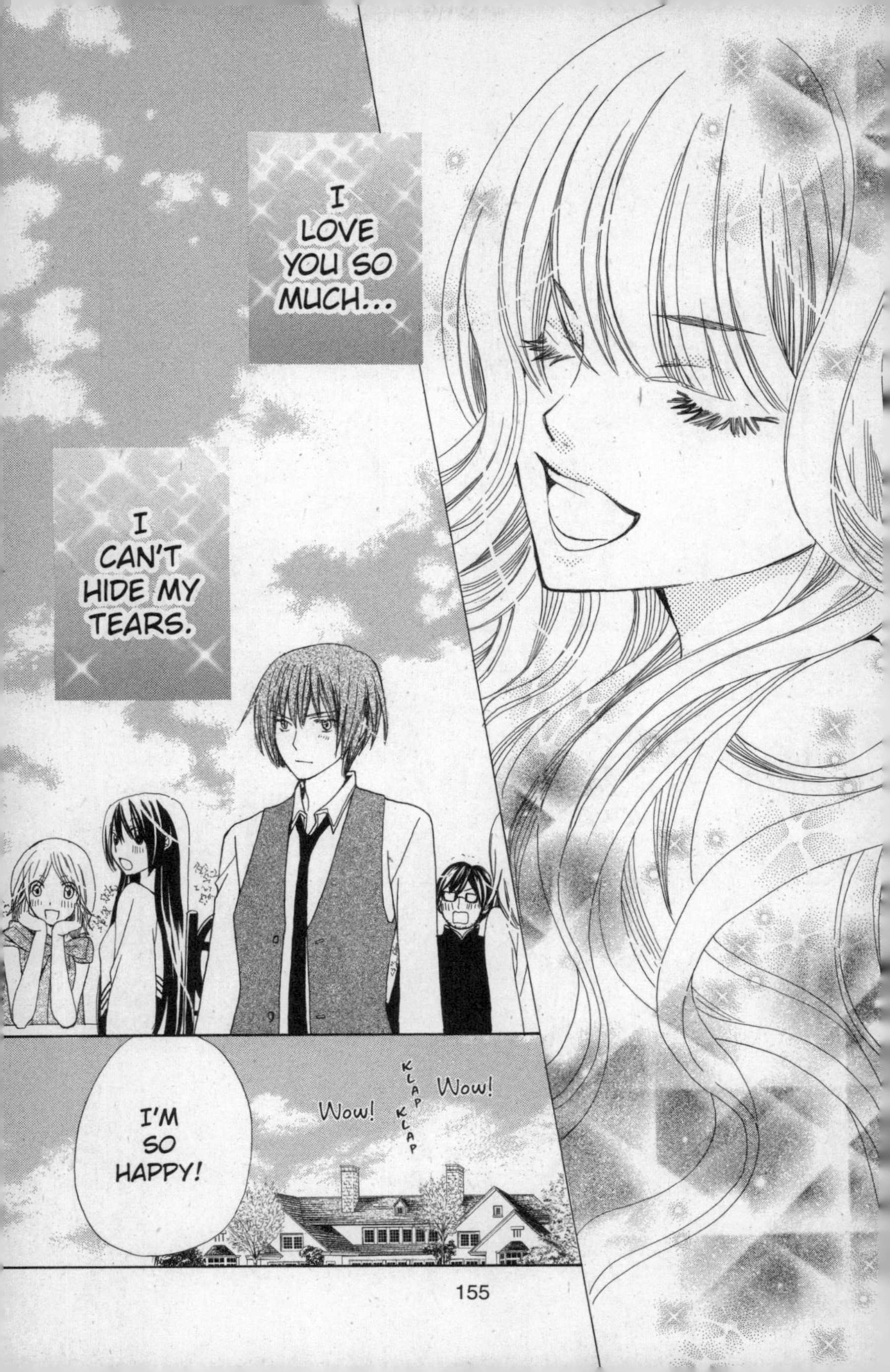
I LOVE YOU SO MUCH...
I CAN'T HIDE MY TEARS.
Wow!
KLAP KLAP
Wow!
I'M SO HAPPY!

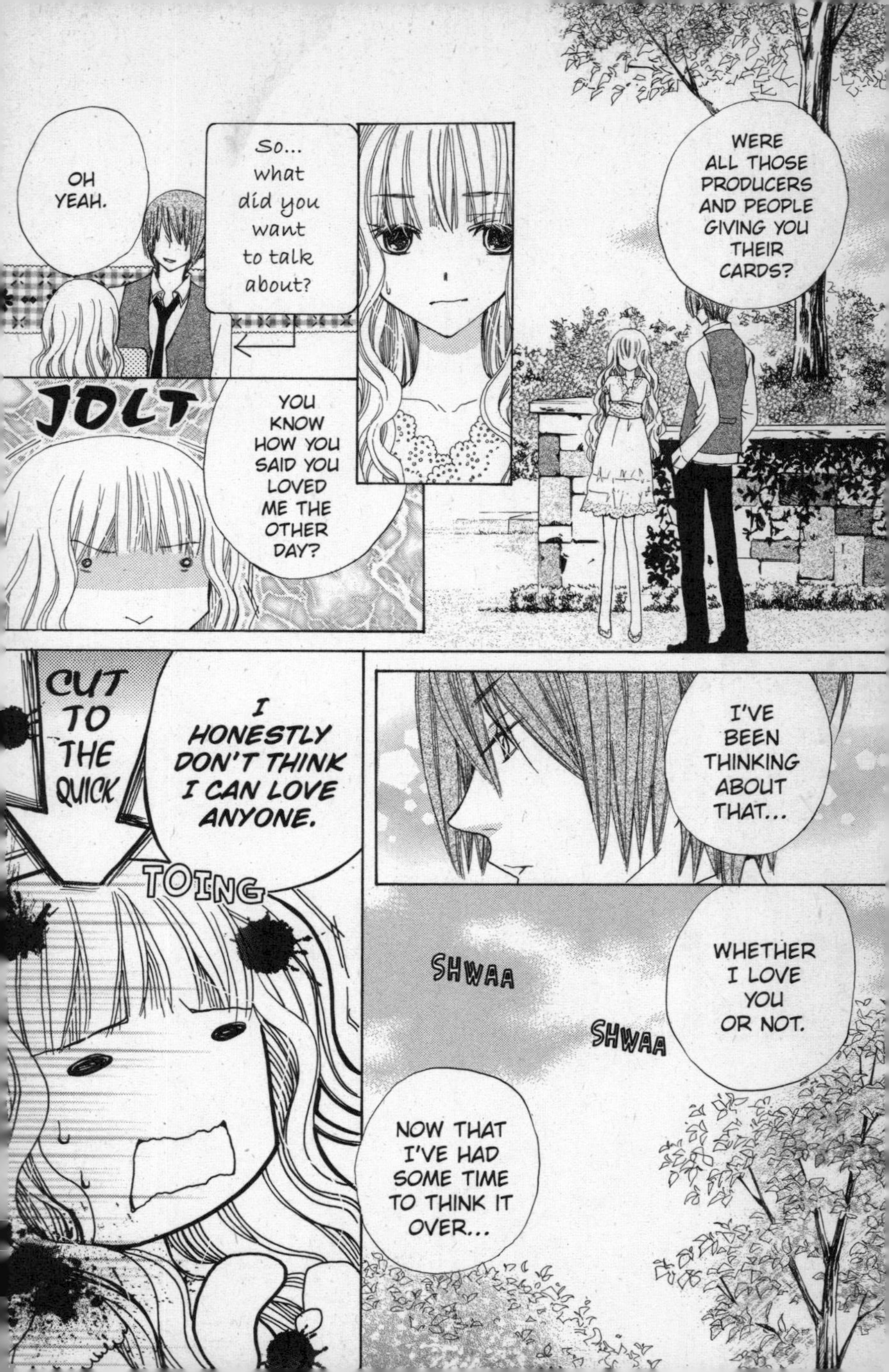
WERE ALL THOSE PRODUCERS AND PEOPLE GIVING YOU THEIR CARDS?
So... what did you want to talk about?
OH YEAH.
YOU KNOW HOW YOU SAID YOU LOVED ME THE OTHER DAY?
JOLT
I'VE BEEN THINKING ABOUT THAT...
WHETHER I LOVE YOU OR NOT.
SHWAA
SHWAA
NOW THAT I'VE HAD SOME TIME TO THINK IT OVER...
I HONESTLY DON'T THINK I CAN LOVE ANYONE.
CUT TO THE QUICK
TOING

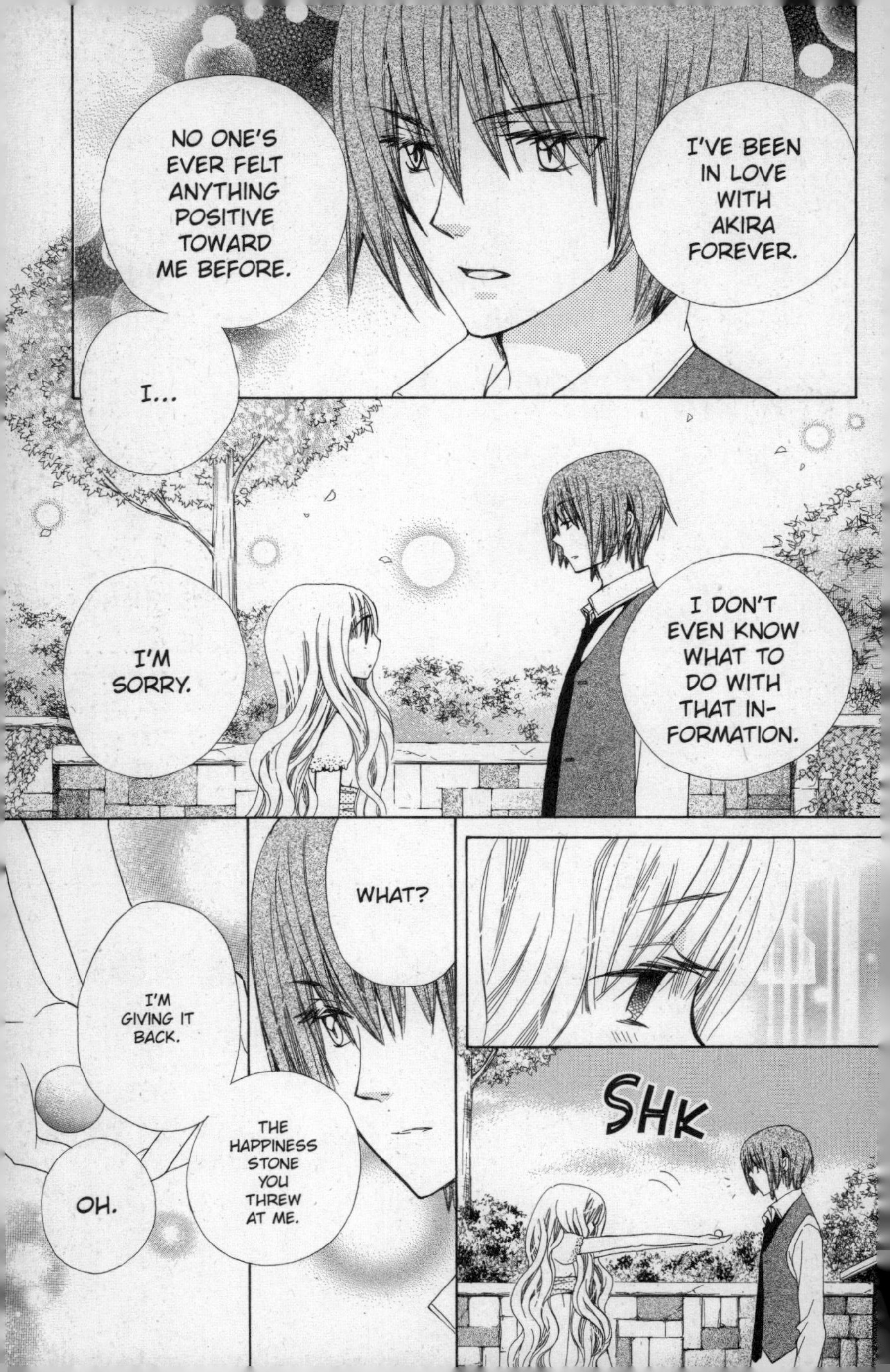
I'VE BEEN IN LOVE WITH AKIRA FOREVER.
NO ONE'S EVER FELT ANYTHING POSITIVE TOWARD ME BEFORE.
I...
I DON'T EVEN KNOW WHAT TO DO WITH THAT IN-FORMATION.
I'M SORRY.
SHK
WHAT?
I'M GIVING IT BACK.
THE HAPPINESS STONE YOU THREW AT ME.
OH.

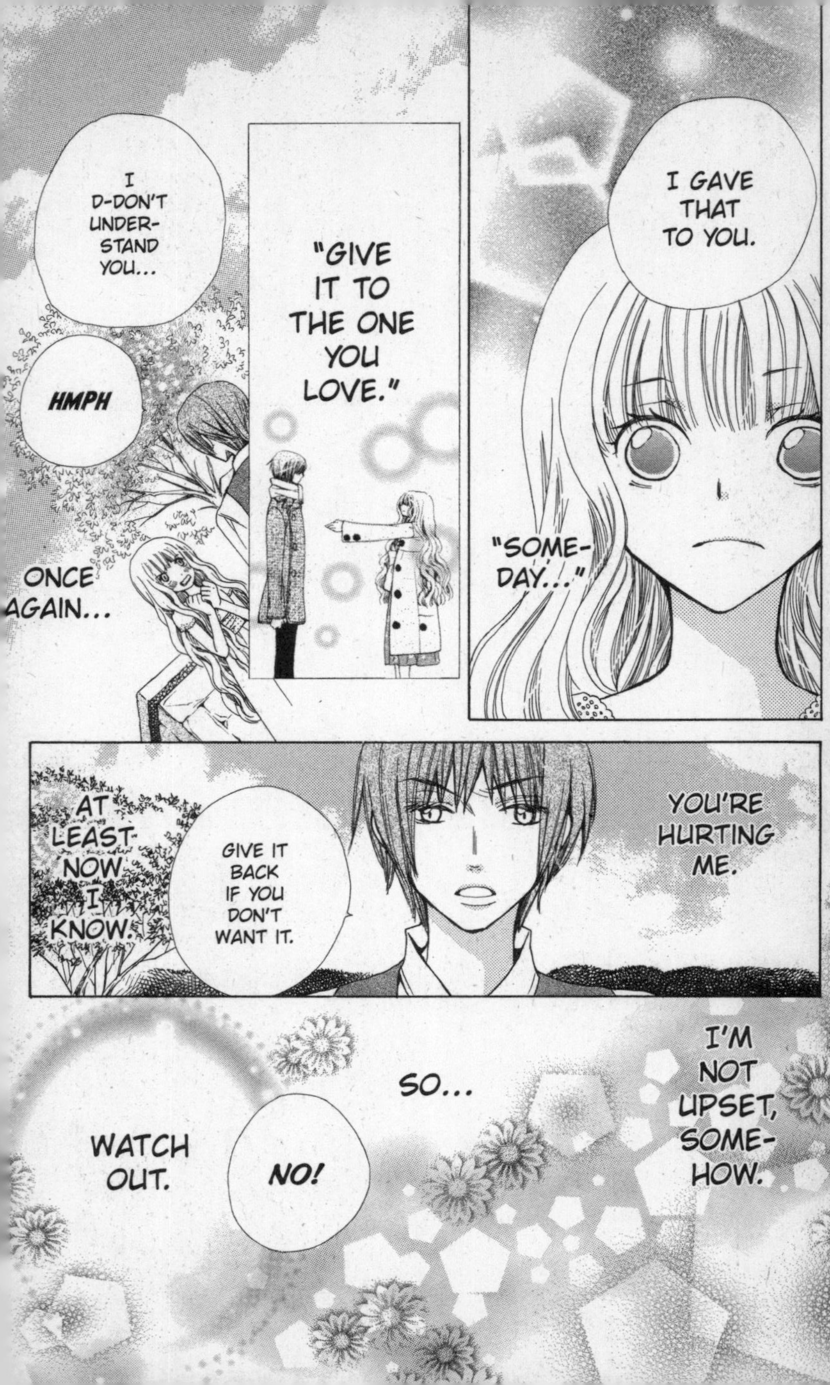
I GAVE THAT TO YOU.
"SOME-DAY..."
"GIVE IT TO THE ONE YOU LOVE."
I D-DON'T UNDER-STAND YOU...
HMPH
ONCE AGAIN...
YOU'RE HURTING ME.
GIVE IT BACK IF YOU DON'T WANT IT.
AT LEAST NOW I KNOW.
I'M NOT UPSET, SOME-HOW.
SO...
NO!
WATCH OUT.

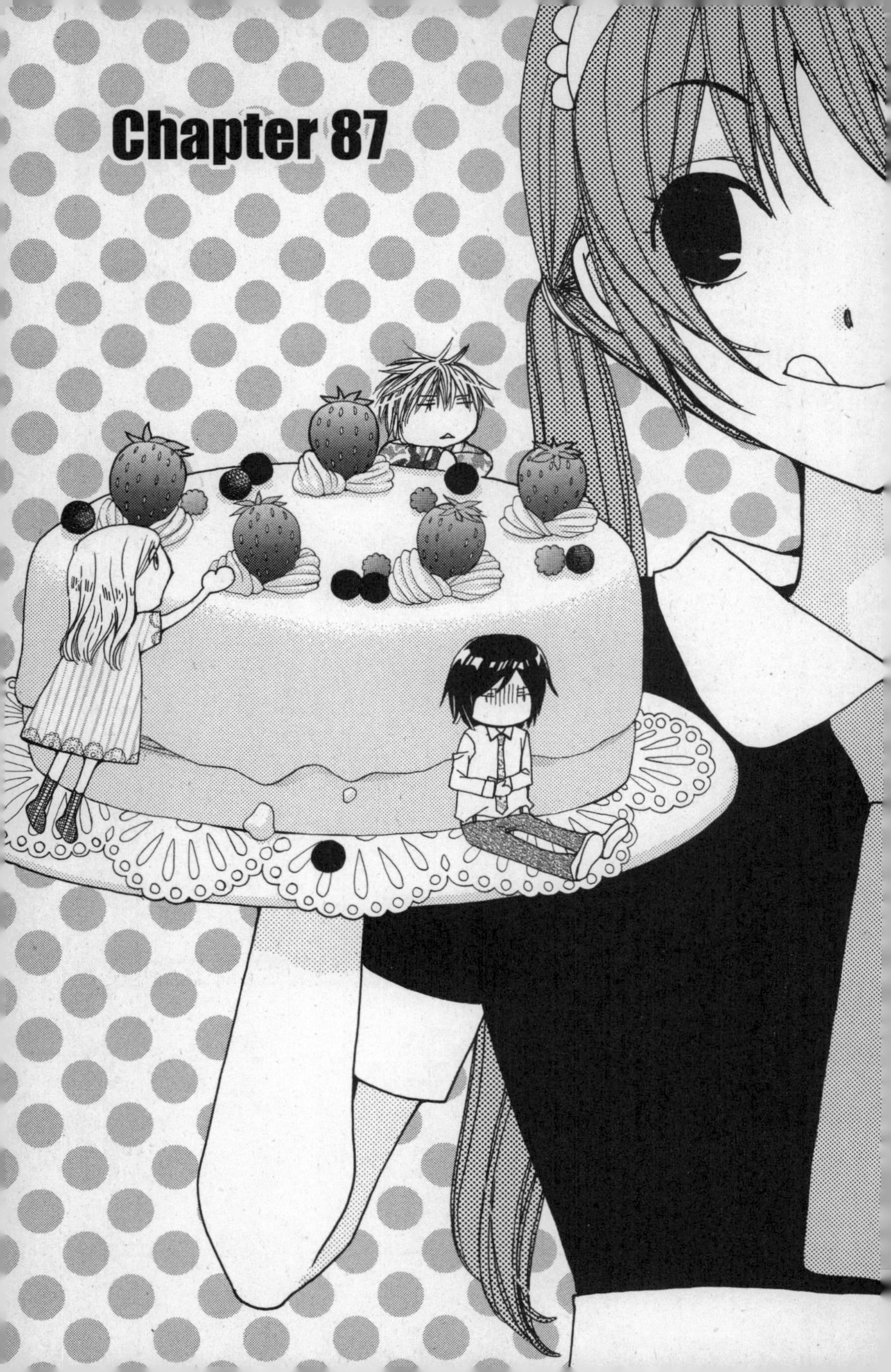
Chapter 87

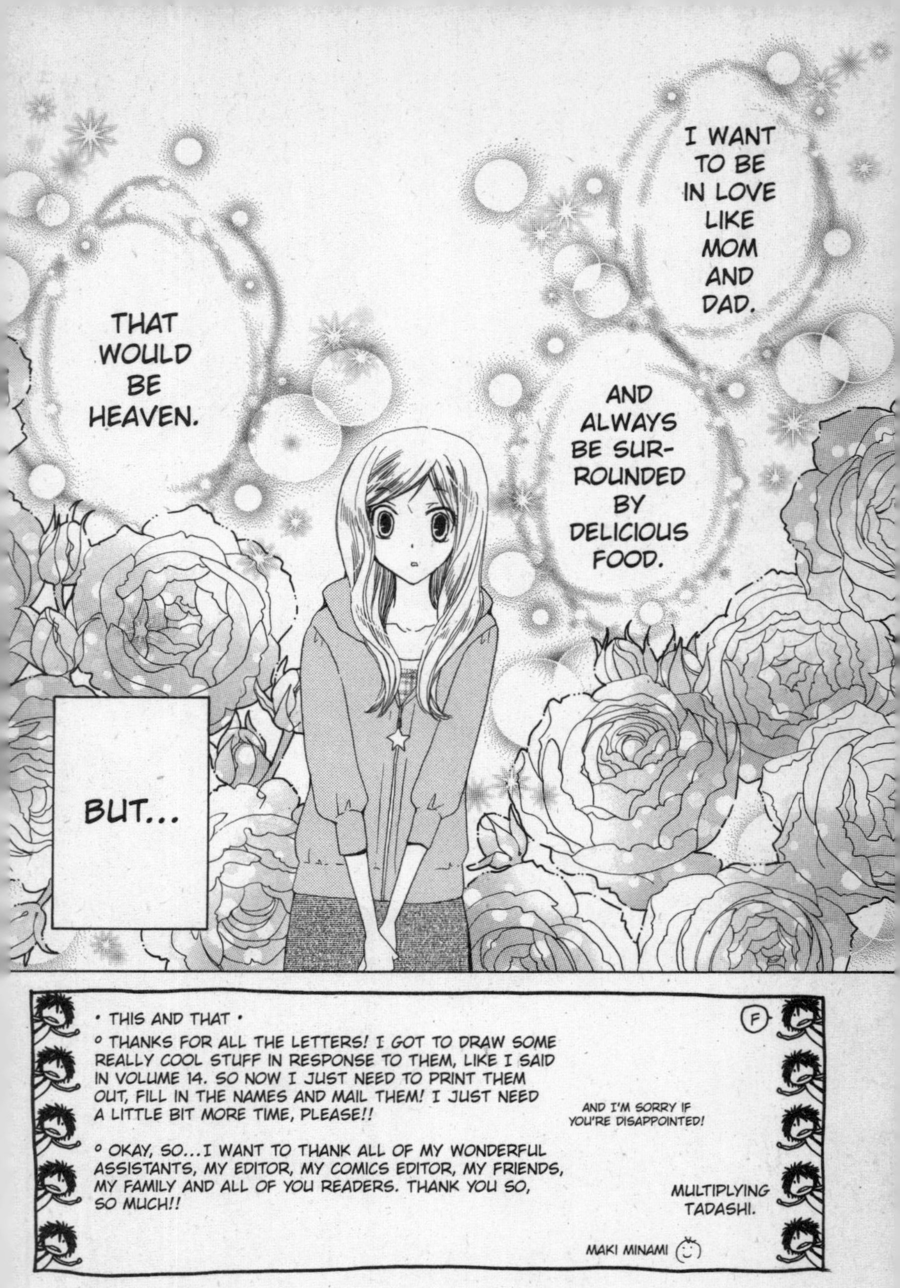
I WANT TO BE IN LOVE LIKE MOM AND DAD.
AND ALWAYS BE SUR-ROUNDED BY DELICIOUS FOOD.
THAT WOULD BE HEAVEN.
BUT...

F

• THIS AND THAT •

○ THANKS FOR ALL THE LETTERS! I GOT TO DRAW SOME REALLY COOL STUFF IN RESPONSE TO THEM, LIKE I SAID IN VOLUME 14. SO NOW I JUST NEED TO PRINT THEM OUT, FILL IN THE NAMES AND MAIL THEM! I JUST NEED A LITTLE BIT MORE TIME, PLEASE!!

AND I'M SORRY IF YOU'RE DISAPPOINTED!

○ OKAY, SO...I WANT TO THANK ALL OF MY WONDERFUL ASSISTANTS, MY EDITOR, MY COMICS EDITOR, MY FRIENDS, MY FAMILY AND ALL OF YOU READERS. THANK YOU SO, SO MUCH!!

MULTIPLYING TADASHI.

MAKI MINAMI

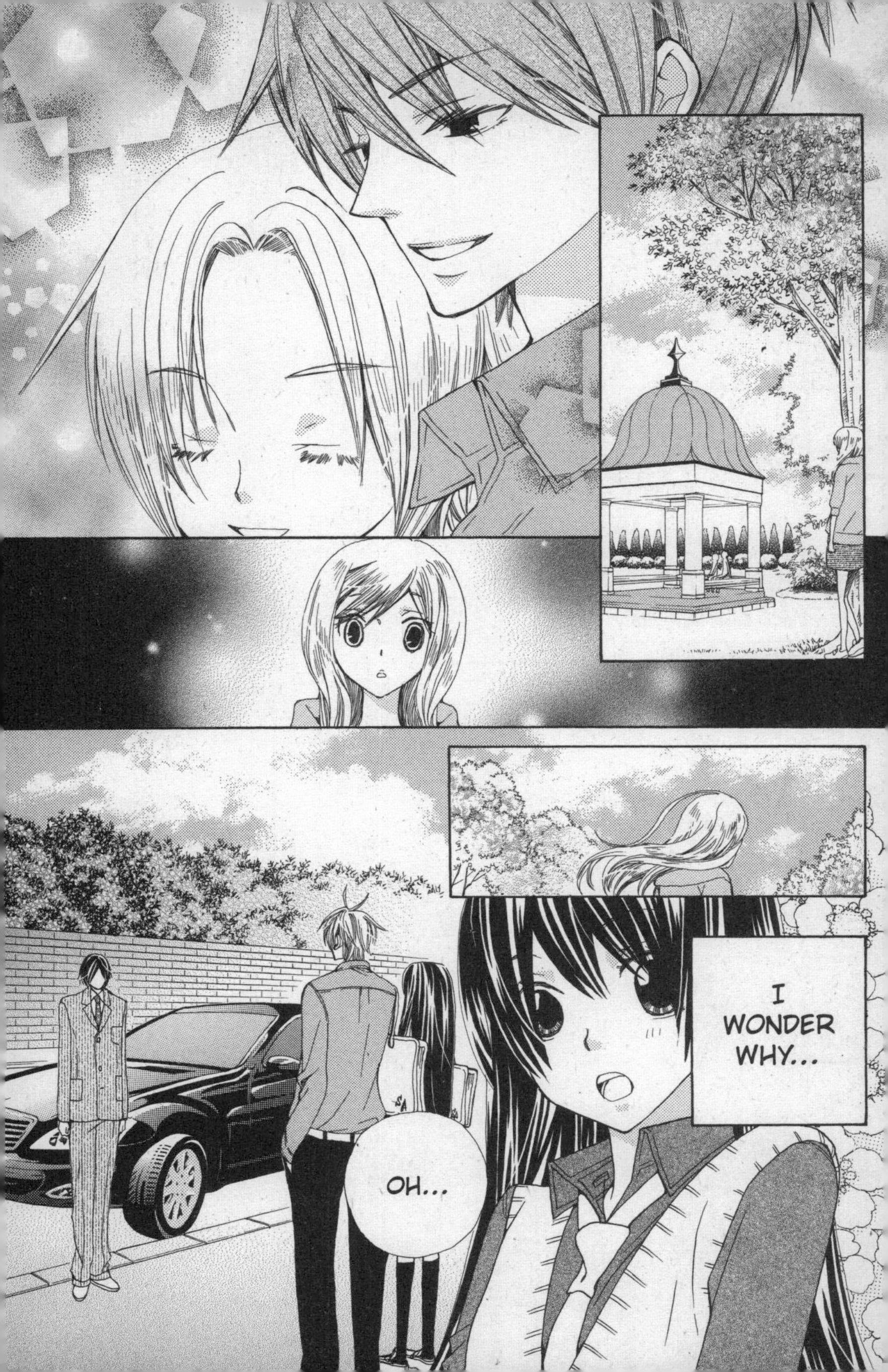
I WONDER WHY...
OH...

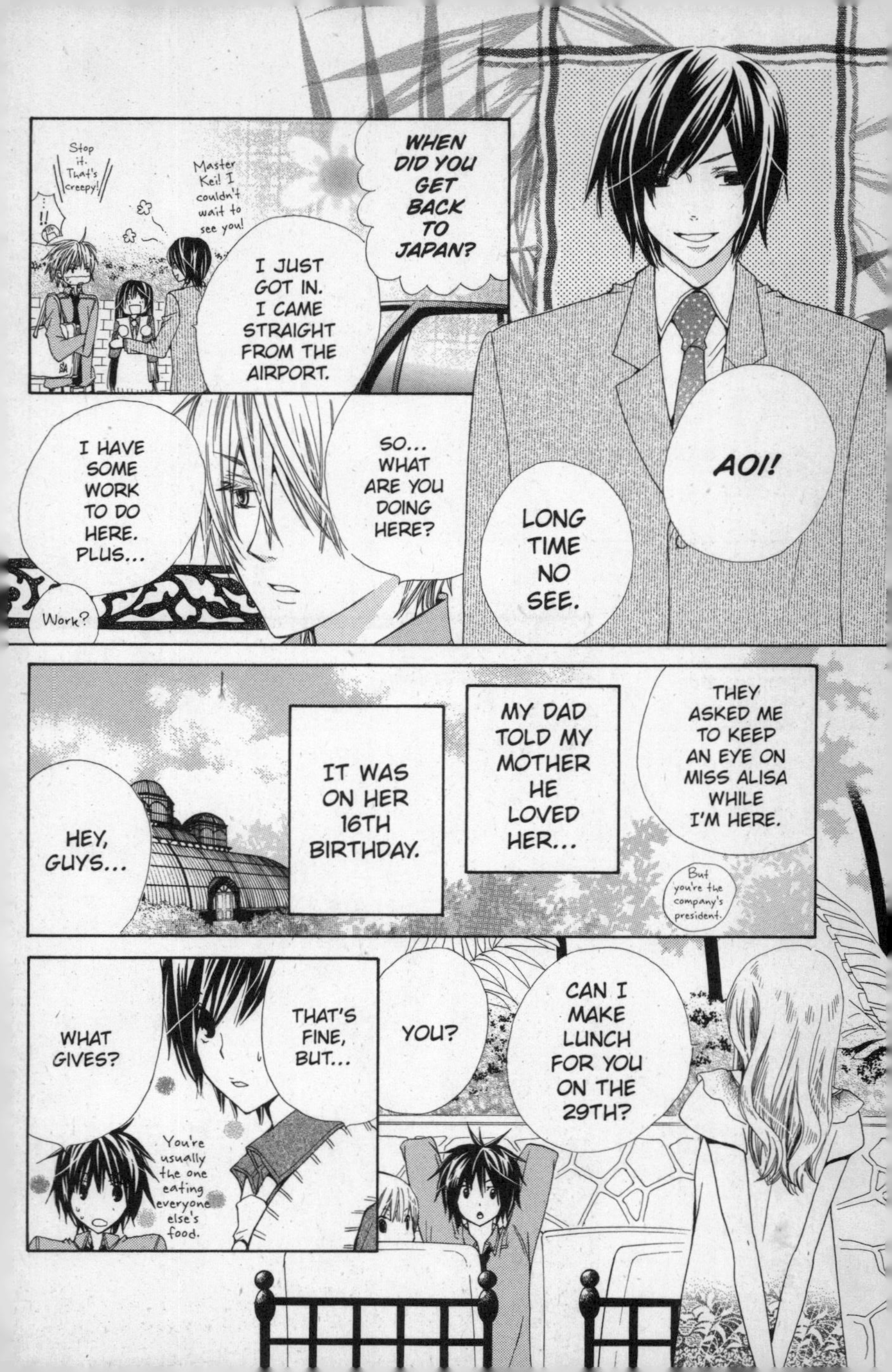
AOI!
LONG TIME NO SEE.
WHEN DID YOU GET BACK TO JAPAN?
I JUST GOT IN. I CAME STRAIGHT FROM THE AIRPORT.
Master Kei! I couldn't wait to see you!
Stop it. That's creepy!
!!
SO... WHAT ARE YOU DOING HERE?
I HAVE SOME WORK TO DO HERE. PLUS...
Work?
THEY ASKED ME TO KEEP AN EYE ON MISS ALISA WHILE I'M HERE.
But you're the company's president.
MY DAD TOLD MY MOTHER HE LOVED HER...
IT WAS ON HER 16TH BIRTHDAY.
HEY, GUYS...
CAN I MAKE LUNCH FOR YOU ON THE 29TH?
YOU?
THAT'S FINE, BUT...
WHAT GIVES?
You're usually the one eating everyone else's food.

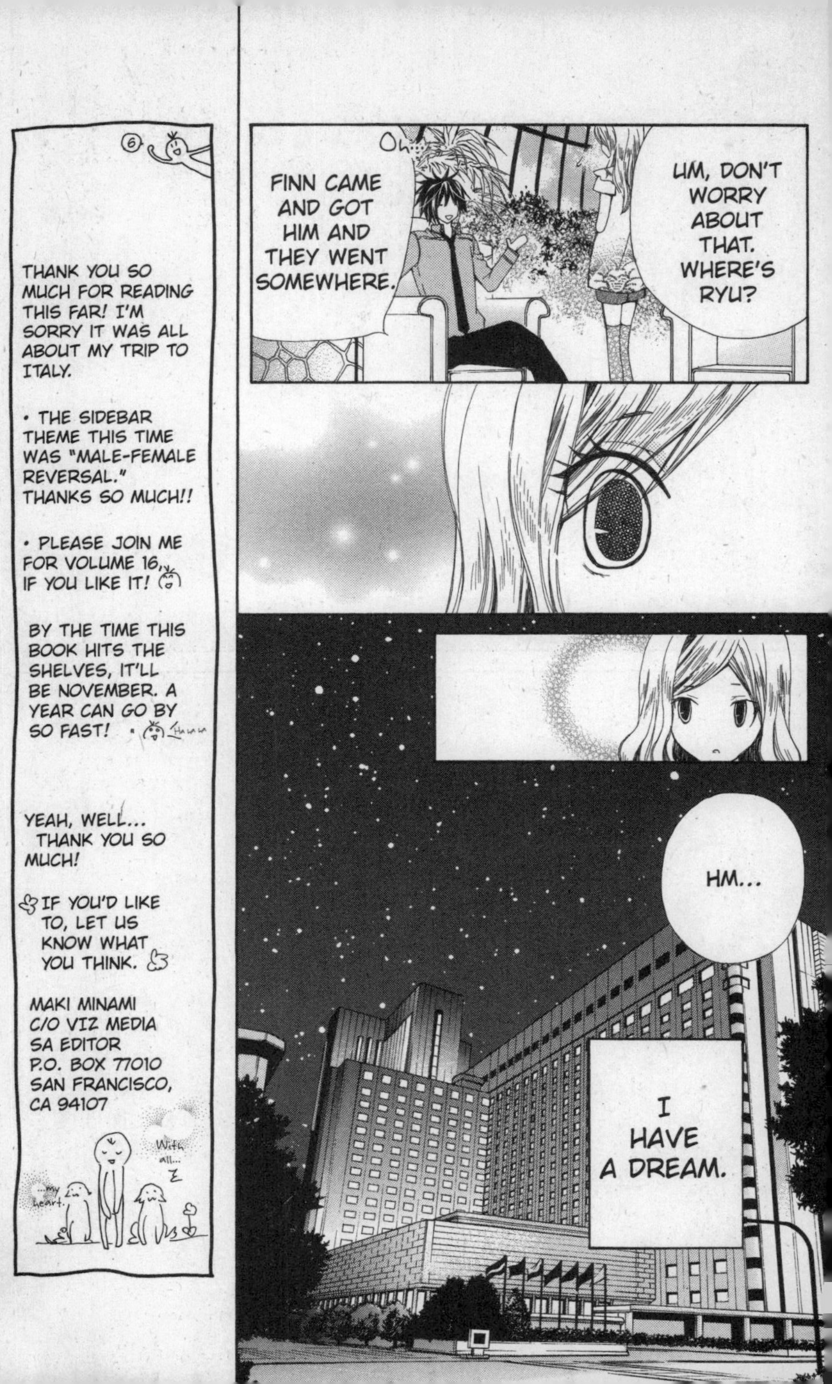
UM, DON'T WORRY ABOUT THAT. WHERE'S RYU?
Oh
FINN CAME AND GOT HIM AND THEY WENT SOMEWHERE.
HM...
I HAVE A DREAM.

⑥

THANK YOU SO MUCH FOR READING THIS FAR! I'M SORRY IT WAS ALL ABOUT MY TRIP TO ITALY.

• THE SIDEBAR THEME THIS TIME WAS "MALE-FEMALE REVERSAL." THANKS SO MUCH!!

• PLEASE JOIN ME FOR VOLUME 16, IF YOU LIKE IT!

BY THE TIME THIS BOOK HITS THE SHELVES, IT'LL BE NOVEMBER. A YEAR CAN GO BY SO FAST! • Hahaha

YEAH, WELL... THANK YOU SO MUCH!

IF YOU'D LIKE TO, LET US KNOW WHAT YOU THINK.

MAKI MINAMI
C/O VIZ MEDIA
SA EDITOR
P.O. BOX 77010
SAN FRANCISCO,
CA 94107

With all... ...my heart.

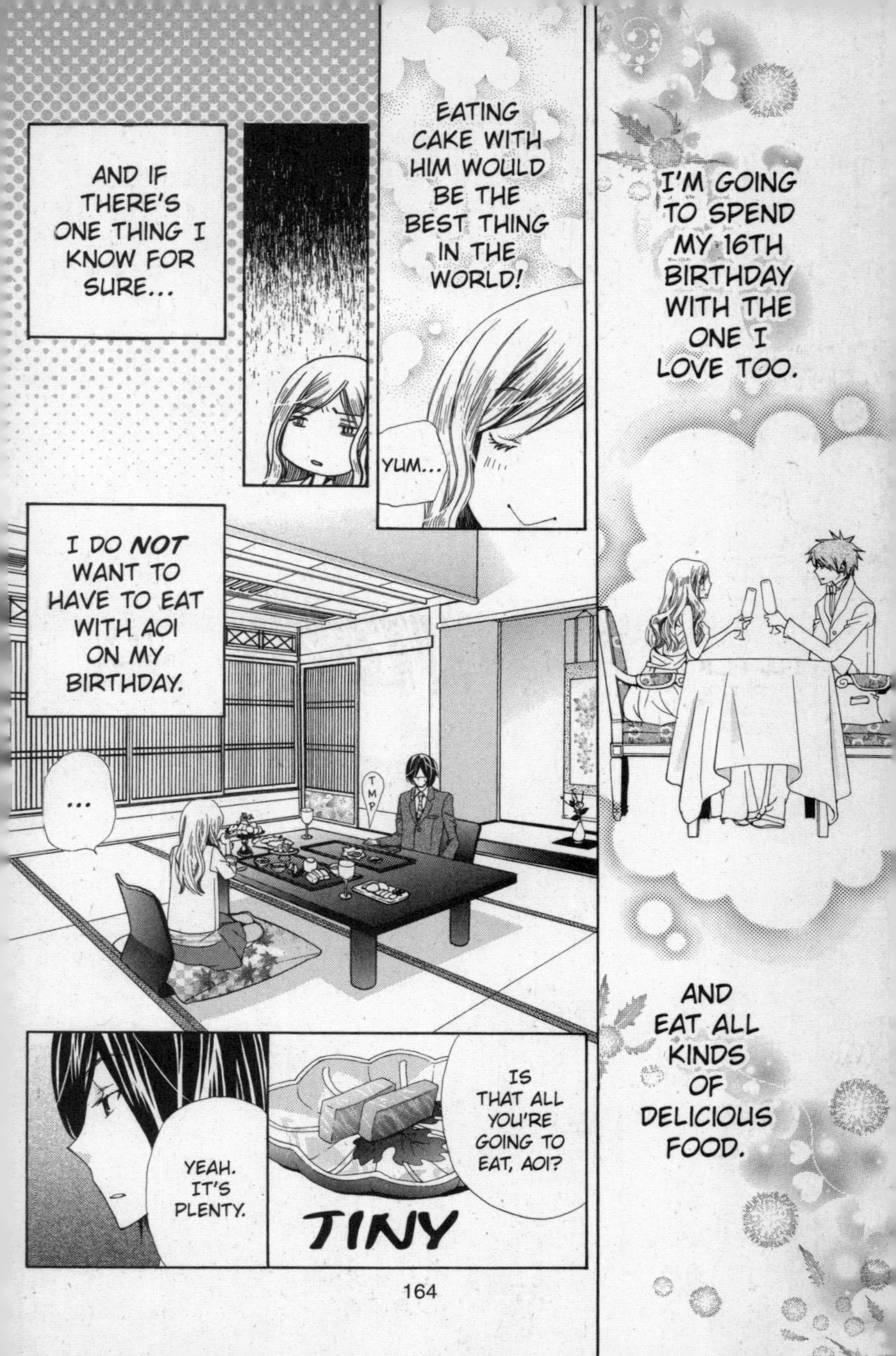
I'M GOING TO SPEND MY 16TH BIRTHDAY WITH THE ONE I LOVE TOO.
AND EAT ALL KINDS OF DELICIOUS FOOD.
EATING CAKE WITH HIM WOULD BE THE BEST THING IN THE WORLD!
YUM...
AND IF THERE'S ONE THING I KNOW FOR SURE...
I DO **NOT** WANT TO HAVE TO EAT WITH AOI ON MY BIRTHDAY.
...
TMP
IS THAT ALL YOU'RE GOING TO EAT, AOI?
TINY
YEAH. IT'S PLENTY.

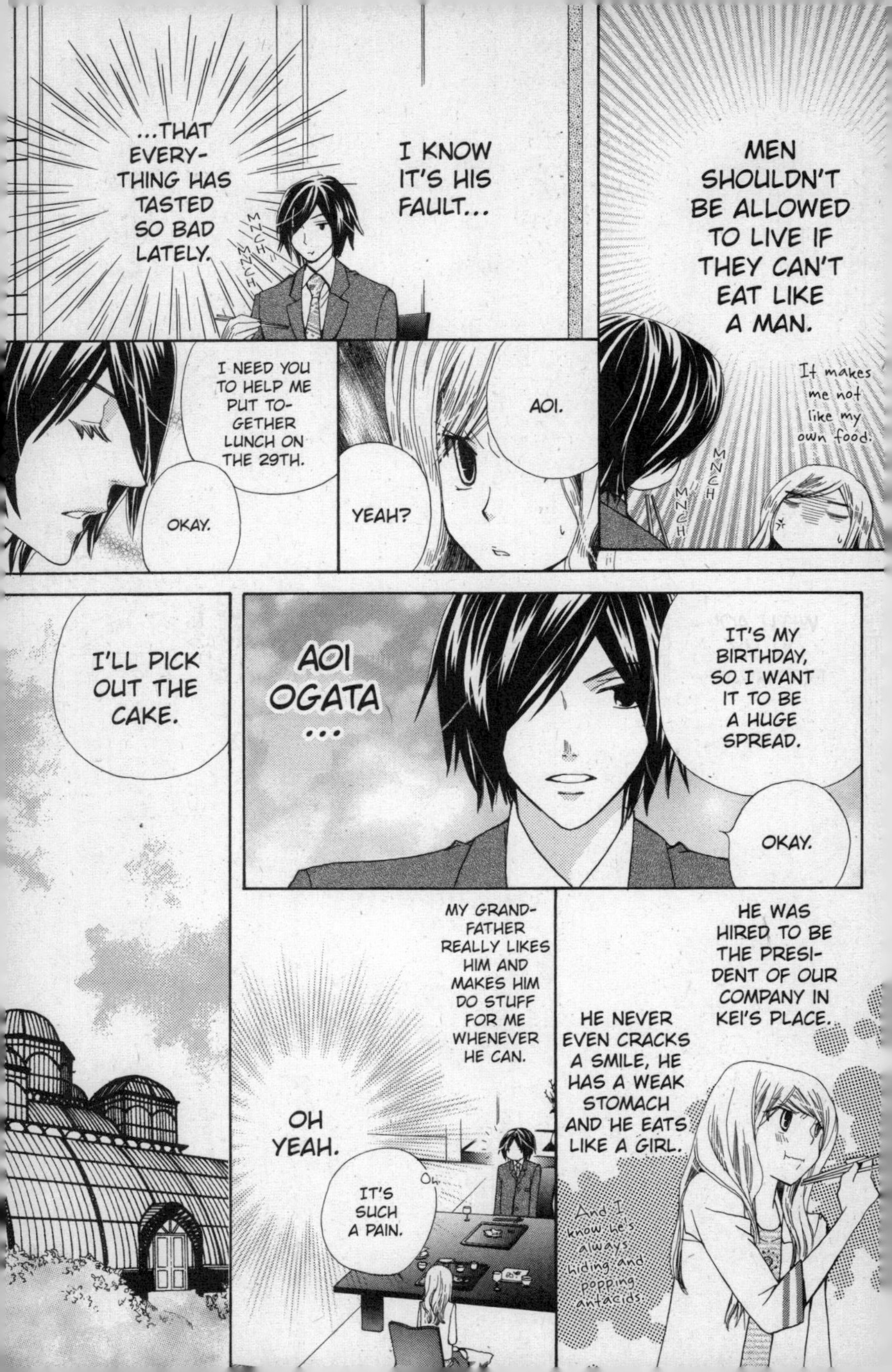
MEN SHOULDN'T BE ALLOWED TO LIVE IF THEY CAN'T EAT LIKE A MAN.
It makes me not like my own food.
MNCH
MNCH
I KNOW IT'S HIS FAULT...
...THAT EVERYTHING HAS TASTED SO BAD LATELY.
MNCH
MNCH
AOI.
YEAH?
I NEED YOU TO HELP ME PUT TOGETHER LUNCH ON THE 29TH.
OKAY.
IT'S MY BIRTHDAY, SO I WANT IT TO BE A HUGE SPREAD.
OKAY.
AOI OGATA...
I'LL PICK OUT THE CAKE.
HE WAS HIRED TO BE THE PRESIDENT OF OUR COMPANY IN KEI'S PLACE.
HE NEVER EVEN CRACKS A SMILE, HE HAS A WEAK STOMACH AND HE EATS LIKE A GIRL.
And I know he's always hiding and popping antacids.
MY GRANDFATHER REALLY LIKES HIM AND MAKES HIM DO STUFF FOR ME WHENEVER HE CAN.
OH YEAH.
Oh
IT'S SUCH A PAIN.

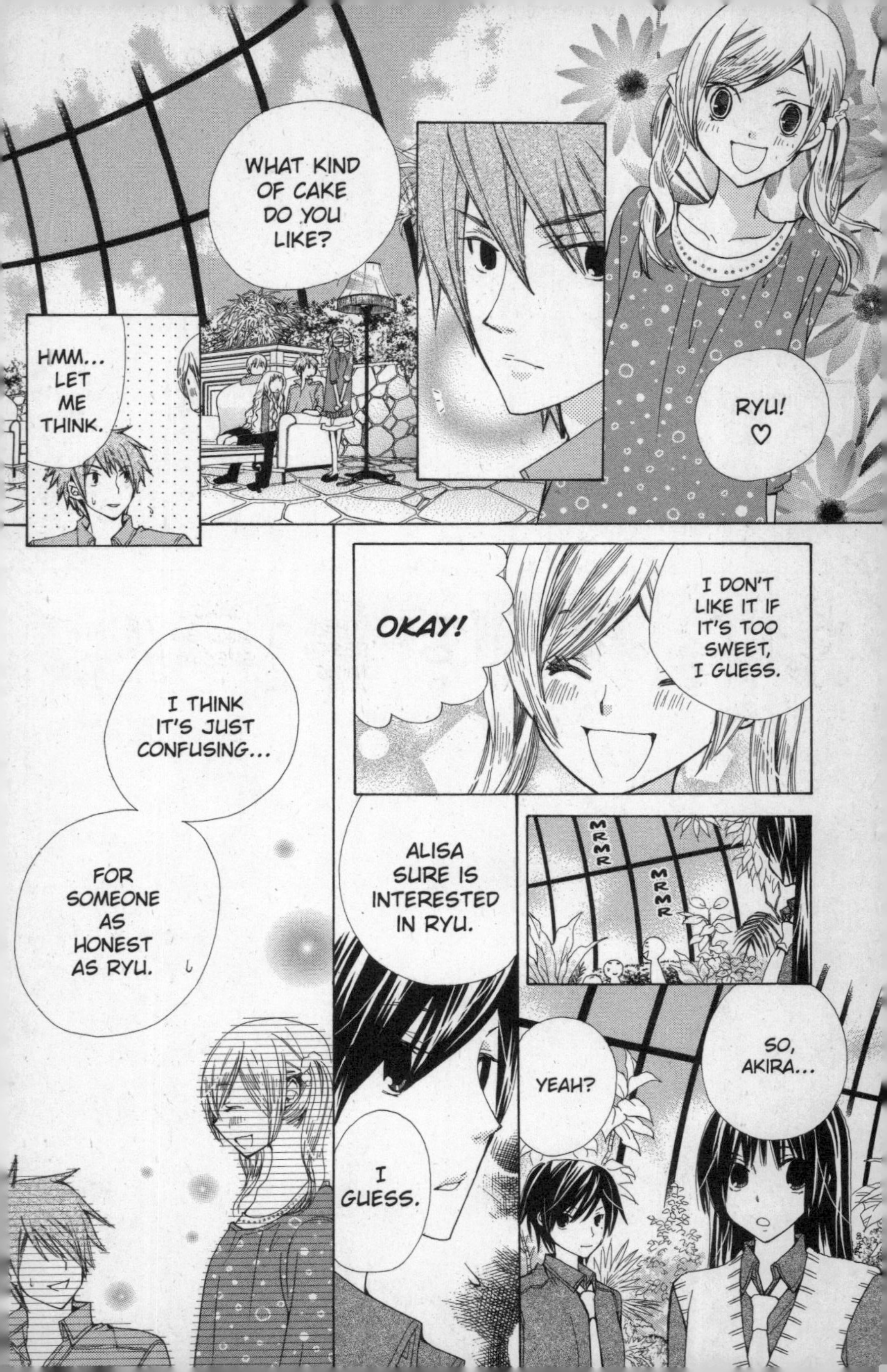
RYU! ♡
WHAT KIND OF CAKE DO YOU LIKE?
HMM... LET ME THINK.
I DON'T LIKE IT IF IT'S TOO SWEET, I GUESS.
OKAY!
MRMR
MRMR
SO, AKIRA...
YEAH?
ALISA SURE IS INTERESTED IN RYU.
I GUESS.
I THINK IT'S JUST CONFUSING...
FOR SOMEONE AS HONEST AS RYU.

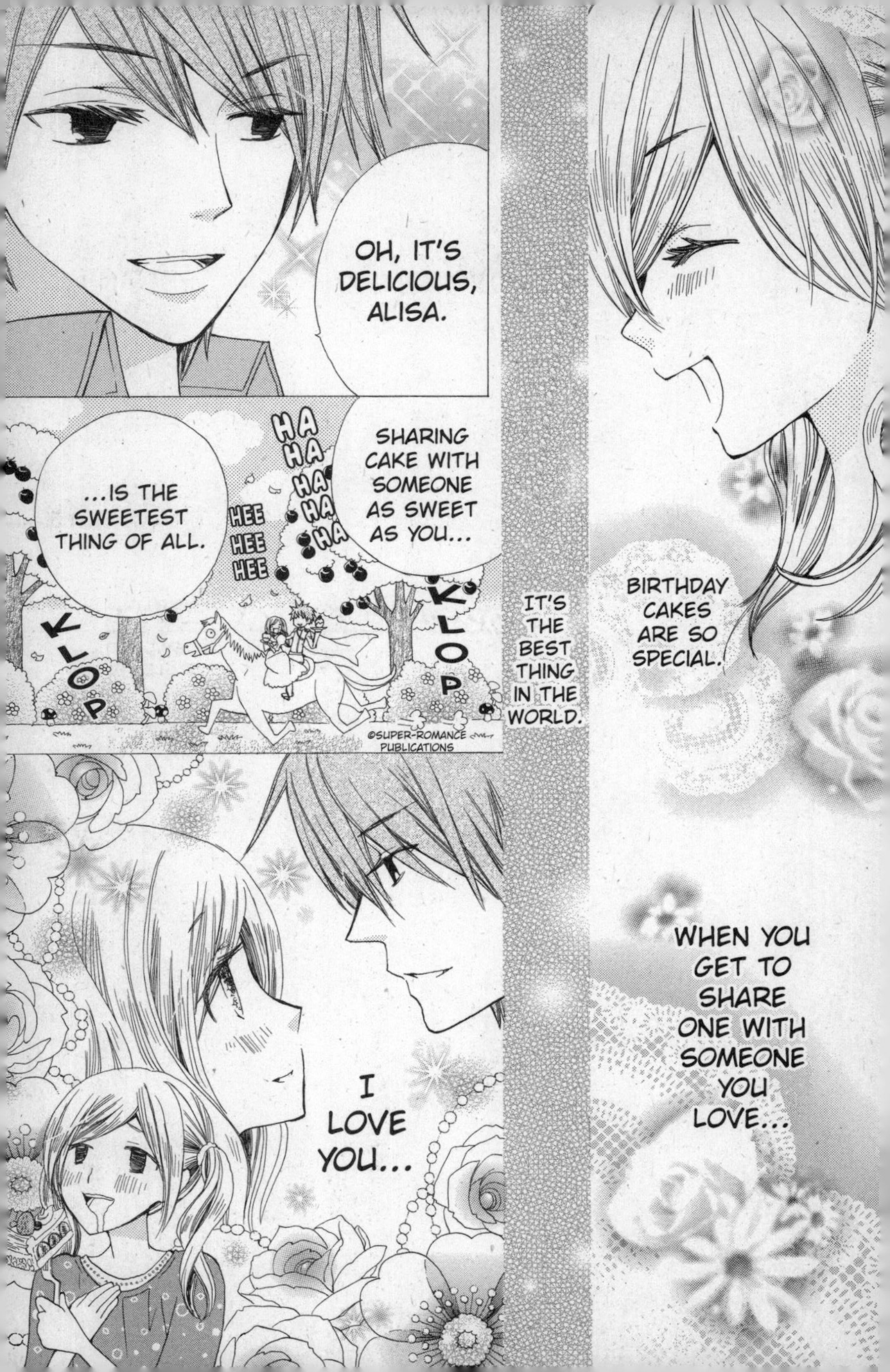
BIRTHDAY CAKES ARE SO SPECIAL.
WHEN YOU GET TO SHARE ONE WITH SOMEONE YOU LOVE...
IT'S THE BEST THING IN THE WORLD.
OH, IT'S DELICIOUS, ALISA.
SHARING CAKE WITH SOMEONE AS SWEET AS YOU...
HA HA HA HA HA
KLOP
HEE HEE HEE
...IS THE SWEETEST THING OF ALL.
KLOP
©SUPER-ROMANCE PUBLICATIONS
I LOVE YOU...

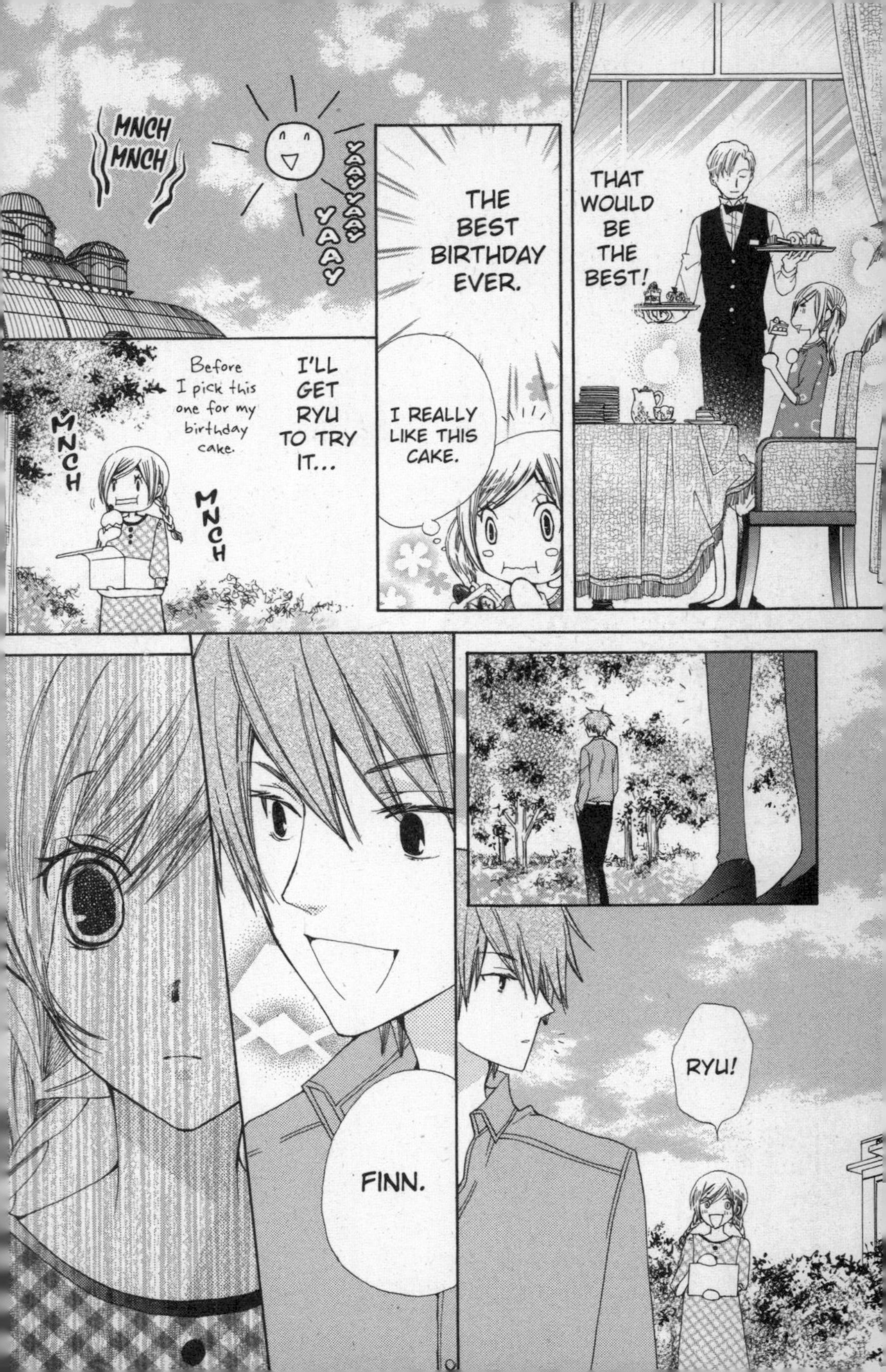
THAT WOULD BE THE BEST!
THE BEST BIRTHDAY EVER.
I REALLY LIKE THIS CAKE.
YAAY YAAY YAAY
MNCH MNCH
I'LL GET RYU TO TRY IT...
Before I pick this one for my birthday cake.
MNCH
MNCH
RYU!
FINN.

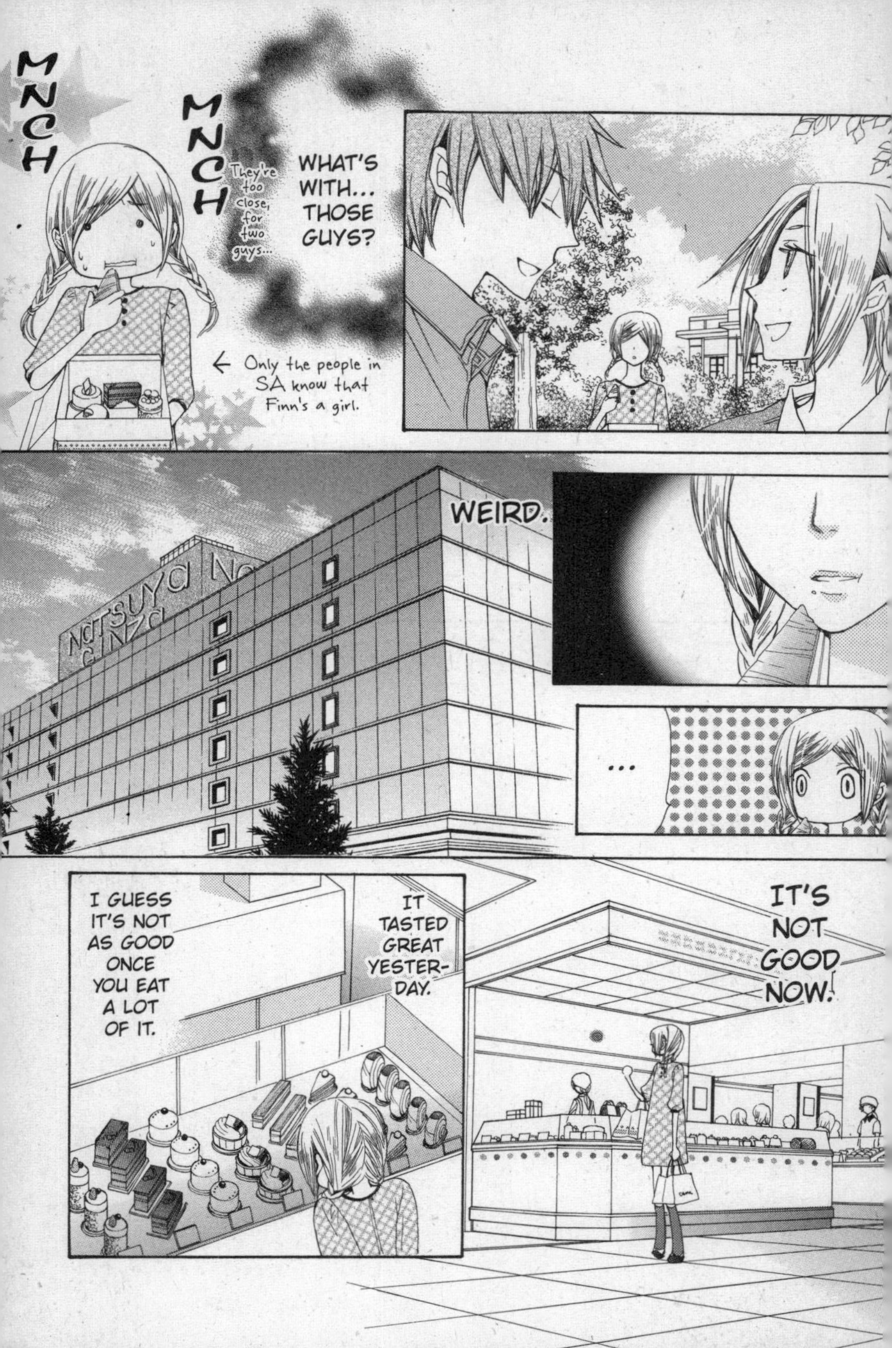
MNCH
MNCH
WHAT'S WITH... THOSE GUYS?
They're too close, for two guys...
← Only the people in SA know that Finn's a girl.
WEIRD.
...
Natsuya Ginza
IT'S NOT GOOD NOW!
IT TASTED GREAT YESTER-DAY.
I GUESS IT'S NOT AS GOOD ONCE YOU EAT A LOT OF IT.

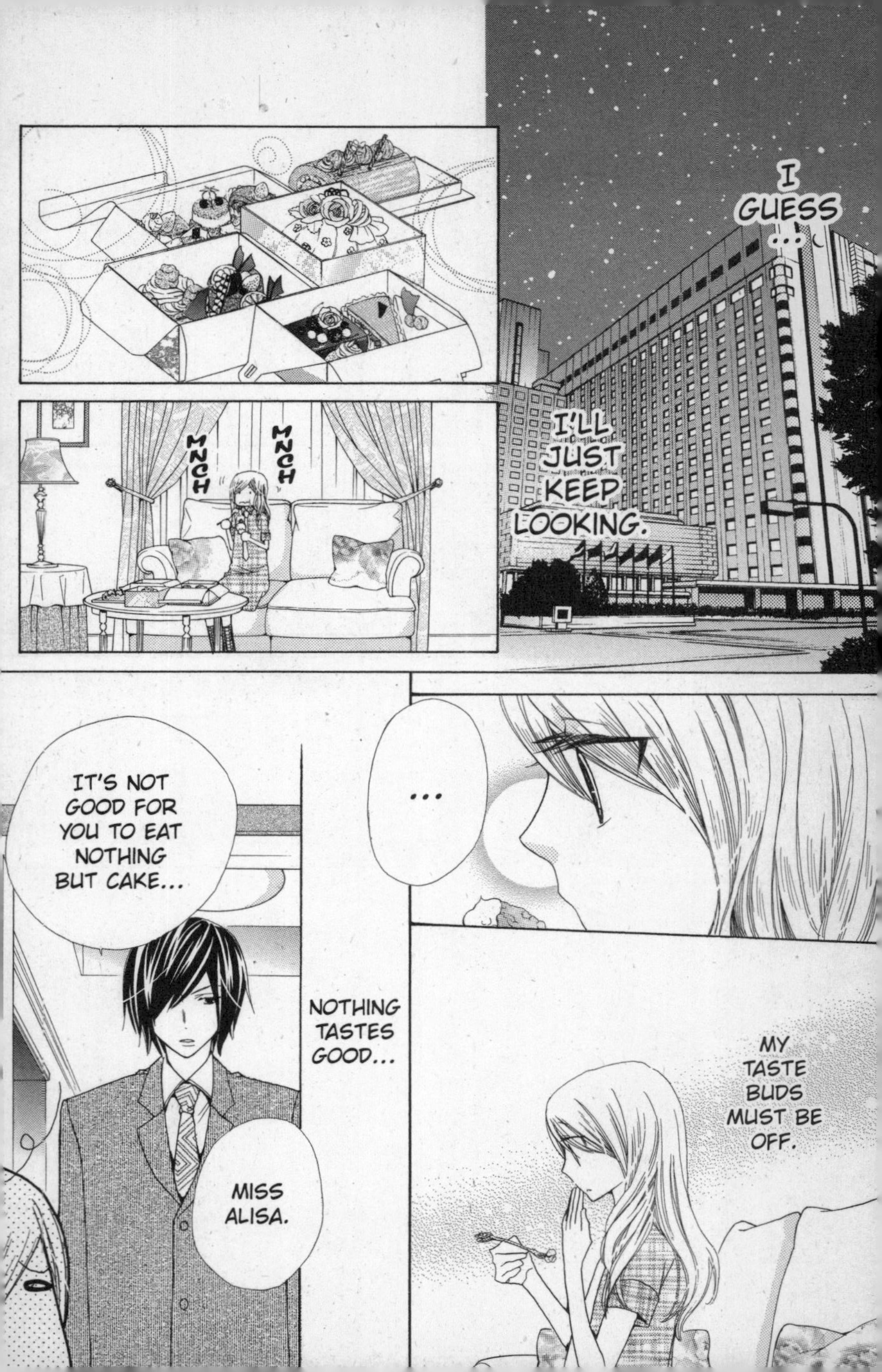
I GUESS...
I'LL JUST KEEP LOOKING.
MNCH
MNCH
...
MY TASTE BUDS MUST BE OFF.
NOTHING TASTES GOOD...
IT'S NOT GOOD FOR YOU TO EAT NOTHING BUT CAKE...
MISS ALISA.

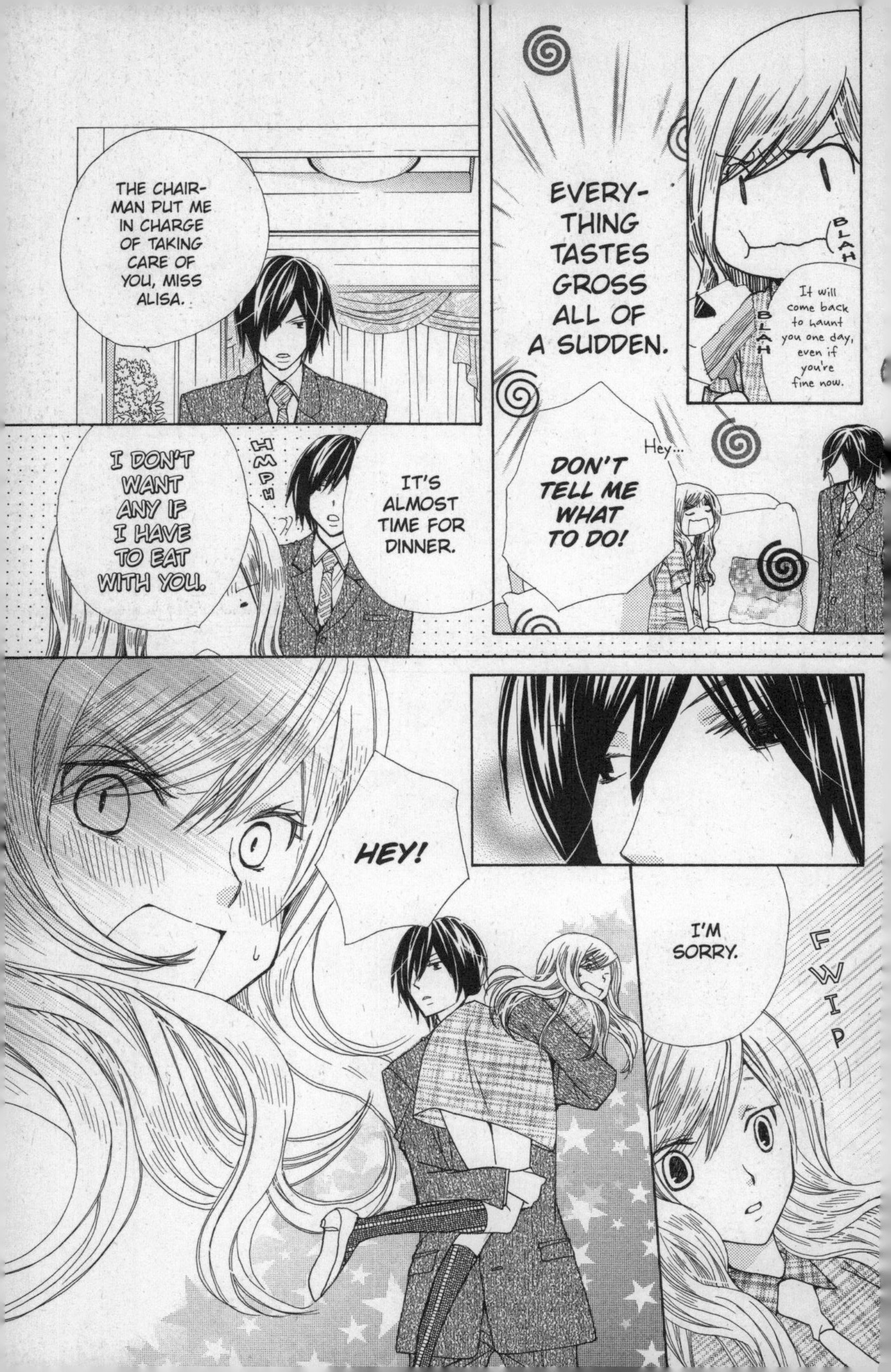
BLAH
BLAH
It will come back to haunt you one day, even if you're fine now.
EVERY-THING TASTES GROSS ALL OF A SUDDEN.
THE CHAIR-MAN PUT ME IN CHARGE OF TAKING CARE OF YOU, MISS ALISA.
Hey...
DON'T TELL ME WHAT TO DO!
IT'S ALMOST TIME FOR DINNER.
HMPH
I DON'T WANT ANY IF I HAVE TO EAT WITH YOU.
FWIP
I'M SORRY.
HEY!

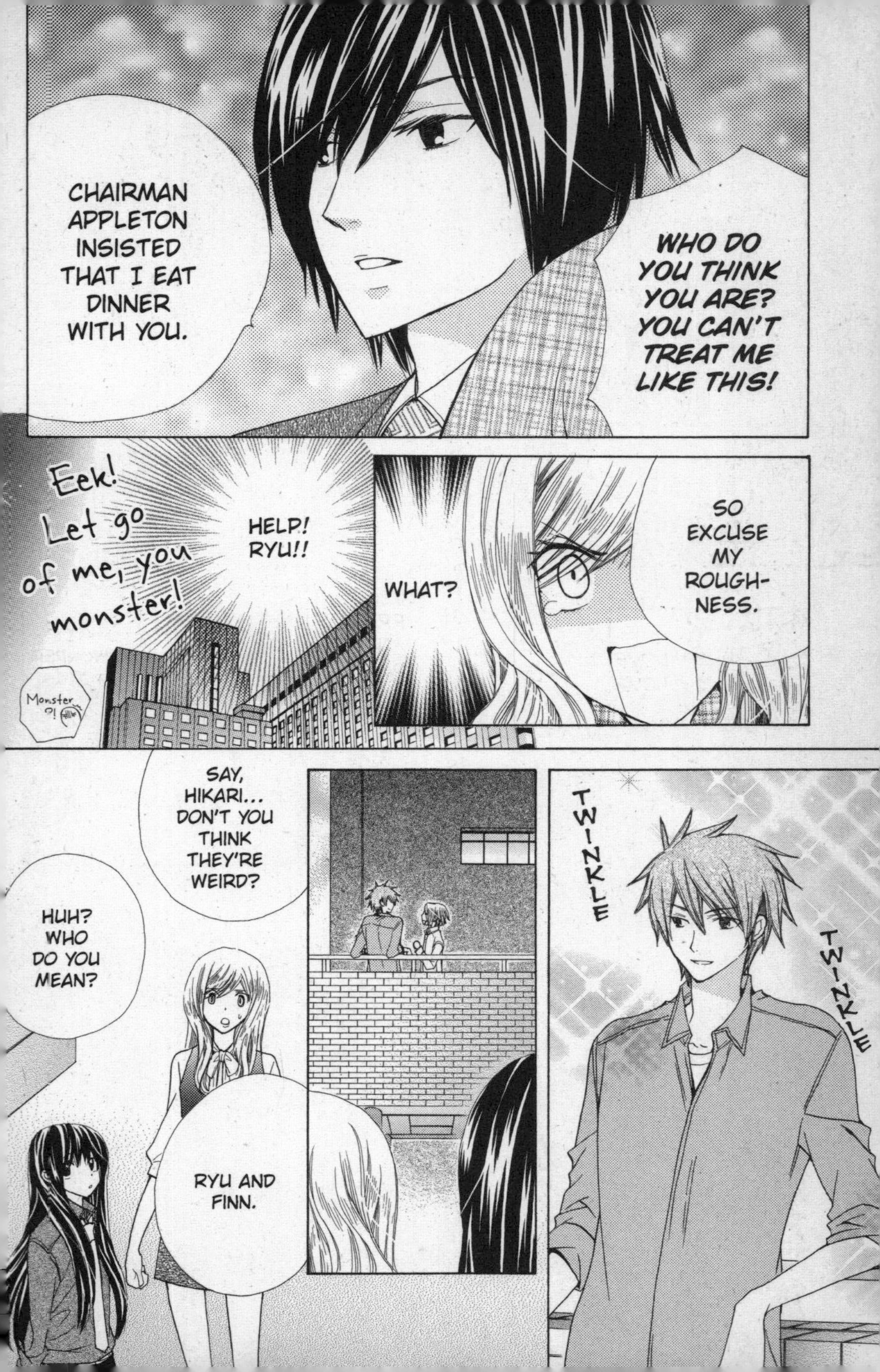
WHO DO YOU THINK YOU ARE? YOU CAN'T TREAT ME LIKE THIS!
CHAIRMAN APPLETON INSISTED THAT I EAT DINNER WITH YOU.
SO EXCUSE MY ROUGHNESS.
WHAT?
HELP! RYU!!
Eek! Let go of me, you monster!
Monster?!
TWINKLE
TWINKLE
SAY, HIKARI... DON'T YOU THINK THEY'RE WEIRD?
HUH? WHO DO YOU MEAN?
RYU AND FINN.

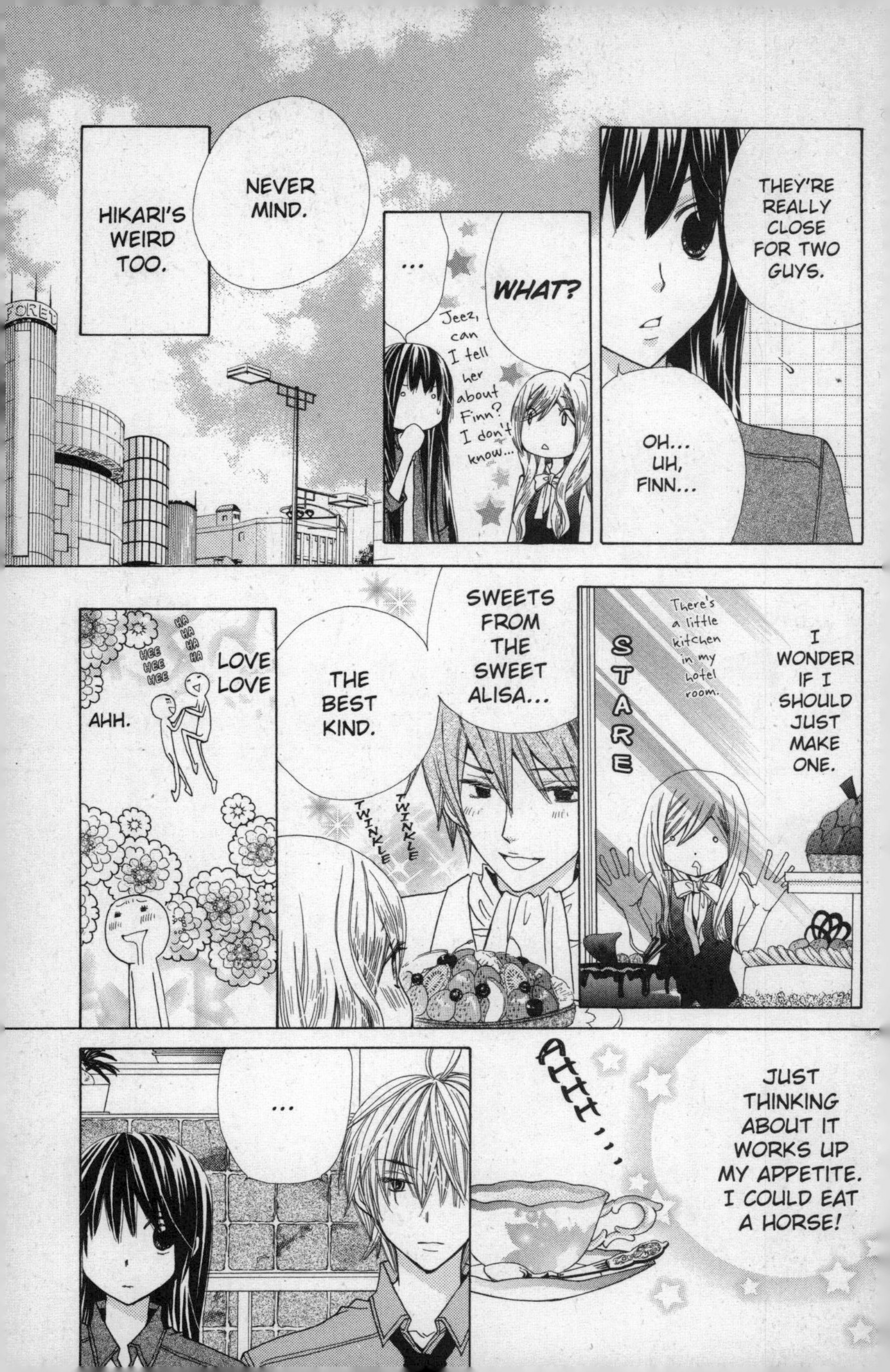
THEY'RE REALLY CLOSE FOR TWO GUYS.
OH... UH, FINN...
WHAT?
...
Jeez, can I tell her about Finn? I don't know...
NEVER MIND.
HIKARI'S WEIRD TOO.
I WONDER IF I SHOULD JUST MAKE ONE.
There's a little kitchen in my hotel room.
STARE
SWEETS FROM THE SWEET ALISA...
THE BEST KIND.
TWINKLE
TWINKLE
LOVE LOVE
HA HA HA HA
HEE HEE HEE
AHH.
JUST THINKING ABOUT IT WORKS UP MY APPETITE. I COULD EAT A HORSE!
AHHH...
...

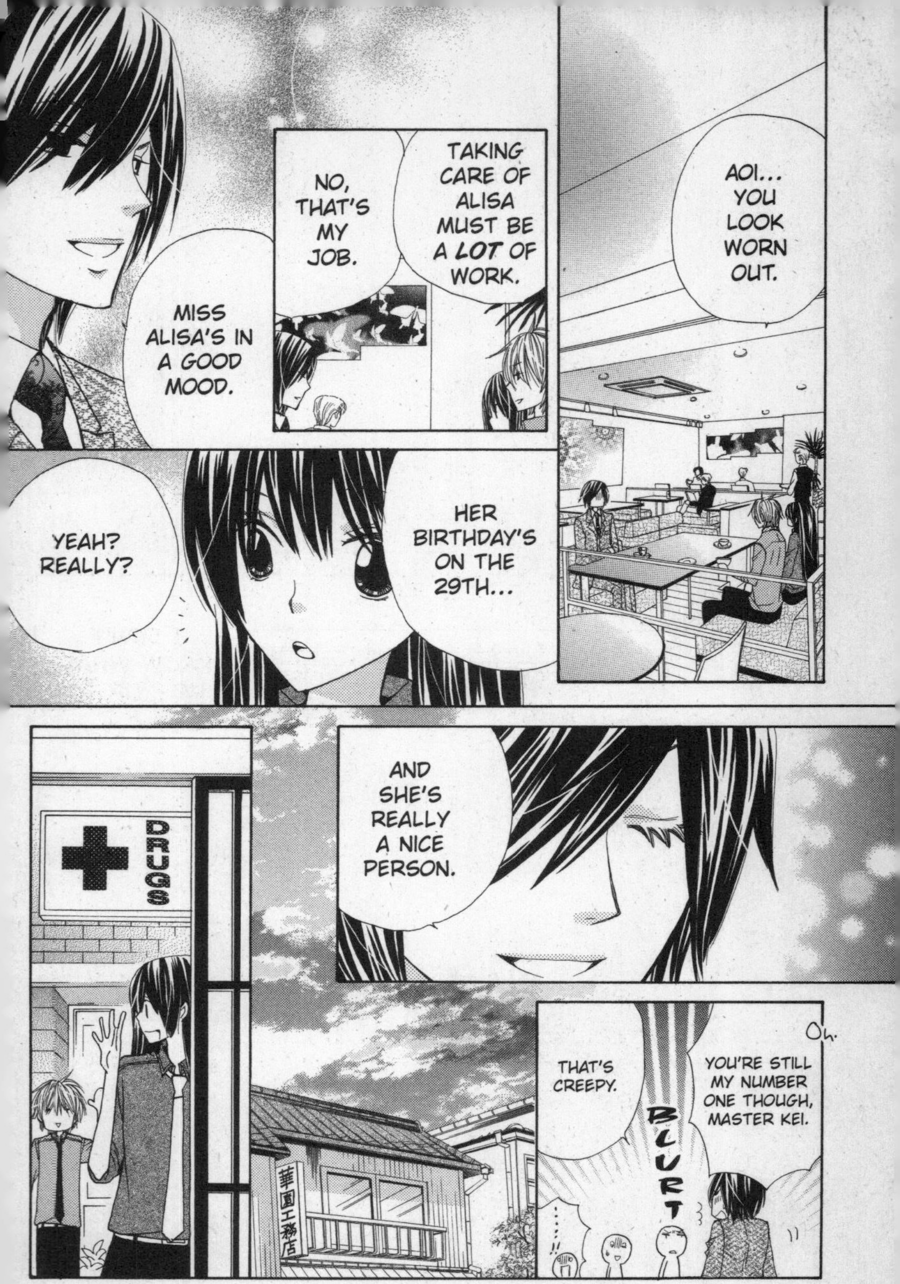
AOI... YOU LOOK WORN OUT.
TAKING CARE OF ALISA MUST BE A *LOT* OF WORK.
NO, THAT'S MY JOB.
MISS ALISA'S IN A GOOD MOOD.
HER BIRTHDAY'S ON THE 29TH...
YEAH? REALLY?
AND SHE'S REALLY A NICE PERSON.
Oh.
YOU'RE STILL MY NUMBER ONE THOUGH, MASTER KEI.
BLURT
THAT'S CREEPY.
......!!
DRUGS
華園工務店

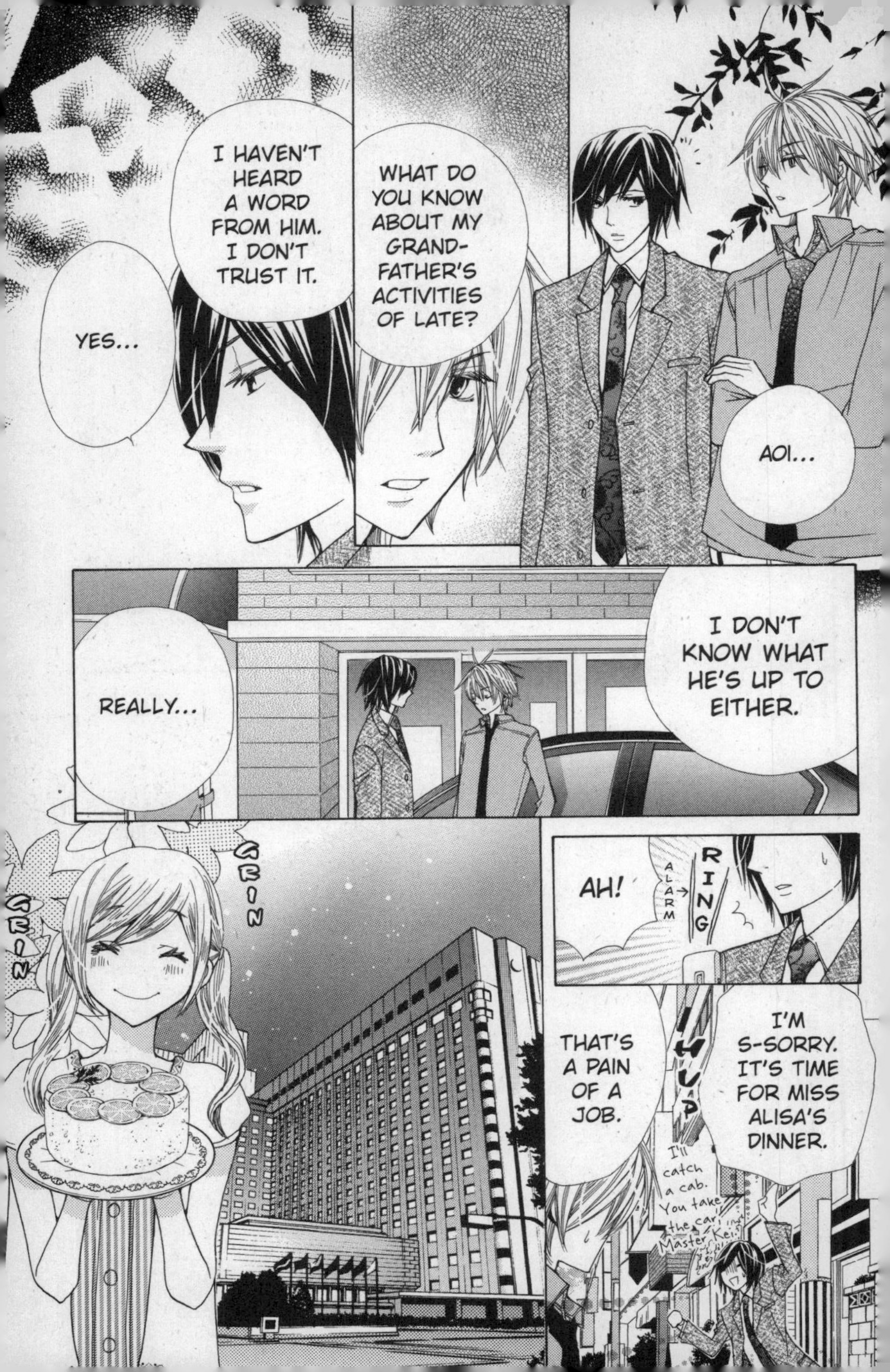
AOI...
WHAT DO YOU KNOW ABOUT MY GRAND-FATHER'S ACTIVITIES OF LATE?
I HAVEN'T HEARD A WORD FROM HIM. I DON'T TRUST IT.
YES...
I DON'T KNOW WHAT HE'S UP TO EITHER.
REALLY...
RING
ALARM
AH!
I'M S-SORRY. IT'S TIME FOR MISS ALISA'S DINNER.
THUP
I'll catch a cab. You take the car, Master Kei.
THAT'S A PAIN OF A JOB.
GRIN
GRIN

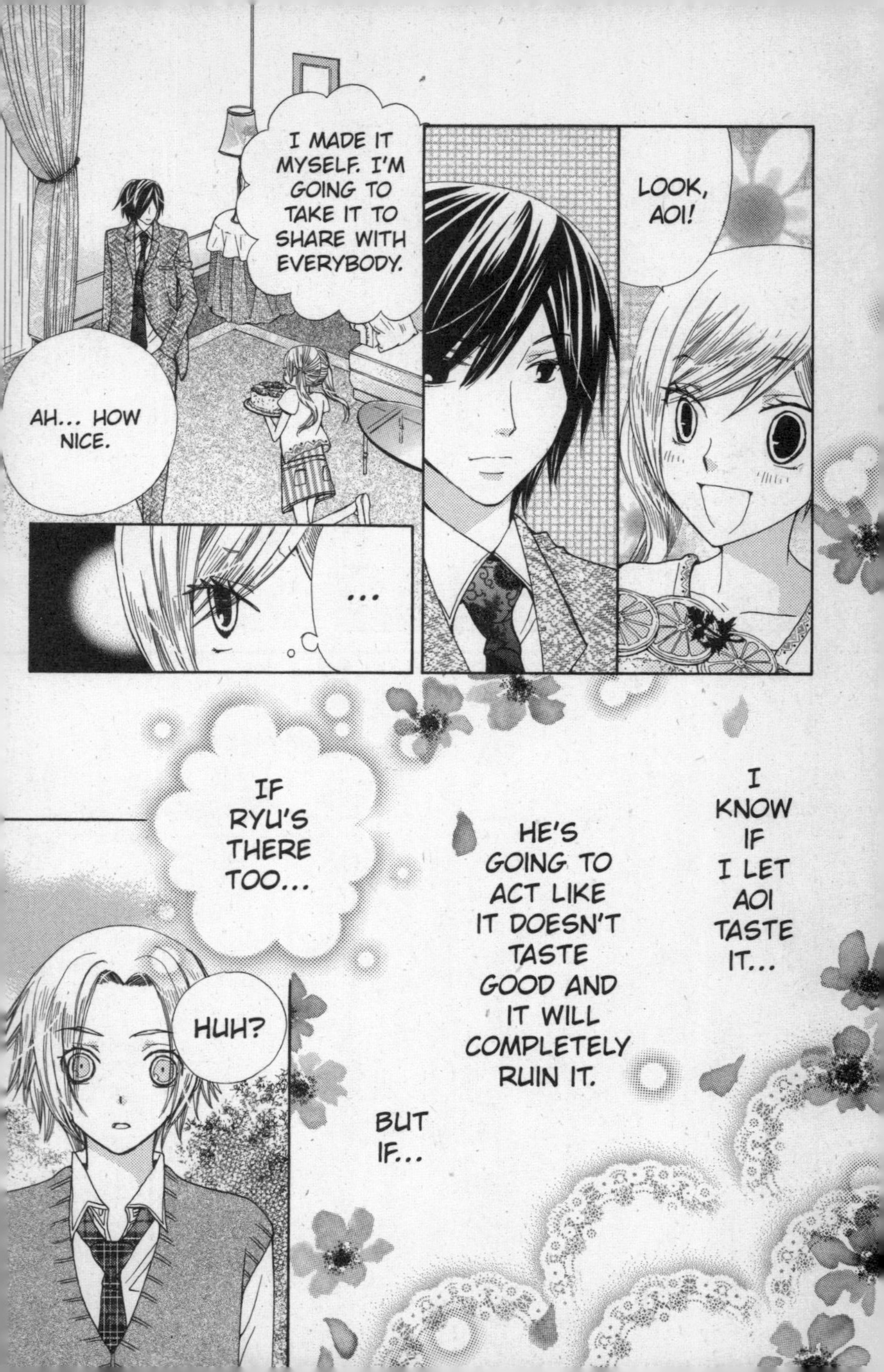
LOOK, AOI!
I MADE IT MYSELF. I'M GOING TO TAKE IT TO SHARE WITH EVERYBODY.
AH... HOW NICE.
...
I KNOW IF I LET AOI TASTE IT...
HE'S GOING TO ACT LIKE IT DOESN'T TASTE GOOD AND IT WILL COMPLETELY RUIN IT.
IF RYU'S THERE TOO...
HUH?
BUT IF...

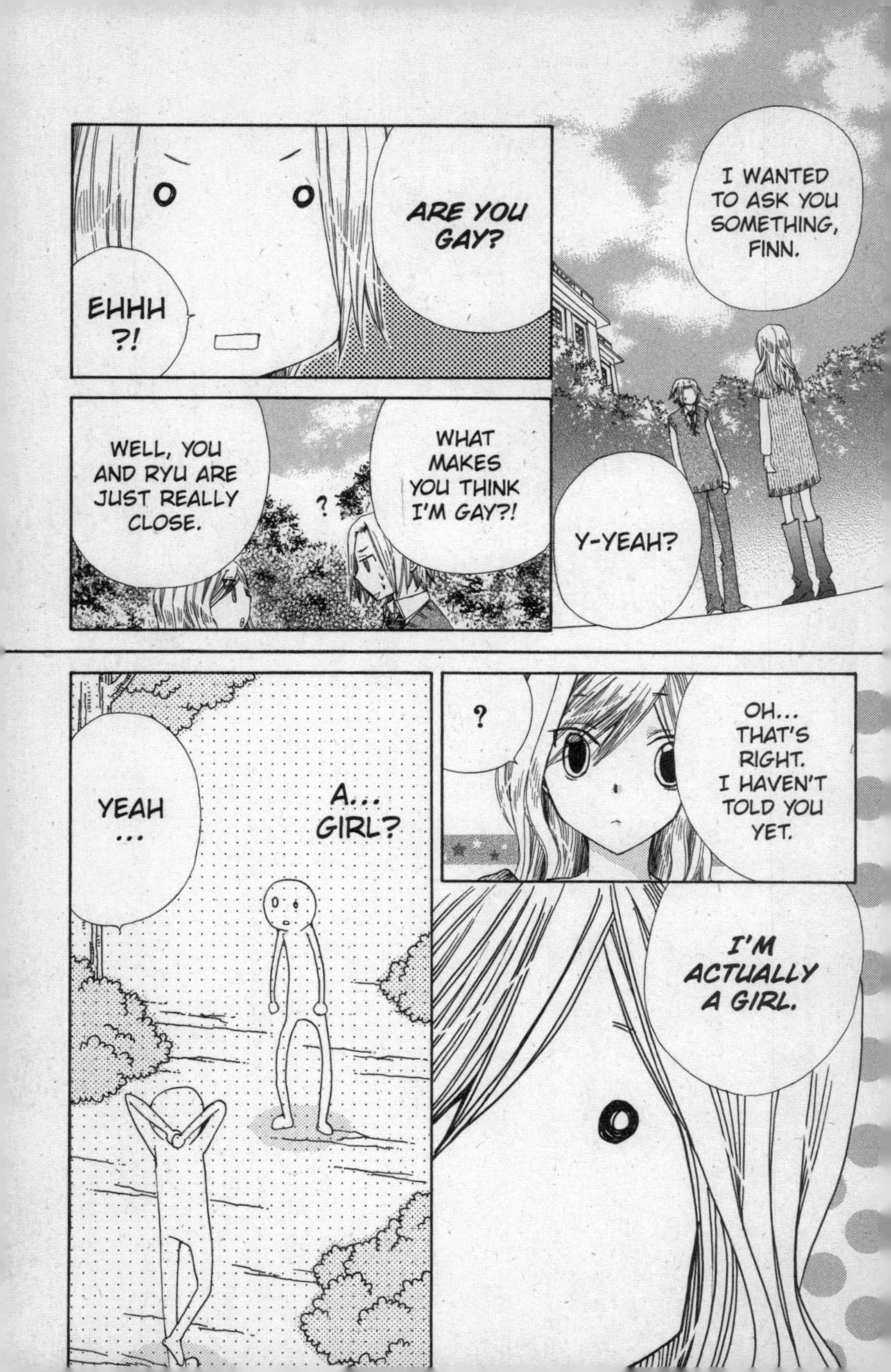
I WANTED TO ASK YOU SOMETHING, FINN.
Y-YEAH?
ARE YOU GAY?
EHHH ?!
WHAT MAKES YOU THINK I'M GAY?!
?
WELL, YOU AND RYU ARE JUST REALLY CLOSE.
OH... THAT'S RIGHT. I HAVEN'T TOLD YOU YET.
?
I'M ACTUALLY A GIRL.
A... GIRL?
YEAH ...

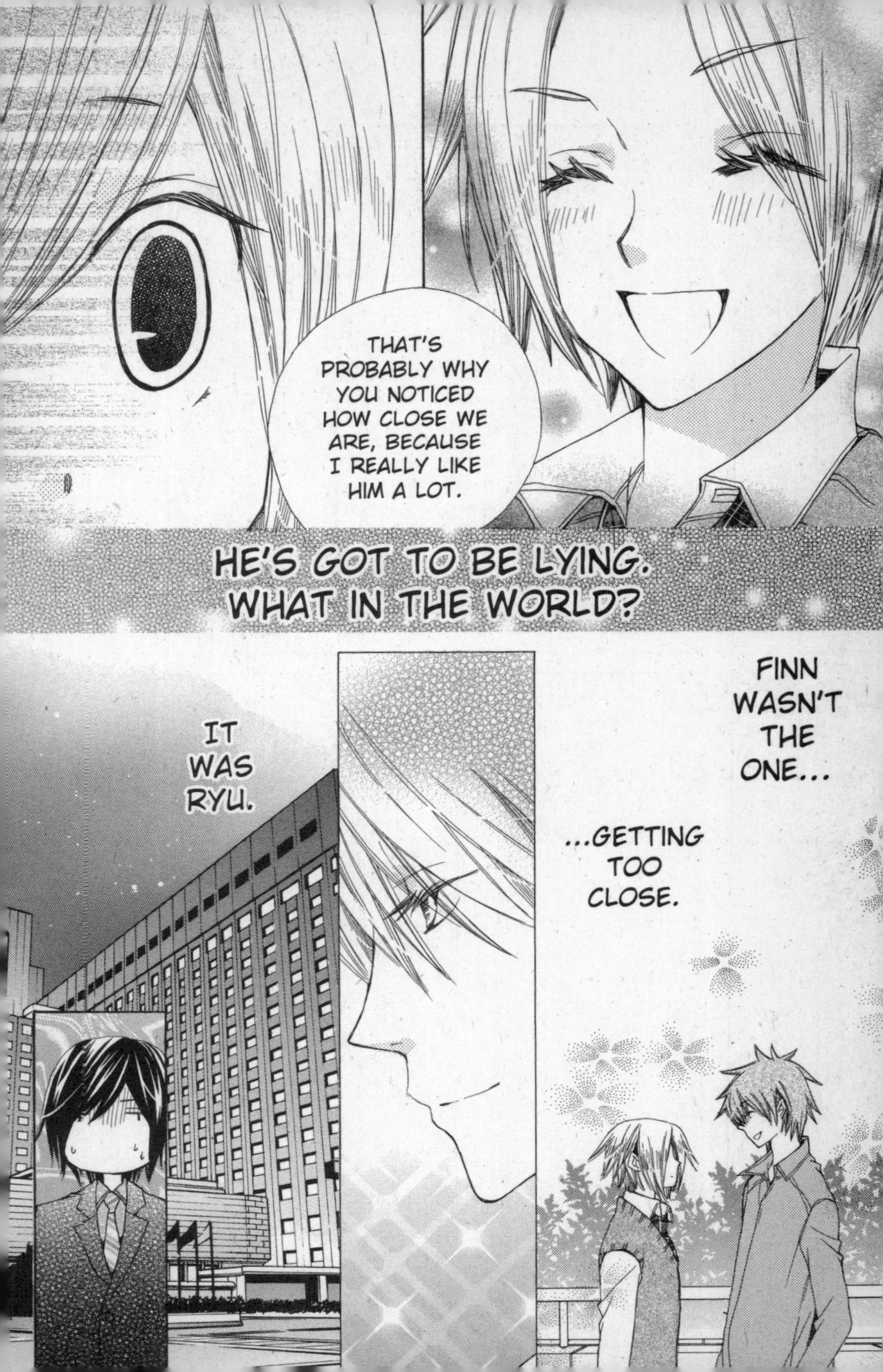
THAT'S PROBABLY WHY YOU NOTICED HOW CLOSE WE ARE, BECAUSE I REALLY LIKE HIM A LOT.
HE'S GOT TO BE LYING. WHAT IN THE WORLD?
FINN WASN'T THE ONE...
...GETTING TOO CLOSE.
IT WAS RYU.

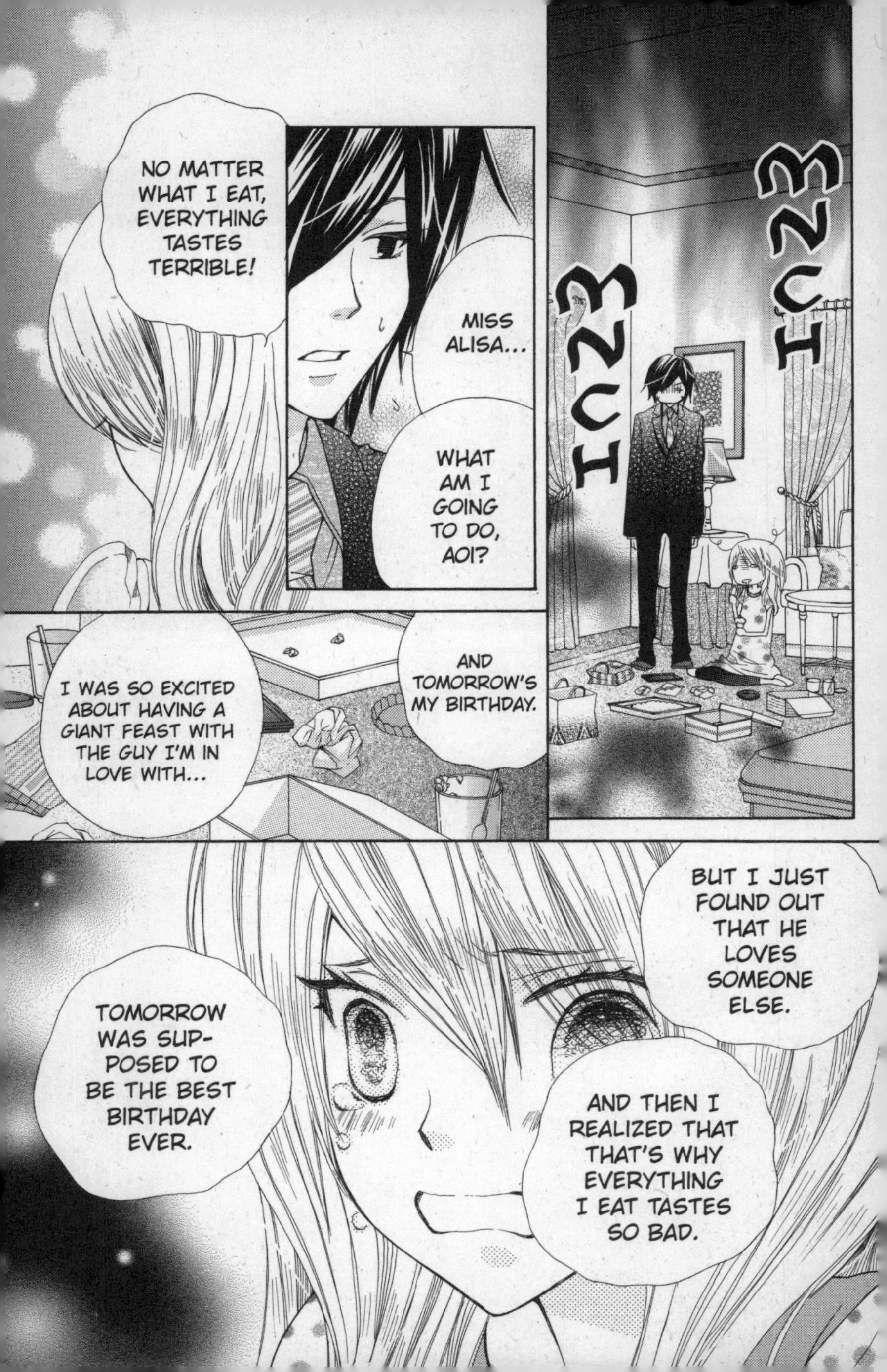
MNCH
MNCH
NO MATTER WHAT I EAT, EVERYTHING TASTES TERRIBLE!
MISS ALISA...
WHAT AM I GOING TO DO, AOI?
AND TOMORROW'S MY BIRTHDAY.
I WAS SO EXCITED ABOUT HAVING A GIANT FEAST WITH THE GUY I'M IN LOVE WITH...
BUT I JUST FOUND OUT THAT HE LOVES SOMEONE ELSE.
TOMORROW WAS SUP-POSED TO BE THE BEST BIRTHDAY EVER.
AND THEN I REALIZED THAT THAT'S WHY EVERYTHING I EAT TASTES SO BAD.

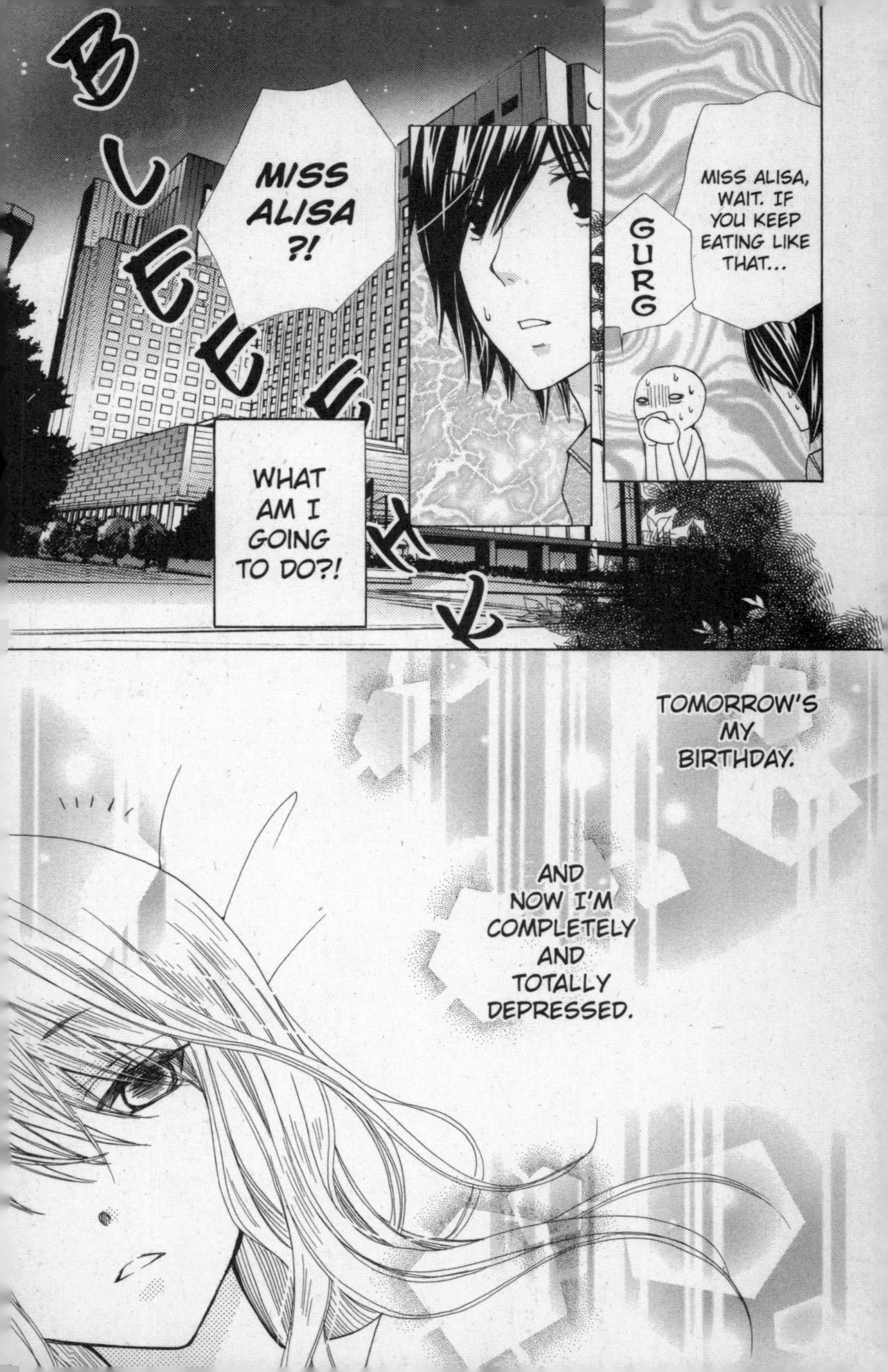
MISS ALISA, WAIT. IF YOU KEEP EATING LIKE THAT...
GURG
MISS ALISA ?!
BLEEEK
WHAT AM I GOING TO DO?!
TOMORROW'S MY BIRTHDAY.
AND NOW I'M COMPLETELY AND TOTALLY DEPRESSED.

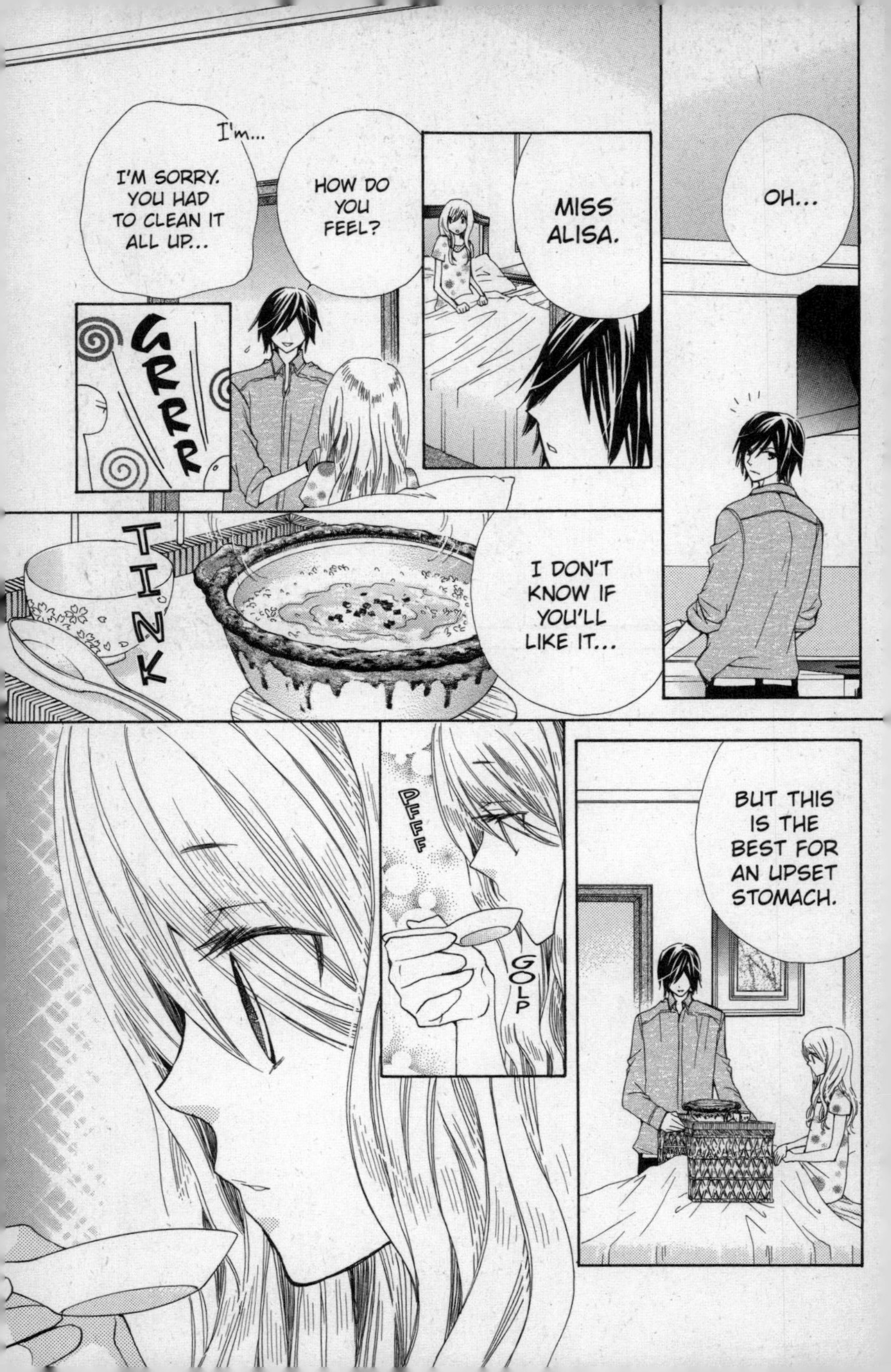
OH...
MISS ALISA.
HOW DO YOU FEEL?
I'M SORRY. YOU HAD TO CLEAN IT ALL UP...
I'm...
GRRR
I DON'T KNOW IF YOU'LL LIKE IT...
TINK
BUT THIS IS THE BEST FOR AN UPSET STOMACH.
PFFF
GOLP

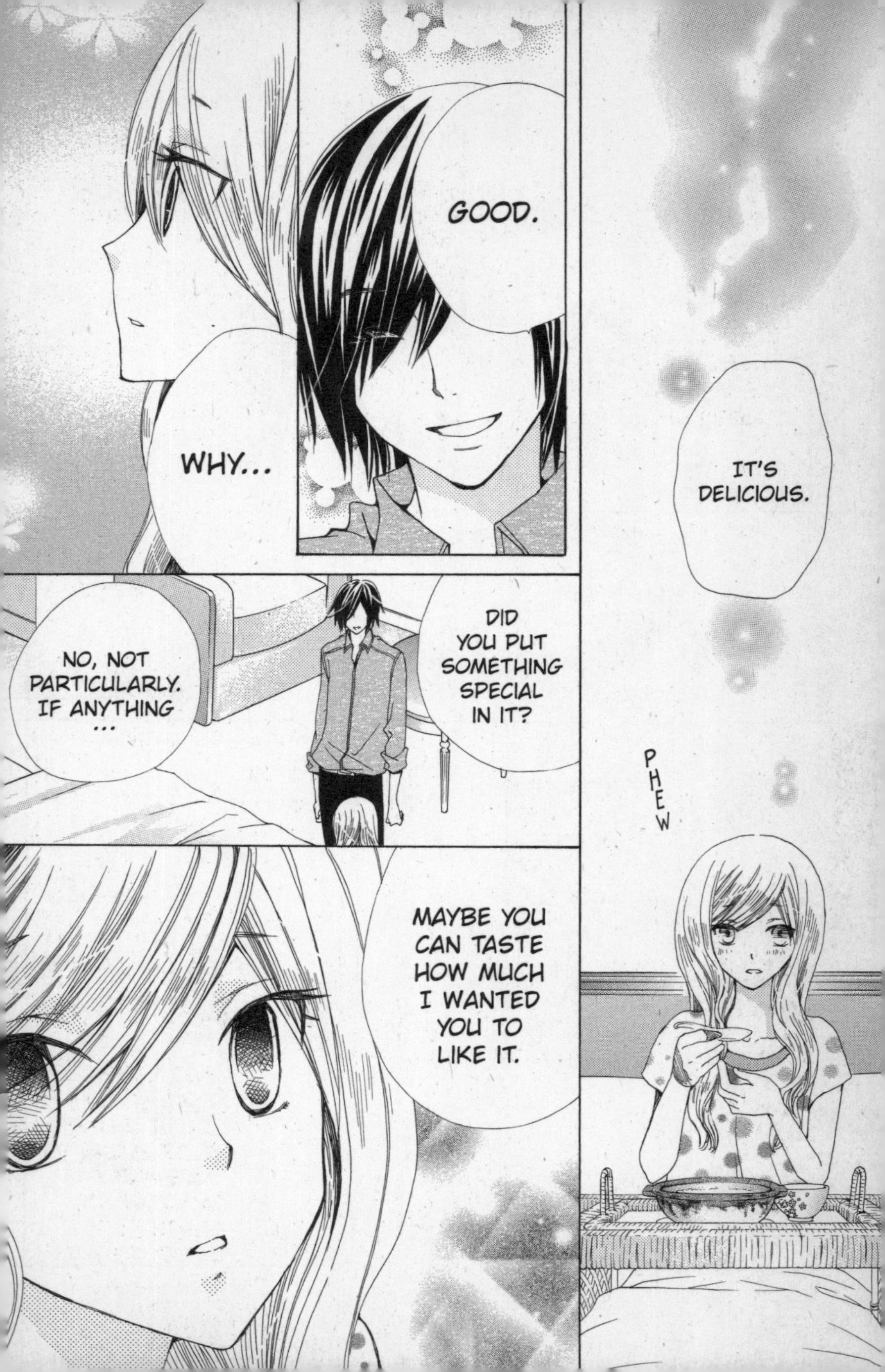
IT'S DELICIOUS.
PHEW
GOOD.
WHY...
DID YOU PUT SOMETHING SPECIAL IN IT?
NO, NOT PARTICULARLY. IF ANYTHING ...
MAYBE YOU CAN TASTE HOW MUCH I WANTED YOU TO LIKE IT.

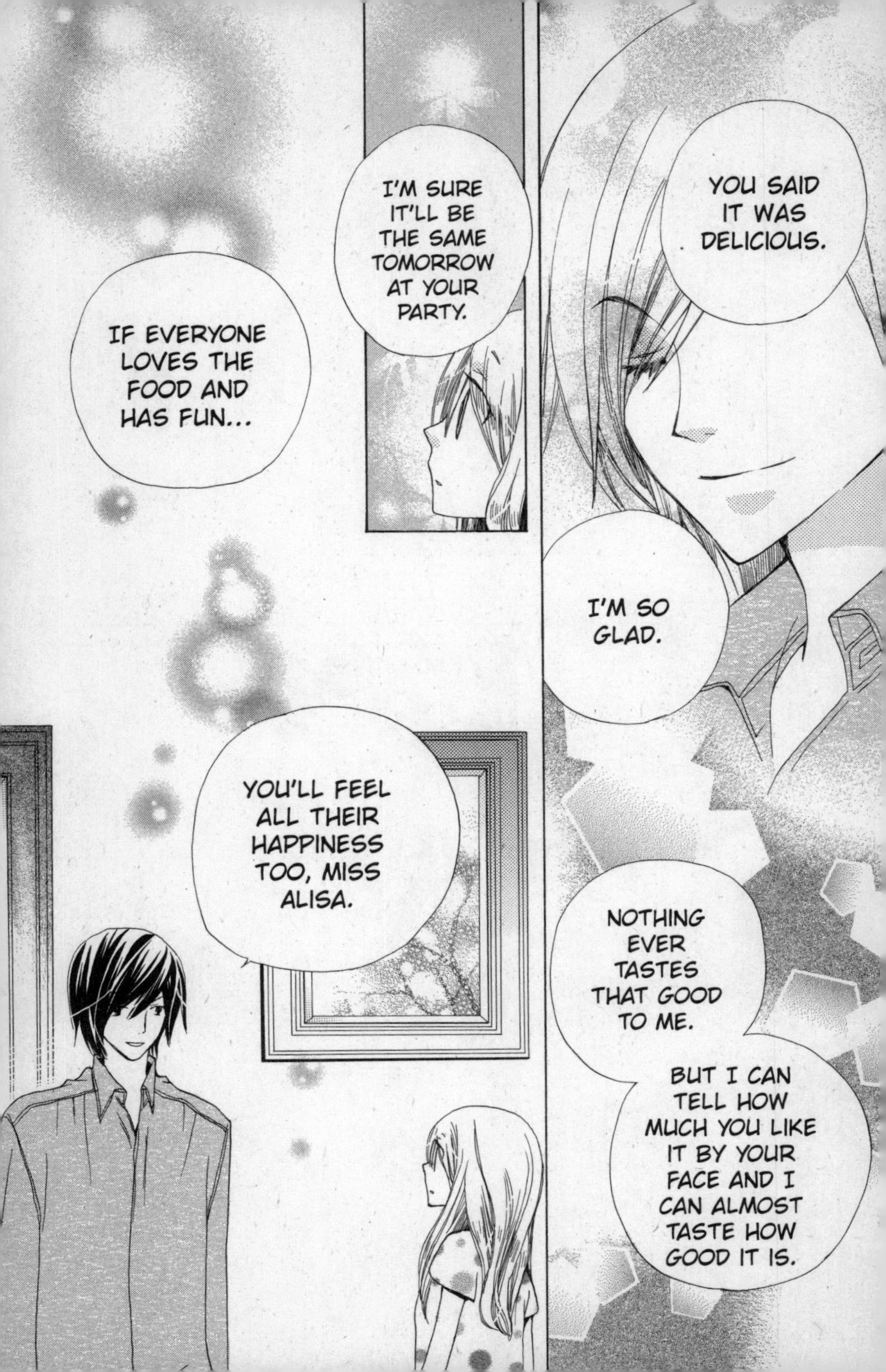
YOU SAID IT WAS DELICIOUS.
I'M SO GLAD.
NOTHING EVER TASTES THAT GOOD TO ME.
BUT I CAN TELL HOW MUCH YOU LIKE IT BY YOUR FACE AND I CAN ALMOST TASTE HOW GOOD IT IS.
I'M SURE IT'LL BE THE SAME TOMORROW AT YOUR PARTY.
IF EVERYONE LOVES THE FOOD AND HAS FUN...
YOU'LL FEEL ALL THEIR HAPPINESS TOO, MISS ALISA.

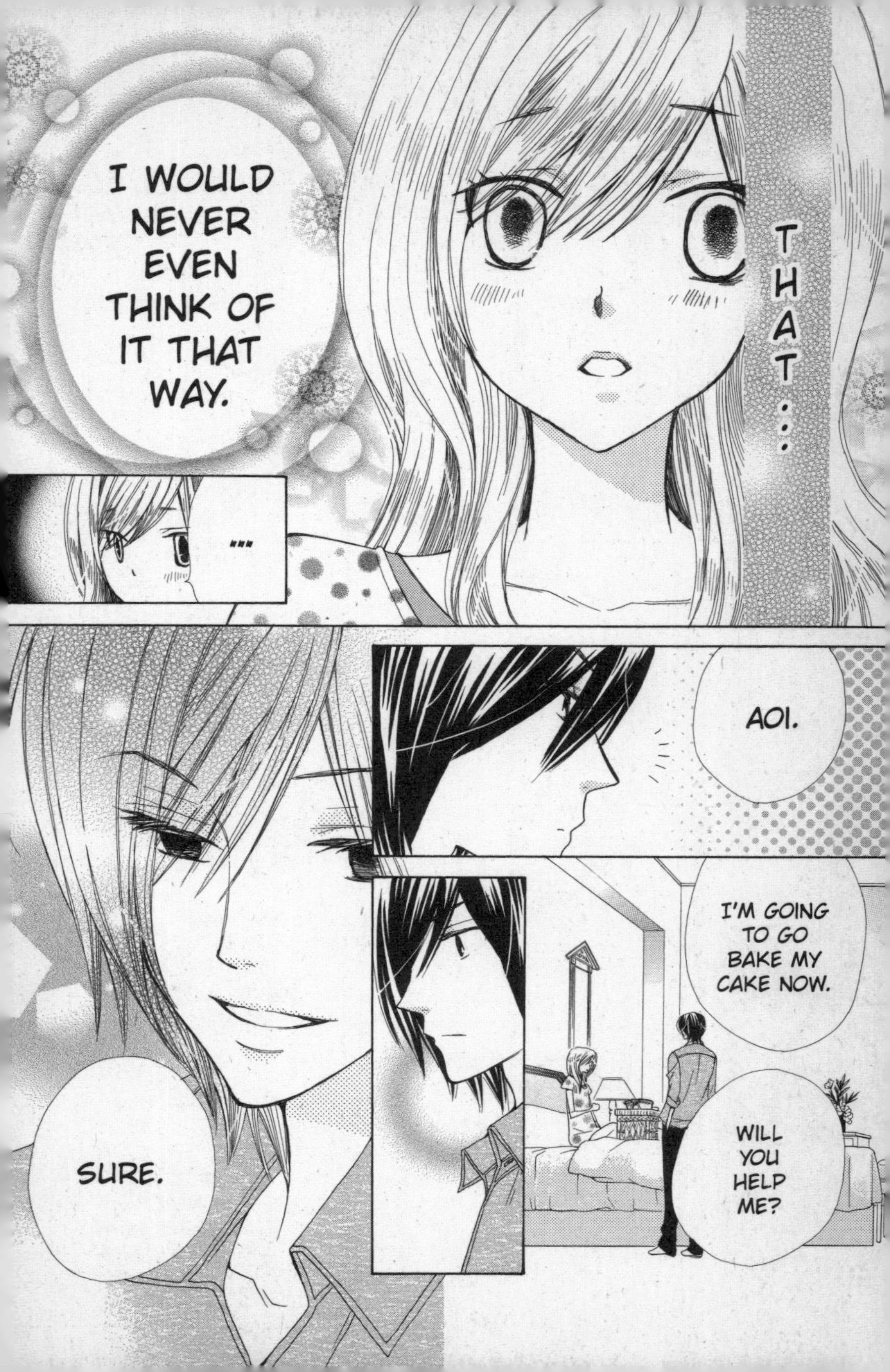
THAT...
I WOULD NEVER EVEN THINK OF IT THAT WAY.
...
AOI.
I'M GOING TO GO BAKE MY CAKE NOW.
WILL YOU HELP ME?
SURE.

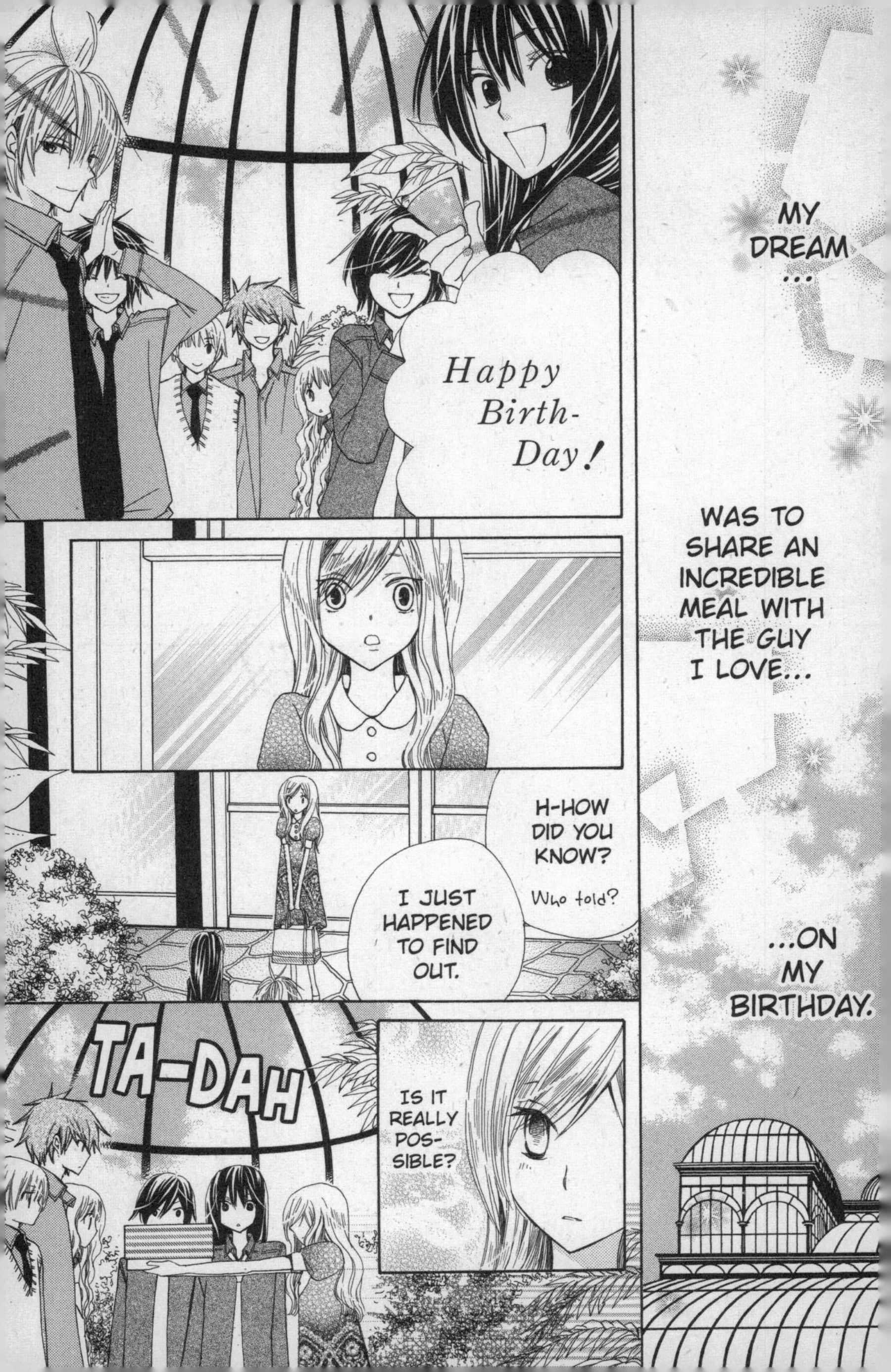
MY DREAM...
WAS TO SHARE AN INCREDIBLE MEAL WITH THE GUY I LOVE...
...ON MY BIRTHDAY.
Happy Birth-Day!
H-HOW DID YOU KNOW?
Who told?
I JUST HAPPENED TO FIND OUT.
IS IT REALLY POS-SIBLE?
TA-DAH

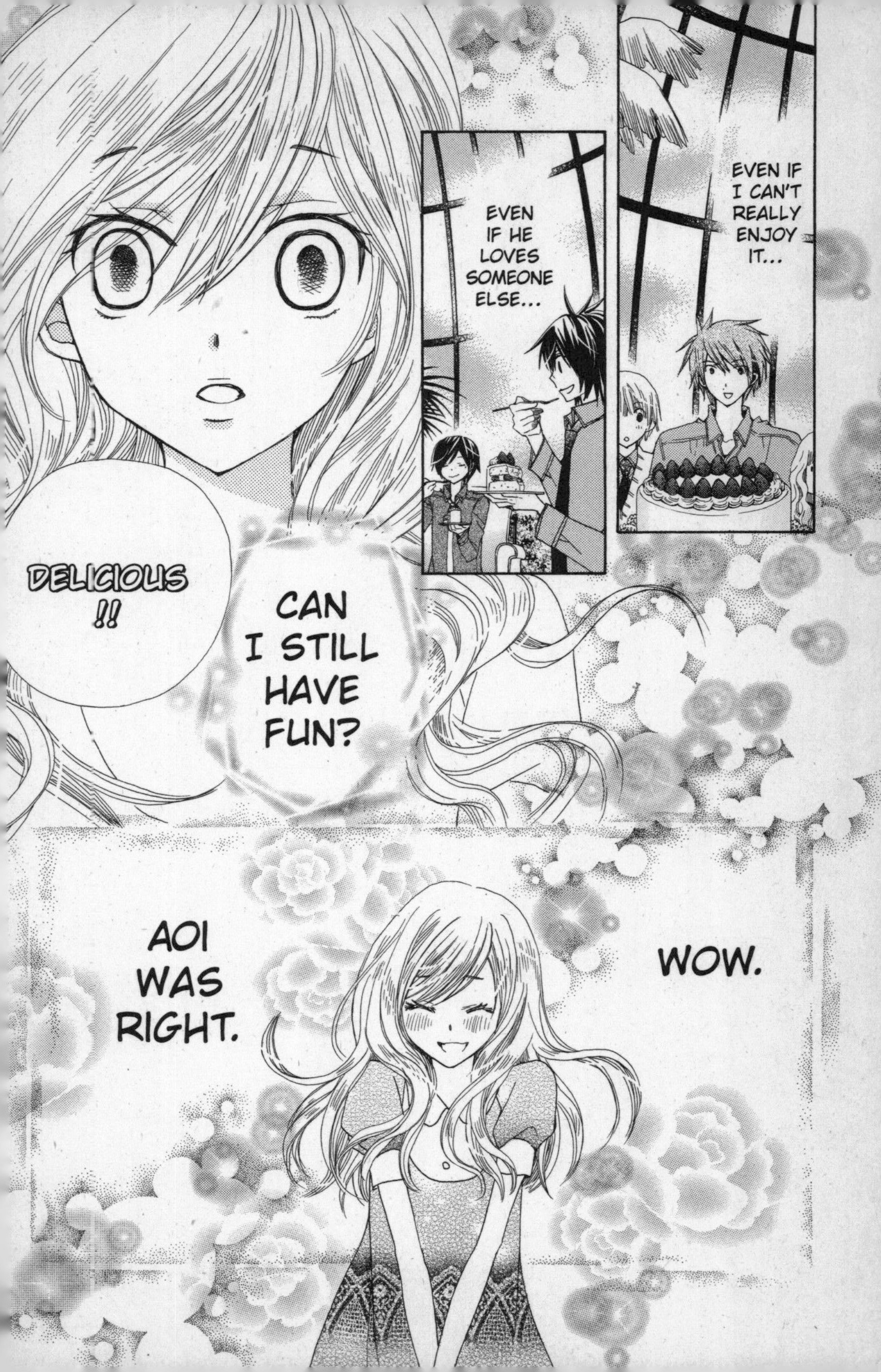
EVEN IF I CAN'T REALLY ENJOY IT...
EVEN IF HE LOVES SOMEONE ELSE...
CAN I STILL HAVE FUN?
DELICIOUS!!
WOW.
AOI WAS RIGHT.

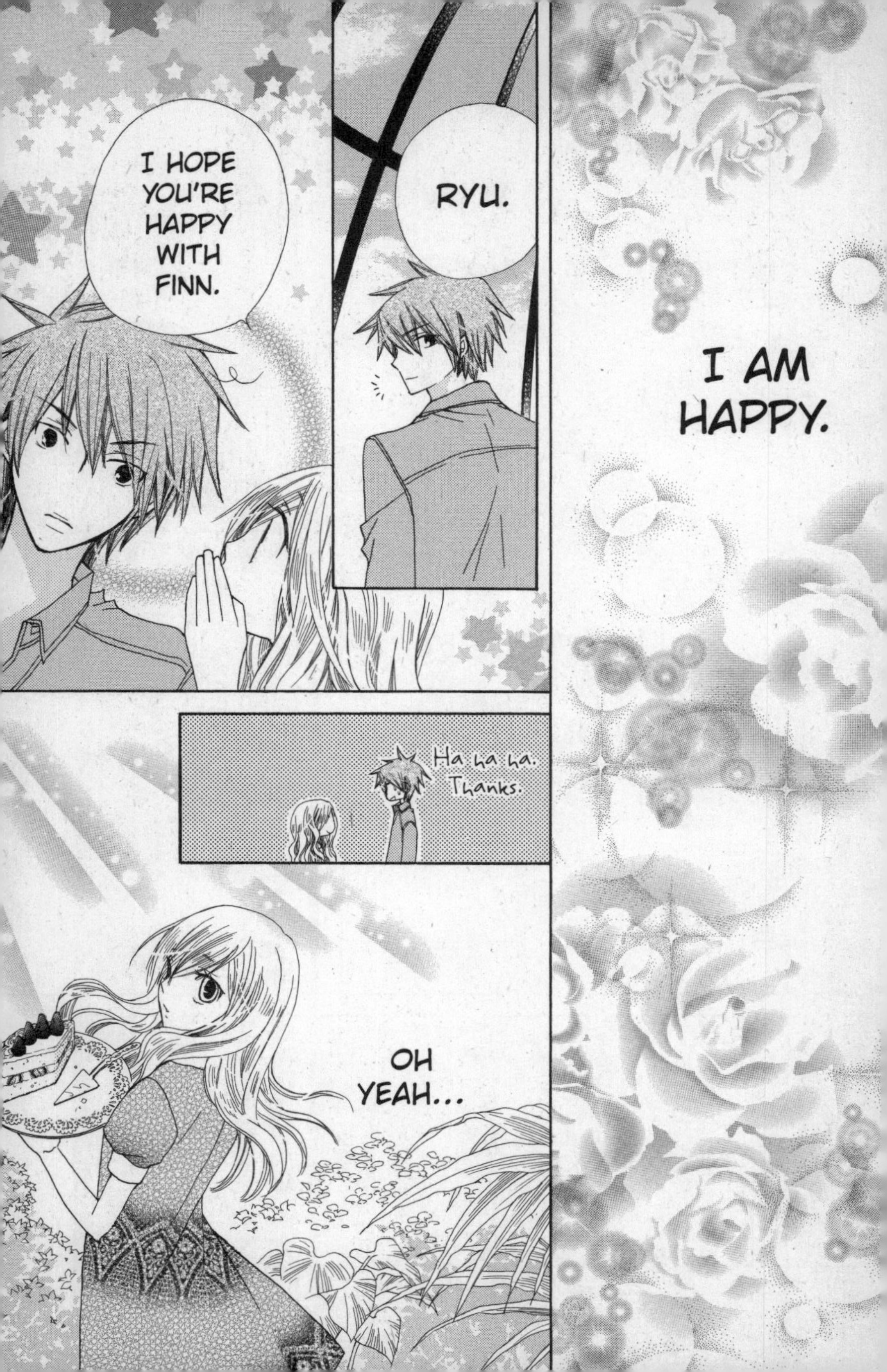
I AM HAPPY.
RYU.
I HOPE YOU'RE HAPPY WITH FINN.
Ha ha ha. Thanks.
OH YEAH...

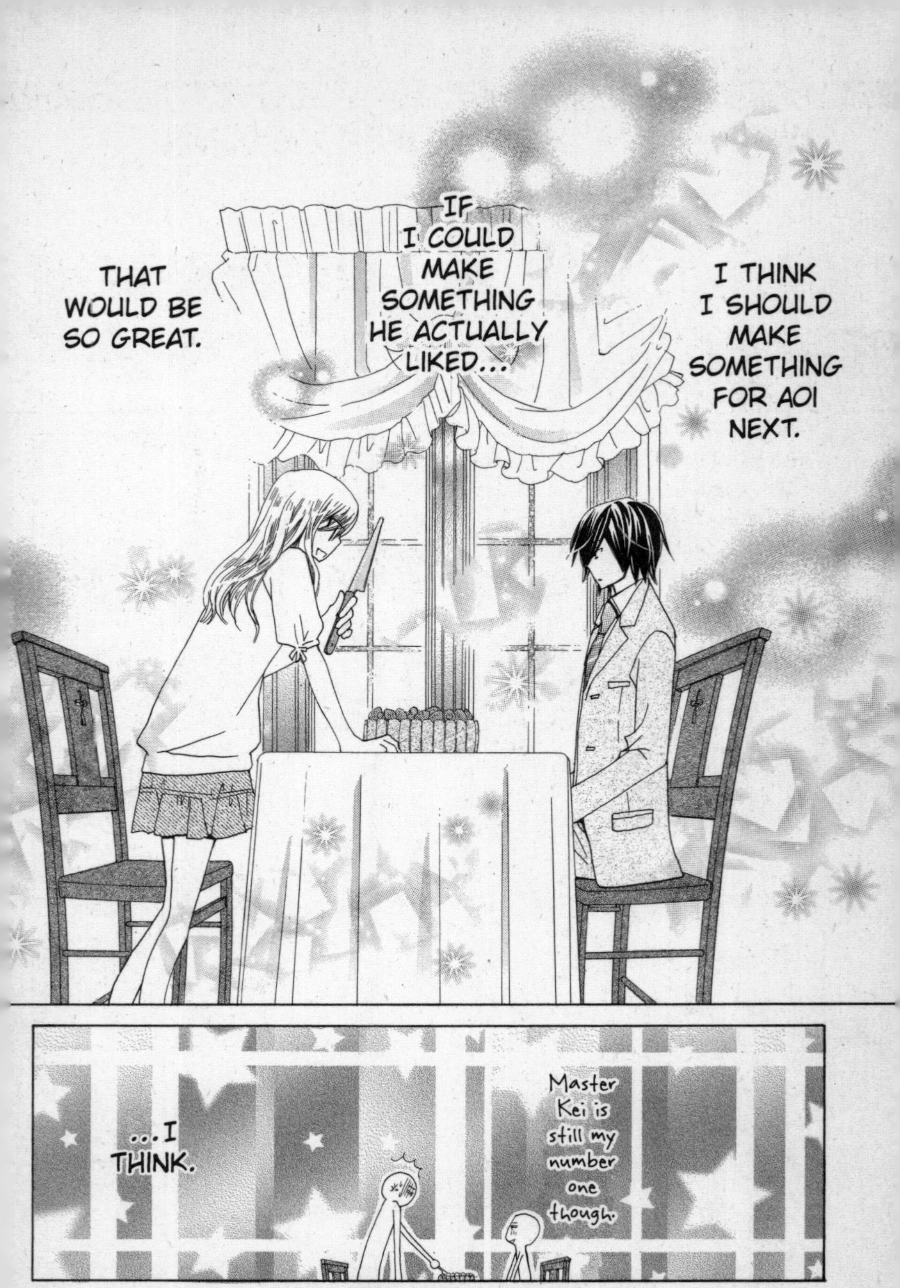
I THINK I SHOULD MAKE SOMETHING FOR AOI NEXT.
IF I COULD MAKE SOMETHING HE ACTUALLY LIKED...
THAT WOULD BE SO GREAT.
Master Kei is still my number one though.
...I THINK.

SA VOLUME 15 / END

WITHOUT WARNING, A TWO-PAGE COMIC.

GO, TADASHI! PART 15!

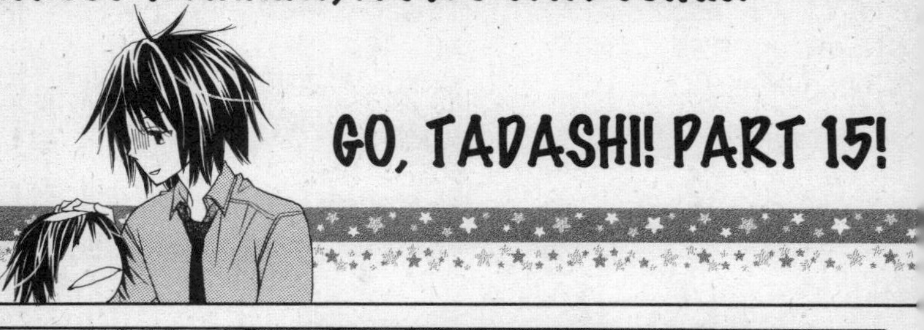

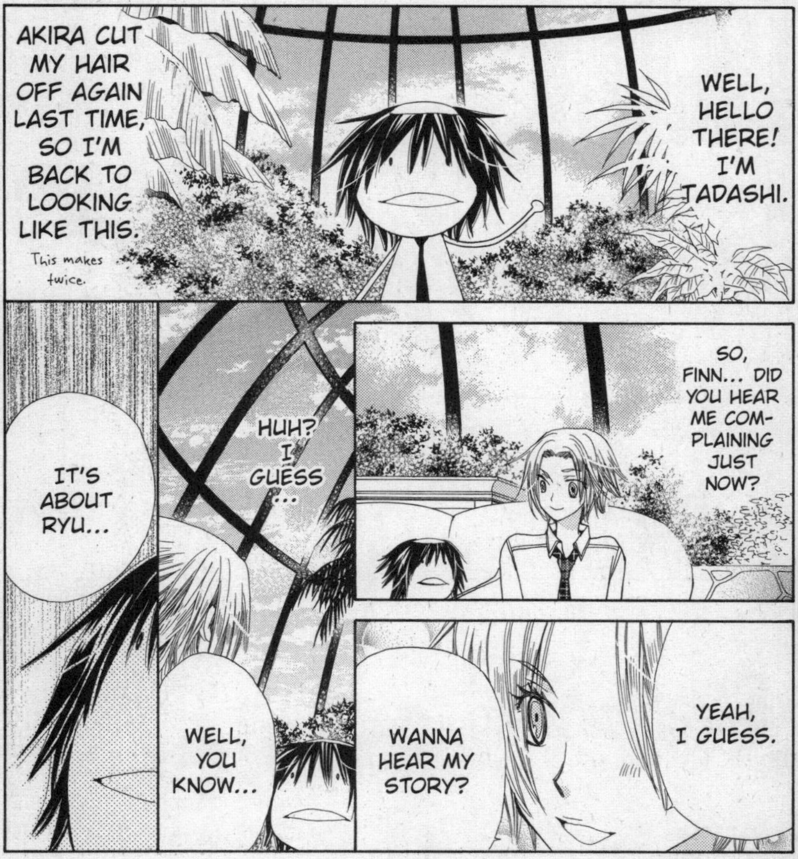
WELL, HELLO THERE! I'M TADASHI.
AKIRA CUT MY HAIR OFF AGAIN LAST TIME, SO I'M BACK TO LOOKING LIKE THIS.
This makes twice.
SO, FINN... DID YOU HEAR ME COM-PLAINING JUST NOW?
YEAH, I GUESS.
WANNA HEAR MY STORY?
HUH? I GUESS...
WELL, YOU KNOW...
IT'S ABOUT RYU...

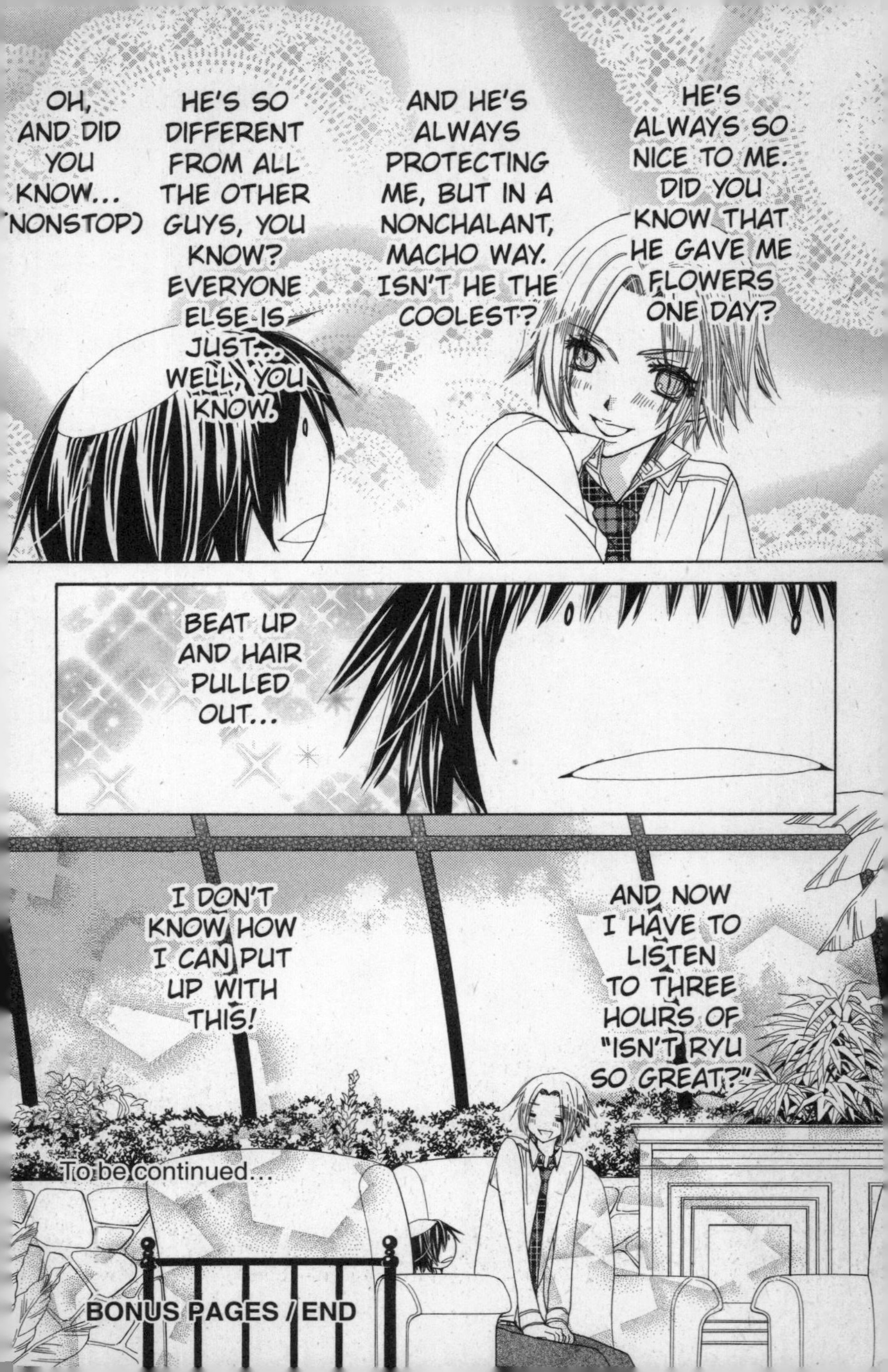
HE'S ALWAYS SO NICE TO ME. DID YOU KNOW THAT HE GAVE ME FLOWERS ONE DAY?
AND HE'S ALWAYS PROTECTING ME, BUT IN A NONCHALANT, MACHO WAY. ISN'T HE THE COOLEST?
HE'S SO DIFFERENT FROM ALL THE OTHER GUYS, YOU KNOW? EVERYONE ELSE IS JUST... WELL, YOU KNOW.
OH, AND DID YOU KNOW... (NONSTOP)
BEAT UP AND HAIR PULLED OUT...
AND NOW I HAVE TO LISTEN TO THREE HOURS OF "ISN'T RYU SO GREAT?"
I DON'T KNOW HOW I CAN PUT UP WITH THIS!
To be continued...
BONUS PAGES / END

Maki Minami is from Saitama
Prefecture in Japan. She debuted
in 2001 with *Kanata no Ao*
(Faraway Blue). Her other works
include *Kimi wa Girlfriend*
(You're My Girlfriend), *Mainichi
ga Takaramono* (Every Day Is a
Treasure) and *Yuki Atataka*
(Warm Winter). *S•A* was serialized in
Japan's *Hana to Yume* magazine and
made into an anime in 2008.

S·A

Vol. 15
Shojo Beat Edition

STORY & ART BY
MAKI MINAMI

English Adaptation/Amanda Hubbard
Translation/JN Productions
Touch-up Art & Lettering/Hudson Yards
Design/Deirdre Shiozawa
Editor/Jonathan Tarbox

VP, Production/Alvin Lu
VP, Sales & Product Marketing/Gonzalo Ferreyra
VP, Creative/Linda Espinosa
Publisher/Hyoe Narita

S·A -Special A- by Maki Minami © Maki Minami 2008. All rights reserved.
First published in Japan in 2008 by HAKUSENSHA, Inc., Tokyo. English
language translation rights arranged with HAKUSENSHA, Inc., Tokyo.

Printed in Canada

Published by VIZ Media, LLC
P.O. Box 77010
San Francisco, CA 94107

10 9 8 7 6 5 4 3 2 1
First printing, March 2010